Shojo Beat

Captive Hearts

Story & Art by
Matsuri Hino

Vol. 4

Captive Hearts
Vol. 4

CONTENTS

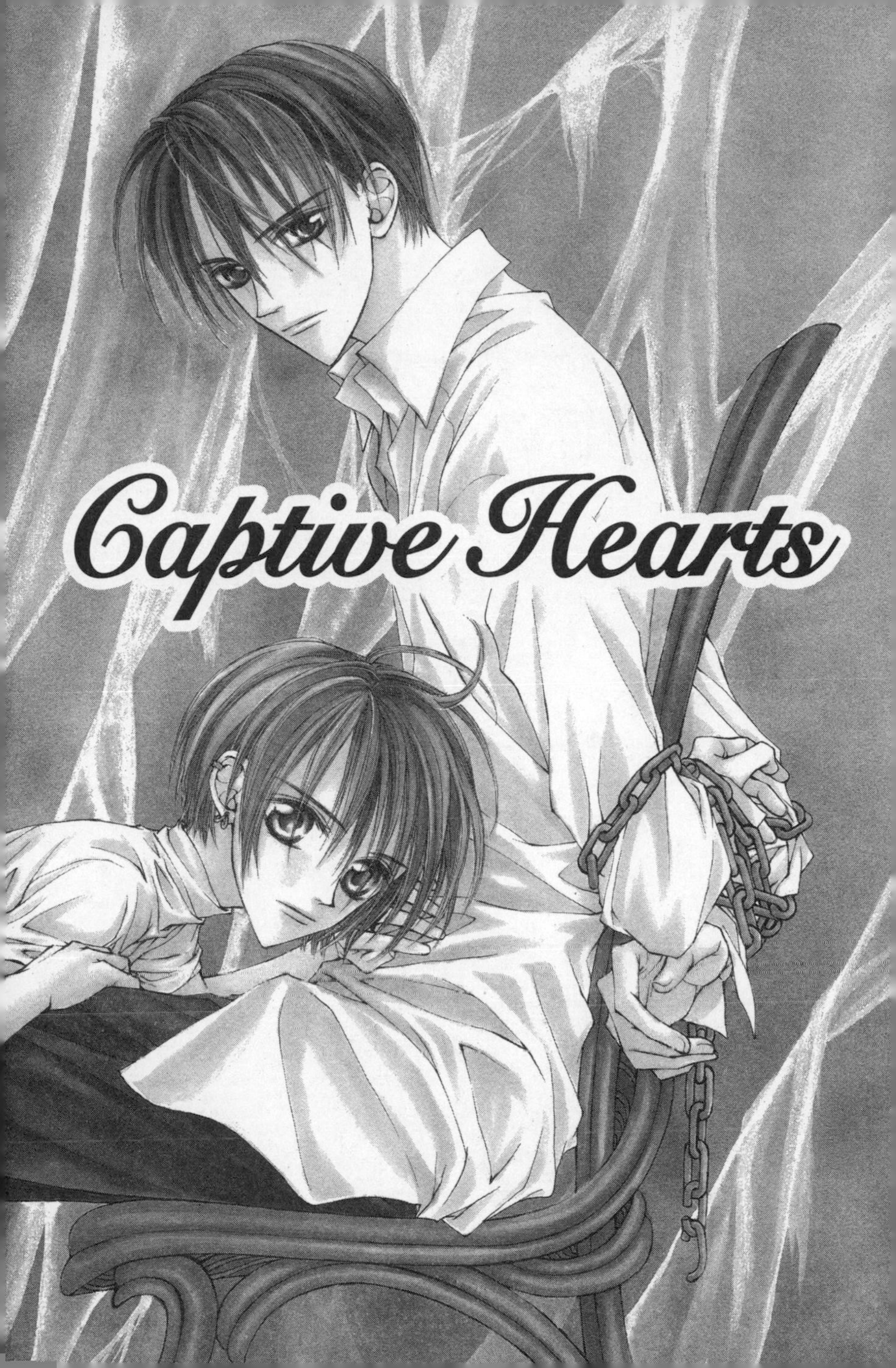
Captive Hearts

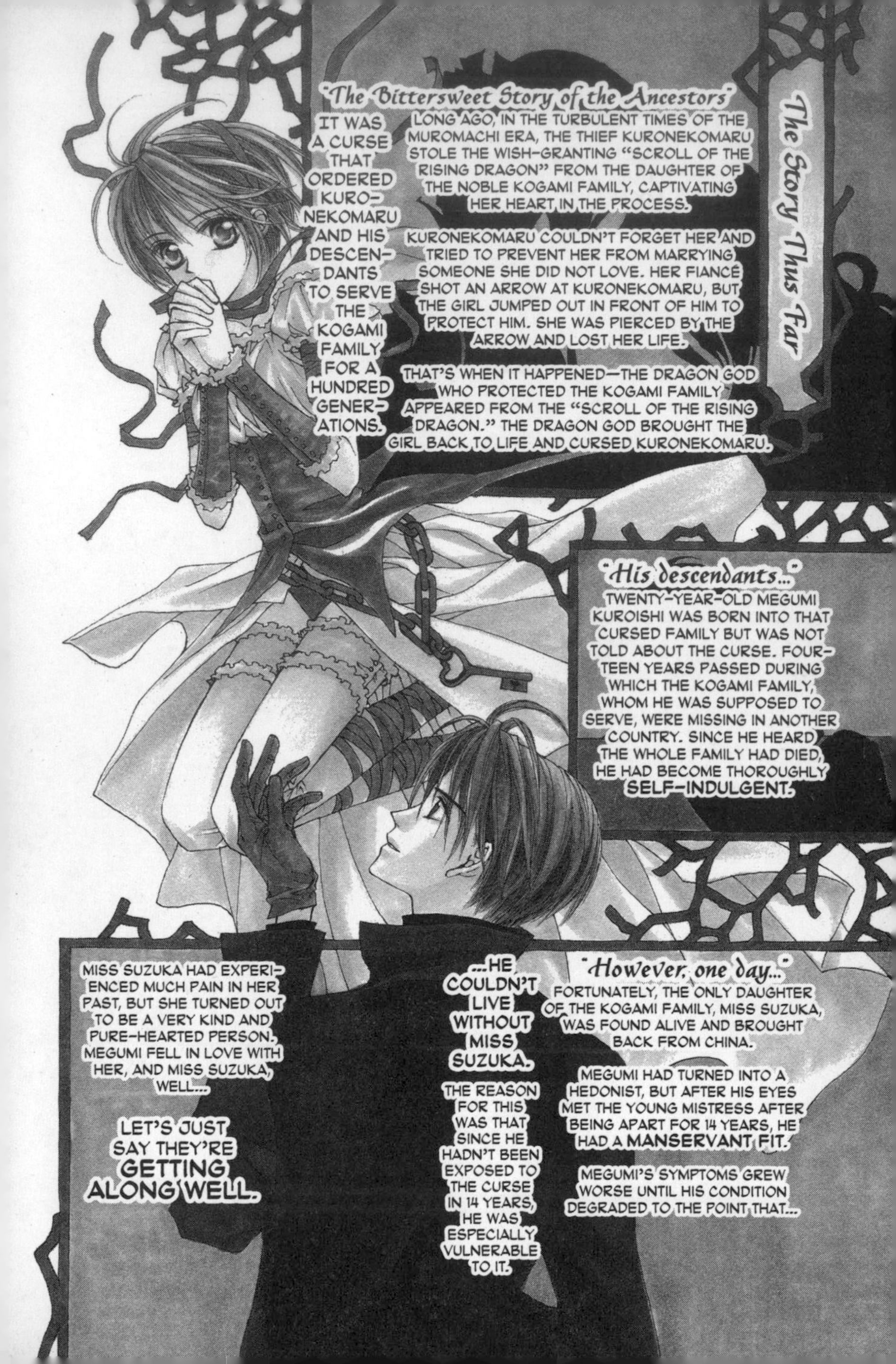
The Story Thus Far
"The Bittersweet Story of the Ancestors"
LONG AGO, IN THE TURBULENT TIMES OF THE MUROMACHI ERA, THE THIEF KURONEKOMARU STOLE THE WISH-GRANTING "SCROLL OF THE RISING DRAGON" FROM THE DAUGHTER OF THE NOBLE KOGAMI FAMILY, CAPTIVATING HER HEART IN THE PROCESS.
KURONEKOMARU COULDN'T FORGET HER AND TRIED TO PREVENT HER FROM MARRYING SOMEONE SHE DID NOT LOVE. HER FIANCÉ SHOT AN ARROW AT KURONEKOMARU, BUT THE GIRL JUMPED OUT IN FRONT OF HIM TO PROTECT HIM. SHE WAS PIERCED BY THE ARROW AND LOST HER LIFE.
THAT'S WHEN IT HAPPENED—THE DRAGON GOD WHO PROTECTED THE KOGAMI FAMILY APPEARED FROM THE "SCROLL OF THE RISING DRAGON." THE DRAGON GOD BROUGHT THE GIRL BACK TO LIFE AND CURSED KURONEKOMARU.
IT WAS A CURSE THAT ORDERED KURONEKOMARU AND HIS DESCENDANTS TO SERVE THE KOGAMI FAMILY FOR A HUNDRED GENERATIONS.
"His descendants..."
TWENTY-YEAR-OLD MEGUMI KUROISHI WAS BORN INTO THAT CURSED FAMILY BUT WAS NOT TOLD ABOUT THE CURSE. FOURTEEN YEARS PASSED DURING WHICH THE KOGAMI FAMILY, WHOM HE WAS SUPPOSED TO SERVE, WERE MISSING IN ANOTHER COUNTRY. SINCE HE HEARD THE WHOLE FAMILY HAD DIED, HE HAD BECOME THOROUGHLY SELF-INDULGENT.
"However, one day..."
FORTUNATELY, THE ONLY DAUGHTER OF THE KOGAMI FAMILY, MISS SUZUKA, WAS FOUND ALIVE AND BROUGHT BACK FROM CHINA.
MEGUMI HAD TURNED INTO A HEDONIST, BUT AFTER HIS EYES MET THE YOUNG MISTRESS AFTER BEING APART FOR 14 YEARS, HE HAD A MANSERVANT FIT.
MEGUMI'S SYMPTOMS GREW WORSE UNTIL HIS CONDITION DEGRADED TO THE POINT THAT...
...HE COULDN'T LIVE WITHOUT MISS SUZUKA.
THE REASON FOR THIS WAS THAT SINCE HE HADN'T BEEN EXPOSED TO THE CURSE IN 14 YEARS, HE WAS ESPECIALLY VULNERABLE TO IT.
MISS SUZUKA HAD EXPERIENCED MUCH PAIN IN HER PAST, BUT SHE TURNED OUT TO BE A VERY KIND AND PURE-HEARTED PERSON. MEGUMI FELL IN LOVE WITH HER, AND MISS SUZUKA, WELL...
LET'S JUST SAY THEY'RE GETTING ALONG WELL.

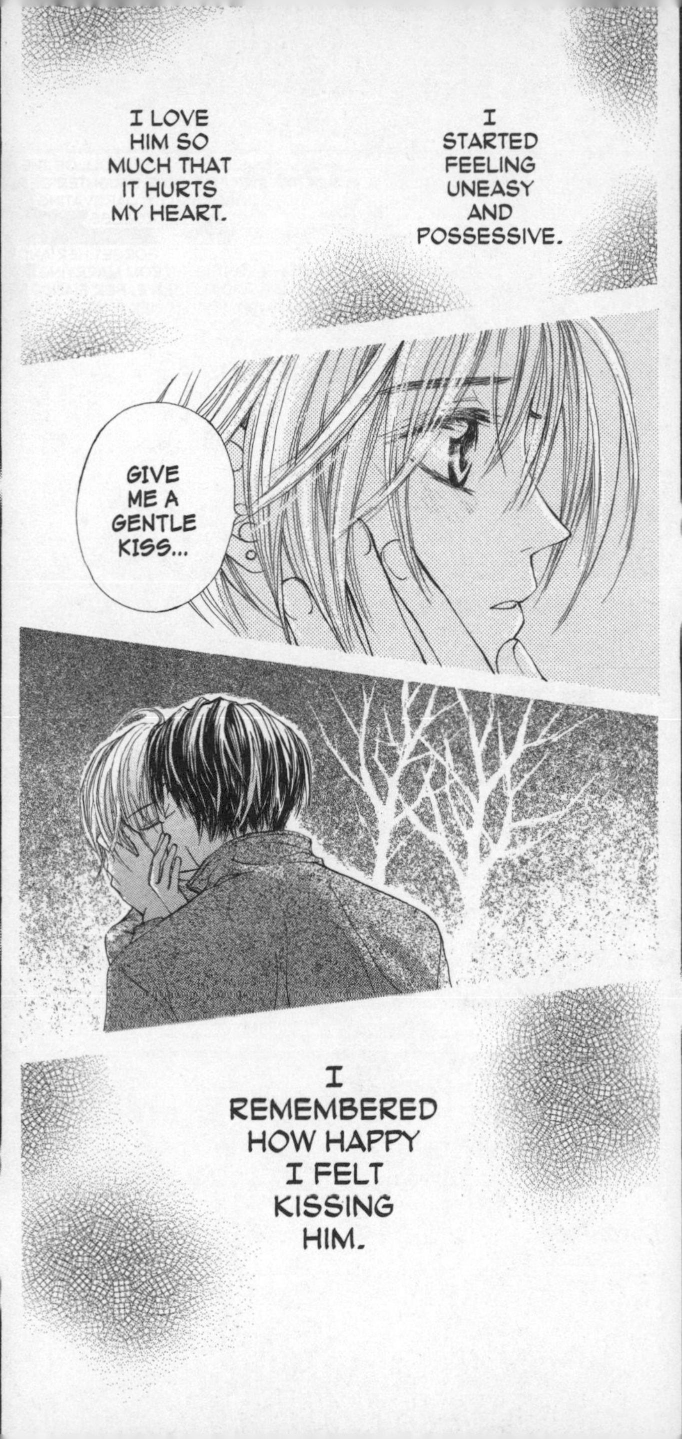
I STARTED FEELING UNEASY AND POSSESSIVE.
I LOVE HIM SO MUCH THAT IT HURTS MY HEART.
GIVE ME A GENTLE KISS...
I REMEMBERED HOW HAPPY I FELT KISSING HIM.

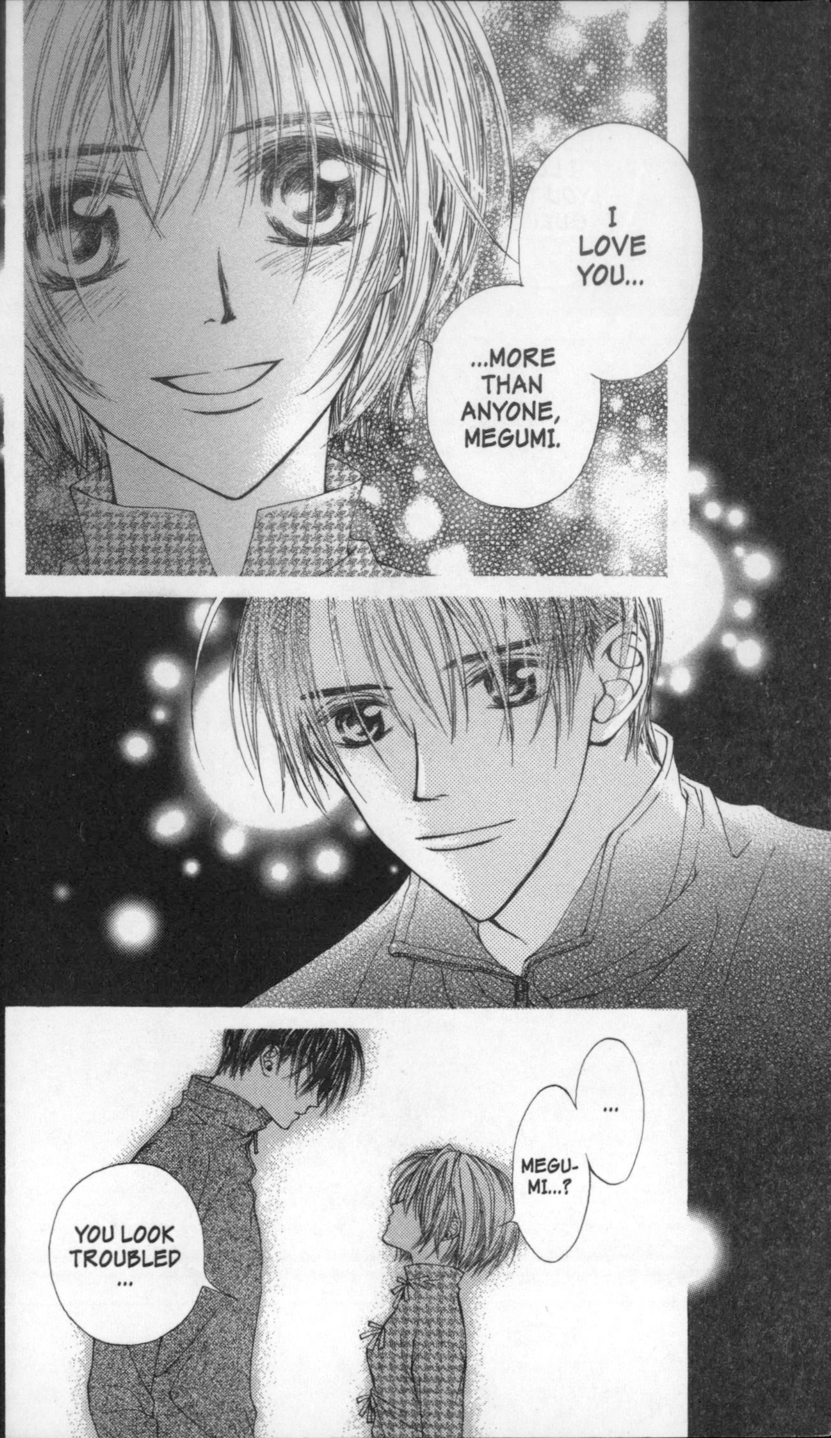
I LOVE YOU...
...MORE THAN ANYONE, MEGUMI.
...
MEGU-MI...?
YOU LOOK TROUBLED ...

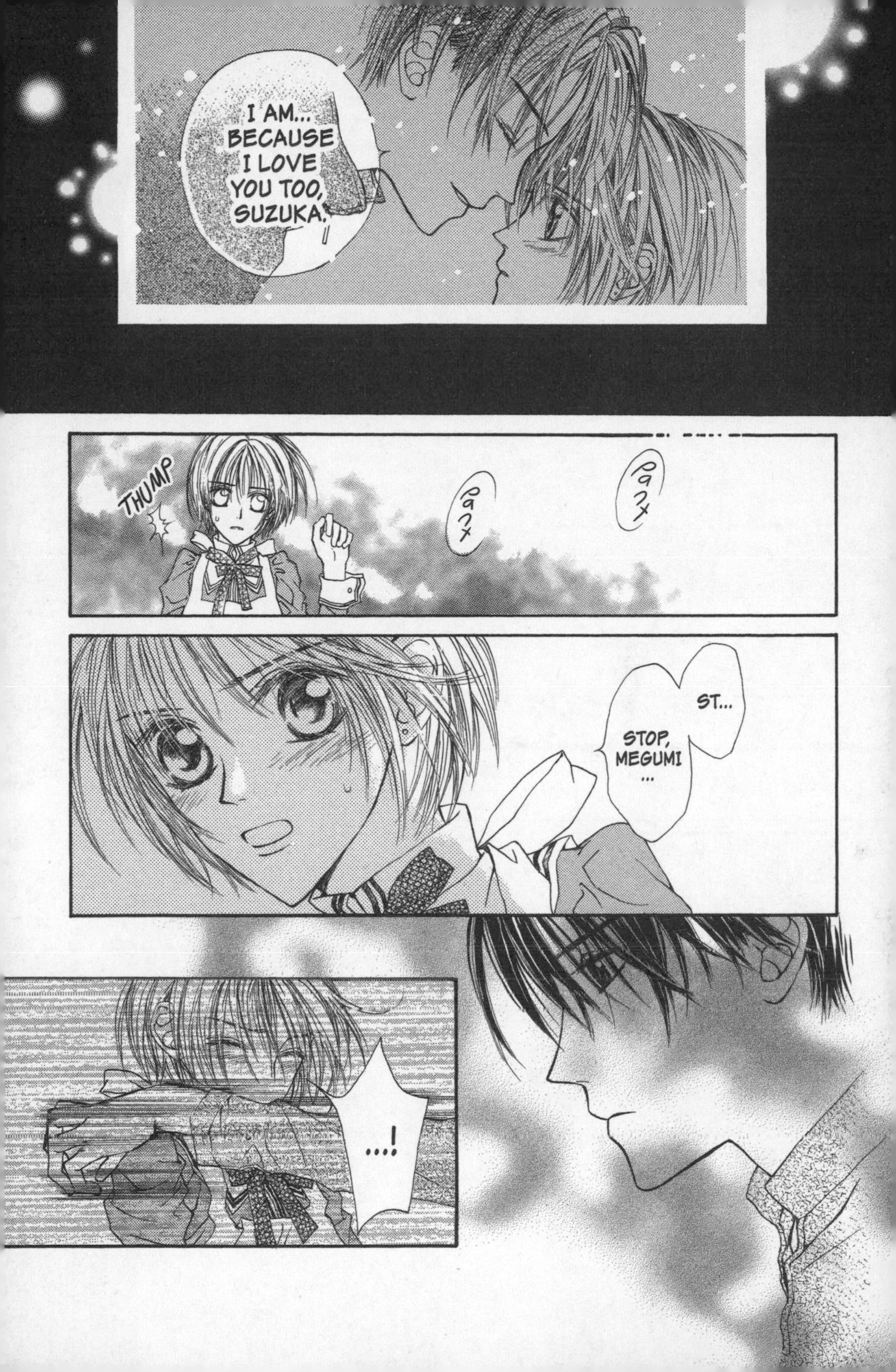
I AM... BECAUSE I LOVE YOU TOO, SUZUKA.
THUMP
ST...
STOP, MEGUMI ...
...!

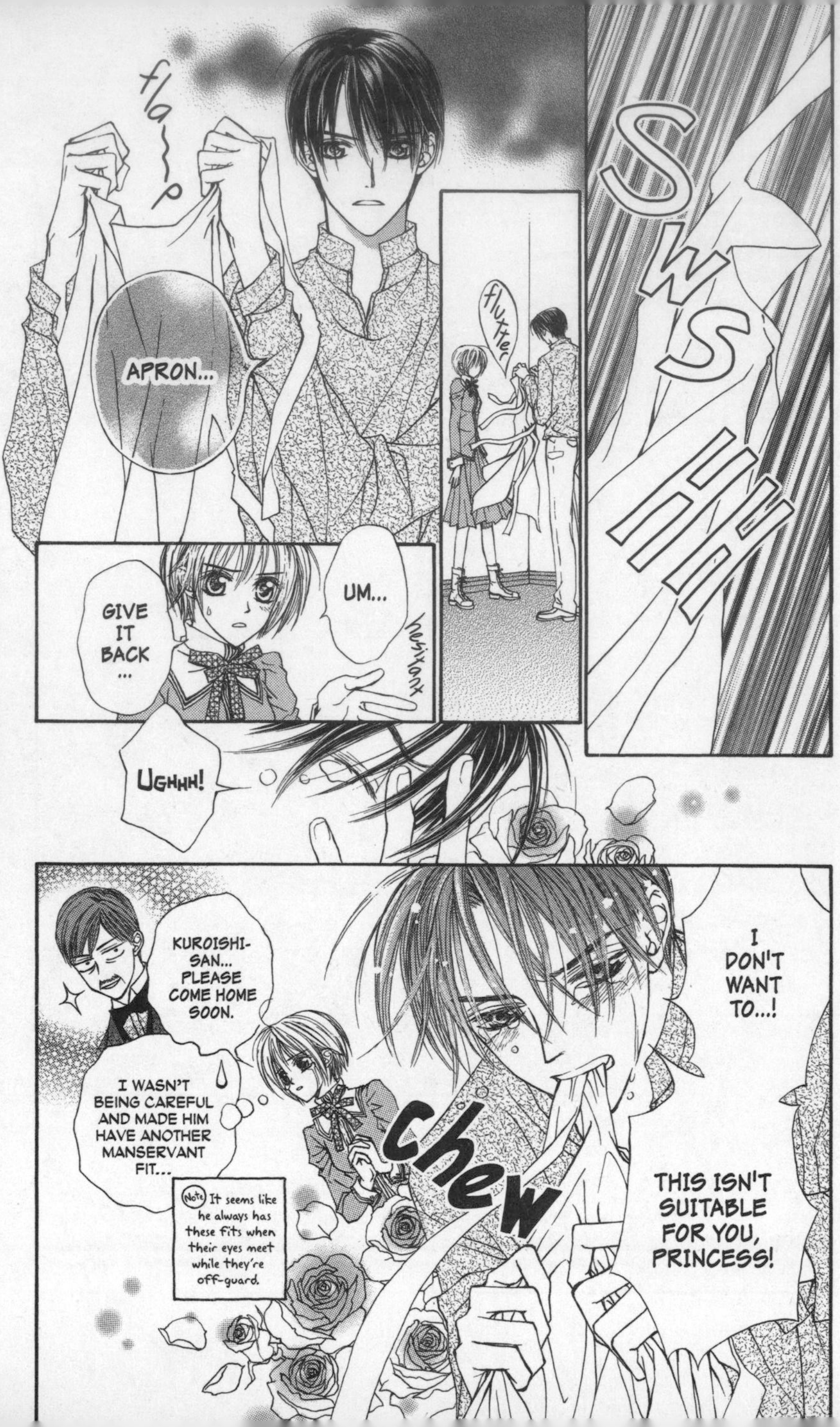

SWSHHH
flutter
fla~p
APRON...
UM...
hesitant
GIVE IT BACK...
UGHHH!
I DON'T WANT TO...!
THIS ISN'T SUITABLE FOR YOU, PRINCESS!
Chew
KUROISHI-SAN... PLEASE COME HOME SOON.
I WASN'T BEING CAREFUL AND MADE HIM HAVE ANOTHER MANSERVANT FIT...
Note It seems like he always has these fits when their eyes meet while they're off-guard.

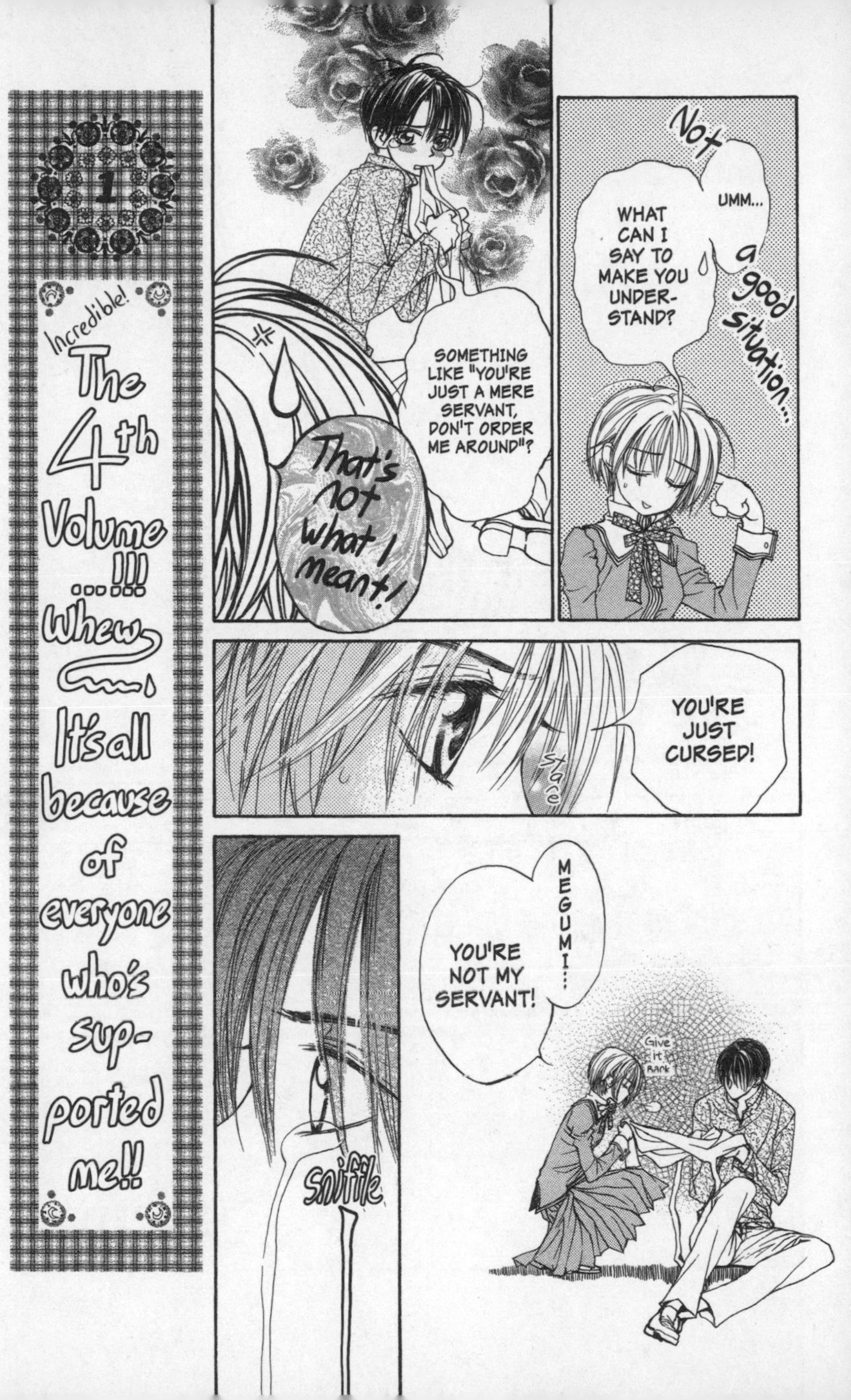

Not a good situation...
UMM...
WHAT CAN I SAY TO MAKE YOU UNDER-STAND?
SOMETHING LIKE "YOU'RE JUST A MERE SERVANT, DON'T ORDER ME AROUND"?
That's not what I meant!
YOU'RE JUST CURSED!
stare
MEGUMI...
YOU'RE NOT MY SERVANT!
Give it back
sniffle

1

Incredible!

The 4th Volume ...!!! Whew~! It's all because of everyone who's sup-ported me!!

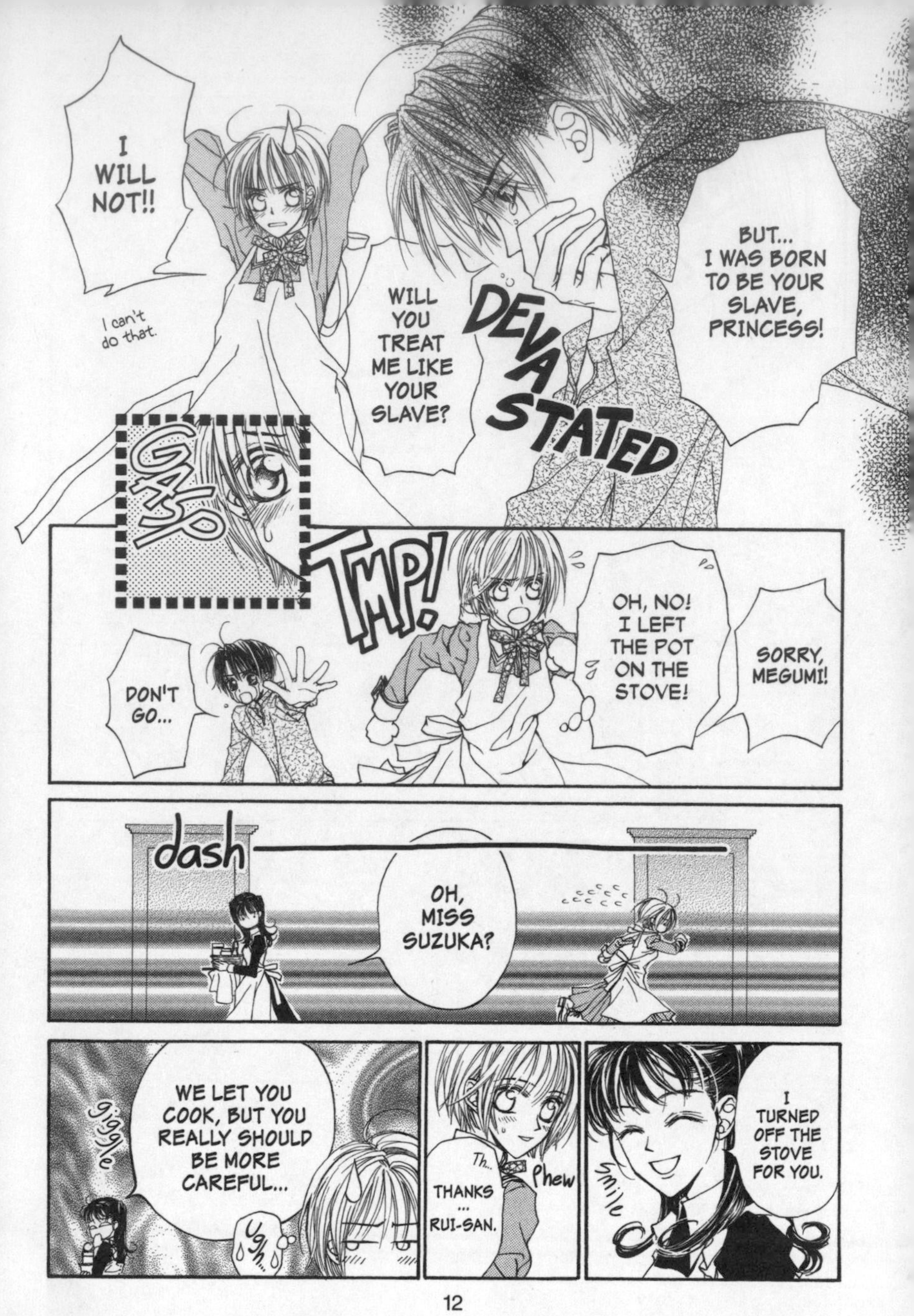
BUT...
I WAS BORN
TO BE YOUR
SLAVE,
PRINCESS!
DEVASTATED
WILL
YOU
TREAT
ME LIKE
YOUR
SLAVE?
I
WILL
NOT!!
I can't
do that.
GASP
SORRY,
MEGUMI!
OH, NO!
I LEFT
THE POT
ON THE
STOVE!
THP!
DON'T
GO...
dash
OH,
MISS
SUZUKA?
I
TURNED
OFF THE
STOVE
FOR YOU.
Smile
Phew
Th...
THANKS
...
RUI-SAN.
WE LET YOU
COOK, BUT YOU
REALLY SHOULD
BE MORE
CAREFUL...
giggle
Ugh

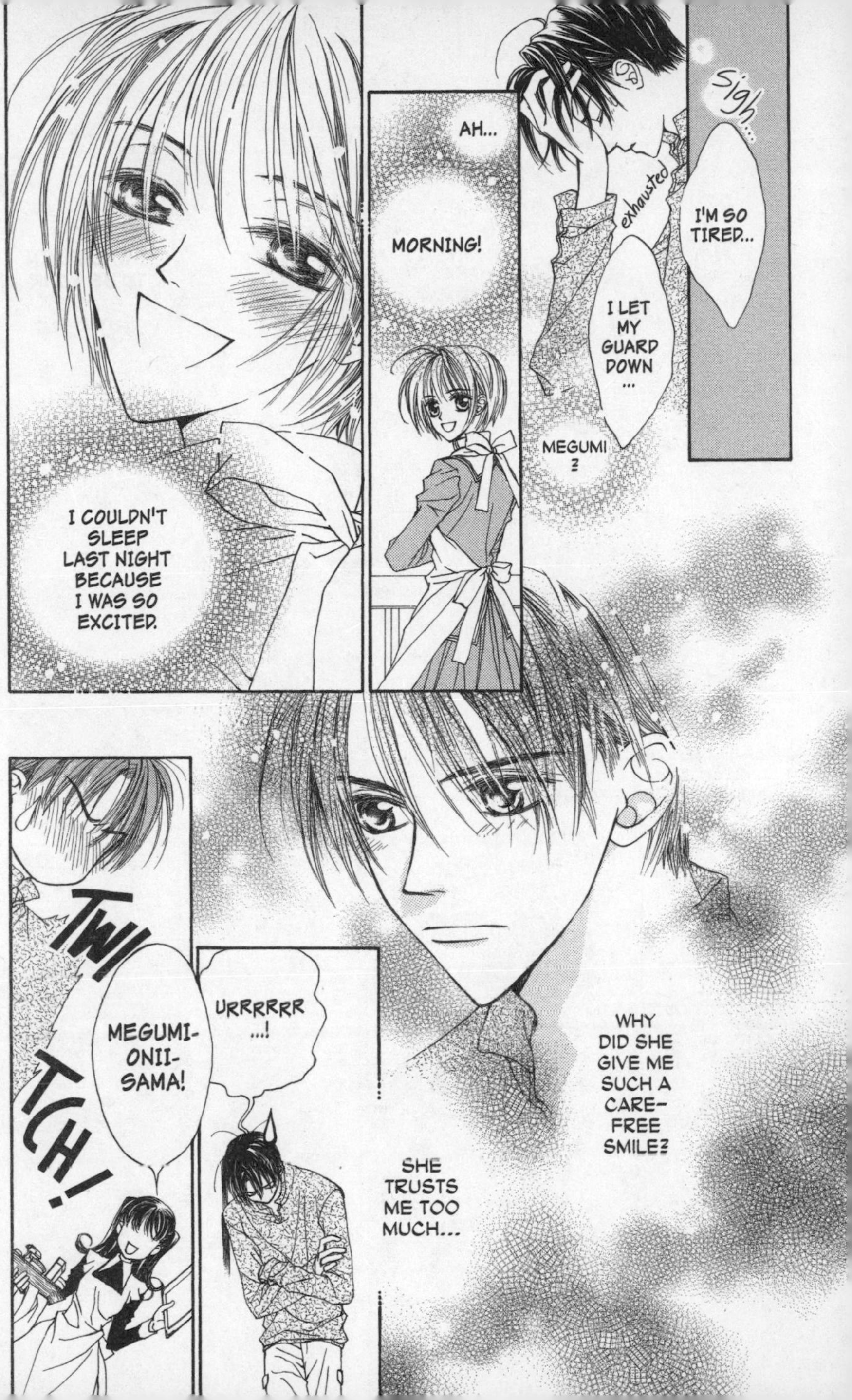
Sigh...
exhausted
I'M SO TIRED...
I LET MY GUARD DOWN ...
MEGUMI?
AH...
MORNING!
I COULDN'T SLEEP LAST NIGHT BECAUSE I WAS SO EXCITED.
WHY DID SHE GIVE ME SUCH A CARE-FREE SMILE?
SHE TRUSTS ME TOO MUCH...
URRRRRR ...!
MEGUMI-ONII-SAMA!
TWITCH!

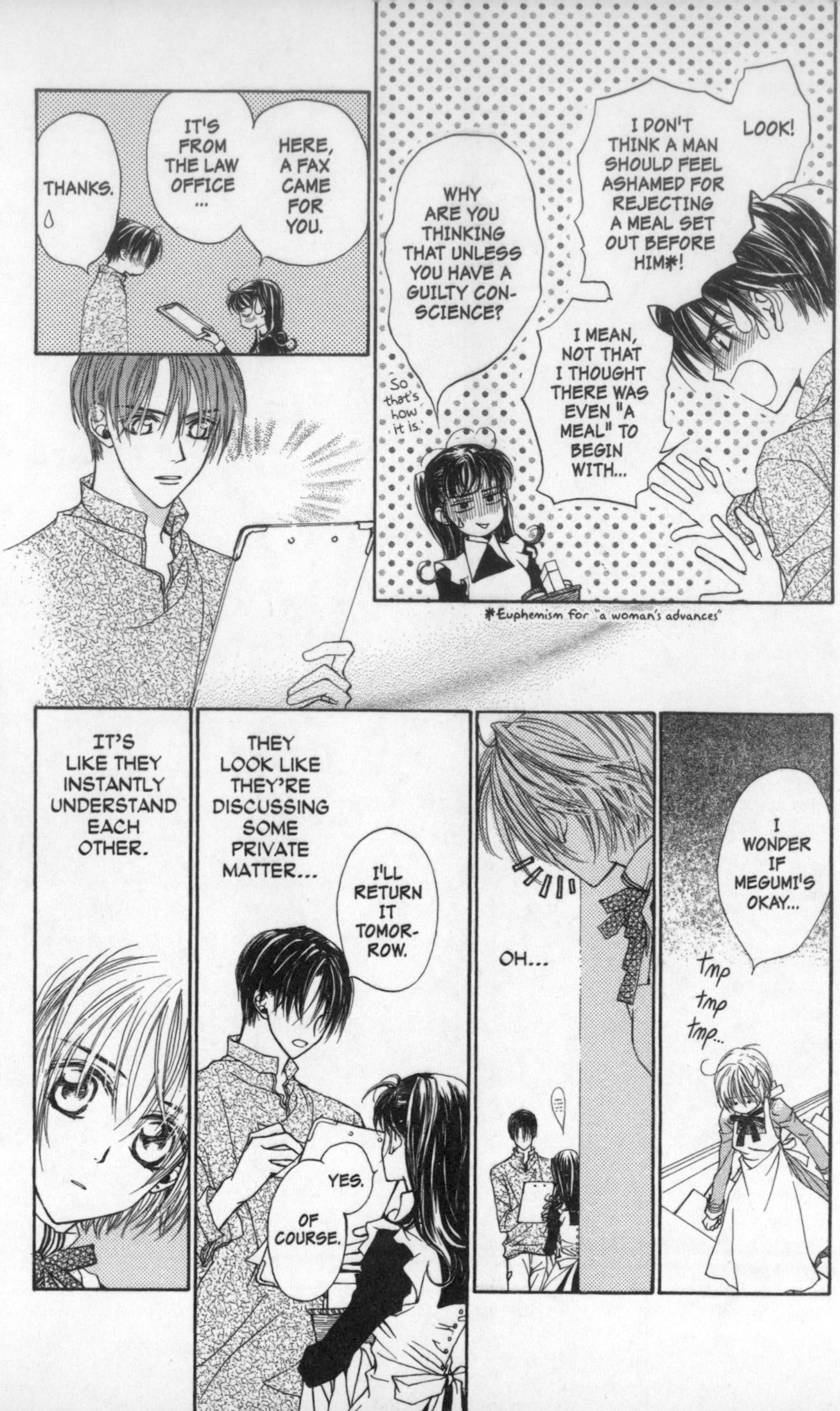
LOOK!
I DON'T THINK A MAN SHOULD FEEL ASHAMED FOR REJECTING A MEAL SET OUT BEFORE HIM*!
I MEAN, NOT THAT I THOUGHT THERE WAS EVEN "A MEAL" TO BEGIN WITH...
WHY ARE YOU THINKING THAT UNLESS YOU HAVE A GUILTY CON-SCIENCE?
So that's how it is.
*Euphemism for "a woman's advances"
HERE, A FAX CAME FOR YOU.
IT'S FROM THE LAW OFFICE ...
THANKS.
I WONDER IF MEGUMI'S OKAY...
tmp tmp tmp...
OH...
THEY LOOK LIKE THEY'RE DISCUSSING SOME PRIVATE MATTER...
I'LL RETURN IT TOMOR-ROW.
YES.
OF COURSE.
IT'S LIKE THEY INSTANTLY UNDERSTAND EACH OTHER.

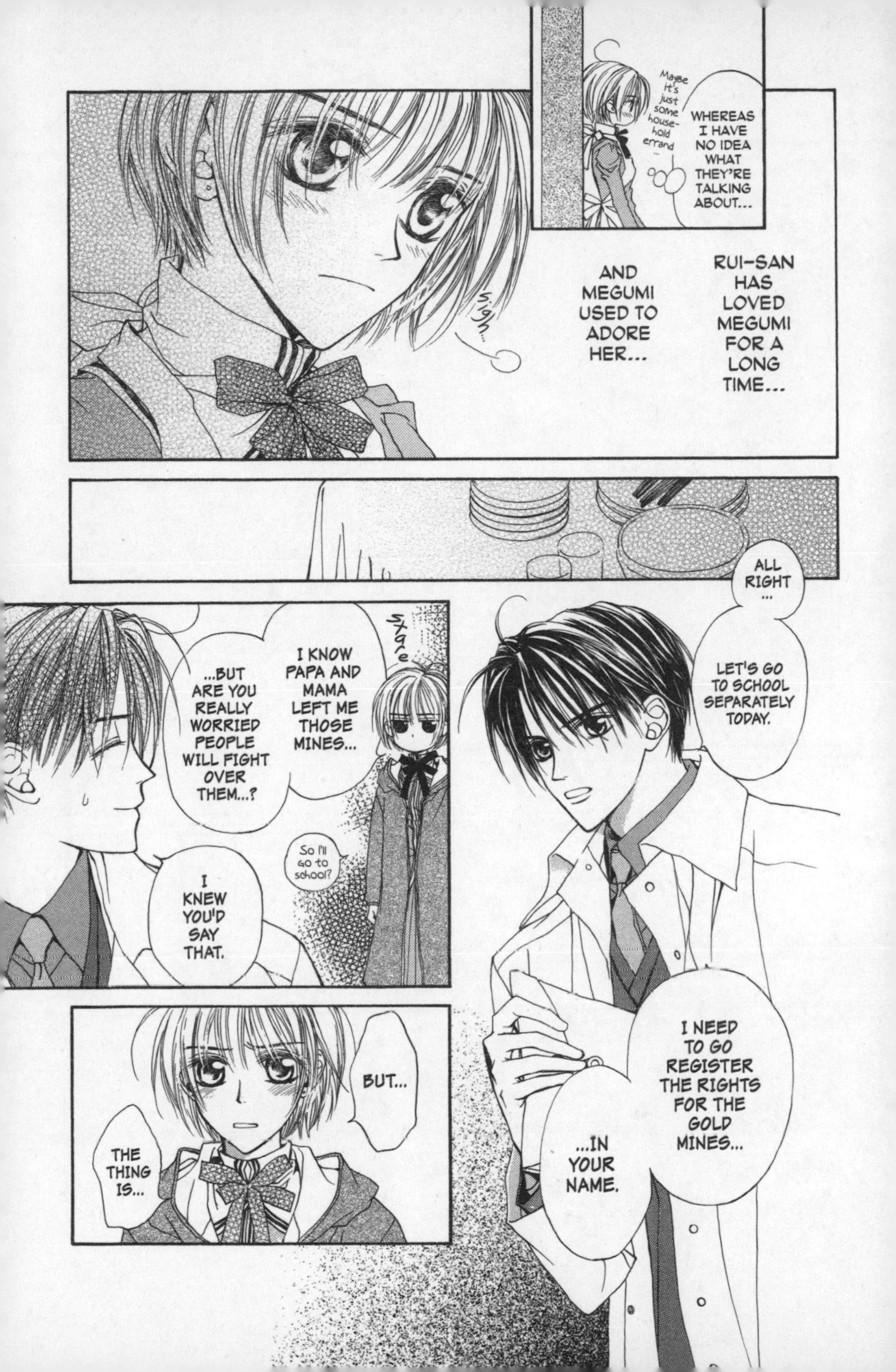
WHEREAS I HAVE NO IDEA WHAT THEY'RE TALKING ABOUT...
Maybe it's just some house-hold errand...
RUI-SAN HAS LOVED MEGUMI FOR A LONG TIME...
AND MEGUMI USED TO ADORE HER...
sigh...
ALL RIGHT...
LET'S GO TO SCHOOL SEPARATELY TODAY.
I NEED TO GO REGISTER THE RIGHTS FOR THE GOLD MINES...
...IN YOUR NAME.
stare
I KNOW PAPA AND MAMA LEFT ME THOSE MINES...
...BUT ARE YOU REALLY WORRIED PEOPLE WILL FIGHT OVER THEM...?
So I'll go to school?
I KNEW YOU'D SAY THAT.
BUT...
THE THING IS...

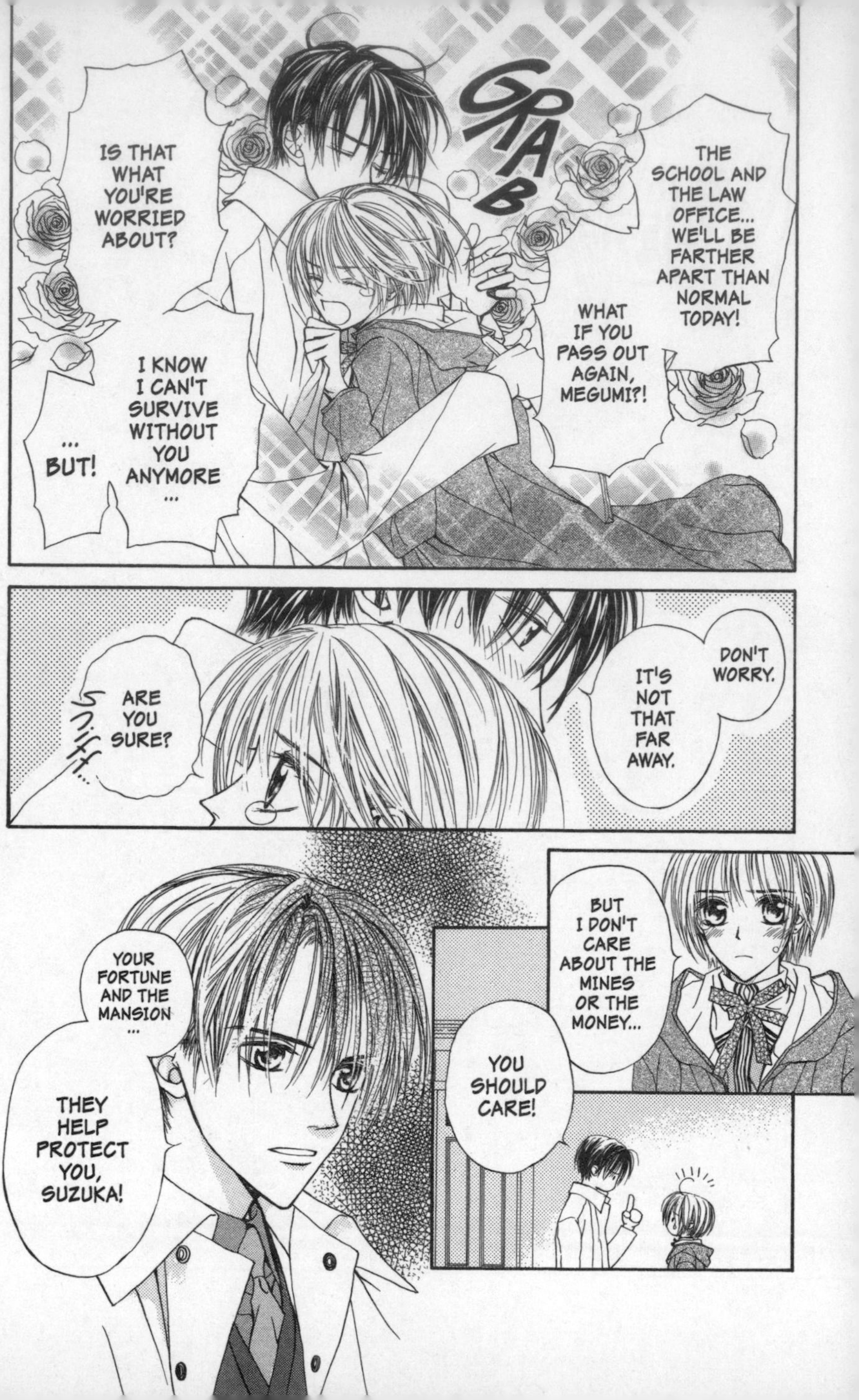
THE SCHOOL AND THE LAW OFFICE... WE'LL BE FARTHER APART THAN NORMAL TODAY!
GRAB
WHAT IF YOU PASS OUT AGAIN, MEGUMI?!
IS THAT WHAT YOU'RE WORRIED ABOUT?
I KNOW I CAN'T SURVIVE WITHOUT YOU ANYMORE ...
... BUT!
DON'T WORRY.
IT'S NOT THAT FAR AWAY.
ARE YOU SURE?
Sniff...
BUT I DON'T CARE ABOUT THE MINES OR THE MONEY...
YOU SHOULD CARE!
YOUR FORTUNE AND THE MANSION ...
THEY HELP PROTECT YOU, SUZUKA!

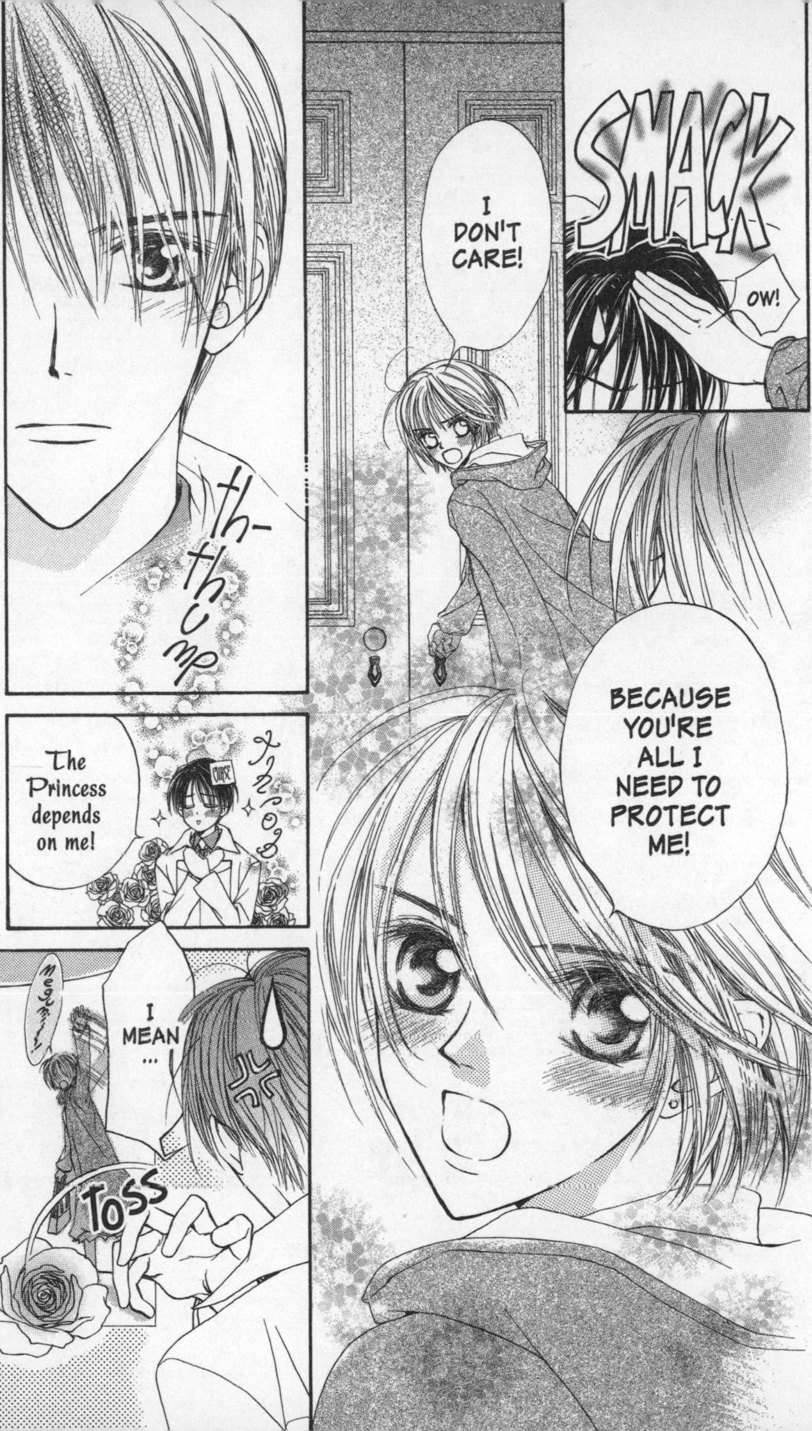
SMACK
OW!
I DON'T CARE!
BECAUSE YOU'RE ALL I NEED TO PROTECT ME!
th-thump
The Princess depends on me!
I MEAN ...
TOSS

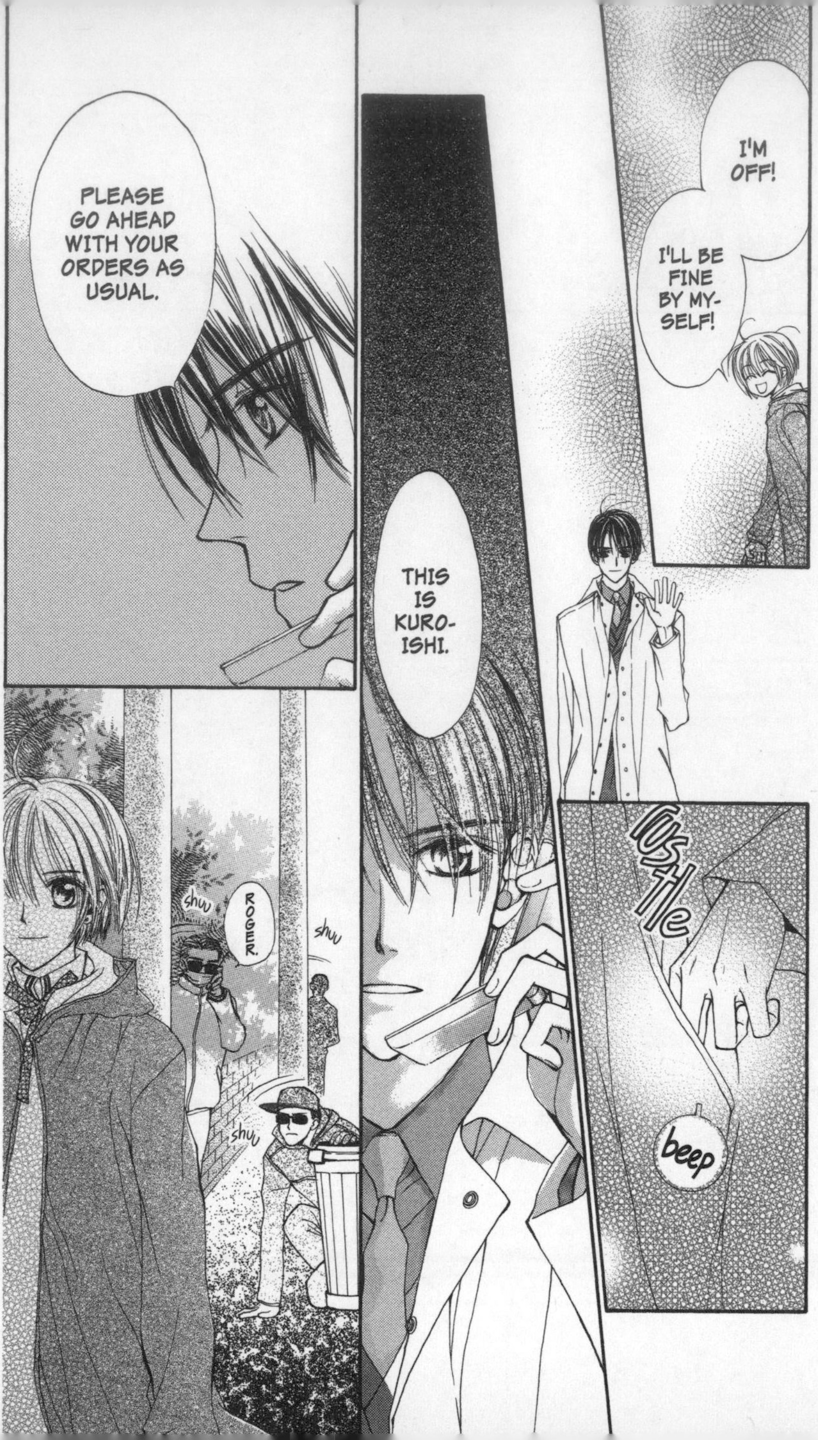
I'M OFF!
I'LL BE FINE BY MY-SELF!
rustle
beep
THIS IS KURO-ISHI.
PLEASE GO AHEAD WITH YOUR ORDERS AS USUAL.
shuu
ROGER.
shuu
shuu

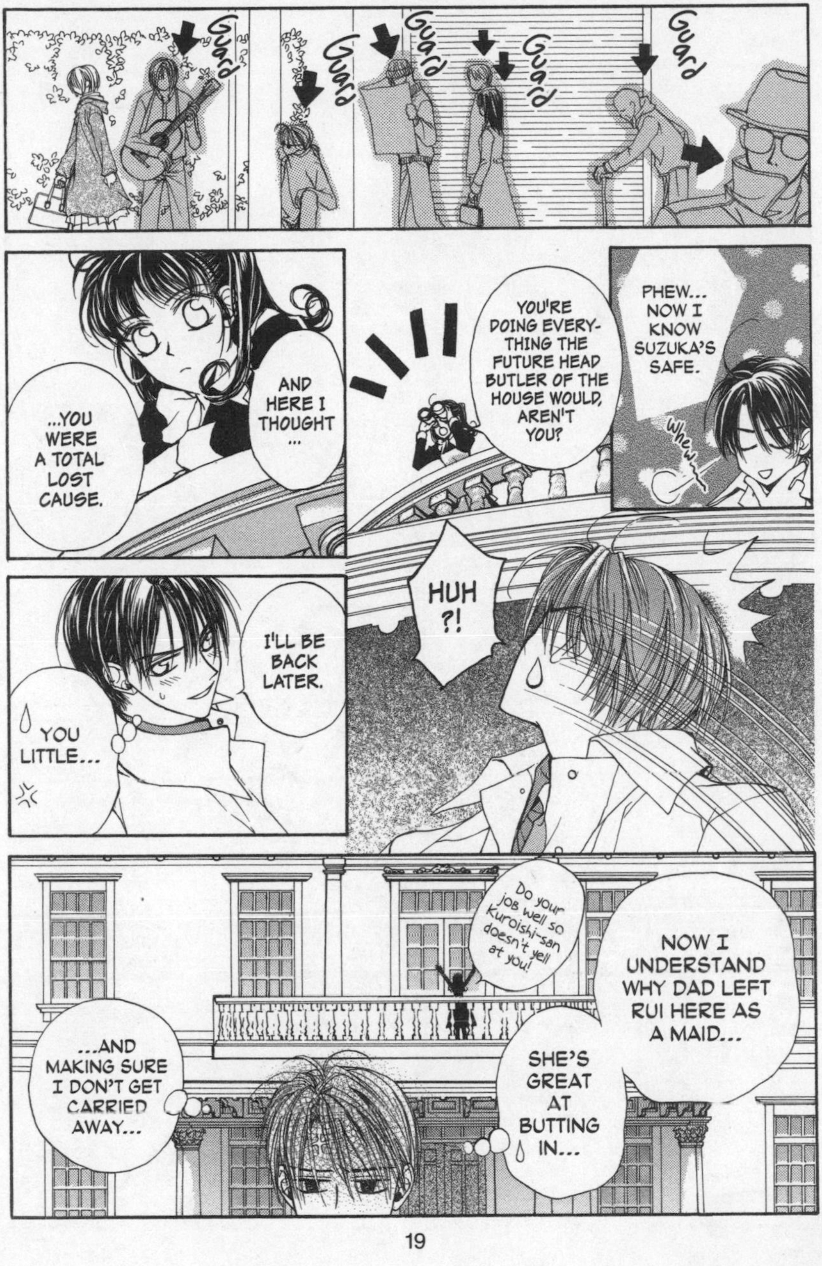
Guard
Guard
Guard
Guard
Guard
PHEW... NOW I KNOW SUZUKA'S SAFE.
Whew...
YOU'RE DOING EVERY-THING THE FUTURE HEAD BUTLER OF THE HOUSE WOULD, AREN'T YOU?
AND HERE I THOUGHT...
...YOU WERE A TOTAL LOST CAUSE.
HUH ?!
I'LL BE BACK LATER.
YOU LITTLE...
NOW I UNDERSTAND WHY DAD LEFT RUI HERE AS A MAID...
Do your job well so Kuroishi-san doesn't yell at you!
SHE'S GREAT AT BUTTING IN...
...AND MAKING SURE I DON'T GET CARRIED AWAY...

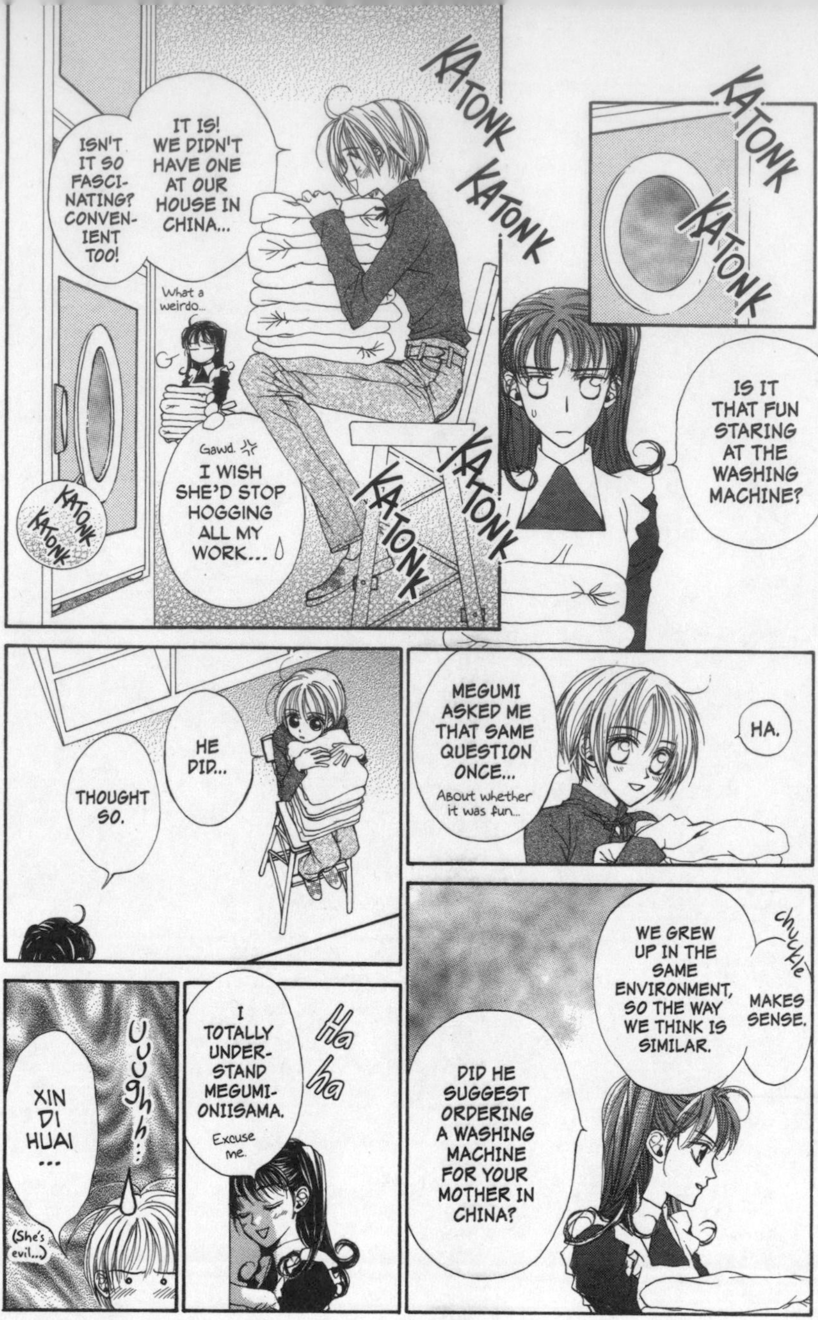
KATONK KATONK
IS IT THAT FUN STARING AT THE WASHING MACHINE?
KATONK KATONK
KATONK KATONK
IT IS! WE DIDN'T HAVE ONE AT OUR HOUSE IN CHINA...
ISN'T IT SO FASCINATING? CONVENIENT TOO!
What a weirdo...
Gawd.
I WISH SHE'D STOP HOGGING ALL MY WORK...
KATONK KATONK
HA.
MEGUMI ASKED ME THAT SAME QUESTION ONCE...
About whether it was fun...
HE DID...
THOUGHT SO.
chuckle
MAKES SENSE.
WE GREW UP IN THE SAME ENVIRONMENT, SO THE WAY WE THINK IS SIMILAR.
DID HE SUGGEST ORDERING A WASHING MACHINE FOR YOUR MOTHER IN CHINA?
Ha ha
I TOTALLY UNDERSTAND MEGUMI-ONIISAMA.
Excuse me.
Uuughh...
XIN DI HUAI...
(She's evil...)

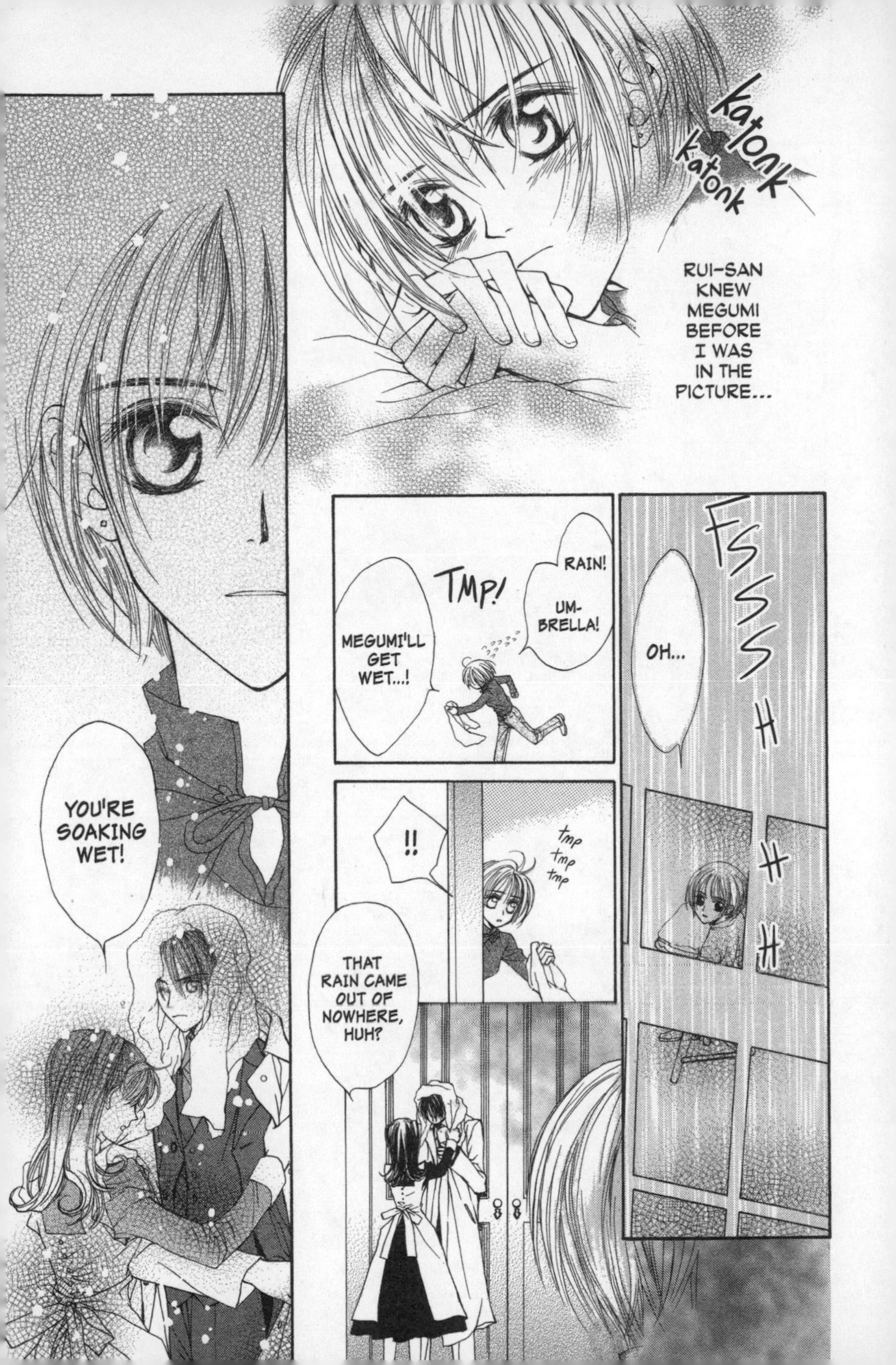
katonk katonk
RUI-SAN KNEW MEGUMI BEFORE I WAS IN THE PICTURE...
FSSSHHH
OH...
RAIN!
UM-BRELLA!
TMP!
MEGUMI'LL GET WET...!
tmp tmp tmp
!!
THAT RAIN CAME OUT OF NOWHERE, HUH?
YOU'RE SOAKING WET!

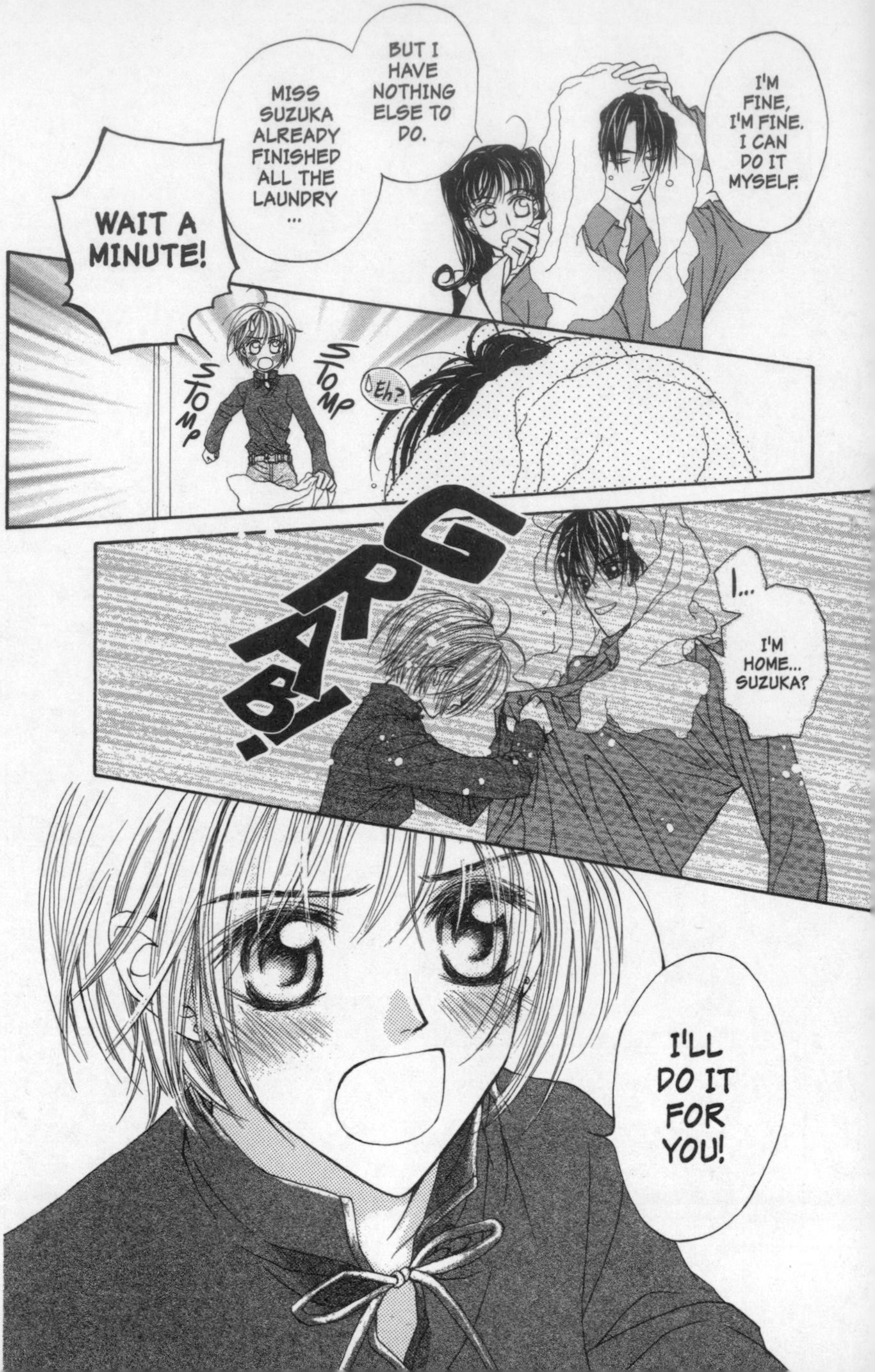
I'M FINE, I'M FINE. I CAN DO IT MYSELF.
MISS SUZUKA ALREADY FINISHED ALL THE LAUNDRY ...
BUT I HAVE NOTHING ELSE TO DO.
WAIT A MINUTE!
Eh?
STOMP
STOMP
I...
I'M HOME... SUZUKA?
GRAB!
I'LL DO IT FOR YOU!

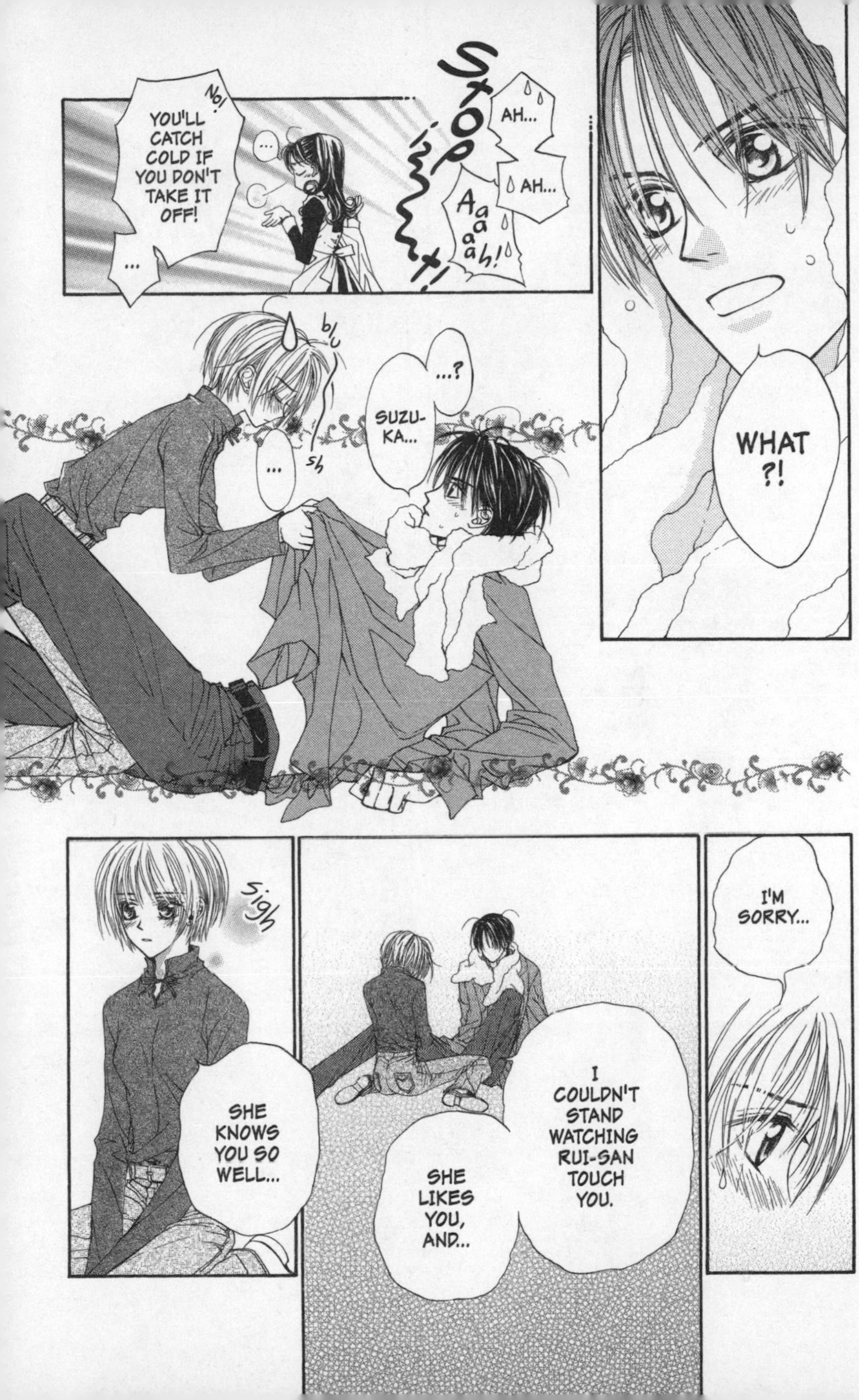
WHAT?!
AH...
AH...
Aaaah!
Stop it!
No!
YOU'LL CATCH COLD IF YOU DON'T TAKE IT OFF!
...
...
...?
SUZU-KA...
blush
...
I'M SORRY...
I COULDN'T STAND WATCHING RUI-SAN TOUCH YOU.
SHE LIKES YOU, AND...
Sigh
SHE KNOWS YOU SO WELL...

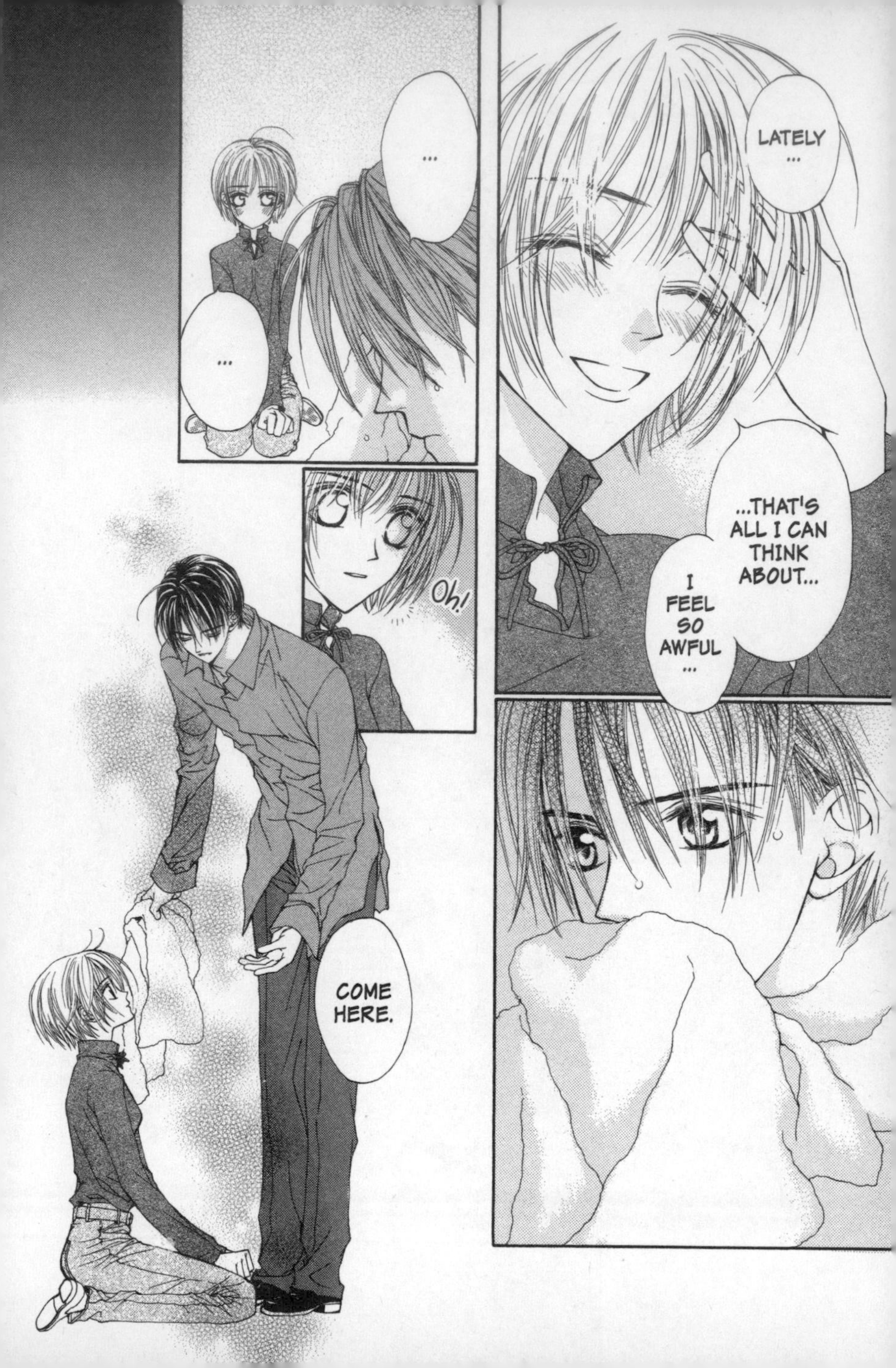
LATELY ...
...THAT'S ALL I CAN THINK ABOUT...
I FEEL SO AWFUL ...
...
...
Oh!
COME HERE.

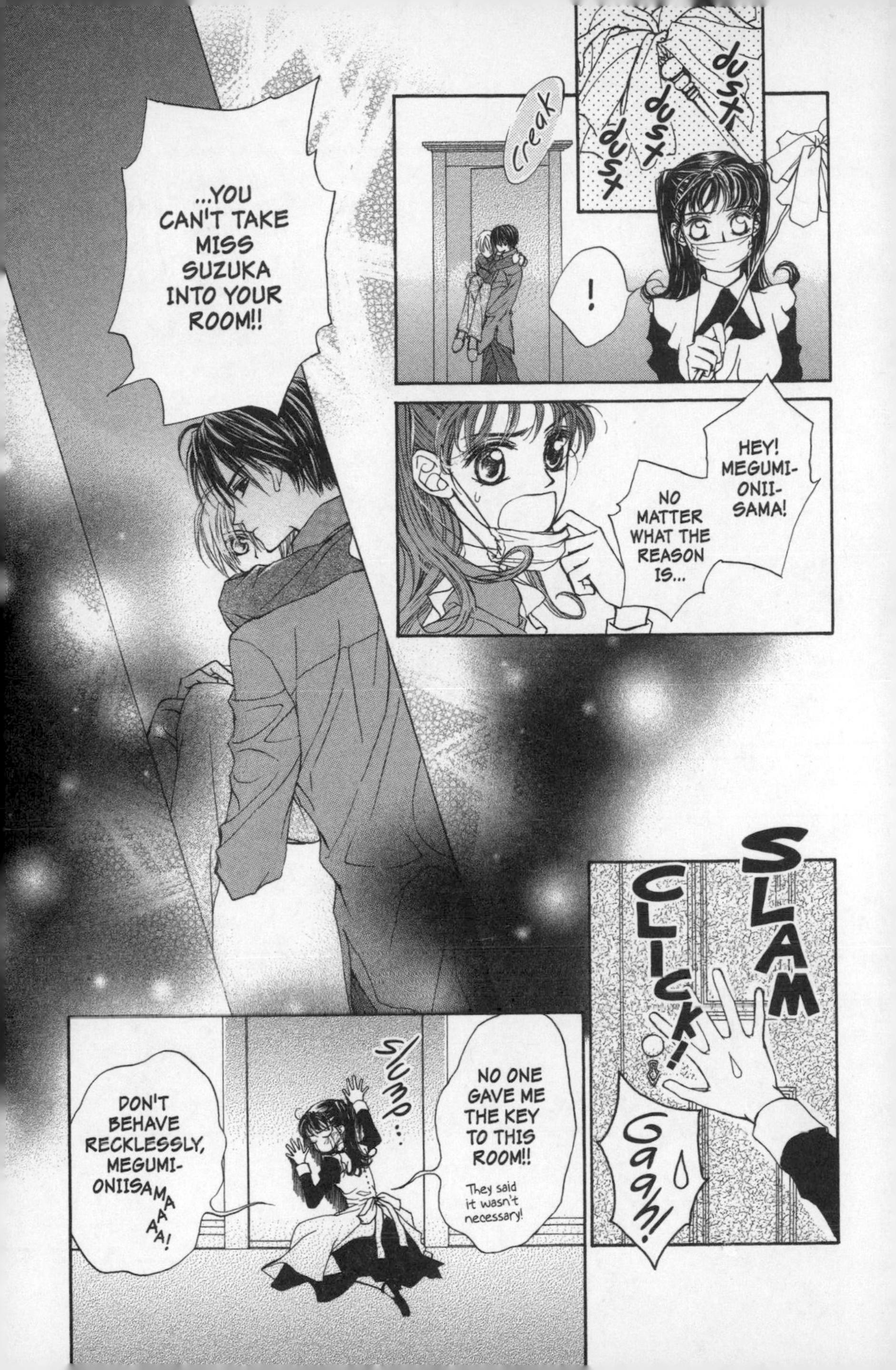
dust dust dust
creak
!
HEY! MEGUMI-ONII-SAMA!
NO MATTER WHAT THE REASON IS...
...YOU CAN'T TAKE MISS SUZUKA INTO YOUR ROOM!!
SLAM
CLICK!
Gaah!
NO ONE GAVE ME THE KEY TO THIS ROOM!!
They said it wasn't necessary!
slump...
DON'T BEHAVE RECKLESSLY, MEGUMI-ONIISAMAAAAA!

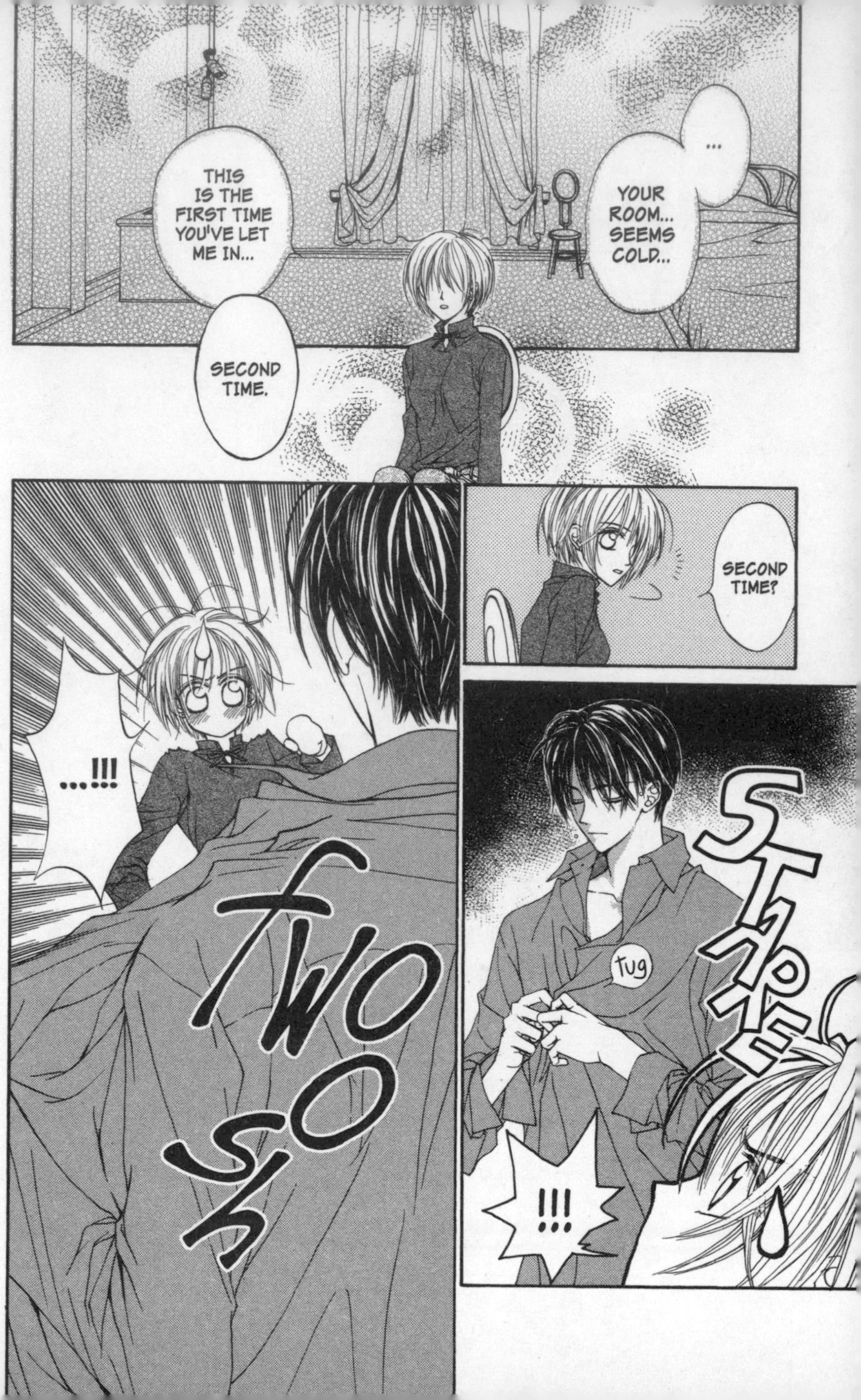
...
YOUR ROOM... SEEMS COLD...
THIS IS THE FIRST TIME YOU'VE LET ME IN...
SECOND TIME.
SECOND TIME?
STRIP
tug
!!!
...!!!
FWOOSH

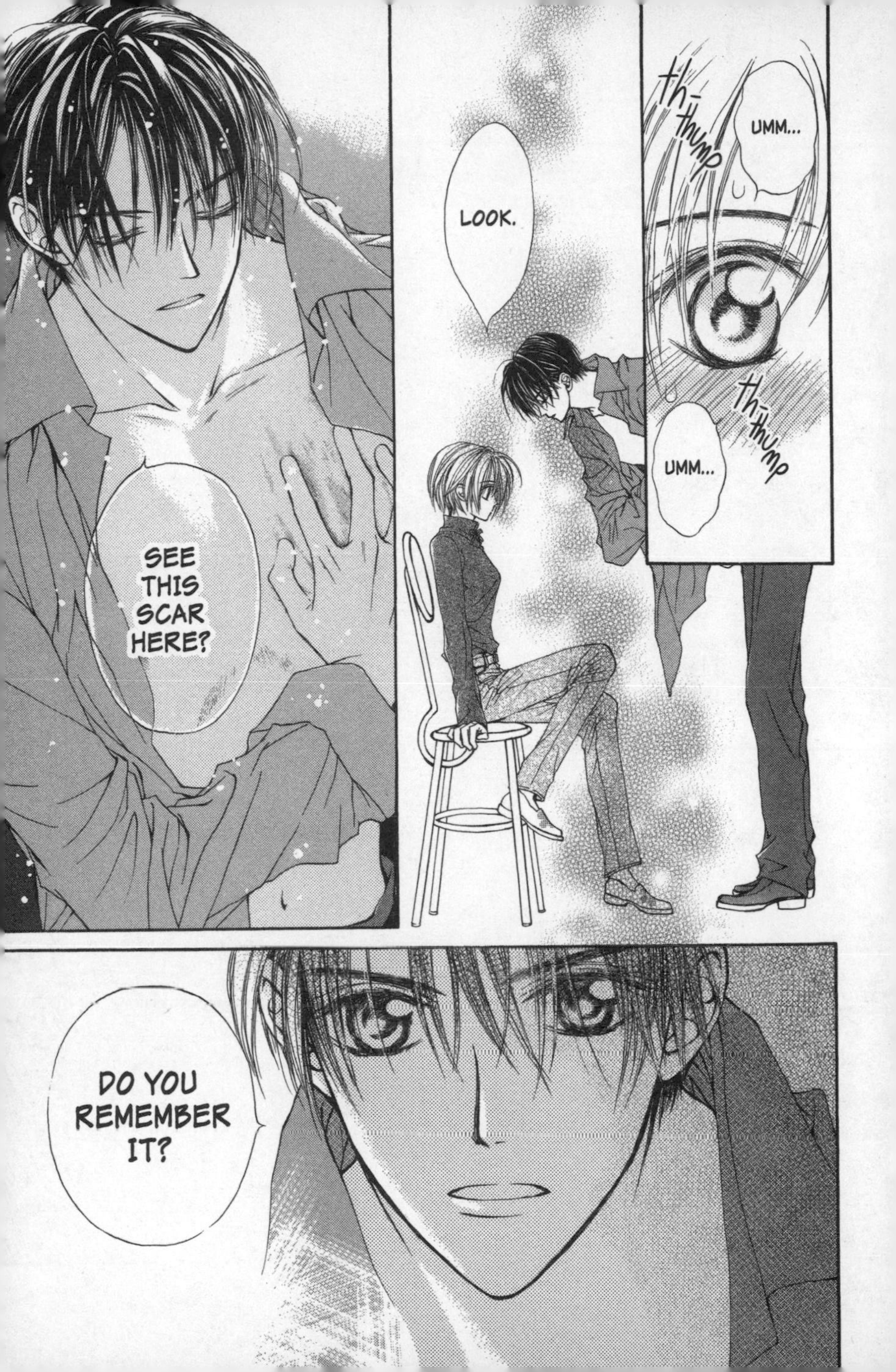
th-thump
UMM...
th-thump
UMM...
LOOK.
SEE THIS SCAR HERE?
DO YOU REMEMBER IT?

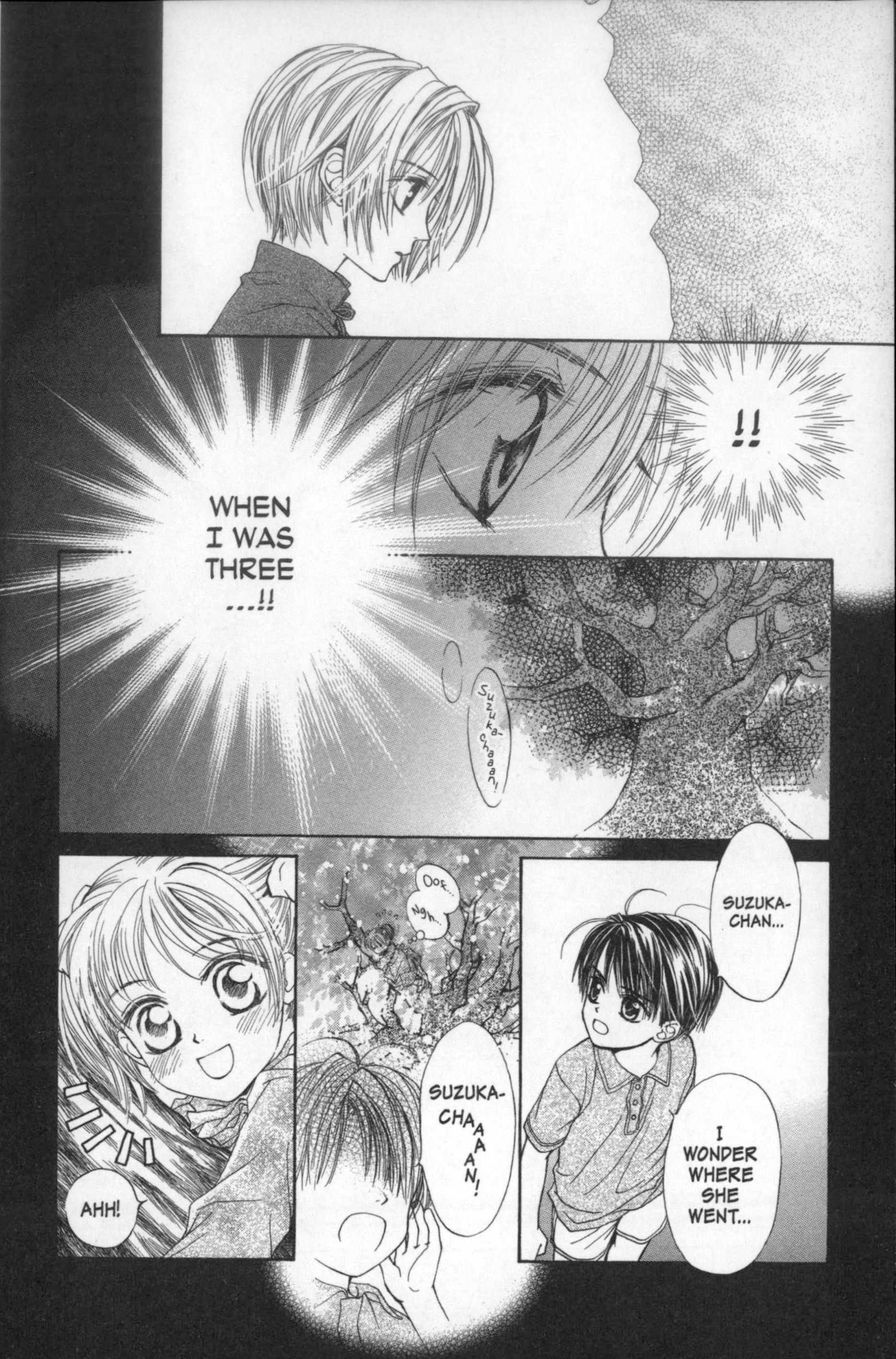
!!
WHEN I WAS THREE ...!!
Suzuka-chaaaan!
SUZUKA-CHAN...
I WONDER WHERE SHE WENT...
SUZUKA-CHAAAAAN!
Oof... Ngh...
AHH!

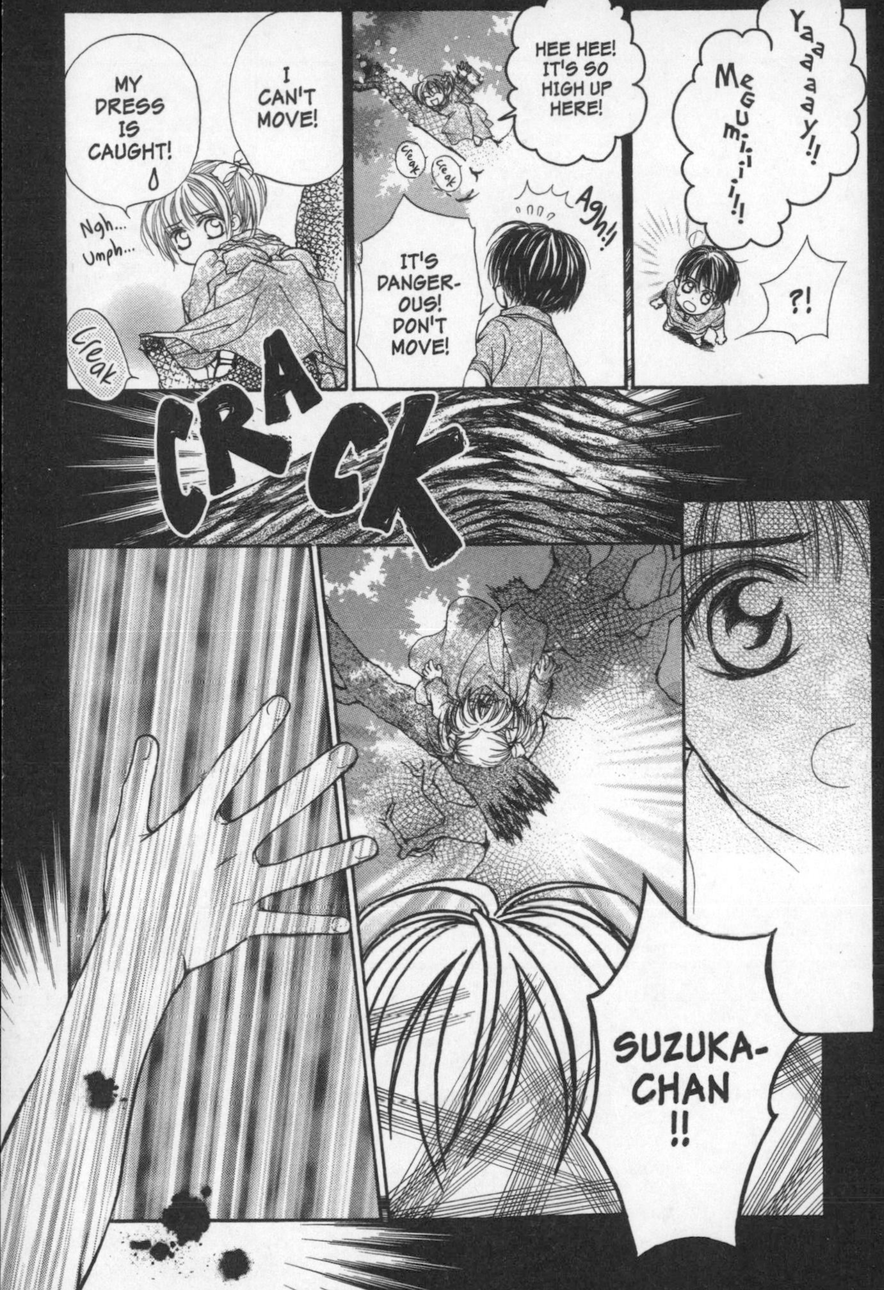
Yaaaaay!!
Megumi-i-i-i!!
?!
HEE HEE! IT'S SO HIGH UP HERE!
creak
creak
Agh!!
IT'S DANGER-OUS! DON'T MOVE!
I CAN'T MOVE!
MY DRESS IS CAUGHT!
Ngh... Umph...
Creak
CRACK
SUZUKA-CHAN!!

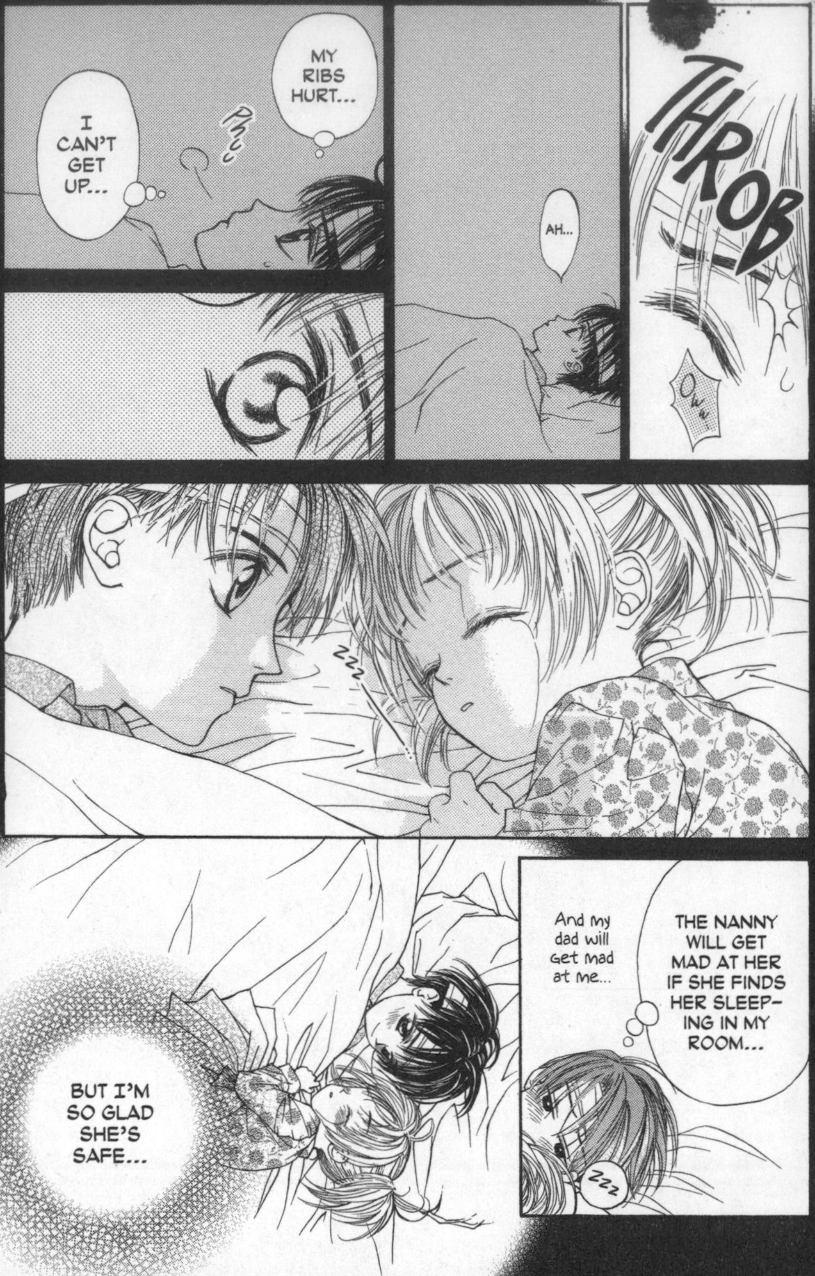
THROB
Oww
AH...
MY RIBS HURT...
I CAN'T GET UP...
ZZZ
THE NANNY WILL GET MAD AT HER IF SHE FINDS HER SLEEP-ING IN MY ROOM...
And my dad will get mad at me...
ZZZ
BUT I'M SO GLAD SHE'S SAFE...

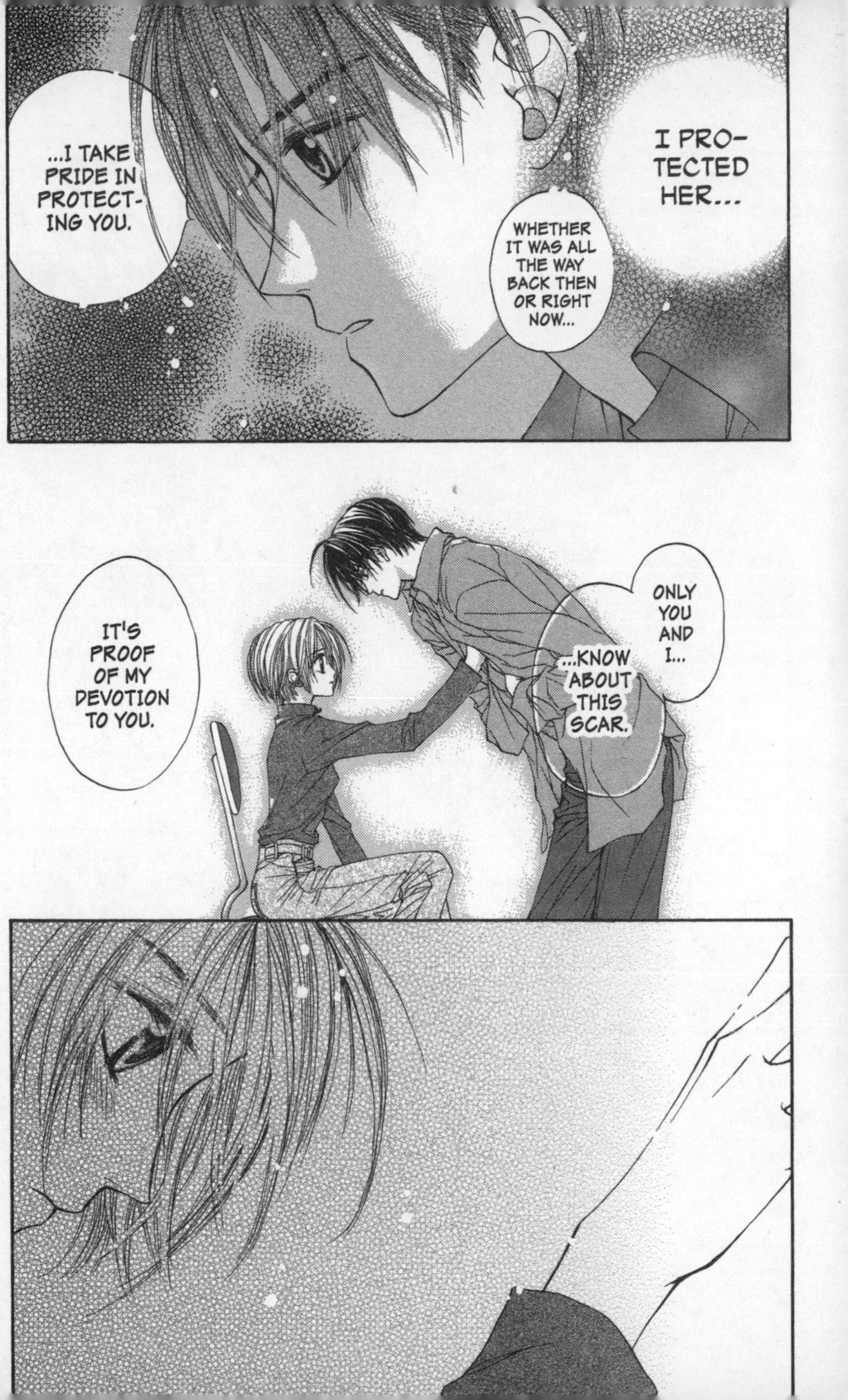
I PROTECTED HER...
WHETHER IT WAS ALL THE WAY BACK THEN OR RIGHT NOW...
...I TAKE PRIDE IN PROTECTING YOU.
ONLY YOU AND I...
...KNOW ABOUT THIS SCAR.
IT'S PROOF OF MY DEVOTION TO YOU.

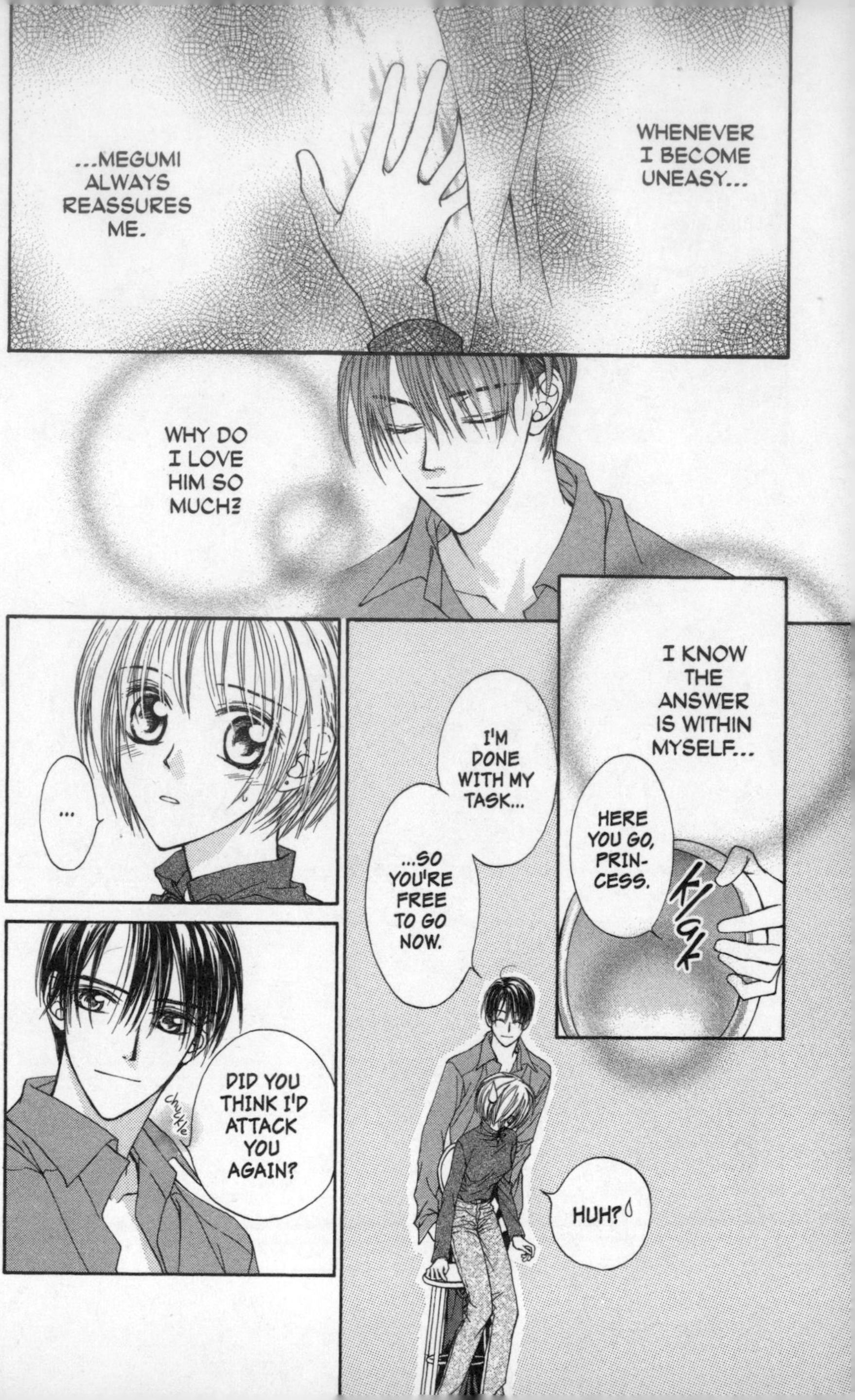
WHENEVER I BECOME UNEASY...
...MEGUMI ALWAYS REASSURES ME.
WHY DO I LOVE HIM SO MUCH?
I KNOW THE ANSWER IS WITHIN MYSELF...
HERE YOU GO, PRIN-CESS.
Klak
I'M DONE WITH MY TASK...
...SO YOU'RE FREE TO GO NOW.
HUH?
...
DID YOU THINK I'D ATTACK YOU AGAIN?
chuckle

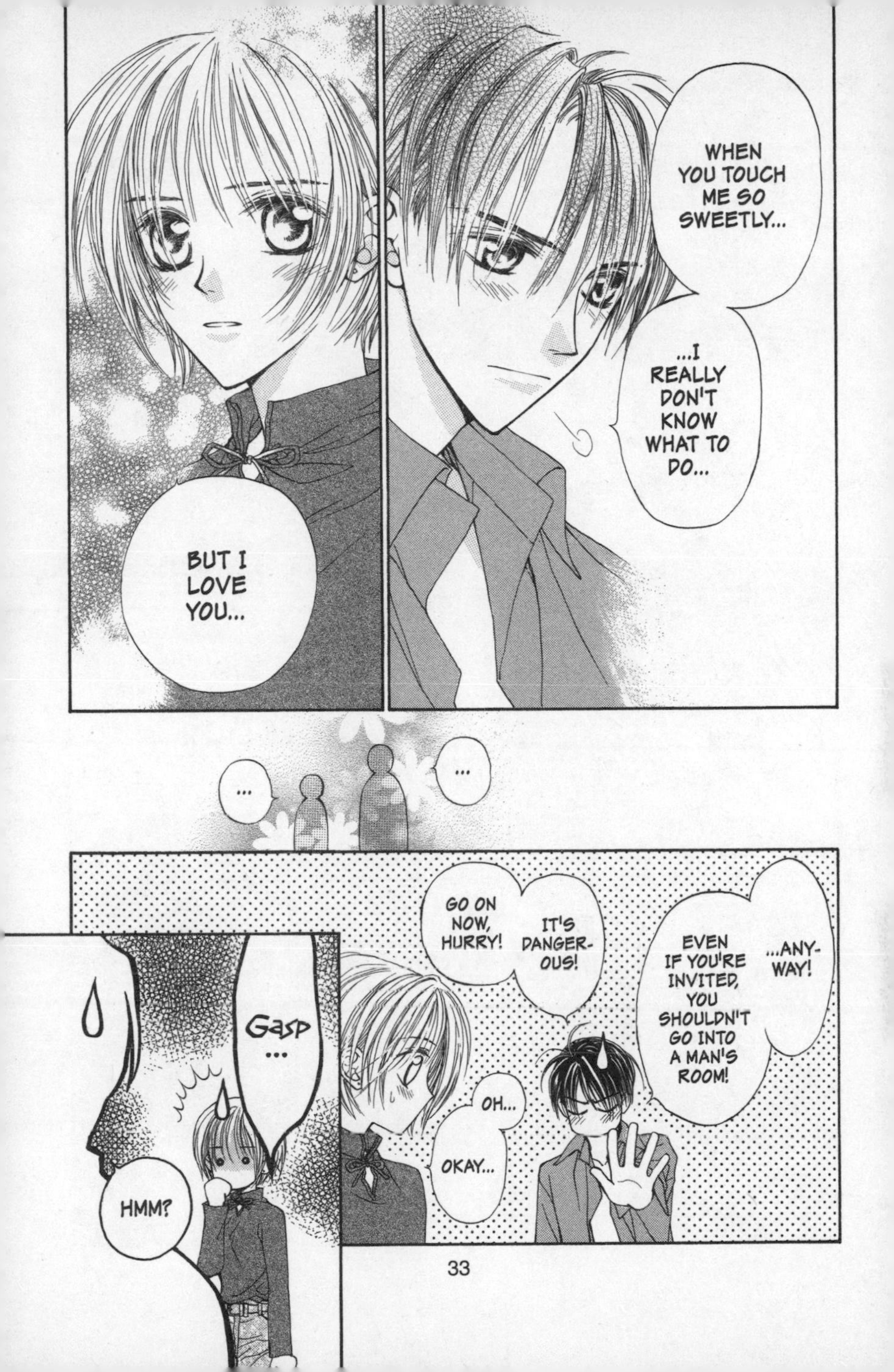
WHEN YOU TOUCH ME SO SWEETLY...
...I REALLY DON'T KNOW WHAT TO DO...
BUT I LOVE YOU...
...
...
...ANY-WAY!
EVEN IF YOU'RE INVITED, YOU SHOULDN'T GO INTO A MAN'S ROOM!
IT'S DANGER-OUS!
GO ON NOW, HURRY!
OH...
OKAY...
Gasp...
HMM?

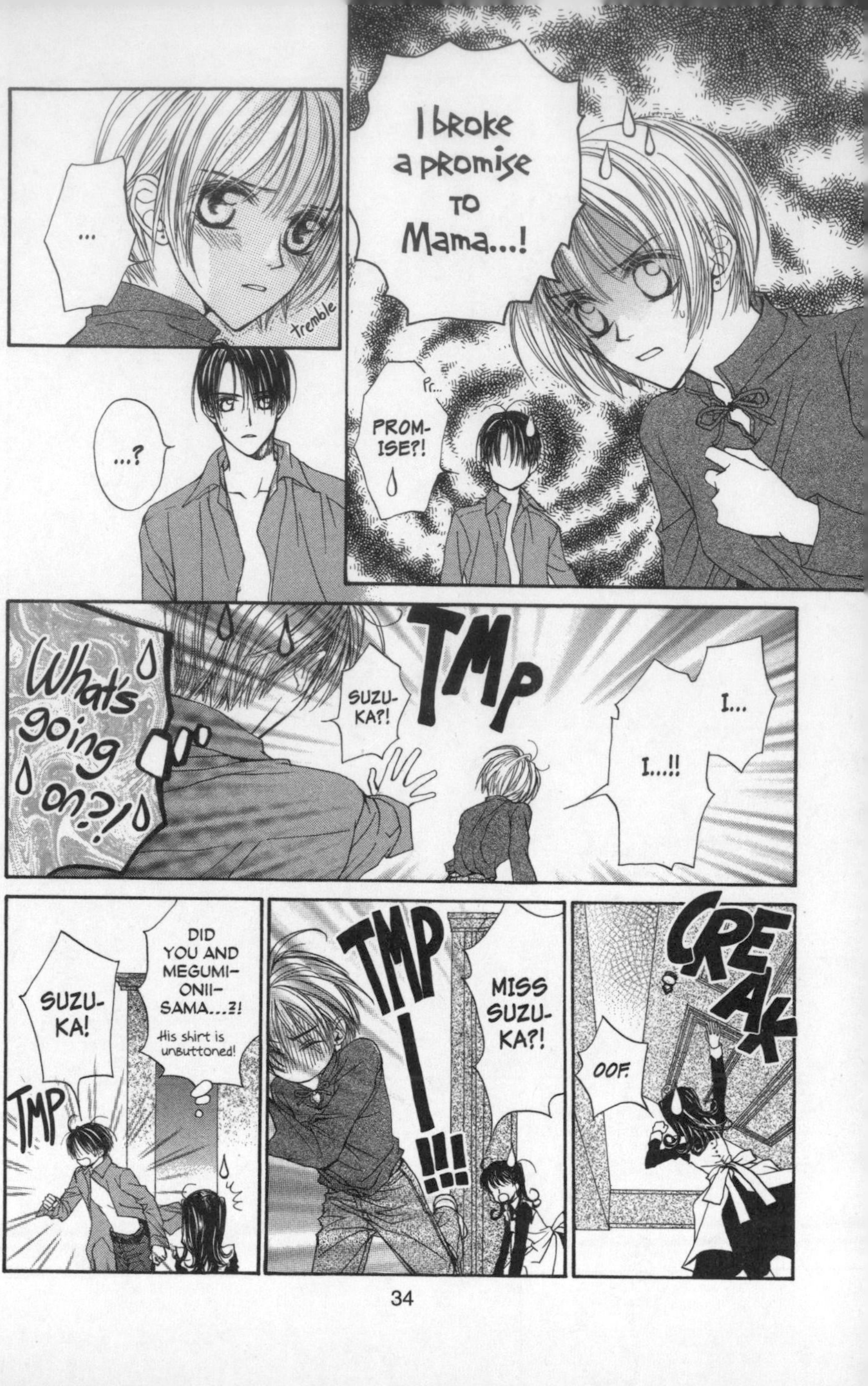
I broke a promise to Mama...!
Pr...
PROMISE?!
...
tremble
...?
I...
I...!!
TMP
SUZUKA?!
What's going on?!
CREAK
OOF.
MISS SUZUKA?!
TMP!!!!
DID YOU AND MEGUMI-ONII-SAMA...?!
His shirt is unbuttoned!
SUZUKA!
TMP

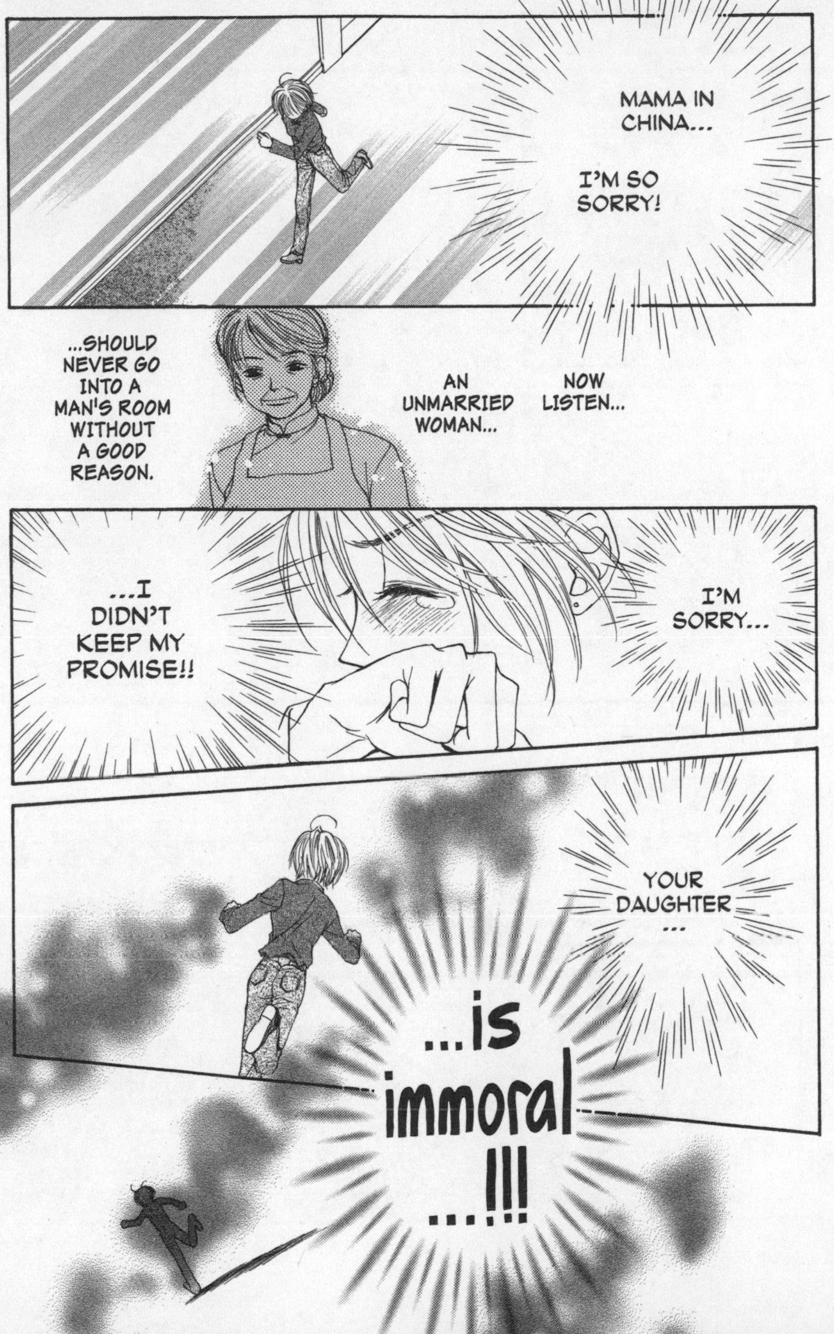
MAMA IN CHINA...
I'M SO SORRY!
NOW LISTEN...
AN UNMARRIED WOMAN...
...SHOULD NEVER GO INTO A MAN'S ROOM WITHOUT A GOOD REASON.
I'M SORRY...
...I DIDN'T KEEP MY PROMISE!!
YOUR DAUGHTER...
...is immoral...!!!

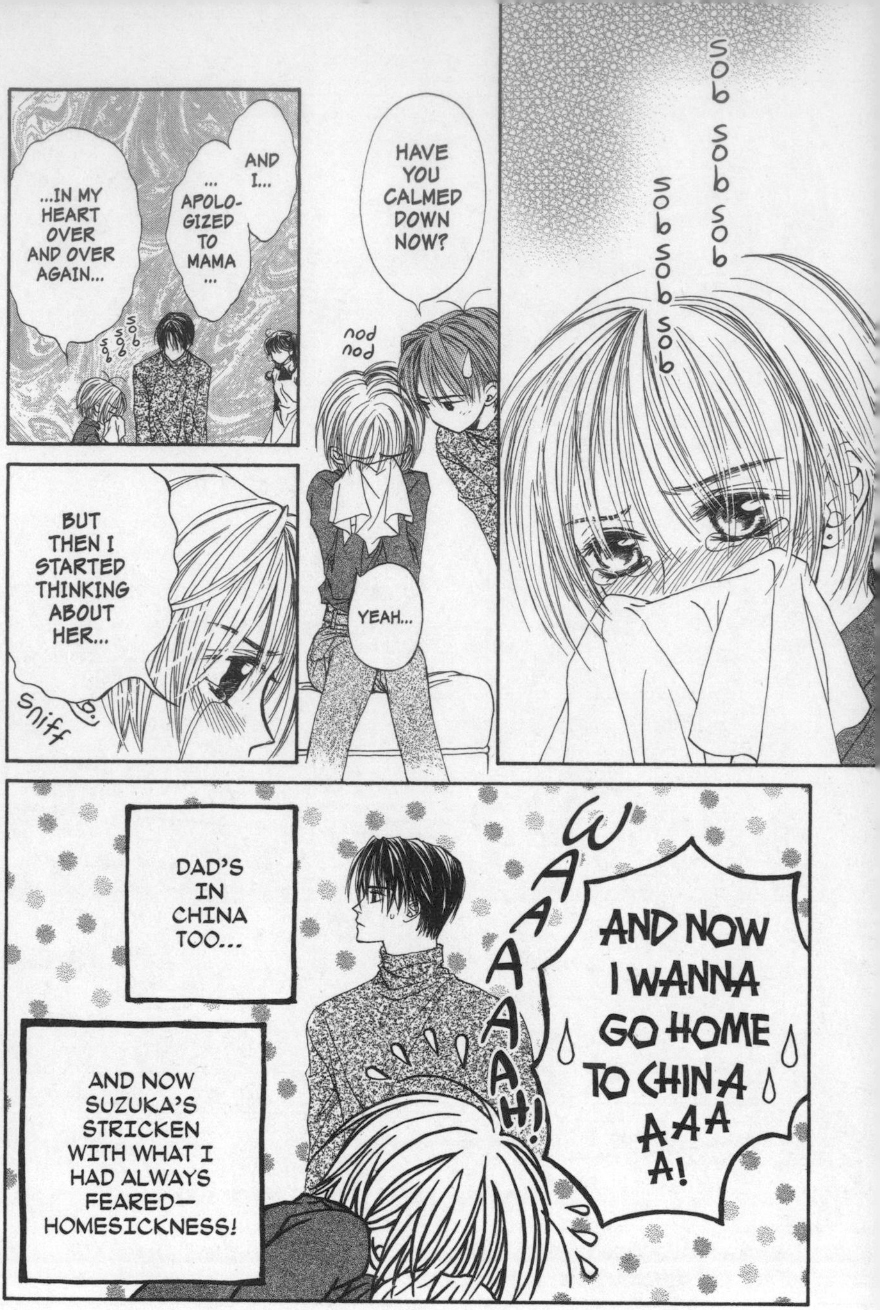
sob sob sob sob sob sob sob sob
HAVE YOU CALMED DOWN NOW?
nod nod
YEAH...
AND I...
... APOLOGIZED TO MAMA ...
...IN MY HEART OVER AND OVER AGAIN...
sob sob sob
BUT THEN I STARTED THINKING ABOUT HER...
sniff
WAAAAAAH!
AND NOW I WANNA GO HOME TO CHINAAAAA!
DAD'S IN CHINA TOO...
AND NOW SUZUKA'S STRICKEN WITH WHAT I HAD ALWAYS FEARED—HOMESICKNESS!

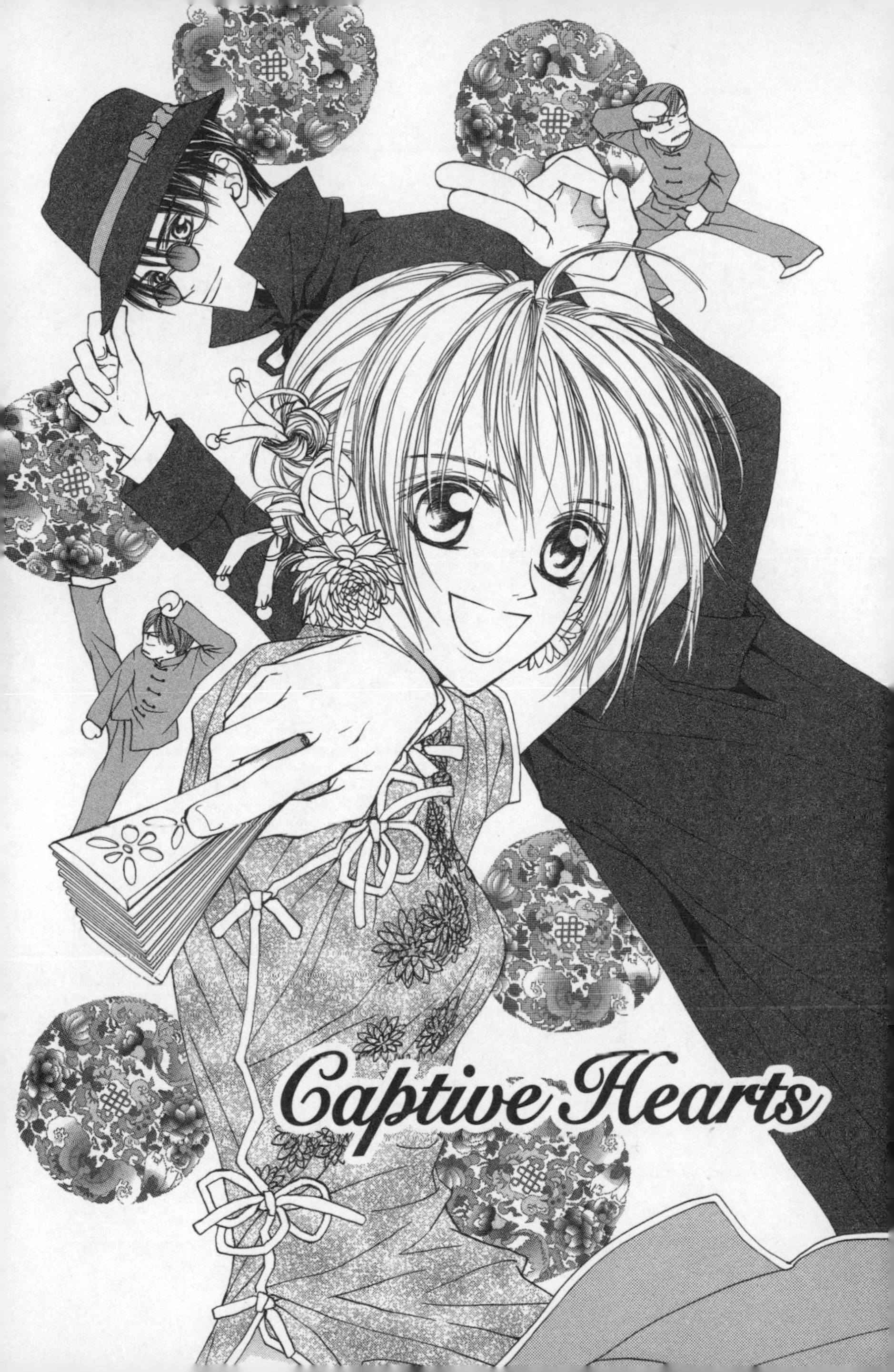
Captive Hearts

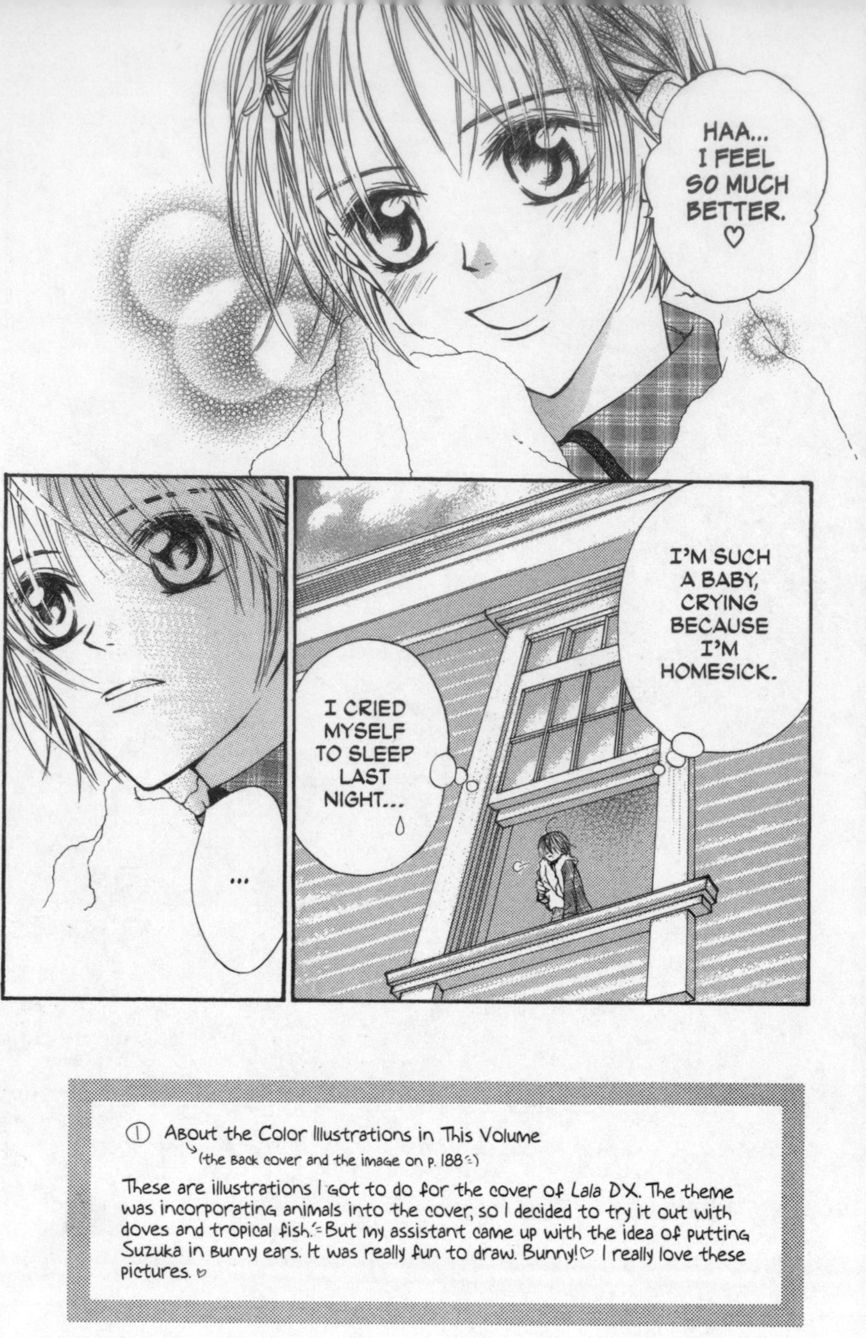
HAA... I FEEL SO MUCH BETTER. ♡
I'M SUCH A BABY, CRYING BECAUSE I'M HOMESICK.
I CRIED MYSELF TO SLEEP LAST NIGHT...
...

① About the Color Illustrations in This Volume
(the back cover and the image on p. 188)

These are illustrations I got to do for the cover of *Lala DX*. The theme was incorporating animals into the cover, so I decided to try it out with doves and tropical fish. But my assistant came up with the idea of putting Suzuka in bunny ears. It was really fun to draw. Bunny! ♡ I really love these pictures. ♡

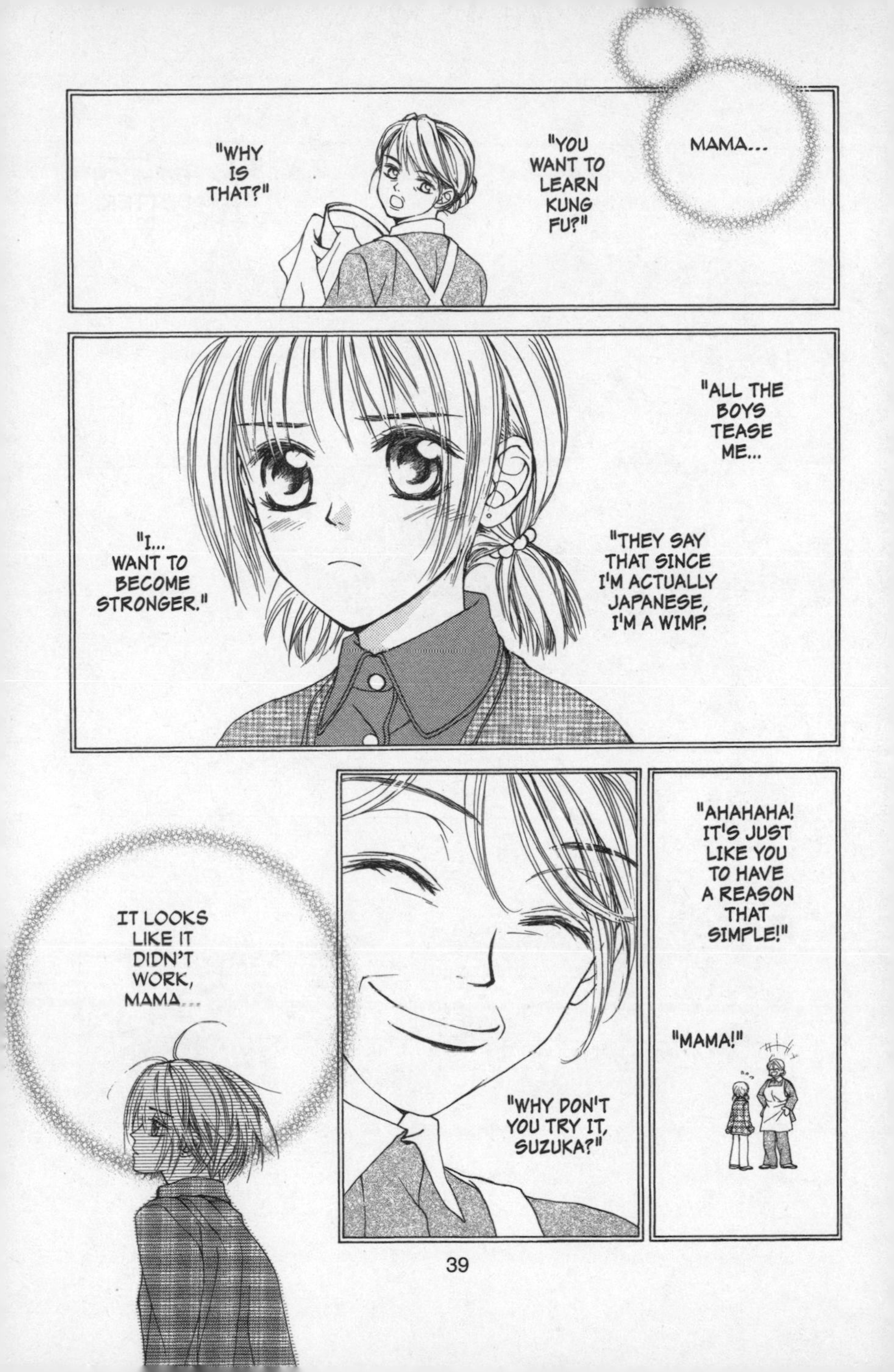
MAMA...
"YOU WANT TO LEARN KUNG FU?"
"WHY IS THAT?"
"ALL THE BOYS TEASE ME...
"THEY SAY THAT SINCE I'M ACTUALLY JAPANESE, I'M A WIMP.
"I... WANT TO BECOME STRONGER."
"AHAHAHA! IT'S JUST LIKE YOU TO HAVE A REASON THAT SIMPLE!"
"MAMA!"
"WHY DON'T YOU TRY IT, SUZUKA?"
IT LOOKS LIKE IT DIDN'T WORK, MAMA...

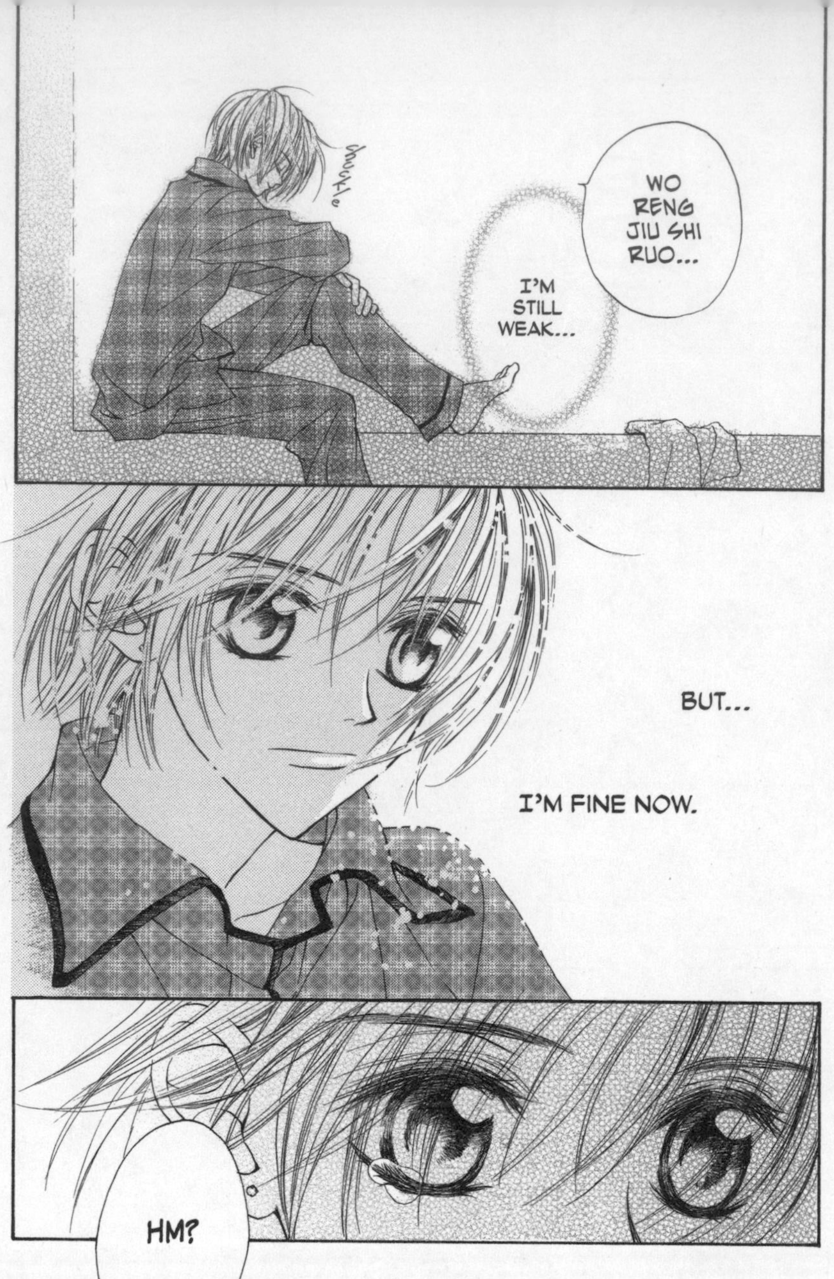
WO RENG JIU SHI RUO...
I'M STILL WEAK...
chuckle
BUT...
I'M FINE NOW.
HM?

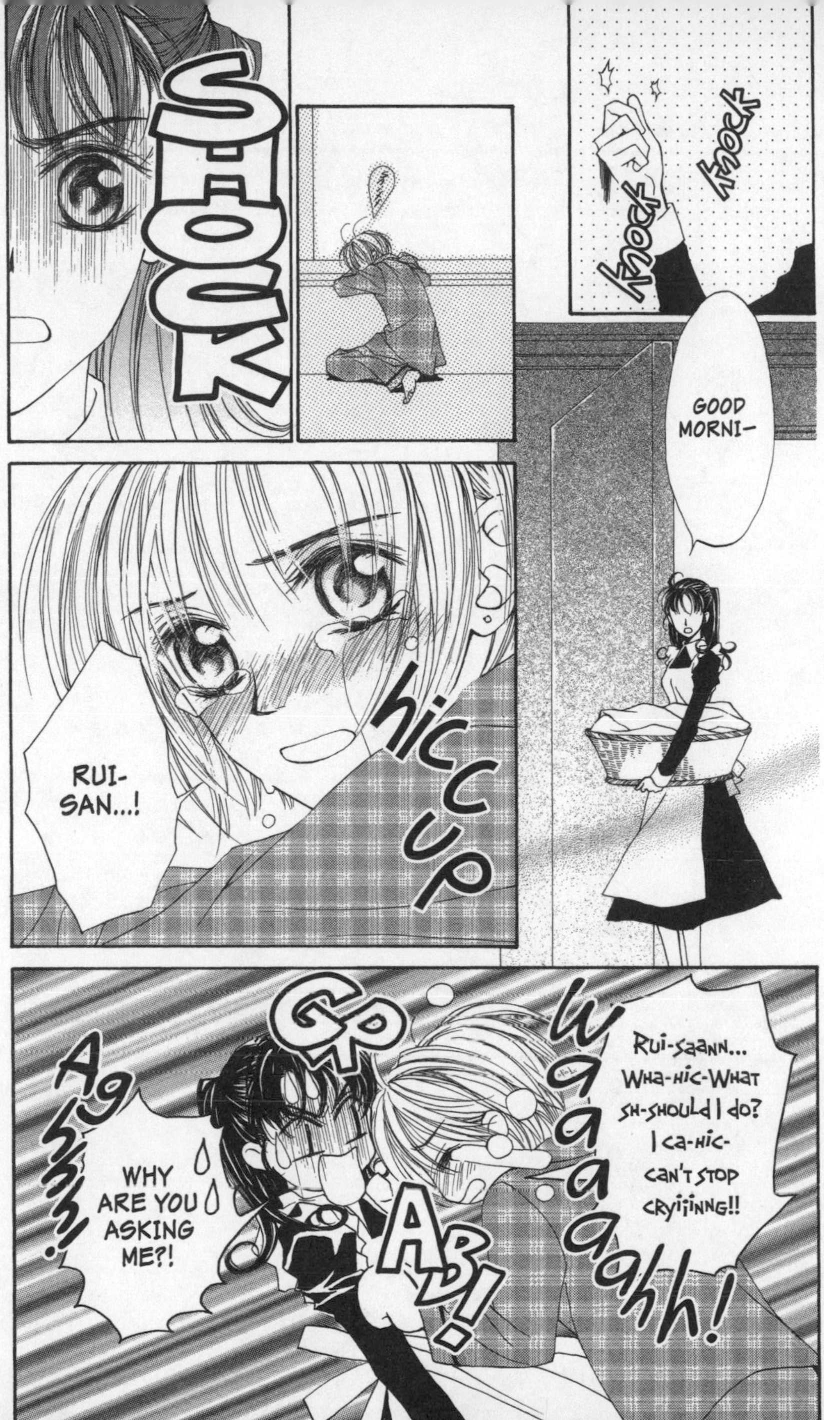
knock
knock
GOOD MORNI-
SHOCK
RUI-SAN...!
hiccup
Rui-saann... Wha-hic-What sh-should I do? I ca-hic-can't stop cryiiinng!!
Waaaaahh!
GRAB!
WHY ARE YOU ASKING ME?!
Aghhh!!

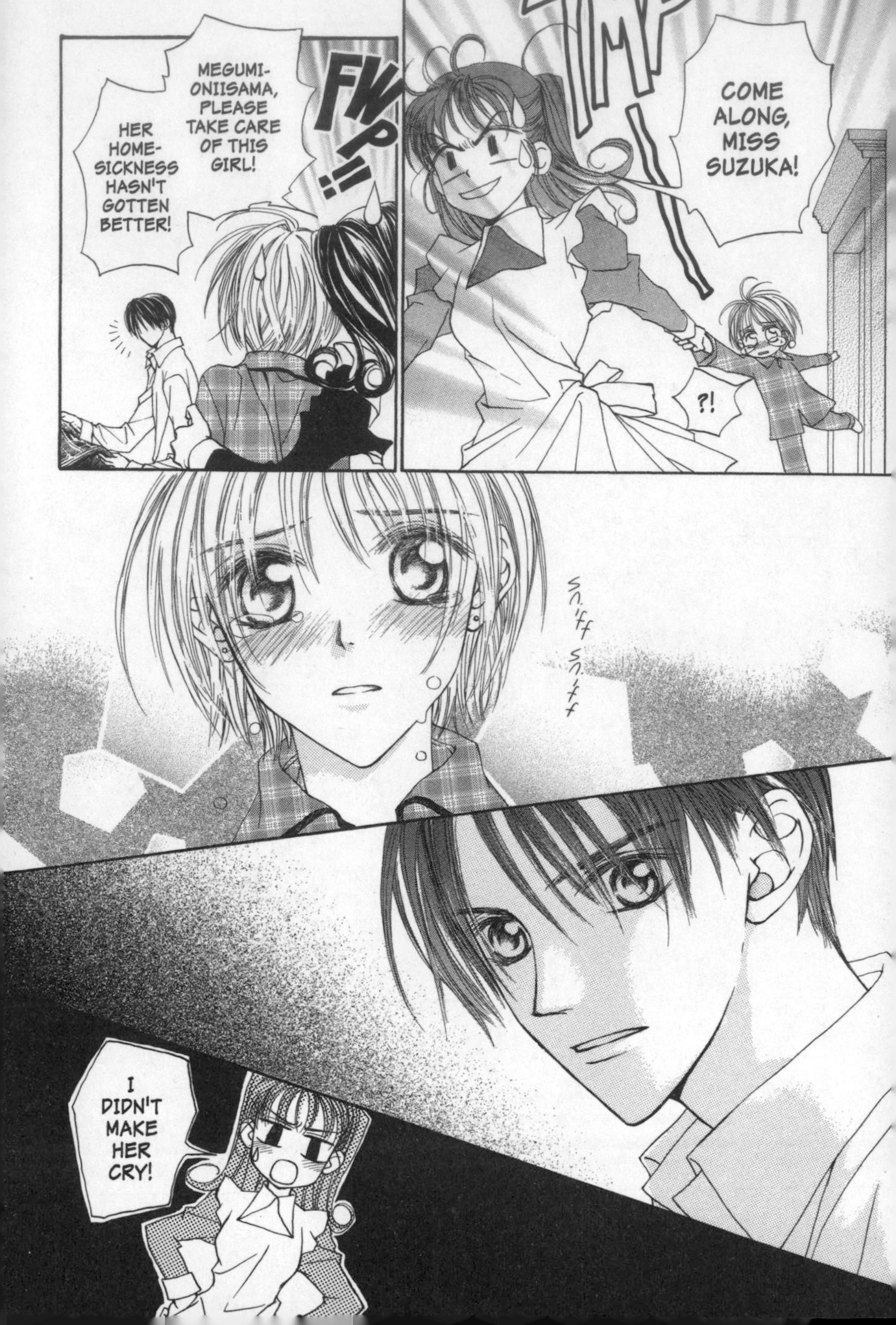
TMP
COME ALONG, MISS SUZUKA!
?!
FWP
MEGUMI-ONIISAMA, PLEASE TAKE CARE OF THIS GIRL!
HER HOMESICKNESS HASN'T GOTTEN BETTER!
sniff sniff
I DIDN'T MAKE HER CRY!

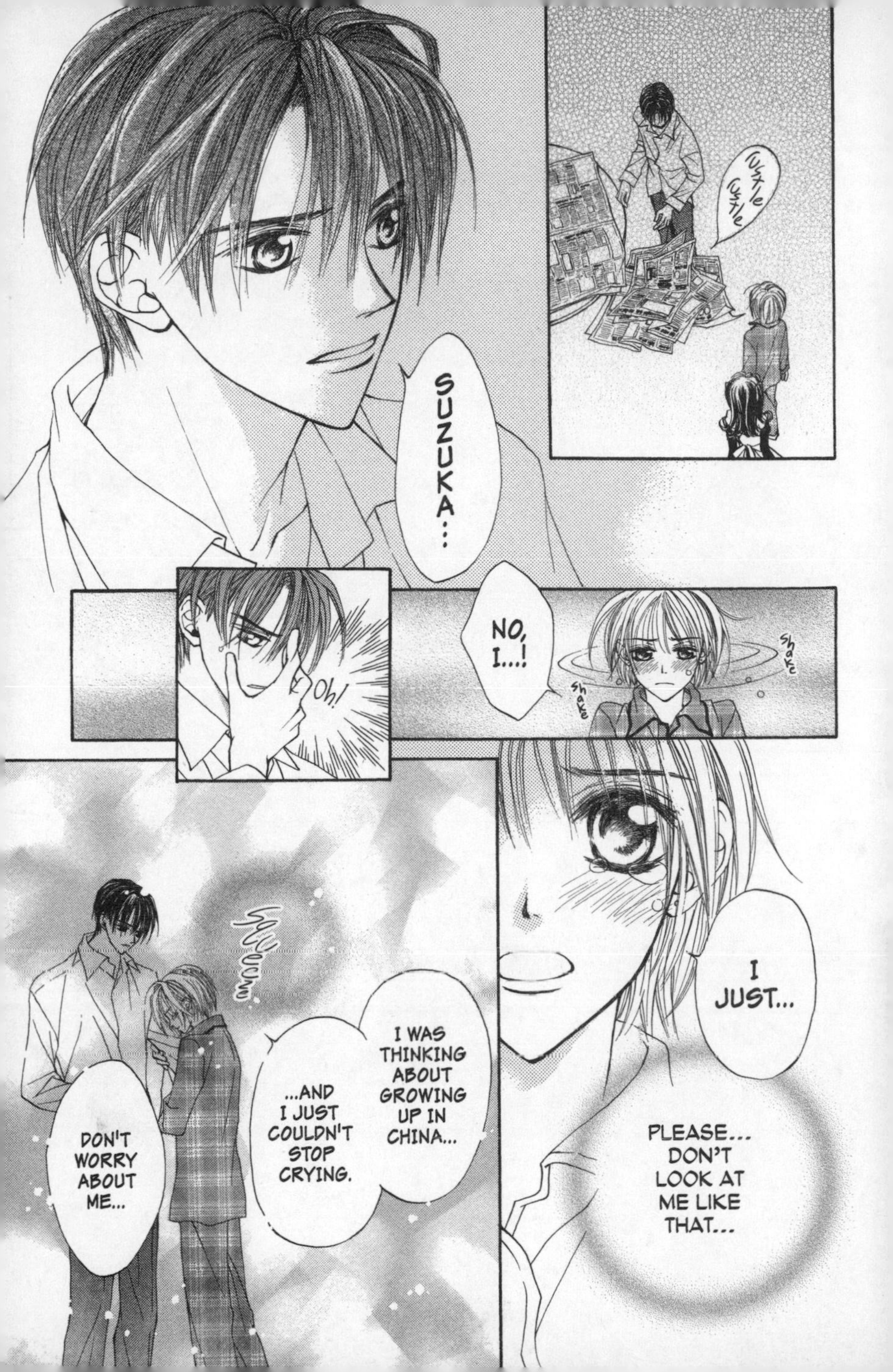
rustle rustle
SUZUKA...
NO, I...!
shake shake
Oh!
I JUST...
PLEASE... DON'T LOOK AT ME LIKE THAT...
I WAS THINKING ABOUT GROWING UP IN CHINA...
...AND I JUST COULDN'T STOP CRYING.
DON'T WORRY ABOUT ME...

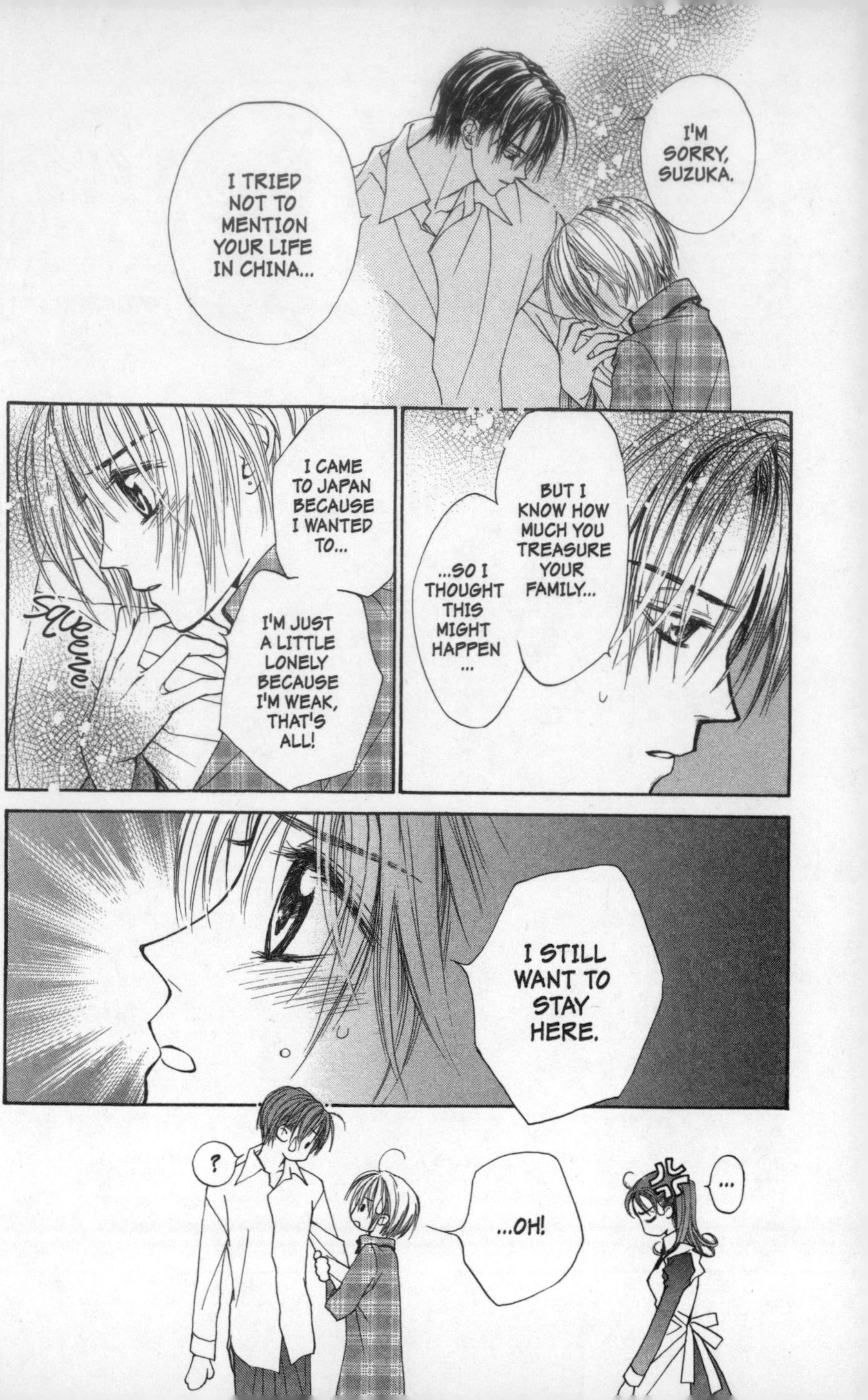
I'M SORRY, SUZUKA.
I TRIED NOT TO MENTION YOUR LIFE IN CHINA...
BUT I KNOW HOW MUCH YOU TREASURE YOUR FAMILY...
...SO I THOUGHT THIS MIGHT HAPPEN ...
I CAME TO JAPAN BECAUSE I WANTED TO...
I'M JUST A LITTLE LONELY BECAUSE I'M WEAK, THAT'S ALL!
squeeze
I STILL WANT TO STAY HERE.
...
...OH!
?

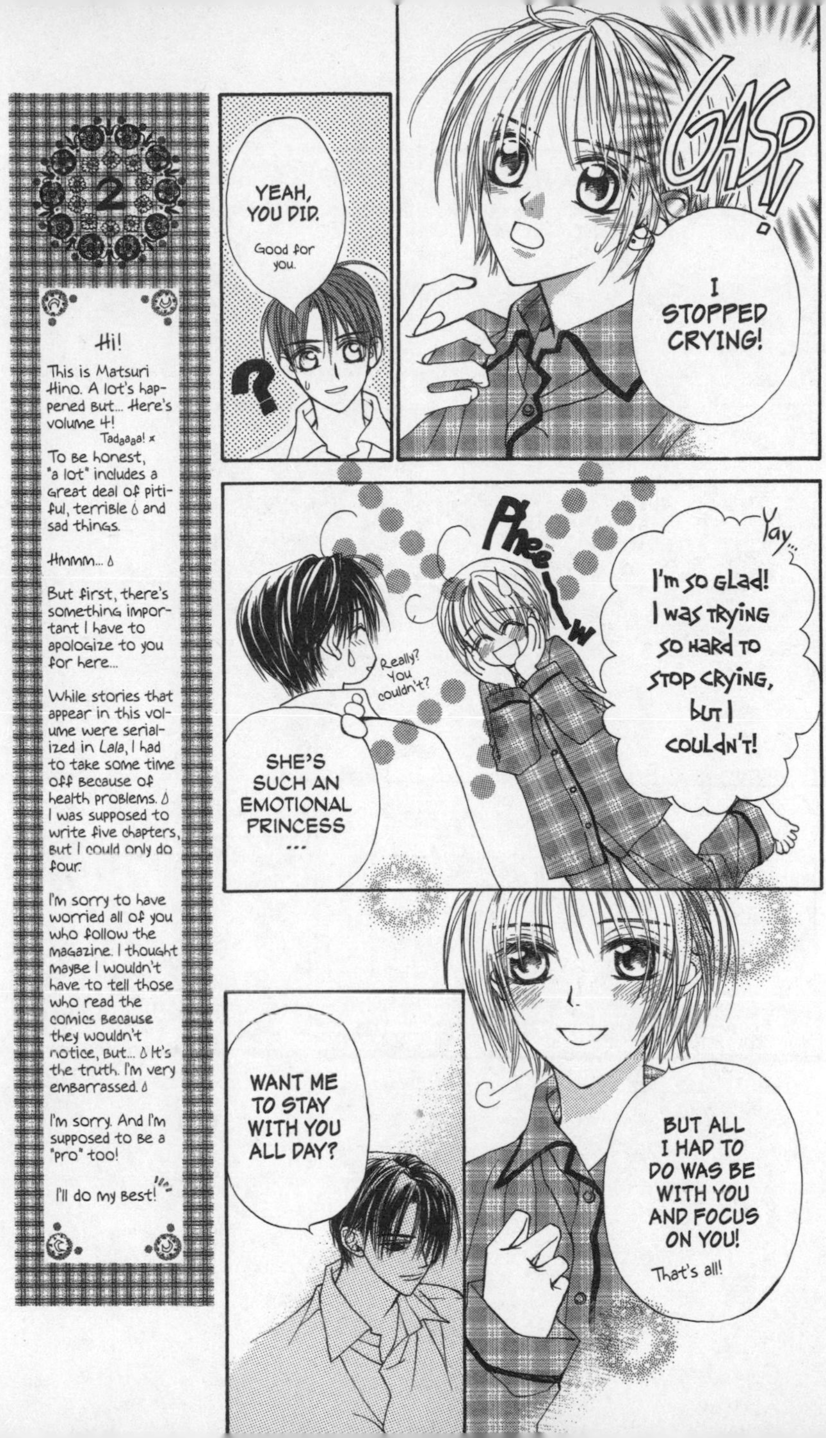
GASP!
I STOPPED CRYING!
YEAH, YOU DID.
Good for you.
Yay...
I'm so glad! I was trying so hard to stop crying, but I couldn't!
Phee~w
Really? You couldn't?
SHE'S SUCH AN EMOTIONAL PRINCESS...
BUT ALL I HAD TO DO WAS BE WITH YOU AND FOCUS ON YOU!
That's all!
WANT ME TO STAY WITH YOU ALL DAY?

2

Hi!

This is Matsuri Hino. A lot's happened but... Here's volume 4! Tadaaa!

To be honest, "a lot" includes a great deal of pitiful, terrible and sad things.

Hmmm...

But first, there's something important I have to apologize to you for here...

While stories that appear in this volume were serialized in *Lala*, I had to take some time off because of health problems. I was supposed to write five chapters, but I could only do four.

I'm sorry to have worried all of you who follow the magazine. I thought maybe I wouldn't have to tell those who read the comics because they wouldn't notice, but... It's the truth. I'm very embarrassed.

I'm sorry. And I'm supposed to be a "pro" too!

I'll do my best!

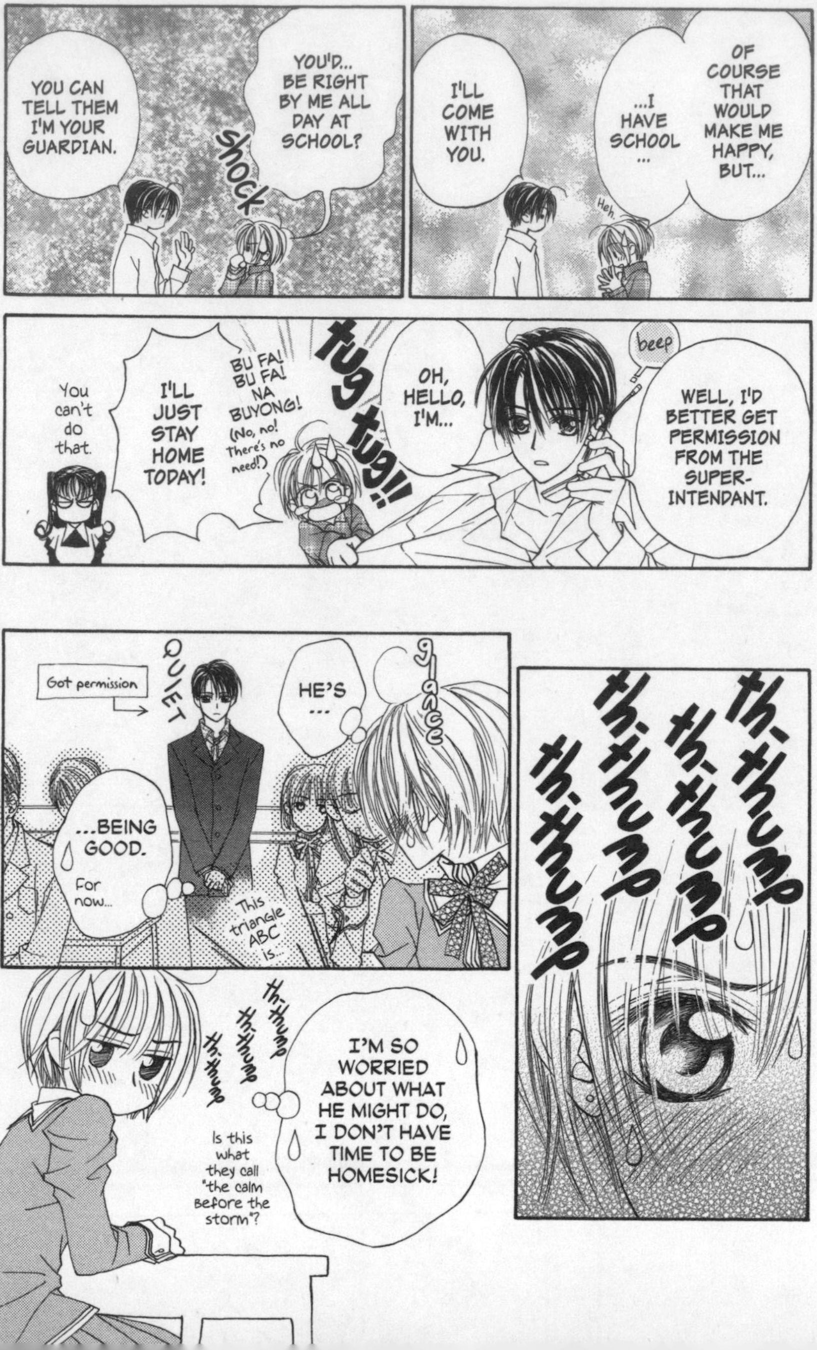

OF COURSE THAT WOULD MAKE ME HAPPY, BUT...
...I HAVE SCHOOL...
I'LL COME WITH YOU.
Heh.
YOU'D... BE RIGHT BY ME ALL DAY AT SCHOOL?
shock
YOU CAN TELL THEM I'M YOUR GUARDIAN.
beep
WELL, I'D BETTER GET PERMISSION FROM THE SUPER-INTENDANT.
OH, HELLO, I'M...
tug tug!!
BU FA! BU FA! NA BUYONG! (No, no! There's no need!)
I'LL JUST STAY HOME TODAY!
You can't do that.
th-thump th-thump th-thump
glance
HE'S...
QUIET
Got permission
...BEING GOOD.
For now...
This triangle ABC is...
I'M SO WORRIED ABOUT WHAT HE MIGHT DO, I DON'T HAVE TIME TO BE HOMESICK!
th-thump th-thump th-thump
Is this what they call "the calm before the storm"?

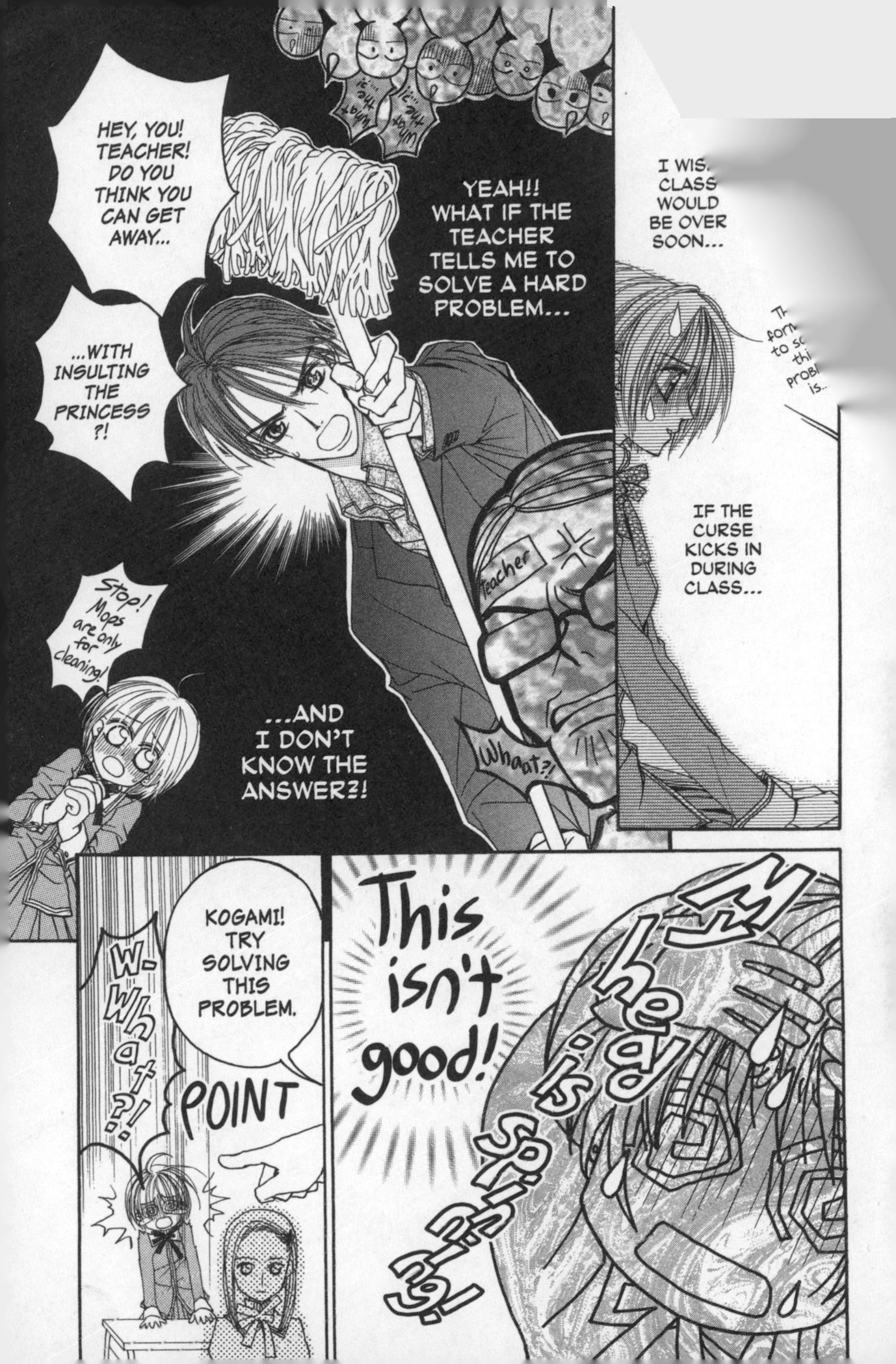

I WIS
CLASS WOULD BE OVER SOON...
IF THE CURSE KICKS IN DURING CLASS...
What the...?!
What the...?!
YEAH!! WHAT IF THE TEACHER TELLS ME TO SOLVE A HARD PROBLEM...
HEY, YOU! TEACHER! DO YOU THINK YOU CAN GET AWAY...
...WITH INSULTING THE PRINCESS?!
Teacher
Stop! Mops are only for cleaning!
Whaat?!
...AND I DON'T KNOW THE ANSWER?!
My head is spinning!
This isn't good!
KOGAMI! TRY SOLVING THIS PROBLEM.
W-What?!
POINT

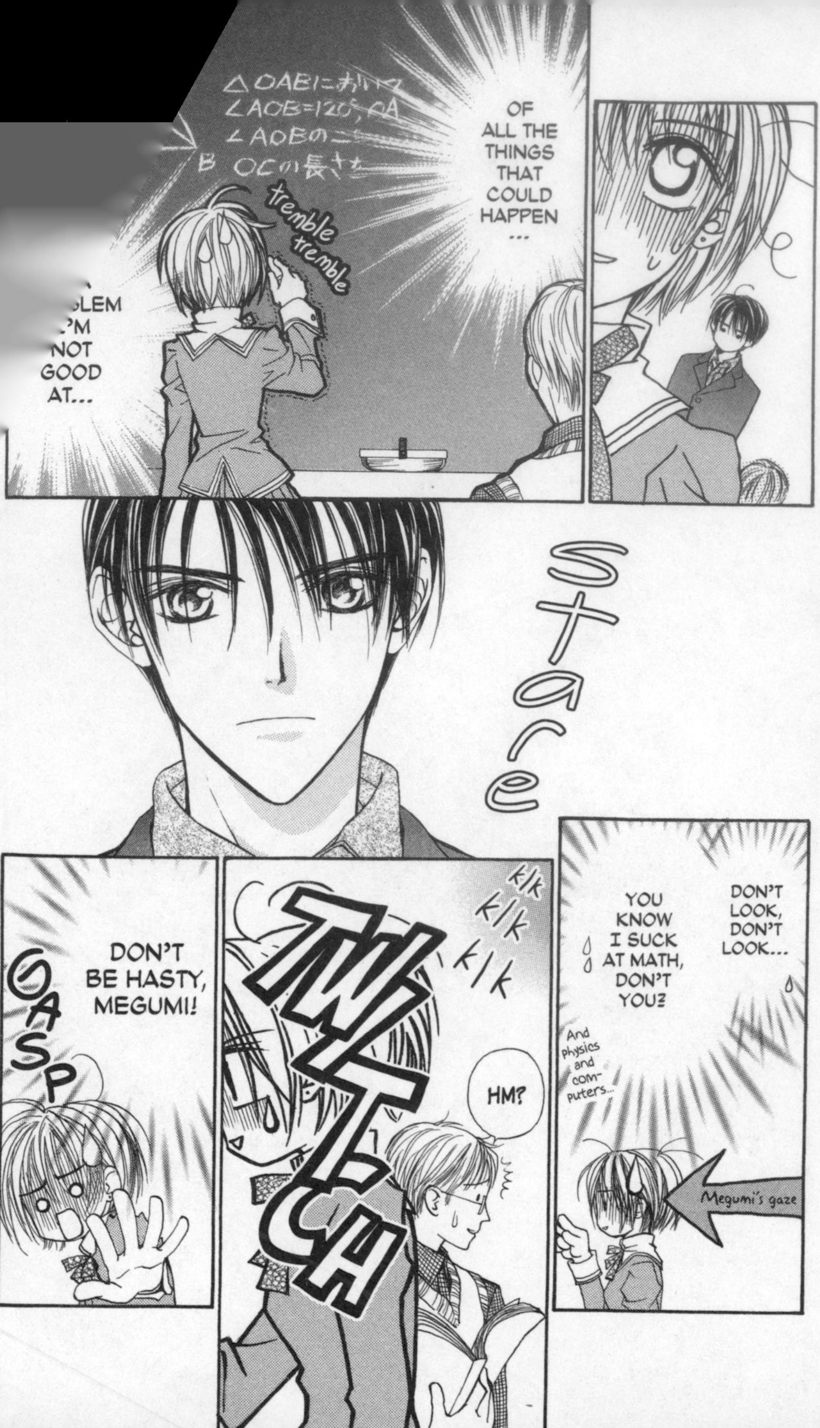
OF ALL THE THINGS THAT COULD HAPPEN...
△OABにおいて
∠AOB=120°, OA
∠AOBの二
B OCの長さを
tremble tremble
BLEM 'M NOT GOOD AT...
stare
DON'T LOOK, DON'T LOOK...
YOU KNOW I SUCK AT MATH, DON'T YOU?
And physics and com-puters...
Megumi's gaze
k/k k/k k/k
TWITCH
HM?
DON'T BE HASTY, MEGUMI!
GASP

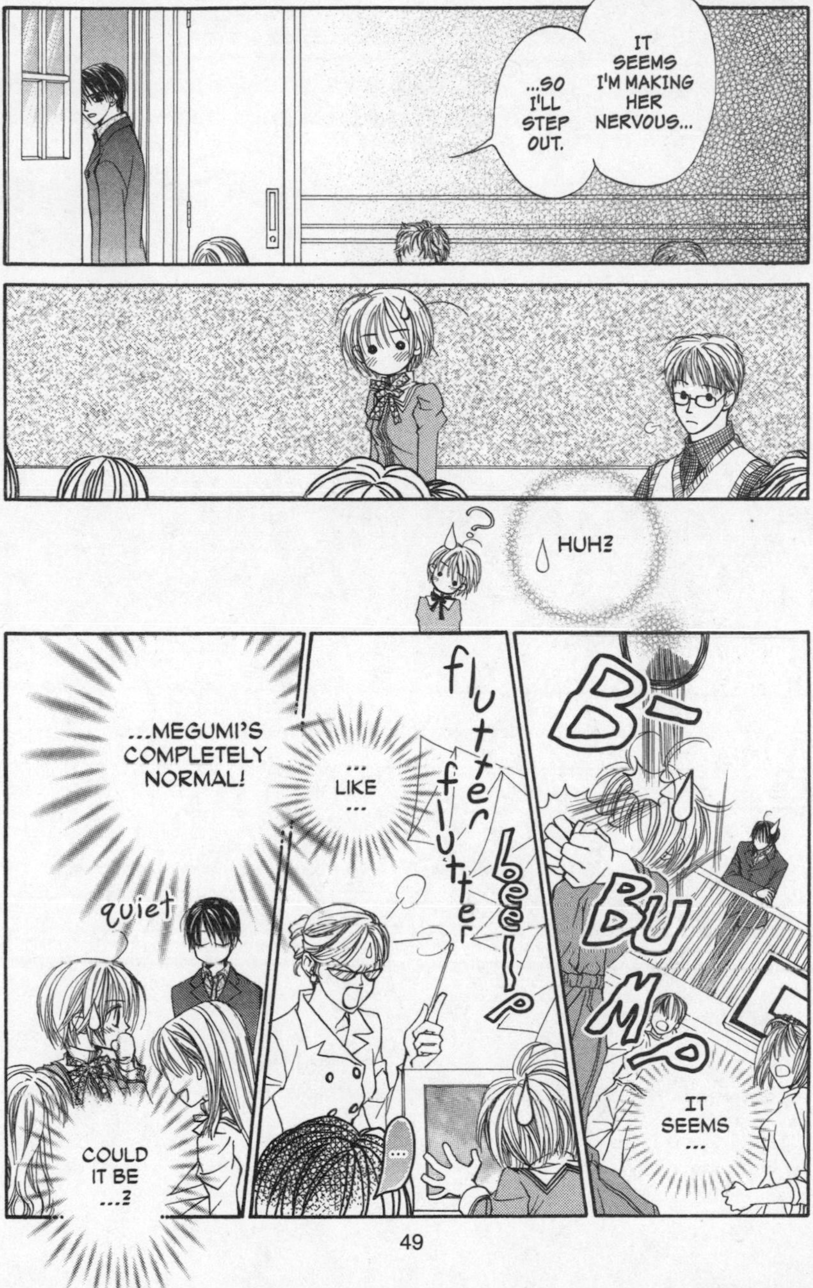
IT SEEMS I'M MAKING HER NERVOUS...
...SO I'LL STEP OUT.
HUH?
B-BUMP
IT SEEMS ...
flutter flutter
beep
... LIKE ...
...
...MEGUMI'S COMPLETELY NORMAL!
quiet
COULD IT BE ...?

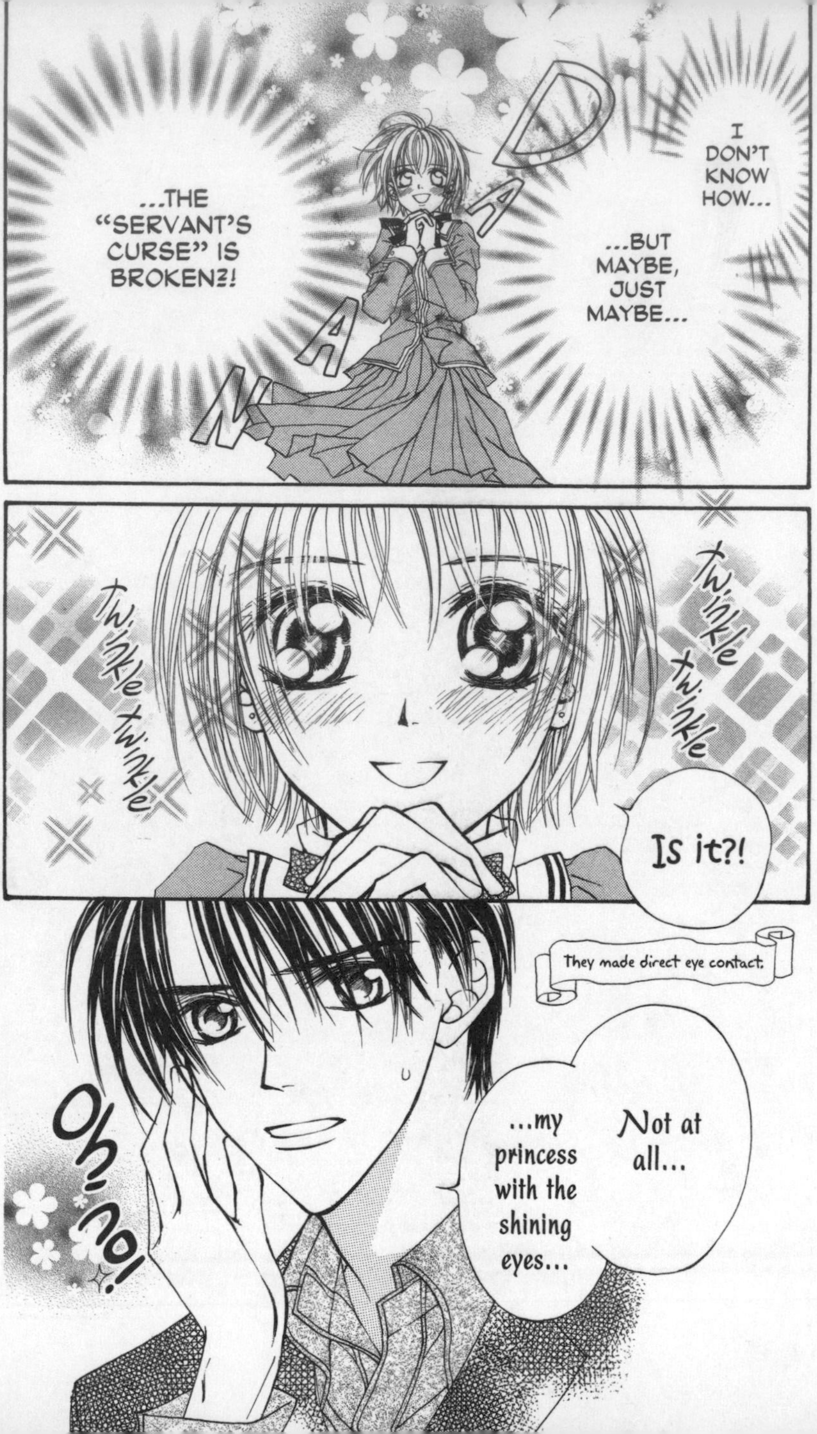
I DON'T KNOW HOW...
...BUT MAYBE, JUST MAYBE...
...THE "SERVANT'S CURSE" IS BROKEN?!
twinkle twinkle
twinkle twinkle
Is it?!
They made direct eye contact.
Not at all...
...my princess with the shining eyes...
Oh no!

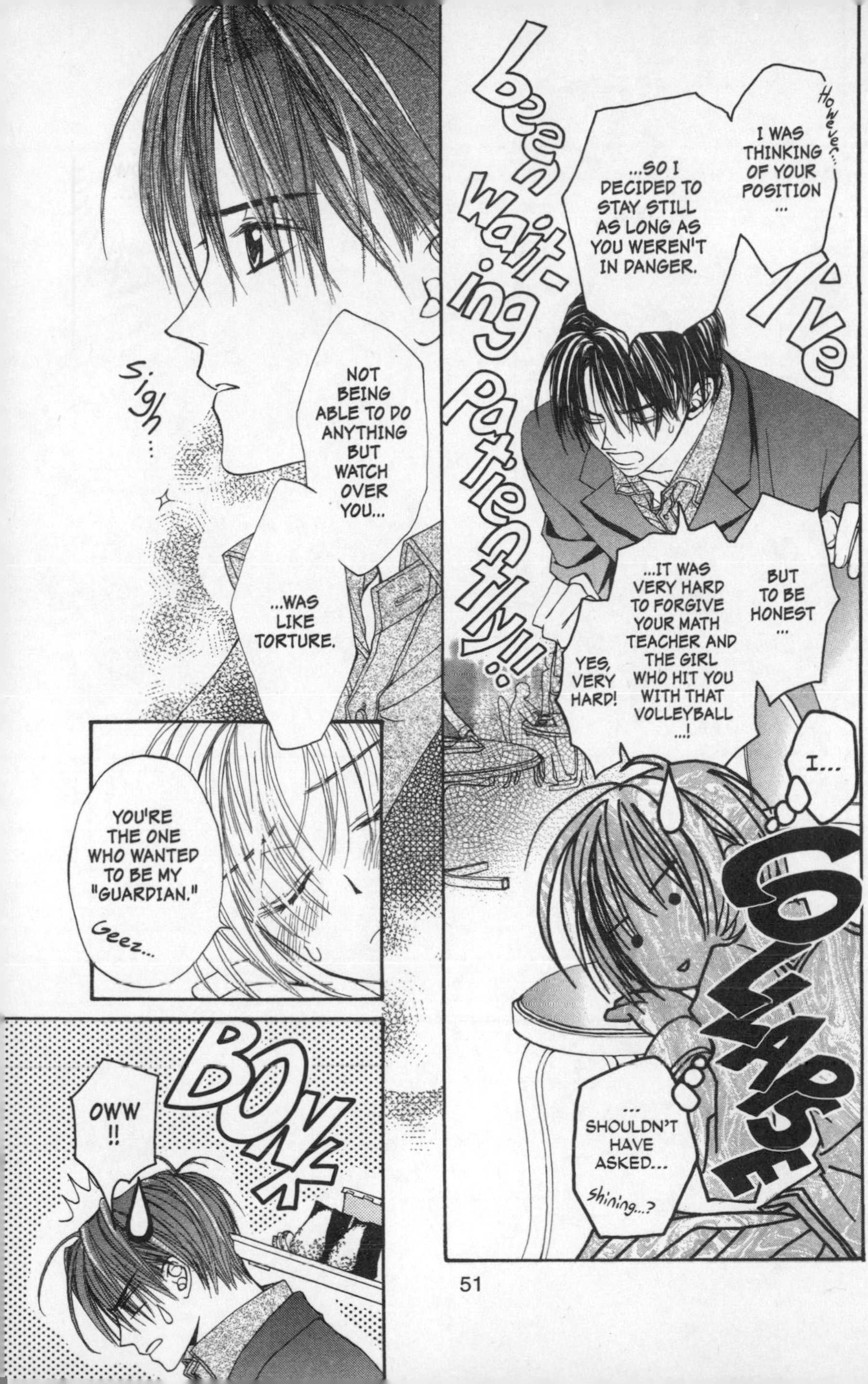
However...
I WAS THINKING OF YOUR POSITION ...
...SO I DECIDED TO STAY STILL AS LONG AS YOU WEREN'T IN DANGER.
I've been wait-ing patiently!!..
BUT TO BE HONEST ...
...IT WAS VERY HARD TO FORGIVE YOUR MATH TEACHER AND THE GIRL WHO HIT YOU WITH THAT VOLLEYBALL ...!
YES, VERY HARD!
I...
COLLAPSE
... SHOULDN'T HAVE ASKED...
Shining...?
Sigh...
NOT BEING ABLE TO DO ANYTHING BUT WATCH OVER YOU...
...WAS LIKE TORTURE.
YOU'RE THE ONE WHO WANTED TO BE MY "GUARDIAN."
Geez...
BONK
OWW !!

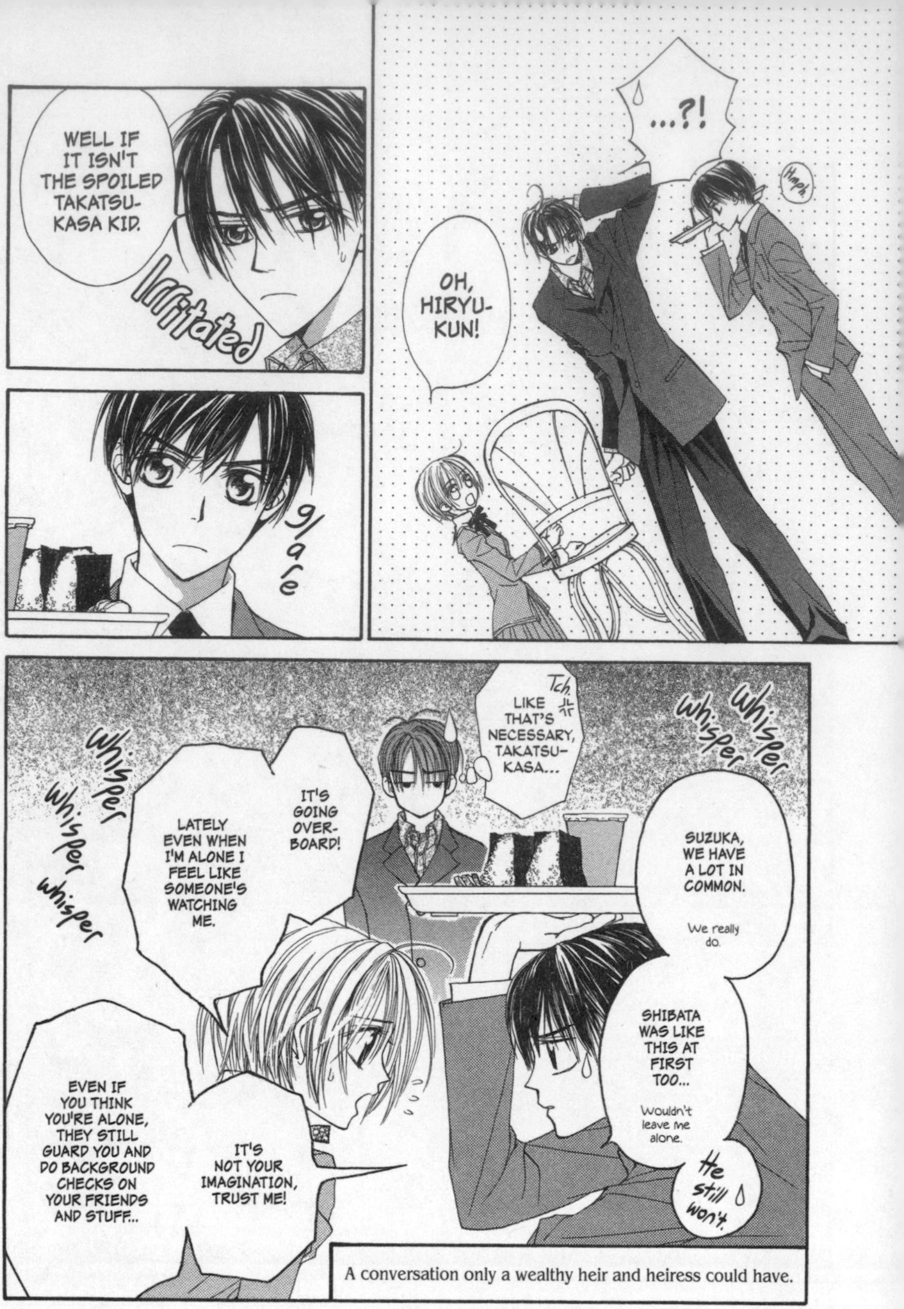
...?!
Hmph.
OH, HIRYU-KUN!
WELL IF IT ISN'T THE SPOILED TAKATSU-KASA KID.
Irritated
glare
whisper whisper
Tch. LIKE THAT'S NECESSARY, TAKATSU-KASA...
SUZUKA, WE HAVE A LOT IN COMMON.
We really do.
IT'S GOING OVER-BOARD!
LATELY EVEN WHEN I'M ALONE I FEEL LIKE SOMEONE'S WATCHING ME.
whisper whisper whisper
SHIBATA WAS LIKE THIS AT FIRST TOO...
Wouldn't leave me alone.
He still won't.
IT'S NOT YOUR IMAGINATION, TRUST ME!
EVEN IF YOU THINK YOU'RE ALONE, THEY STILL GUARD YOU AND DO BACKGROUND CHECKS ON YOUR FRIENDS AND STUFF...
A conversation only a wealthy heir and heiress could have.

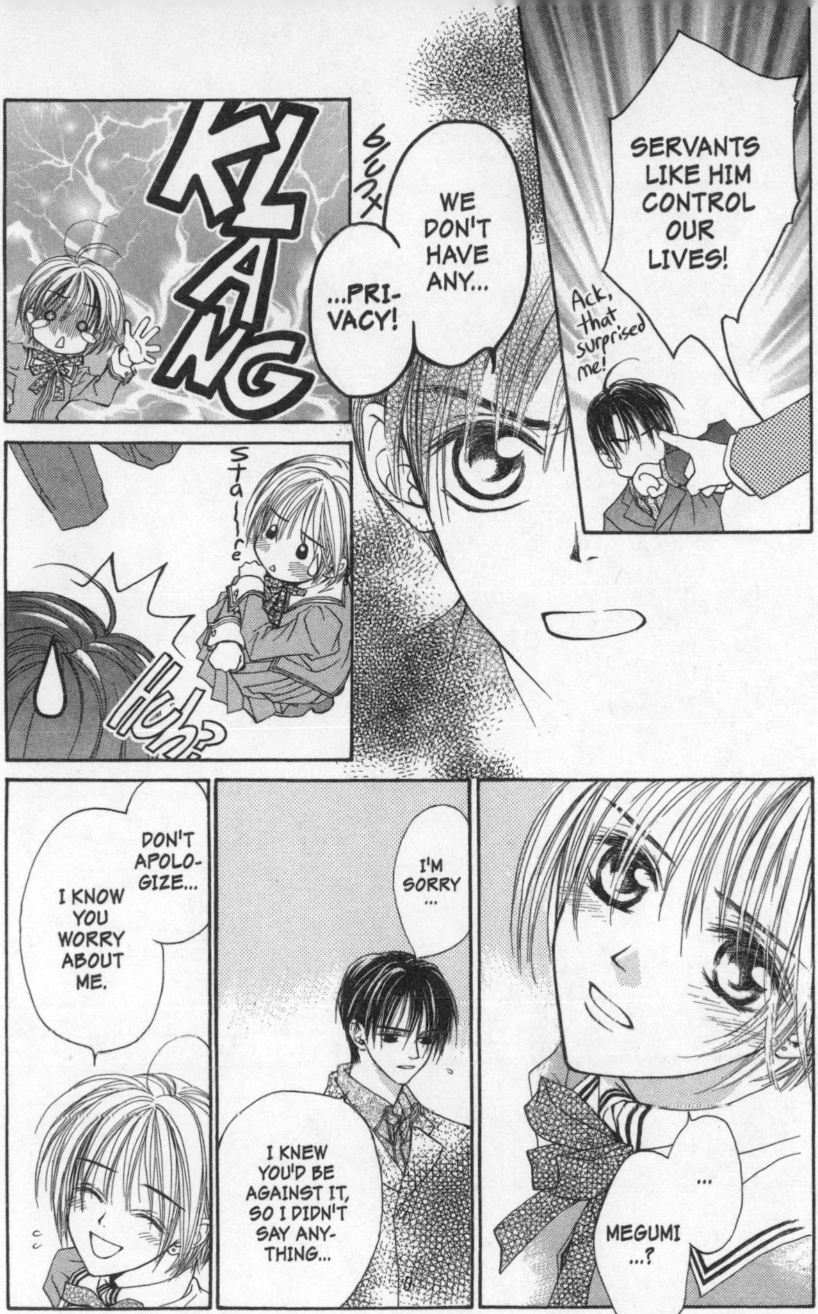
SERVANTS LIKE HIM CONTROL OUR LIVES!
Ack, that surprised me!
WE DON'T HAVE ANY...
...PRI-VACY!
KLANG
Stare
Huh?
...
MEGUMI ...?
I'M SORRY ...
I KNEW YOU'D BE AGAINST IT, SO I DIDN'T SAY ANY-THING...
DON'T APOLO-GIZE...
I KNOW YOU WORRY ABOUT ME.

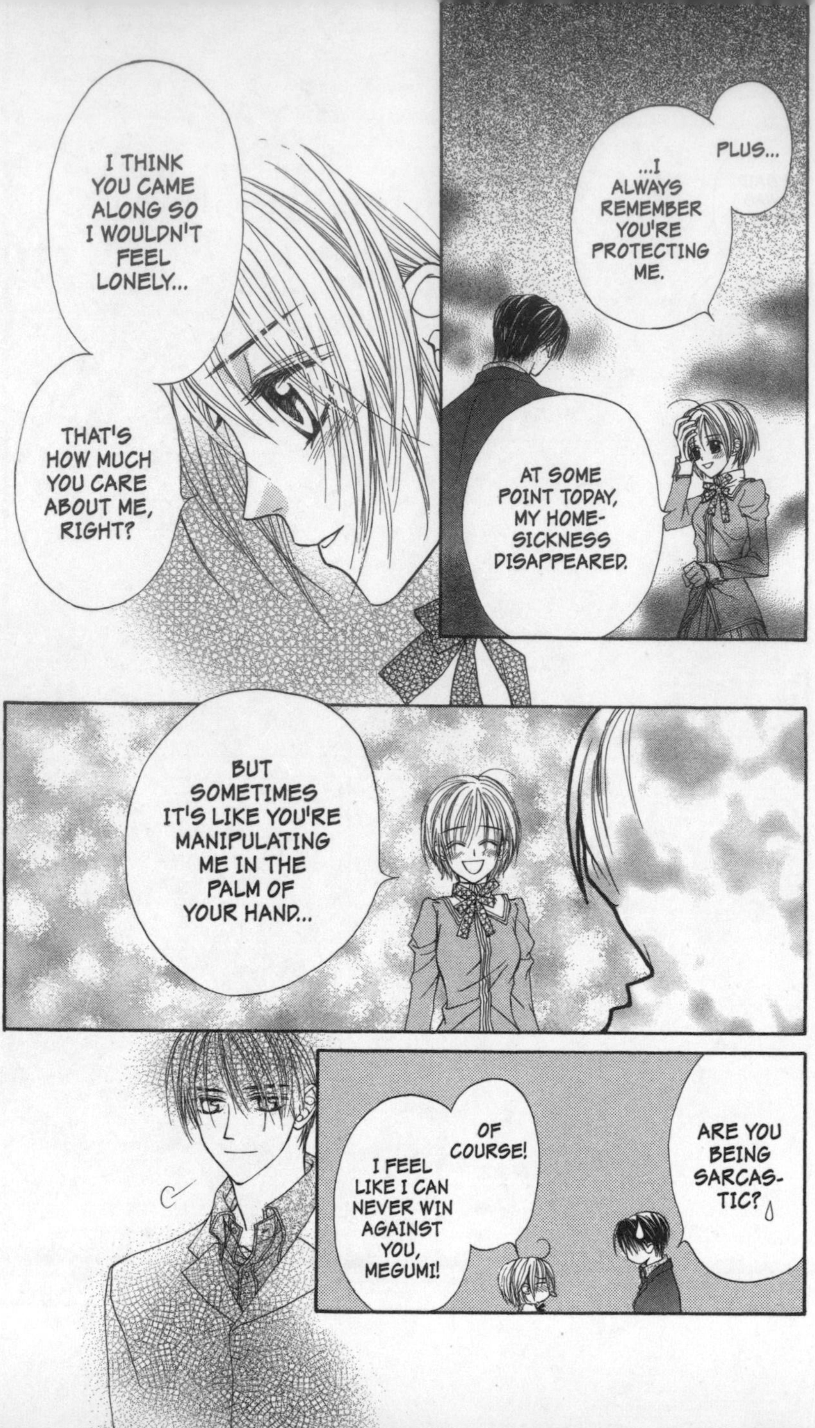
PLUS...
...I ALWAYS REMEMBER YOU'RE PROTECTING ME.
AT SOME POINT TODAY, MY HOME-SICKNESS DISAPPEARED.
I THINK YOU CAME ALONG SO I WOULDN'T FEEL LONELY...
THAT'S HOW MUCH YOU CARE ABOUT ME, RIGHT?
BUT SOMETIMES IT'S LIKE YOU'RE MANIPULATING ME IN THE PALM OF YOUR HAND...
ARE YOU BEING SARCAS-TIC?
OF COURSE!
I FEEL LIKE I CAN NEVER WIN AGAINST YOU, MEGUMI!

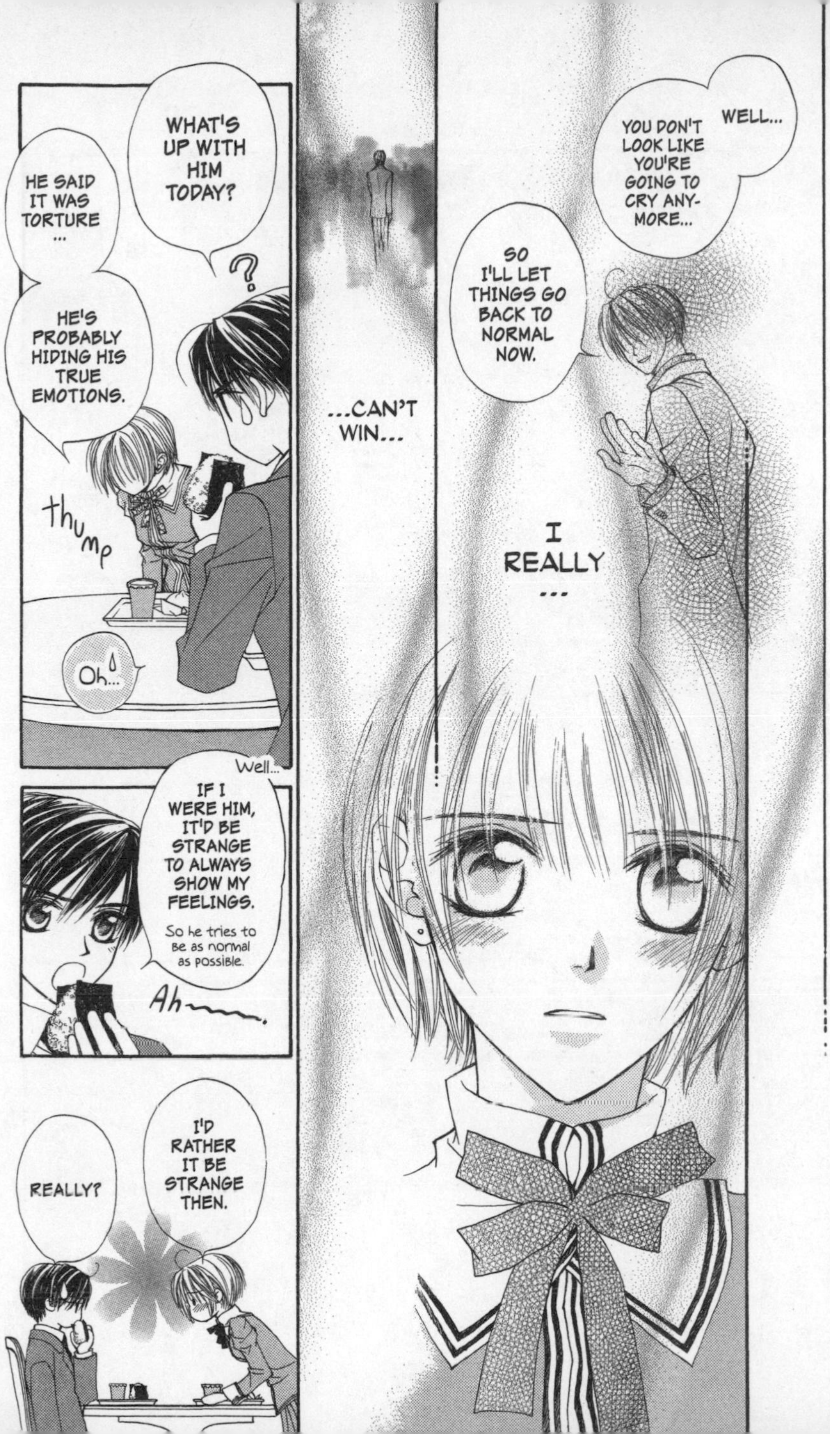
WELL...
YOU DON'T LOOK LIKE YOU'RE GOING TO CRY ANY-MORE...
SO I'LL LET THINGS GO BACK TO NORMAL NOW.
I REALLY ...
...CAN'T WIN...
WHAT'S UP WITH HIM TODAY?
?
HE SAID IT WAS TORTURE ...
HE'S PROBABLY HIDING HIS TRUE EMOTIONS.
thump
Oh...
Well...
IF I WERE HIM, IT'D BE STRANGE TO ALWAYS SHOW MY FEELINGS.
So he tries to be as normal as possible.
Ah
I'D RATHER IT BE STRANGE THEN.
REALLY?

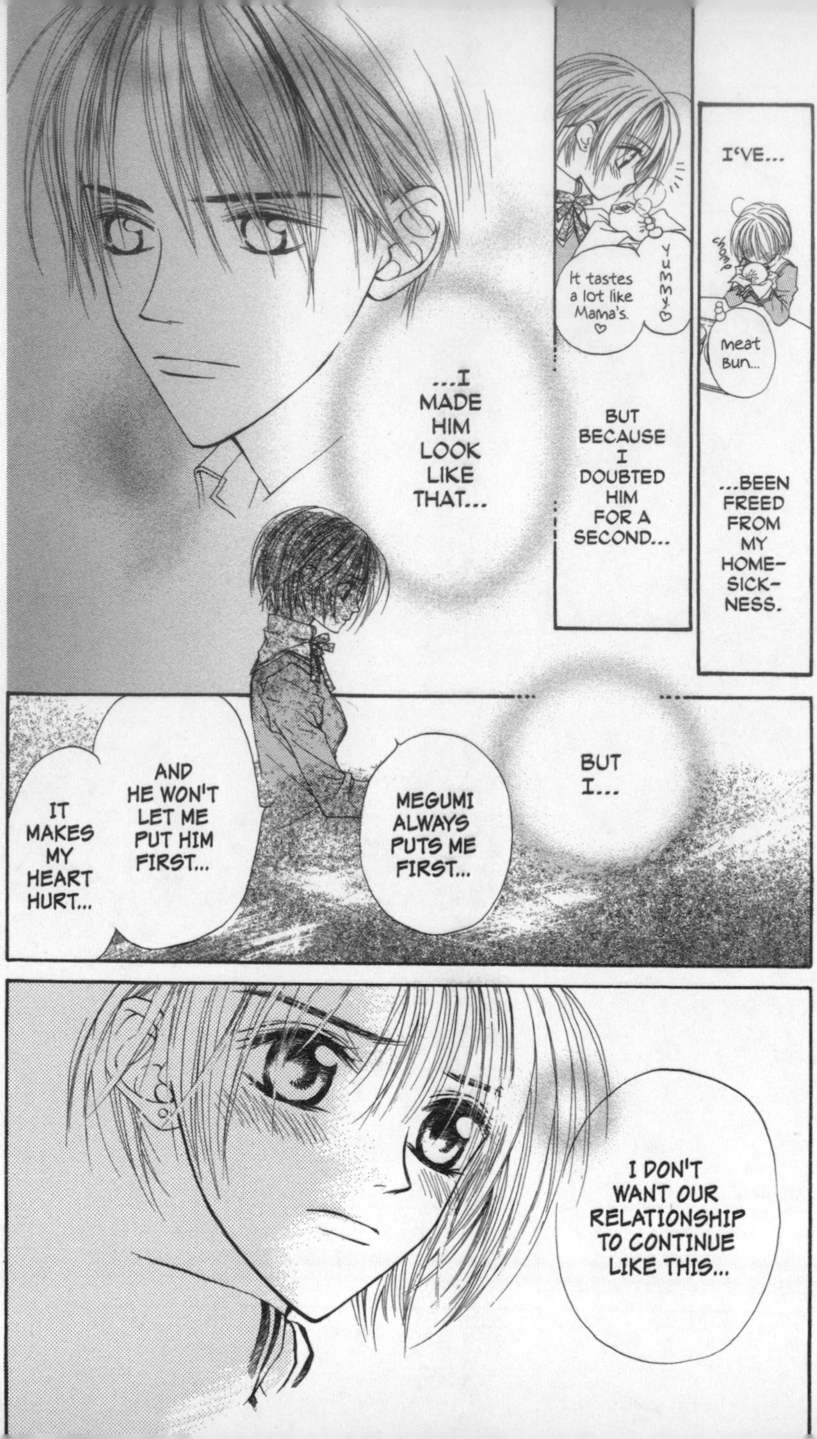
I'VE...
chomp
Meat Bun...
...BEEN FREED FROM MY HOME-SICKNESS.
Yummy ♡
It tastes a lot like Mama's. ♡
BUT BECAUSE I DOUBTED HIM FOR A SECOND...
...I MADE HIM LOOK LIKE THAT...
BUT I...
MEGUMI ALWAYS PUTS ME FIRST...
AND HE WON'T LET ME PUT HIM FIRST...
IT MAKES MY HEART HURT...
I DON'T WANT OUR RELATIONSHIP TO CONTINUE LIKE THIS...

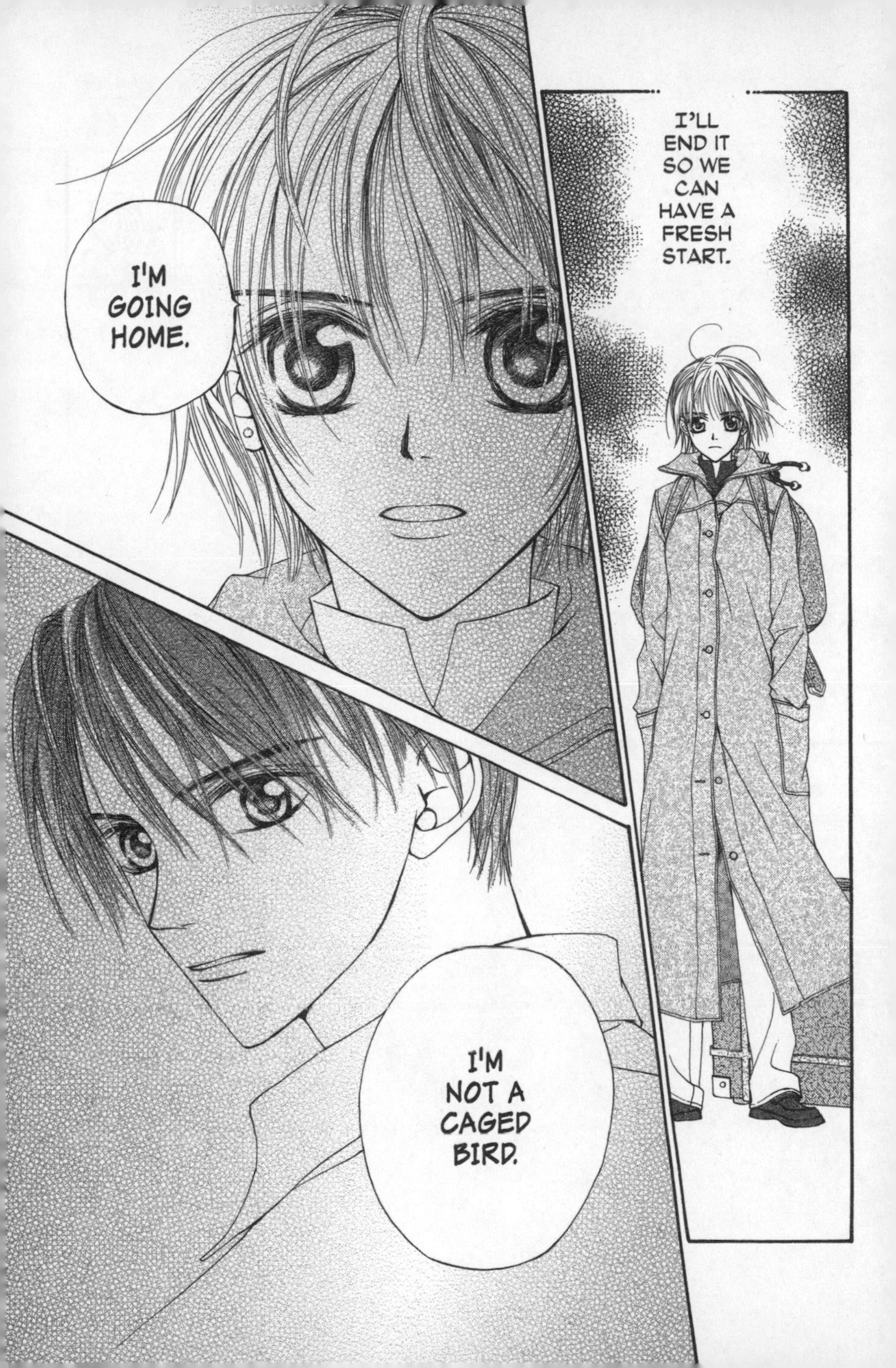
I'LL END IT SO WE CAN HAVE A FRESH START.
I'M GOING HOME.
I'M NOT A CAGED BIRD.

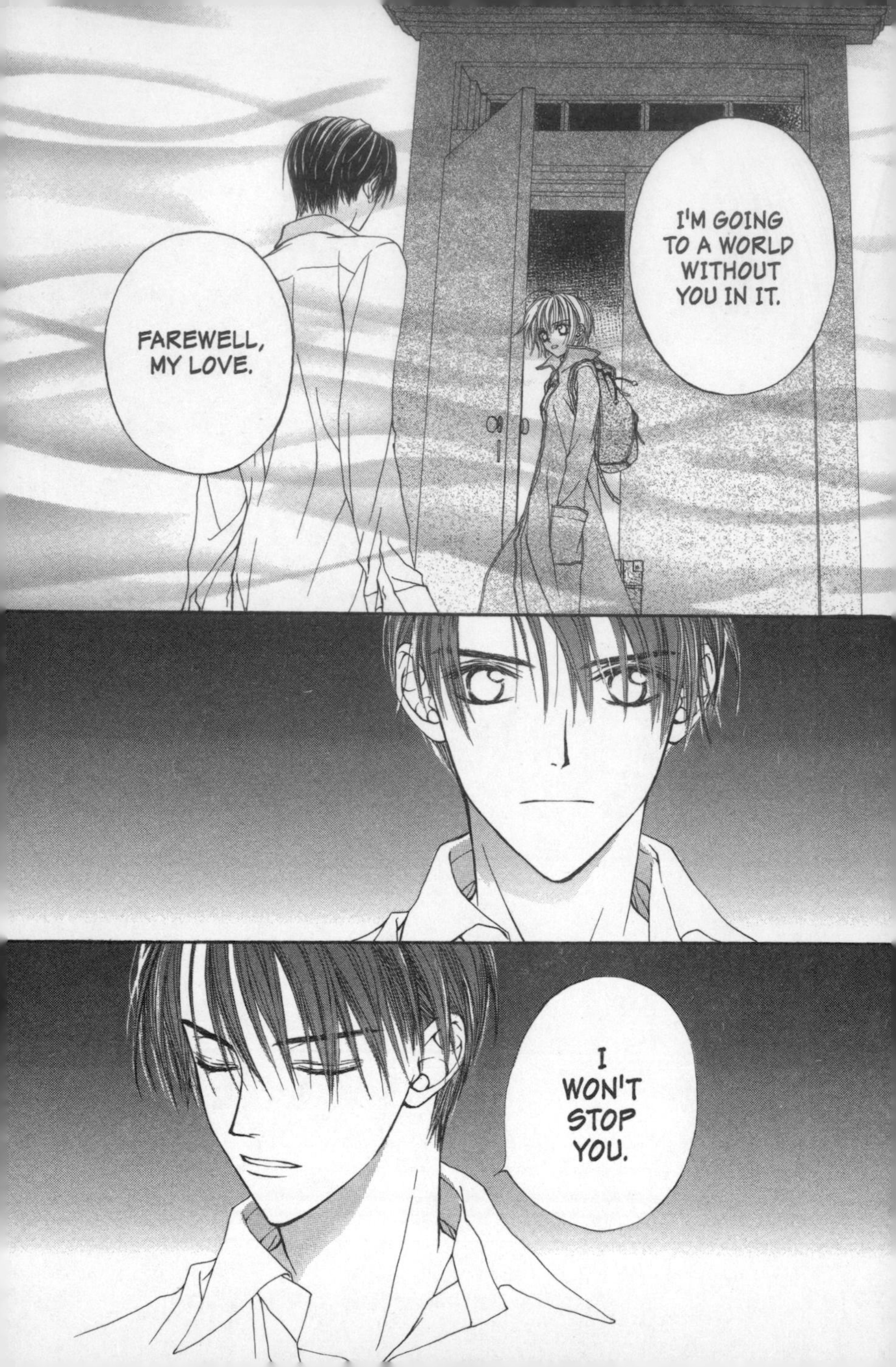
I'M GOING TO A WORLD WITHOUT YOU IN IT.
FAREWELL, MY LOVE.
I WON'T STOP YOU.

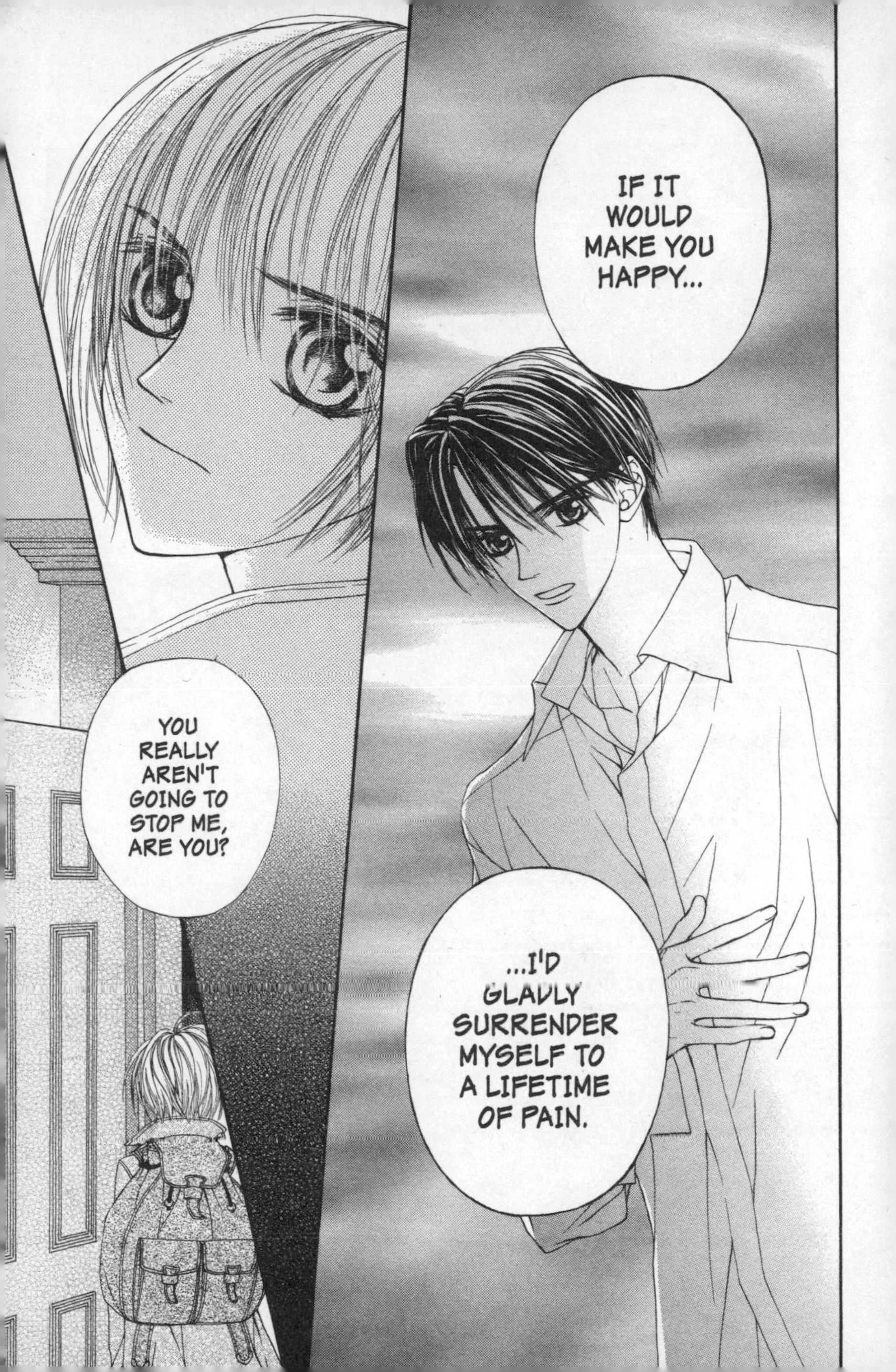
IF IT WOULD MAKE YOU HAPPY...
...I'D GLADLY SURRENDER MYSELF TO A LIFETIME OF PAIN.
YOU REALLY AREN'T GOING TO STOP ME, ARE YOU?

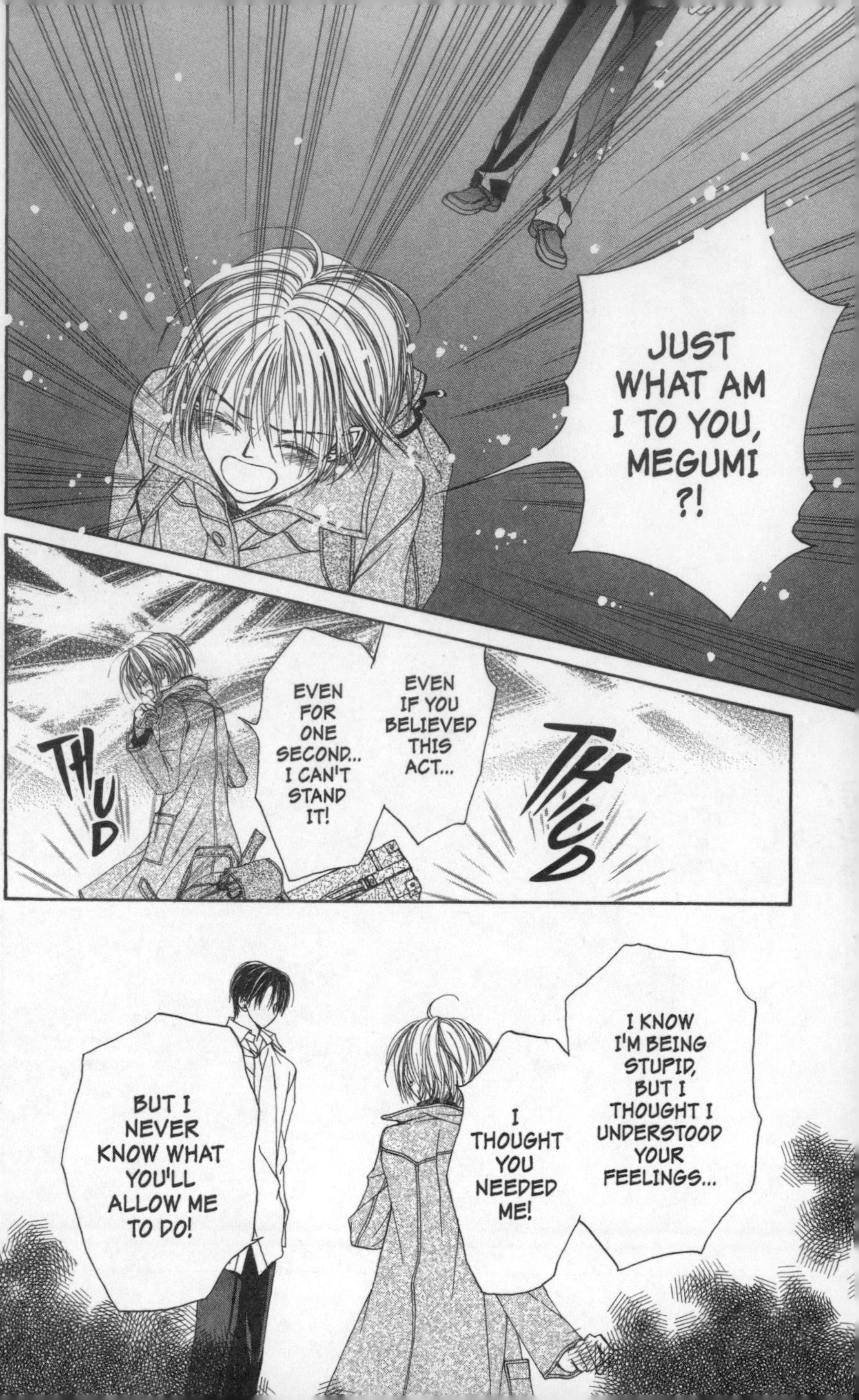
JUST WHAT AM I TO YOU, MEGUMI ?!
THUD
EVEN IF YOU BELIEVED THIS ACT...
EVEN FOR ONE SECOND... I CAN'T STAND IT!
THUD
I KNOW I'M BEING STUPID, BUT I THOUGHT I UNDERSTOOD YOUR FEELINGS...
I THOUGHT YOU NEEDED ME!
BUT I NEVER KNOW WHAT YOU'LL ALLOW ME TO DO!

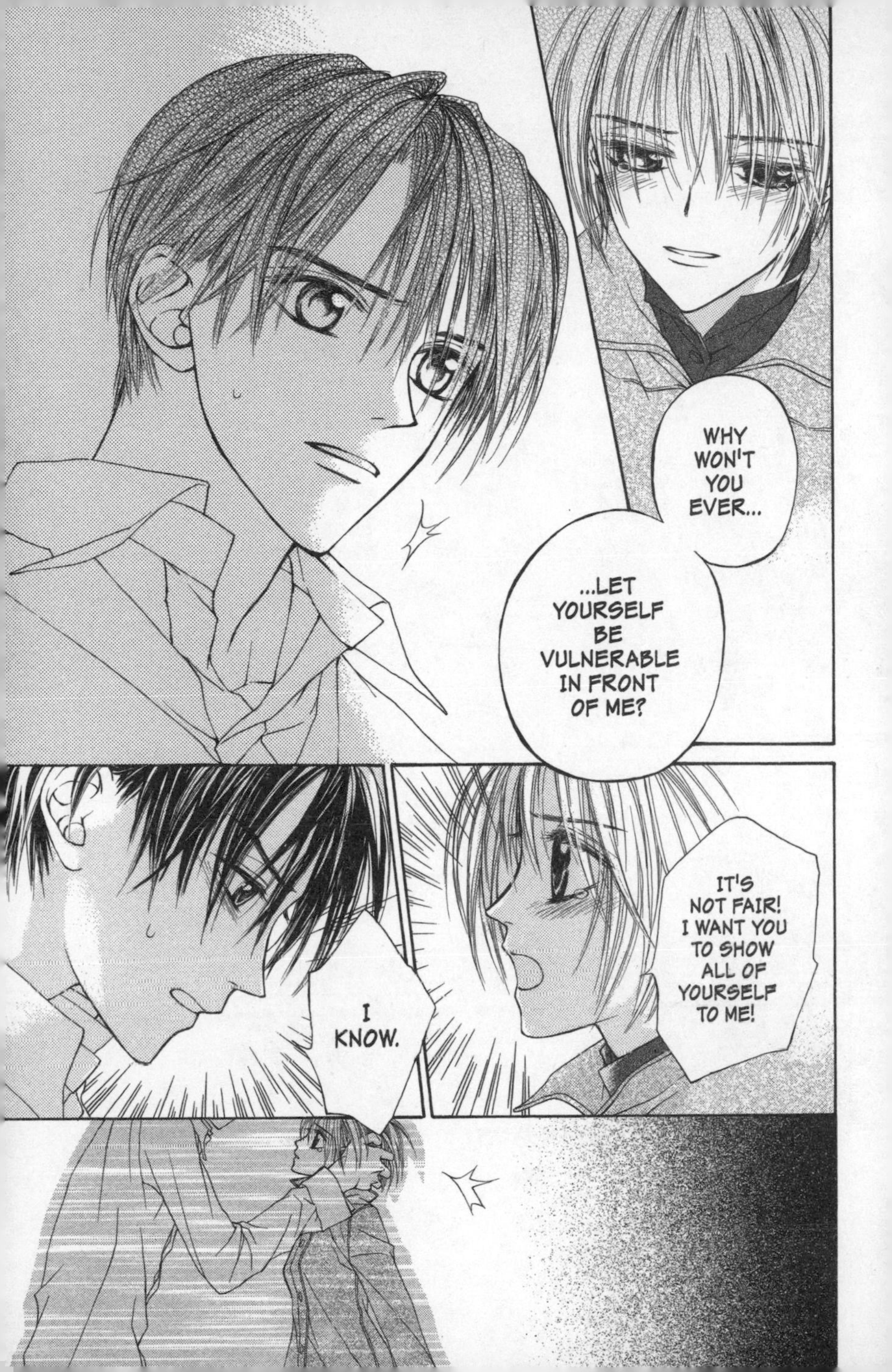
WHY WON'T YOU EVER...
...LET YOURSELF BE VULNERABLE IN FRONT OF ME?
IT'S NOT FAIR! I WANT YOU TO SHOW ALL OF YOURSELF TO ME!
I KNOW.

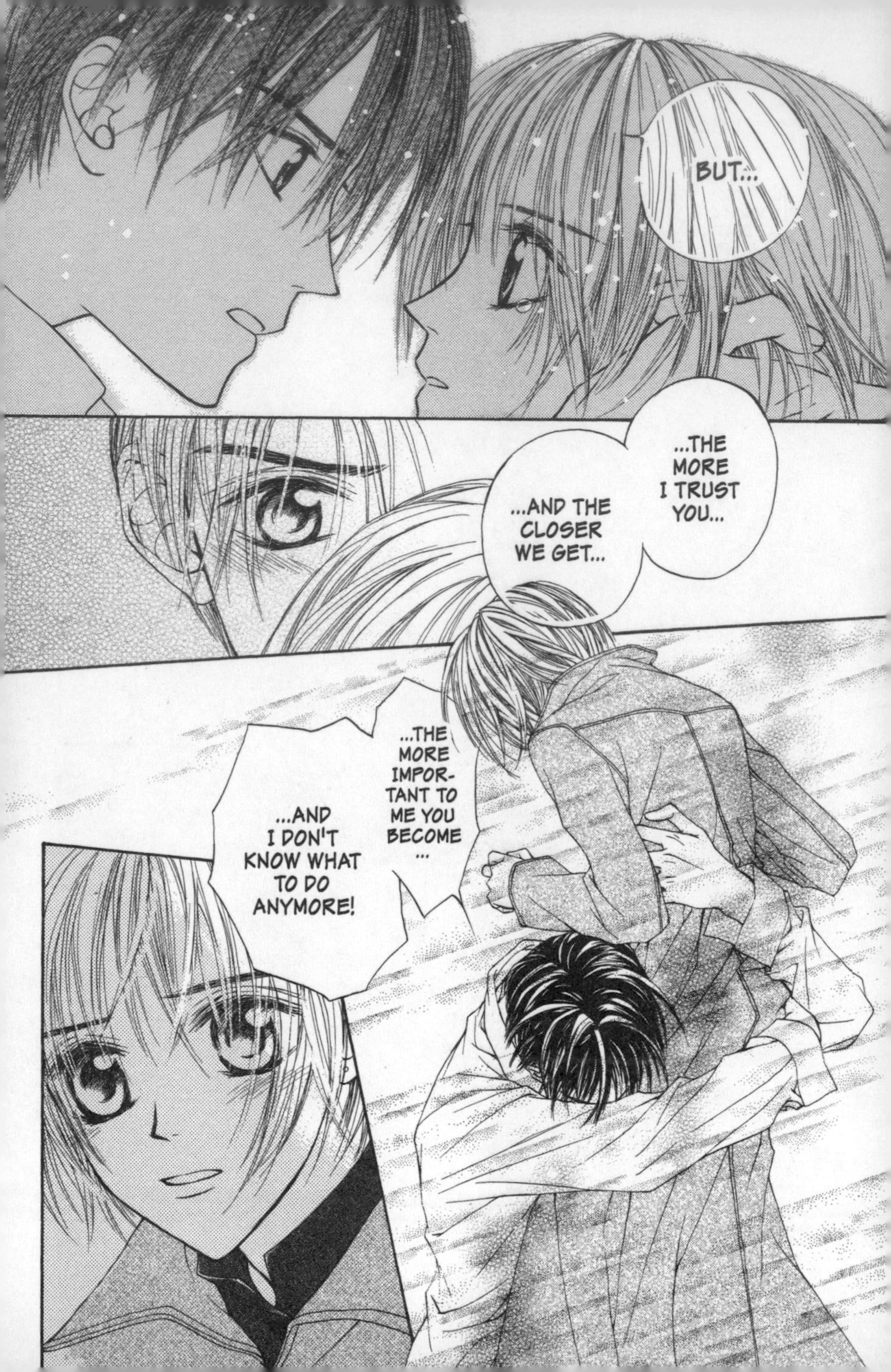
BUT...
...THE MORE I TRUST YOU...
...AND THE CLOSER WE GET...
...THE MORE IMPORTANT TO ME YOU BECOME...
...AND I DON'T KNOW WHAT TO DO ANYMORE!

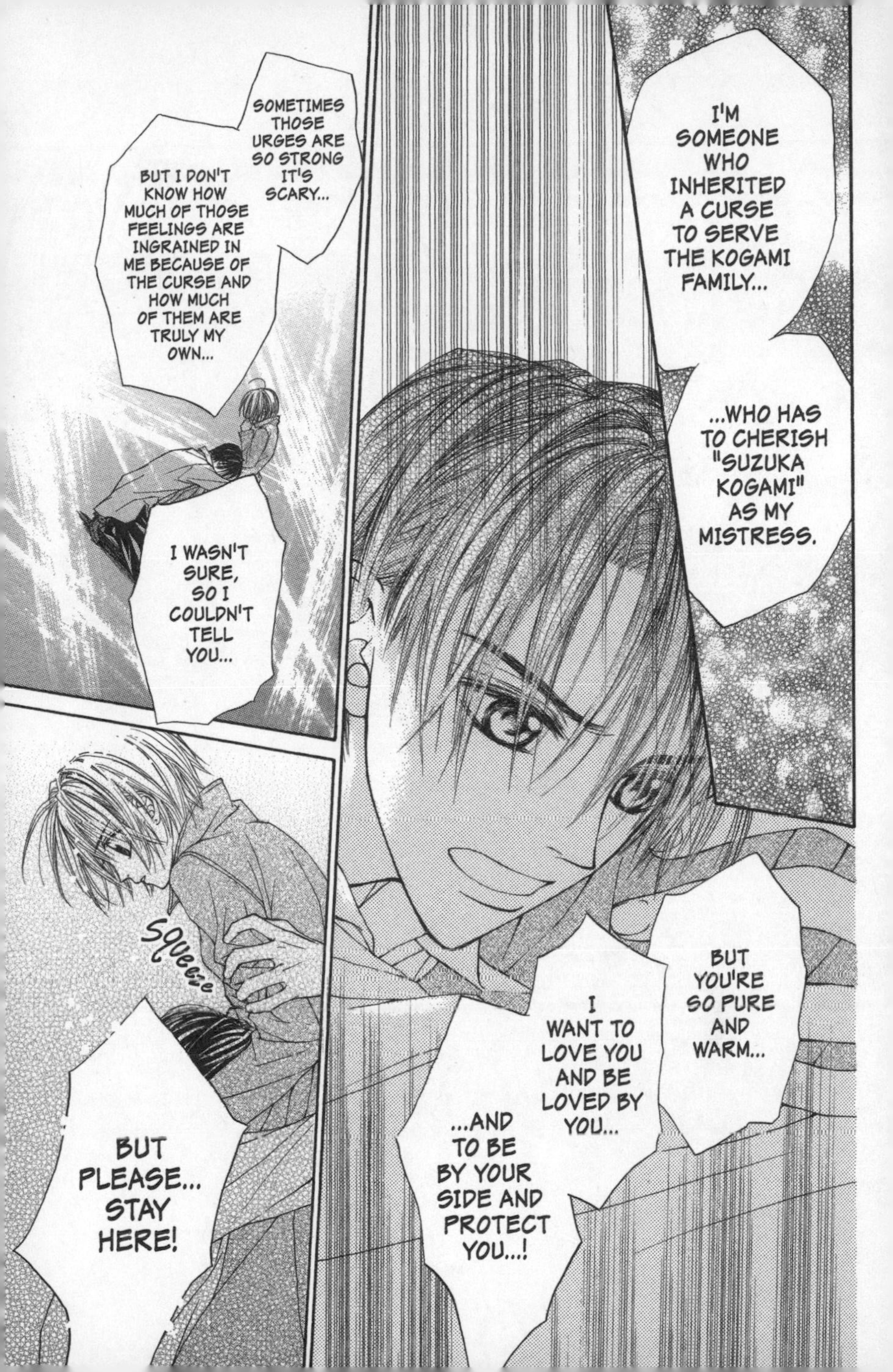
I'M SOMEONE WHO INHERITED A CURSE TO SERVE THE KOGAMI FAMILY...
...WHO HAS TO CHERISH "SUZUKA KOGAMI" AS MY MISTRESS.
BUT YOU'RE SO PURE AND WARM...
I WANT TO LOVE YOU AND BE LOVED BY YOU...
...AND TO BE BY YOUR SIDE AND PROTECT YOU...!
SOMETIMES THOSE URGES ARE SO STRONG IT'S SCARY...
BUT I DON'T KNOW HOW MUCH OF THOSE FEELINGS ARE INGRAINED IN ME BECAUSE OF THE CURSE AND HOW MUCH OF THEM ARE TRULY MY OWN...
I WASN'T SURE, SO I COULDN'T TELL YOU...
Squeeze
BUT PLEASE... STAY HERE!

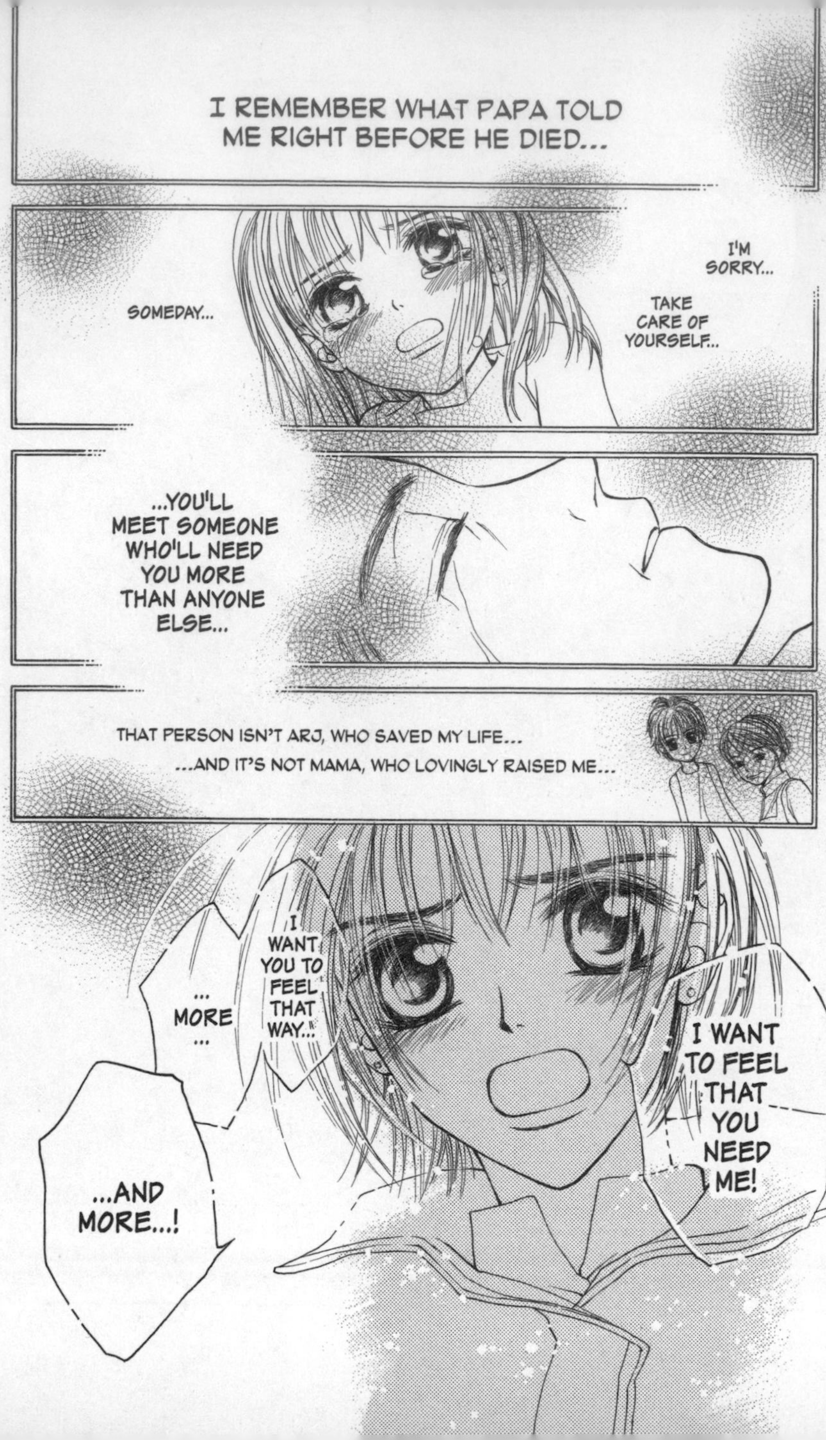
I REMEMBER WHAT PAPA TOLD ME RIGHT BEFORE HE DIED...
I'M SORRY...
TAKE CARE OF YOURSELF...
SOMEDAY...
...YOU'LL MEET SOMEONE WHO'LL NEED YOU MORE THAN ANYONE ELSE...
THAT PERSON ISN'T ARJ, WHO SAVED MY LIFE...
...AND IT'S NOT MAMA, WHO LOVINGLY RAISED ME...
I WANT TO FEEL THAT YOU NEED ME!
I WANT YOU TO FEEL THAT WAY...
...MORE...
...AND MORE...!

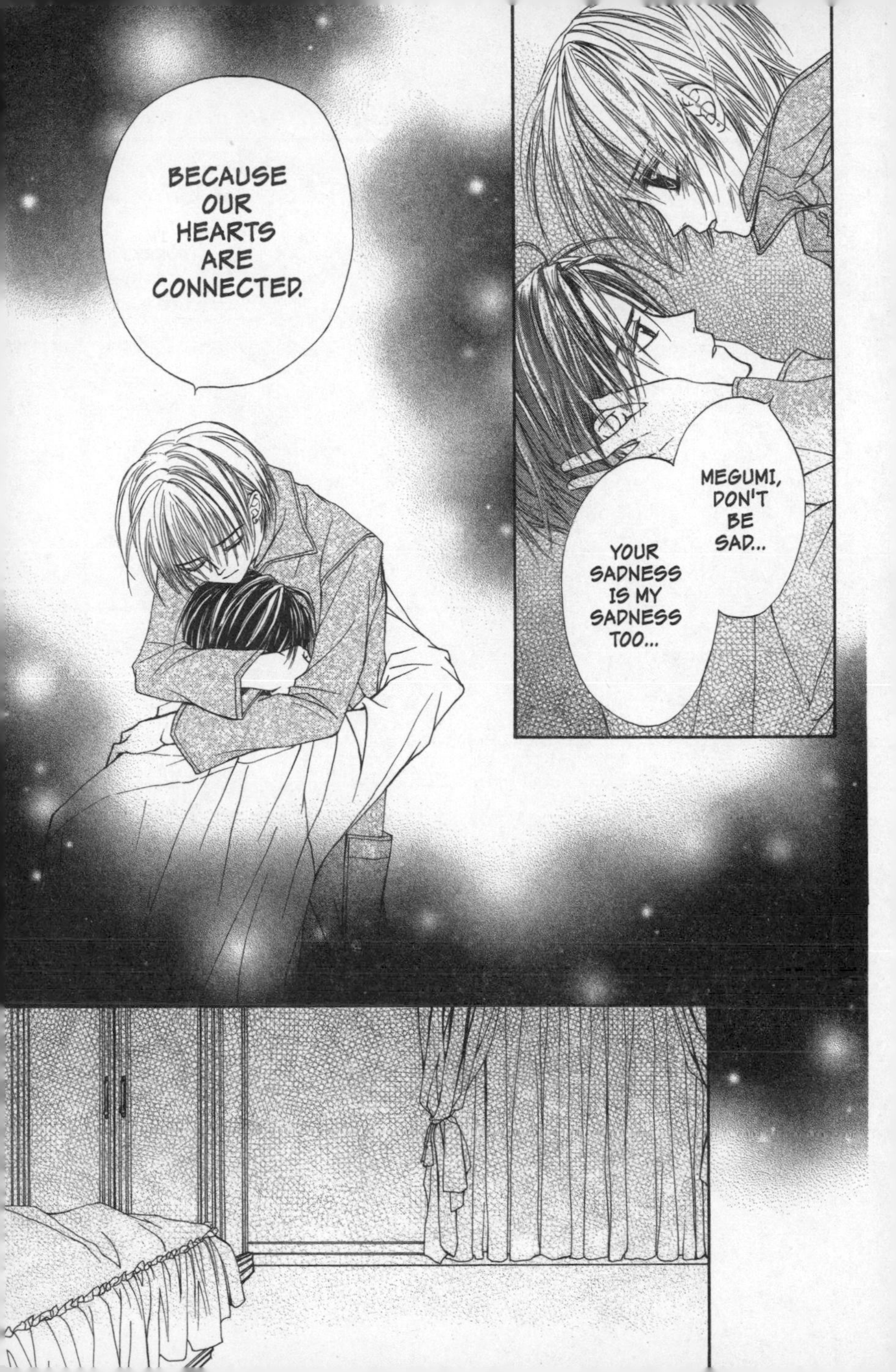
MEGUMI, DON'T BE SAD...
YOUR SADNESS IS MY SADNESS TOO...
BECAUSE OUR HEARTS ARE CONNECTED.

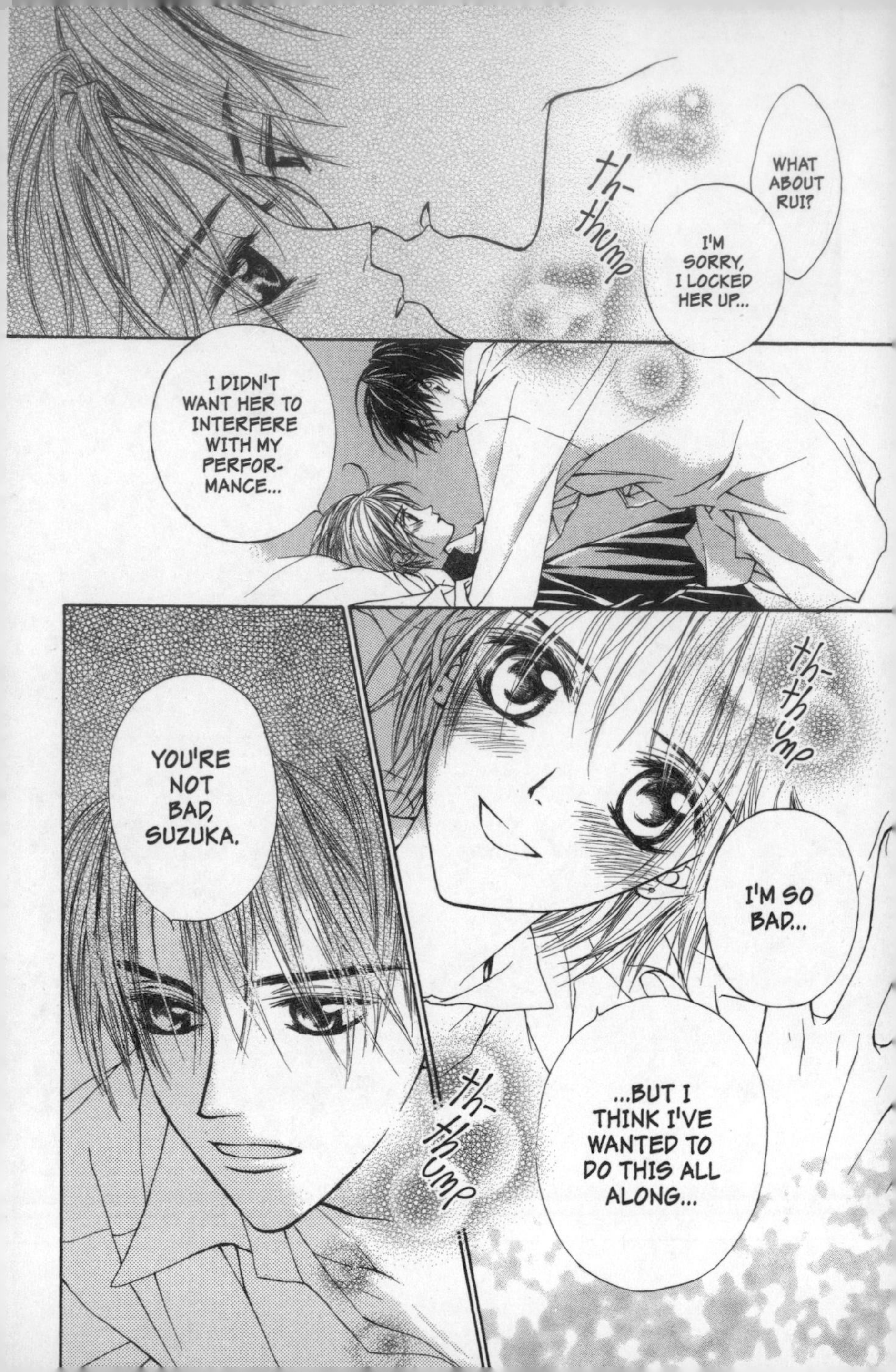
WHAT ABOUT RUI?
th-thump
I'M SORRY, I LOCKED HER UP...
I DIDN'T WANT HER TO INTERFERE WITH MY PERFORMANCE...
th-thump
I'M SO BAD...
...BUT I THINK I'VE WANTED TO DO THIS ALL ALONG...
th-thump
YOU'RE NOT BAD, SUZUKA.

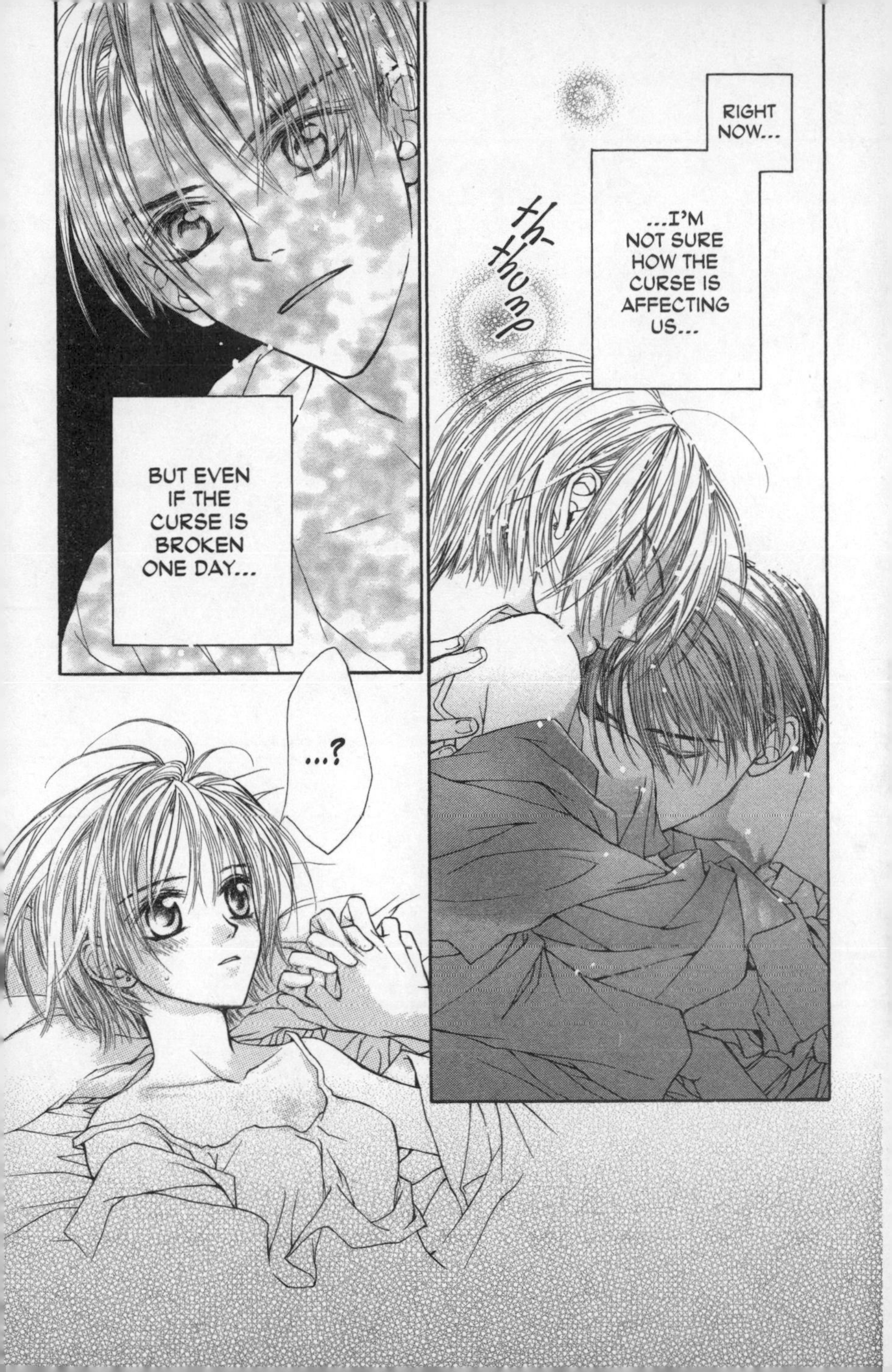
RIGHT NOW...
...I'M NOT SURE HOW THE CURSE IS AFFECTING US...
th-thump
BUT EVEN IF THE CURSE IS BROKEN ONE DAY...
...?

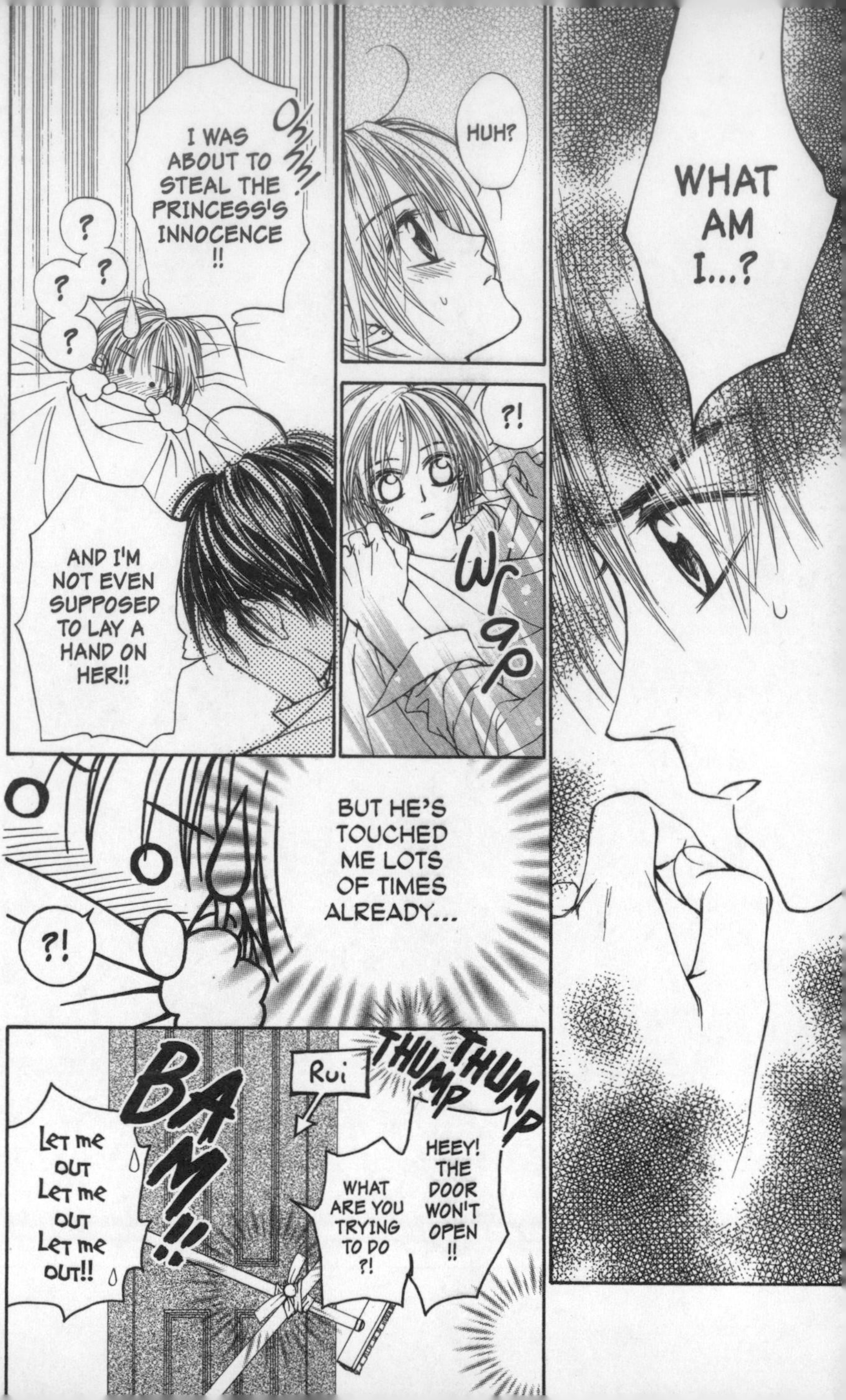
WHAT AM I...?
HUH?
?!
Wrap
Ohhh!
I WAS ABOUT TO STEAL THE PRINCESS'S INNOCENCE !!
? ? ? ?
AND I'M NOT EVEN SUPPOSED TO LAY A HAND ON HER!!
BUT HE'S TOUCHED ME LOTS OF TIMES ALREADY...
?!
THUMP THUMP
HEEY! THE DOOR WON'T OPEN !!
WHAT ARE YOU TRYING TO DO ?!
Rui
BAM!!
Let me out Let me out Let me out!!

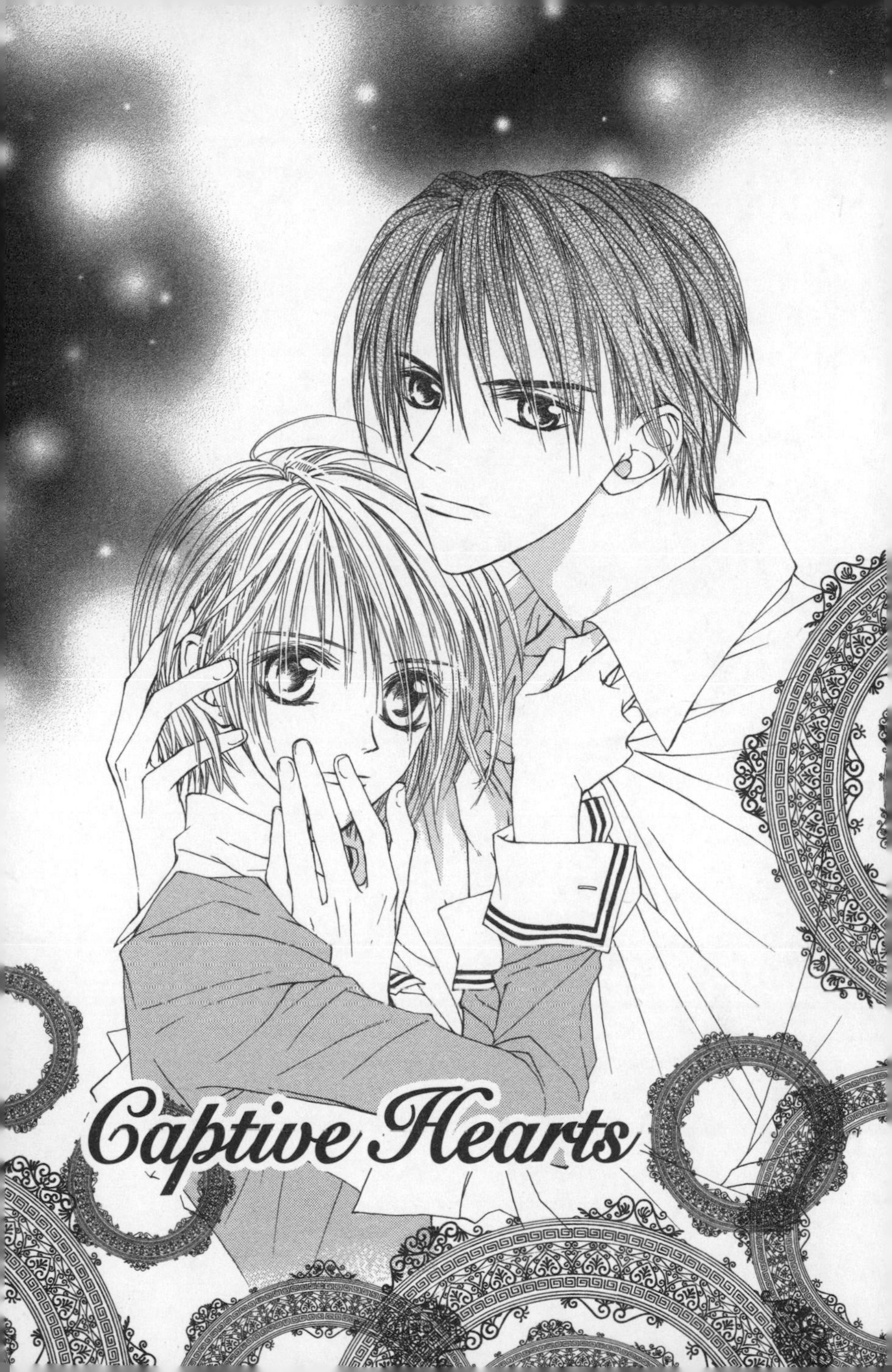
Captive Hearts

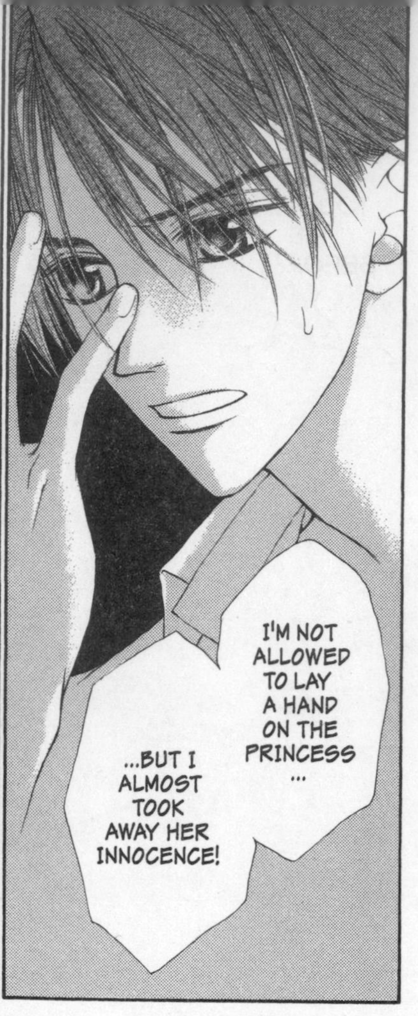
I'M NOT ALLOWED TO LAY A HAND ON THE PRINCESS...
...BUT I ALMOST TOOK AWAY HER INNOCENCE!

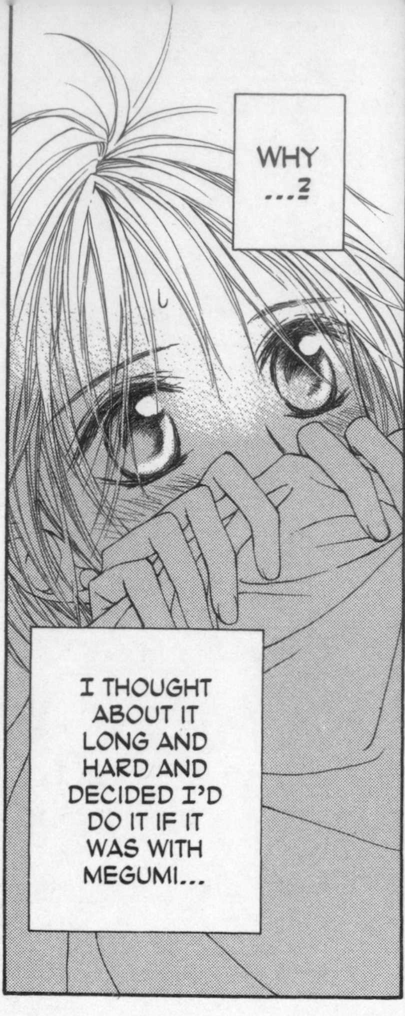
WHY...?
I THOUGHT ABOUT IT LONG AND HARD AND DECIDED I'D DO IT IF IT WAS WITH MEGUMI...

② I think I've started using colors a bit differently ever since I went to China.

Yeah, I think I have. It might be temporary, but I feel like I can't work in color like I did before! I think it was the influence from my China trip. Images like "desert nation," "Space," "Trees," "Vast land" and "Wind mixing with music" are in my head...♪ I felt even more connected to *Captive Hearts* after going to China. I think I might want to travel more...♪

My China travel diary is in the back of the book—check it out!♡

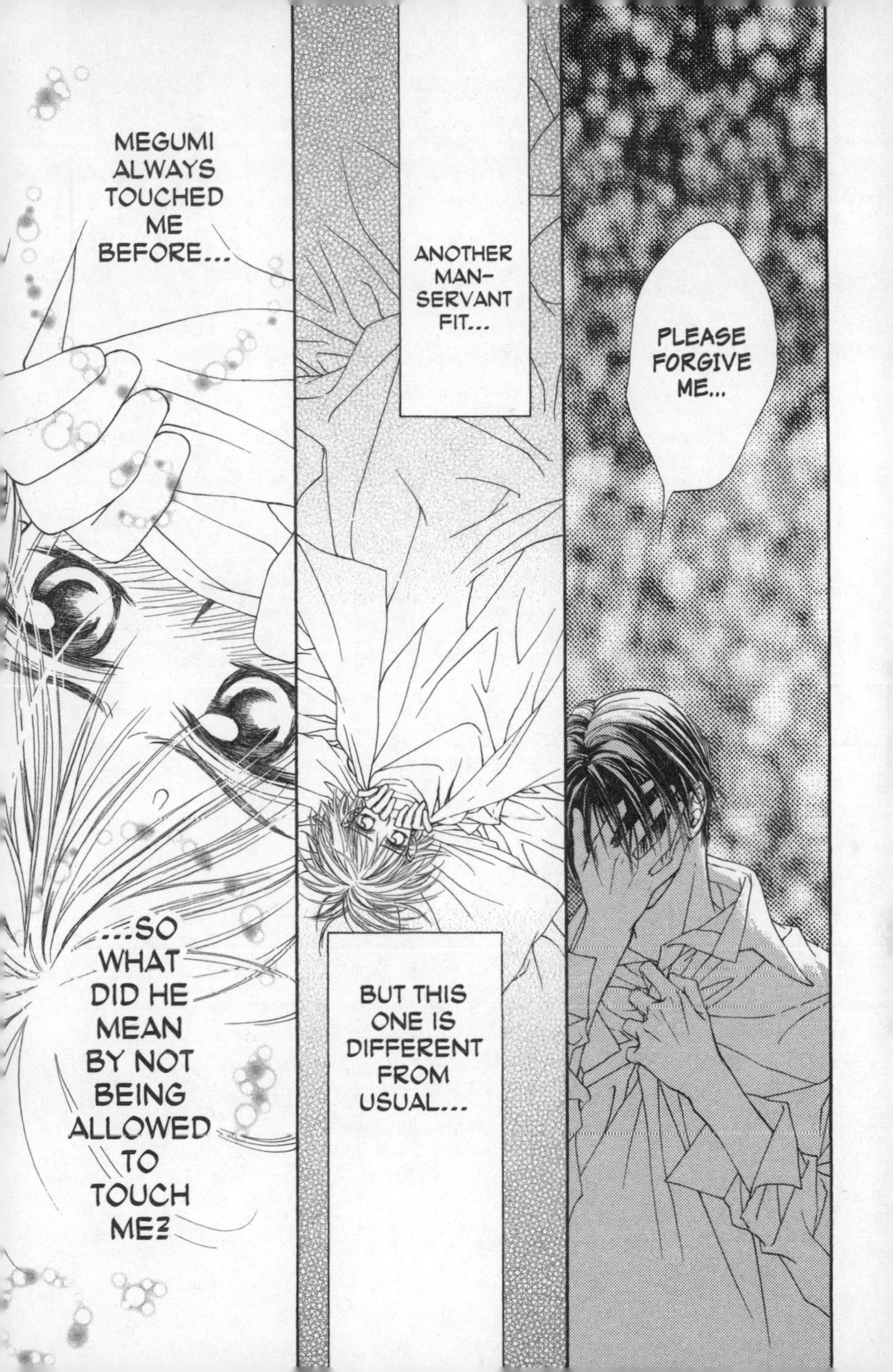
PLEASE FORGIVE ME...
ANOTHER MAN-SERVANT FIT...
BUT THIS ONE IS DIFFERENT FROM USUAL...
MEGUMI ALWAYS TOUCHED ME BEFORE...
...SO WHAT DID HE MEAN BY NOT BEING ALLOWED TO TOUCH ME?

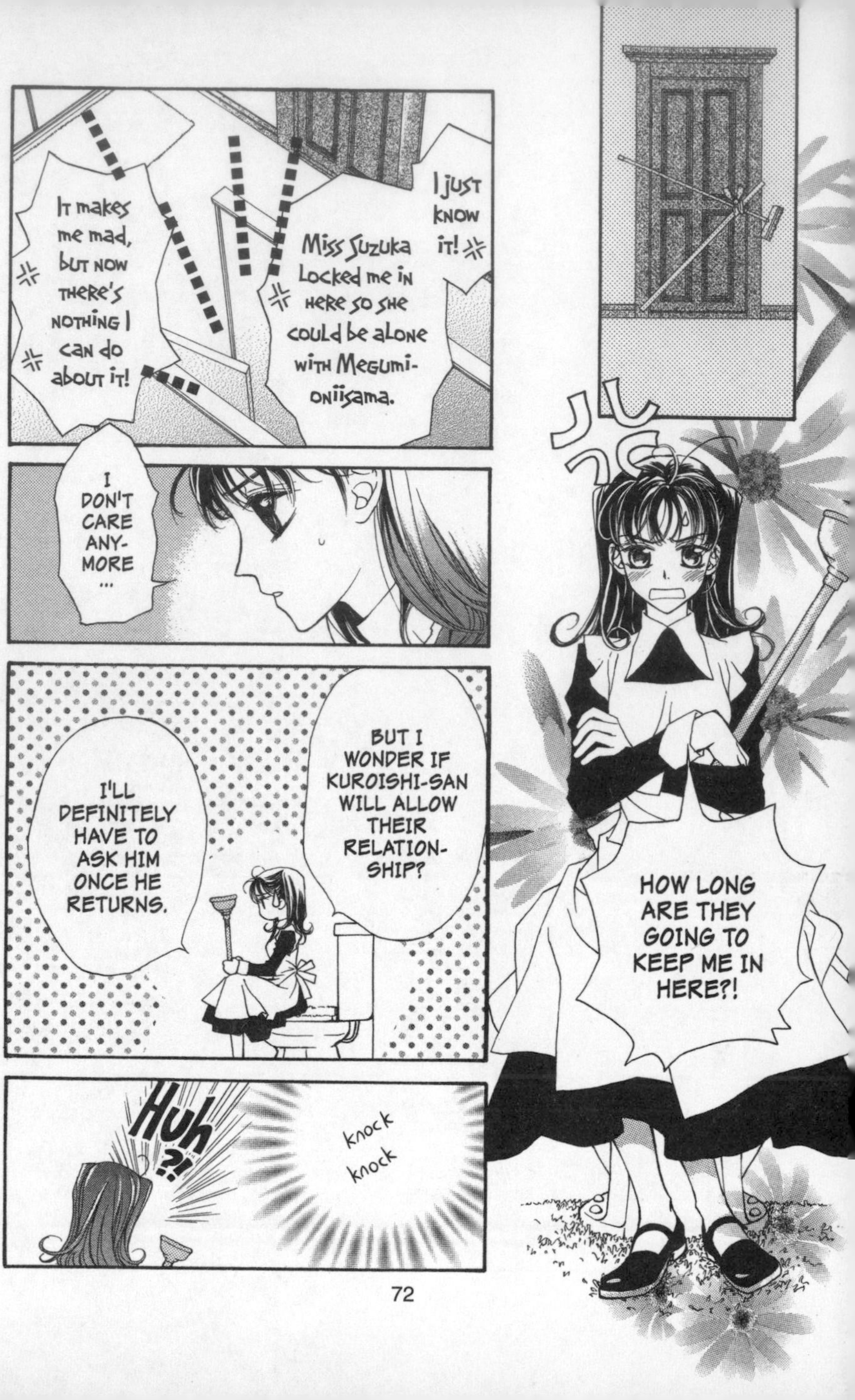
HOW LONG ARE THEY GOING TO KEEP ME IN HERE?!
I just know it!
Miss Suzuka Locked me in here so she could be alone with Megumi-oniisama.
It makes me mad, but now there's nothing I can do about it!
I DON'T CARE ANYMORE...
BUT I WONDER IF KUROISHI-SAN WILL ALLOW THEIR RELATIONSHIP?
I'LL DEFINITELY HAVE TO ASK HIM ONCE HE RETURNS.
knock knock
Huh?!

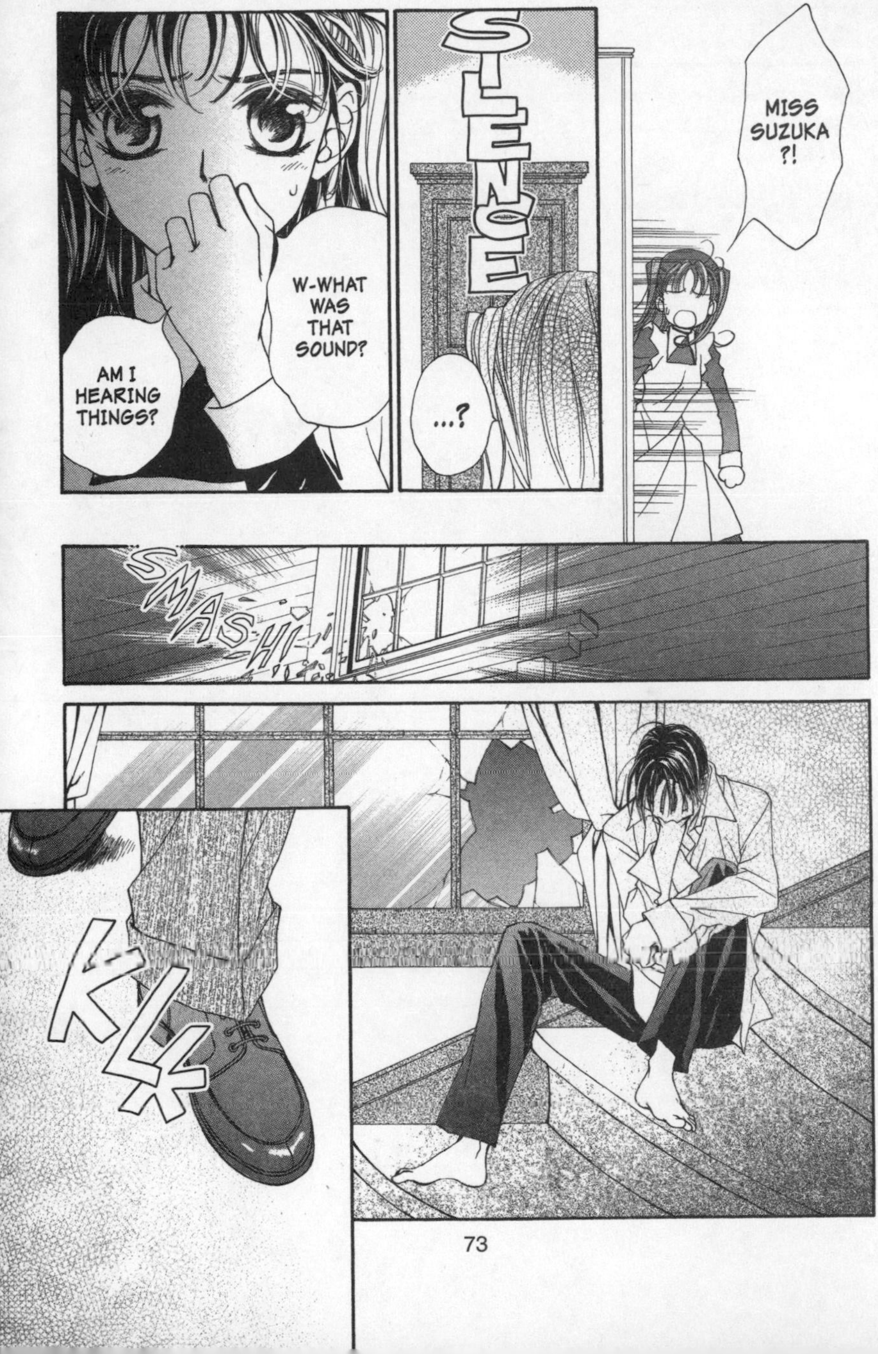
MISS SUZUKA ?!
SILENCE
...?
W-WHAT WAS THAT SOUND?
AM I HEARING THINGS?
SMASH!
KLK

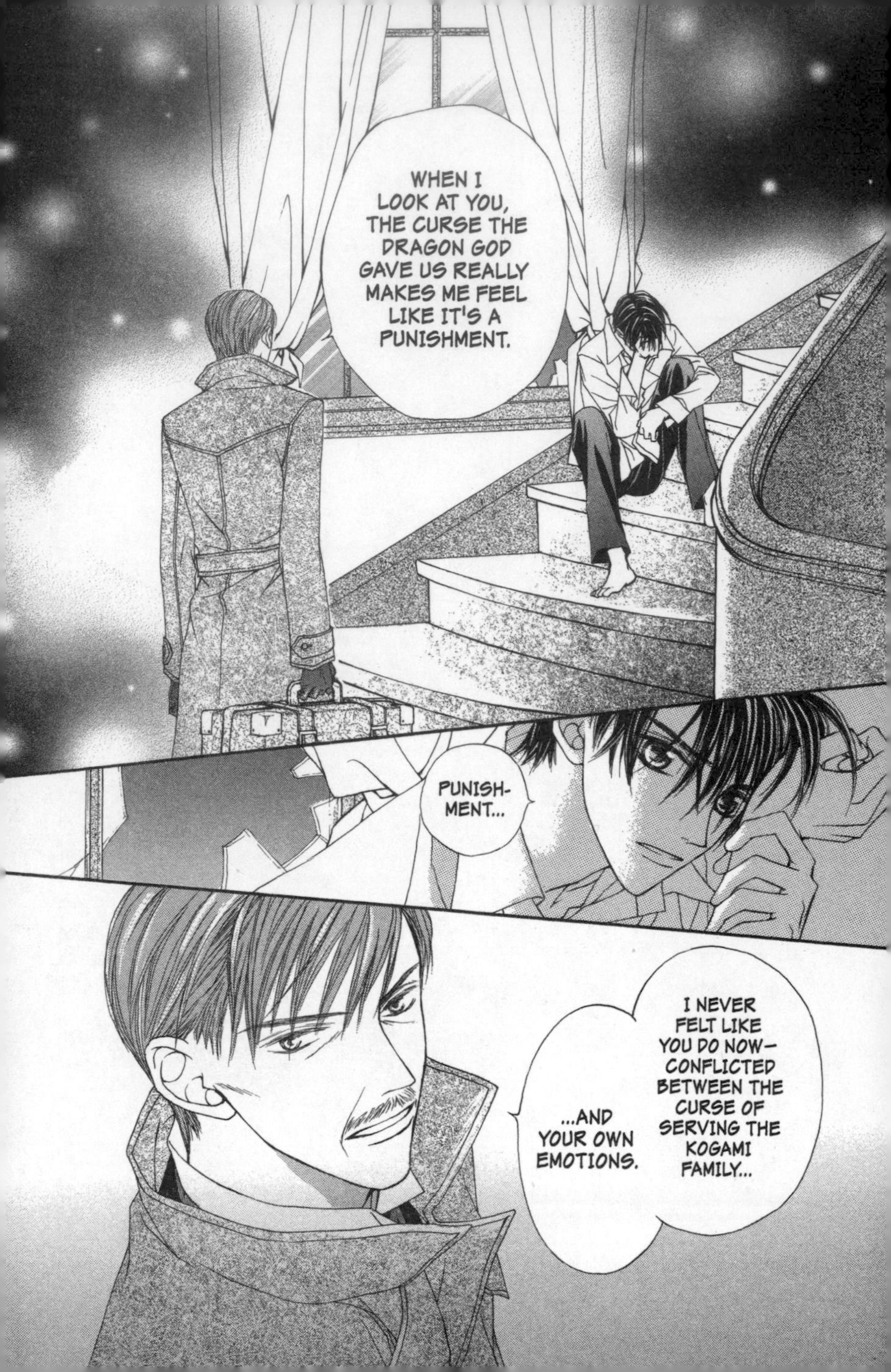
WHEN I LOOK AT YOU, THE CURSE THE DRAGON GOD GAVE US REALLY MAKES ME FEEL LIKE IT'S A PUNISHMENT.
PUNISH-MENT...
I NEVER FELT LIKE YOU DO NOW—CONFLICTED BETWEEN THE CURSE OF SERVING THE KOGAMI FAMILY...
...AND YOUR OWN EMOTIONS.

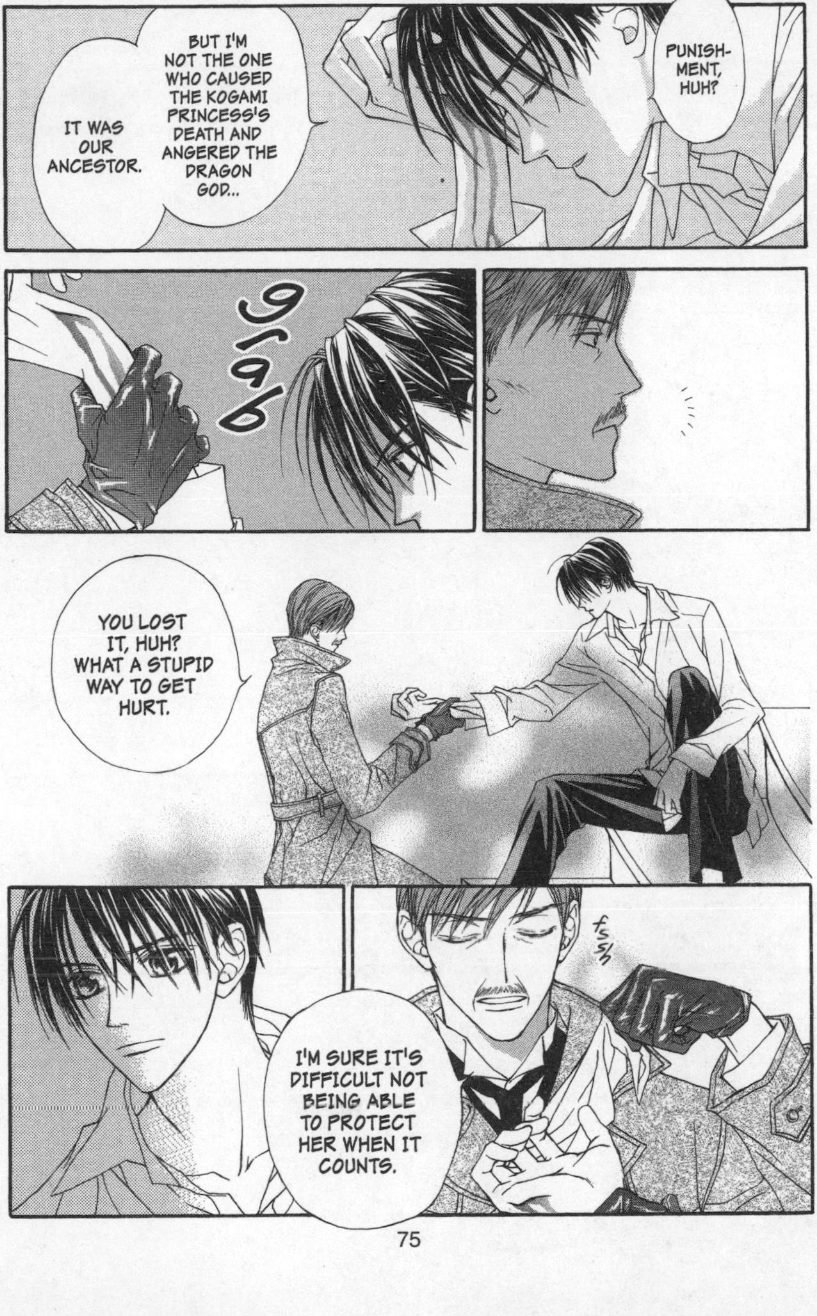
PUNISH-MENT, HUH?
BUT I'M NOT THE ONE WHO CAUSED THE KOGAMI PRINCESS'S DEATH AND ANGERED THE DRAGON GOD...
IT WAS OUR ANCESTOR.
grab
YOU LOST IT, HUH? WHAT A STUPID WAY TO GET HURT.
fssh
I'M SURE IT'S DIFFICULT NOT BEING ABLE TO PROTECT HER WHEN IT COUNTS.

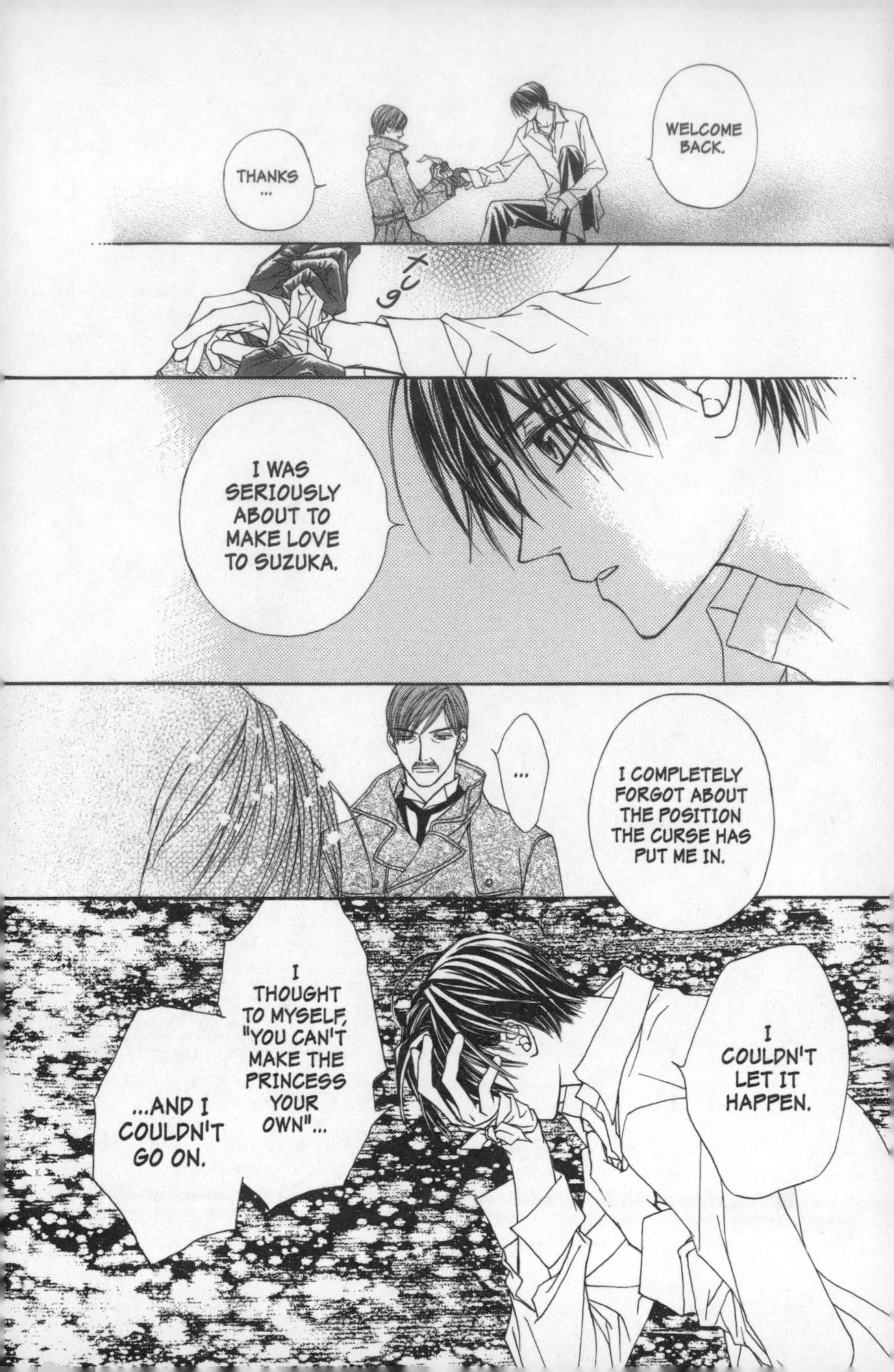

WELCOME BACK.
THANKS ...
TUG
I WAS SERIOUSLY ABOUT TO MAKE LOVE TO SUZUKA.
I COMPLETELY FORGOT ABOUT THE POSITION THE CURSE HAS PUT ME IN.
...
I COULDN'T LET IT HAPPEN.
I THOUGHT TO MYSELF, "YOU CAN'T MAKE THE PRINCESS YOUR OWN"...
...AND I COULDN'T GO ON.

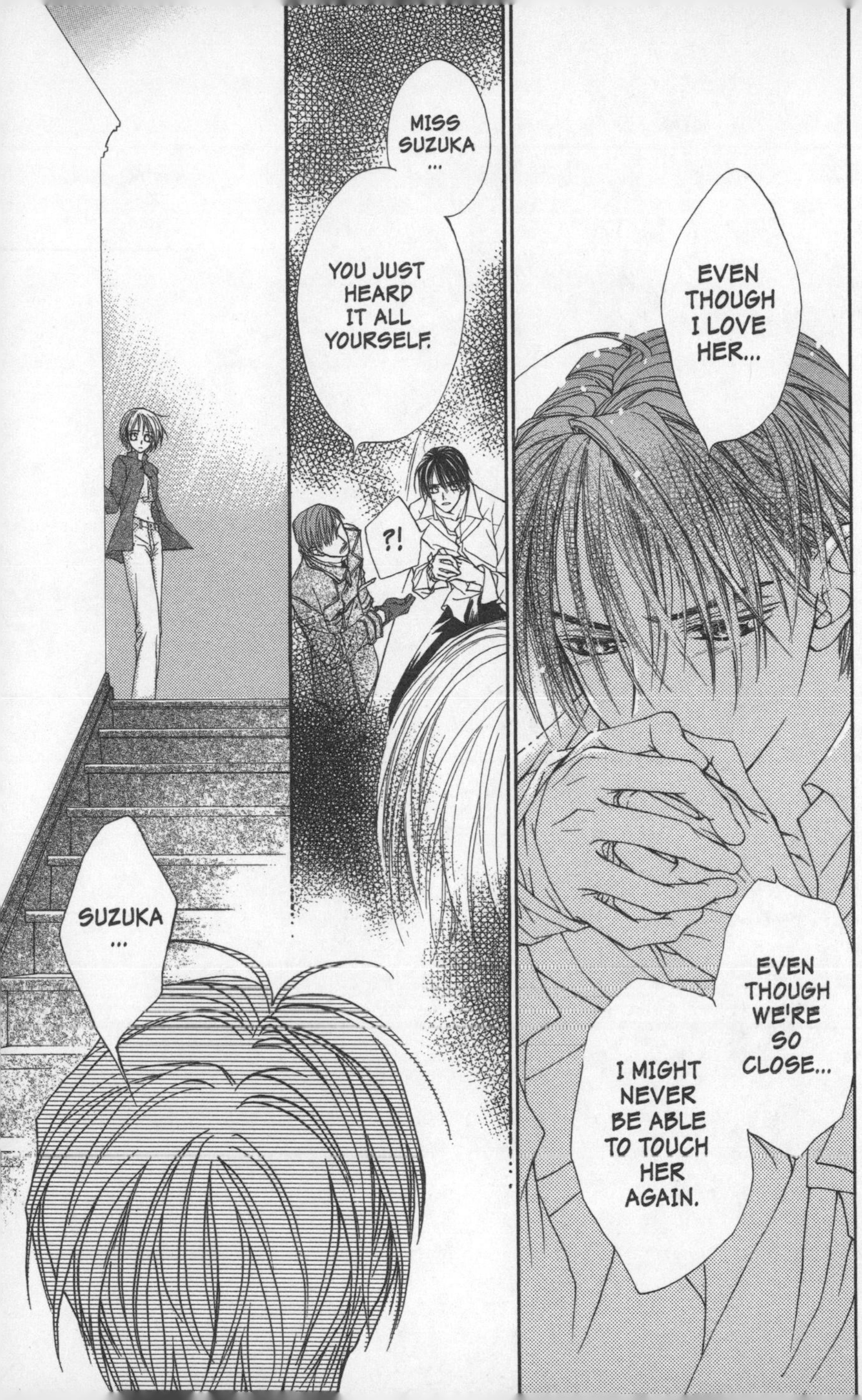
EVEN THOUGH I LOVE HER...
EVEN THOUGH WE'RE SO CLOSE...
I MIGHT NEVER BE ABLE TO TOUCH HER AGAIN.
MISS SUZUKA ...
YOU JUST HEARD IT ALL YOURSELF.
?!
SUZUKA ...

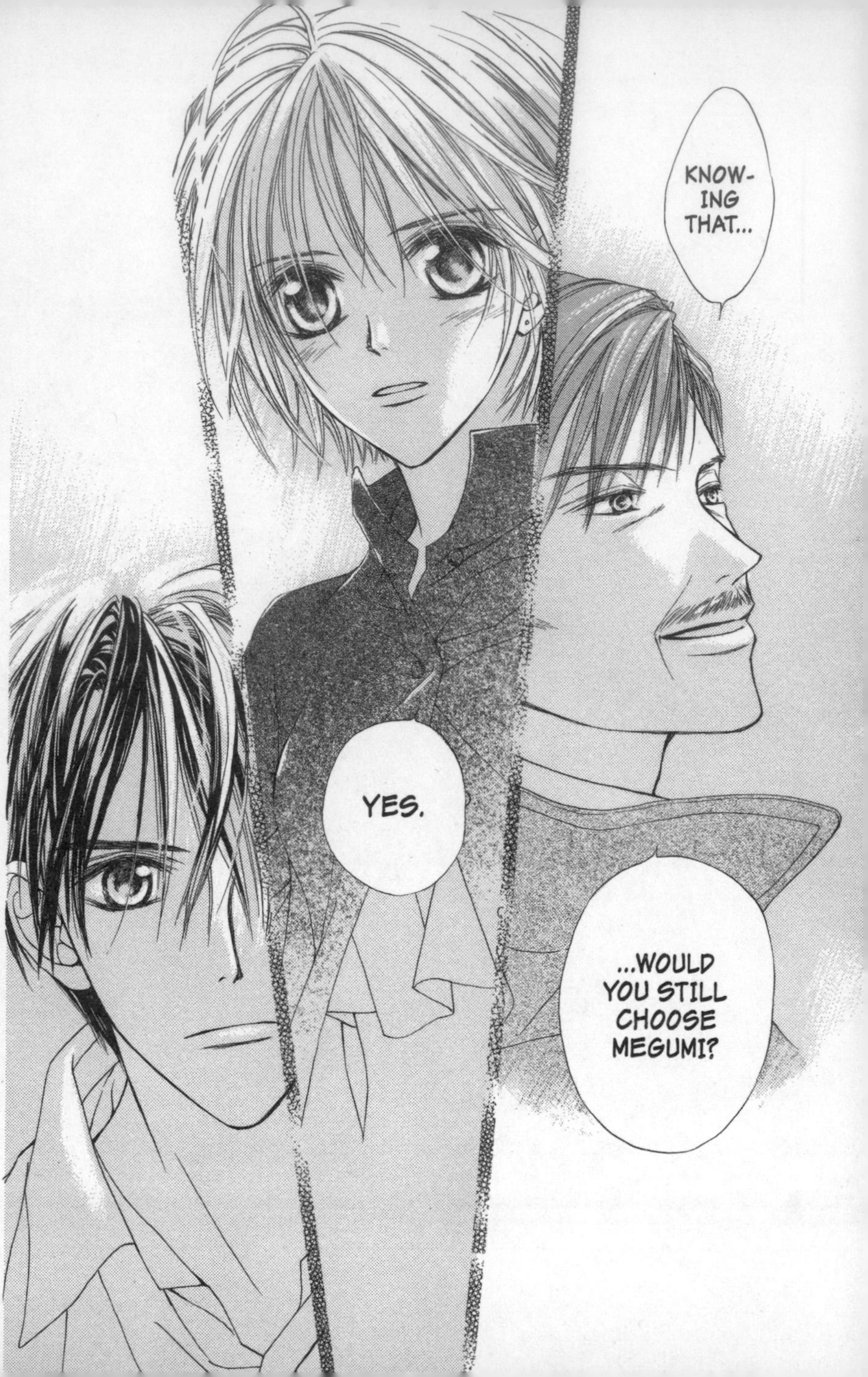
KNOW-ING THAT...
...WOULD YOU STILL CHOOSE MEGUMI?
YES.

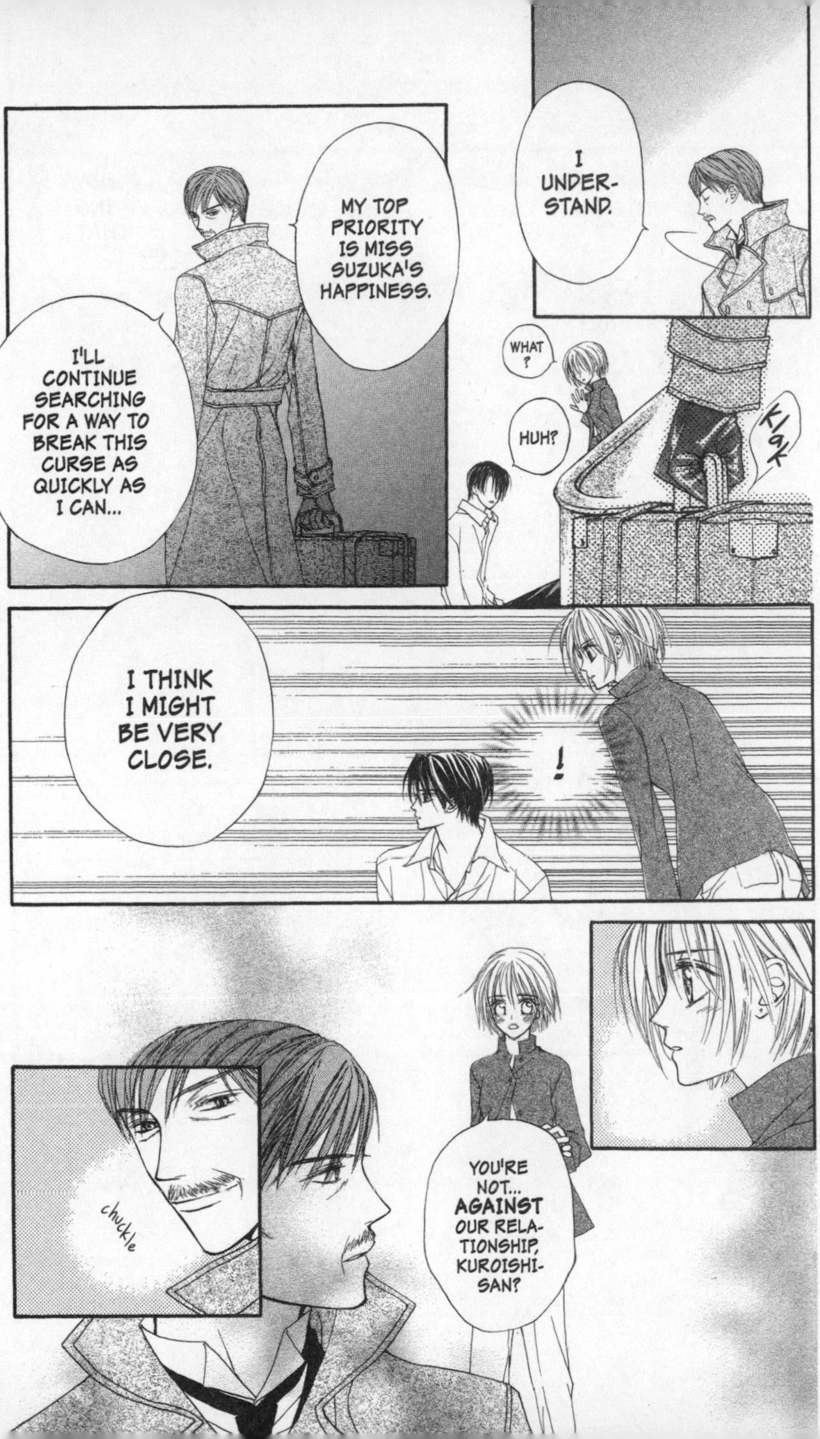
I UNDER-STAND.
WHAT?
HUH?
KLAK
MY TOP PRIORITY IS MISS SUZUKA'S HAPPINESS.
I'LL CONTINUE SEARCHING FOR A WAY TO BREAK THIS CURSE AS QUICKLY AS I CAN...
!
I THINK I MIGHT BE VERY CLOSE.
YOU'RE NOT... AGAINST OUR RELA-TIONSHIP, KUROISHI-SAN?
chuckle

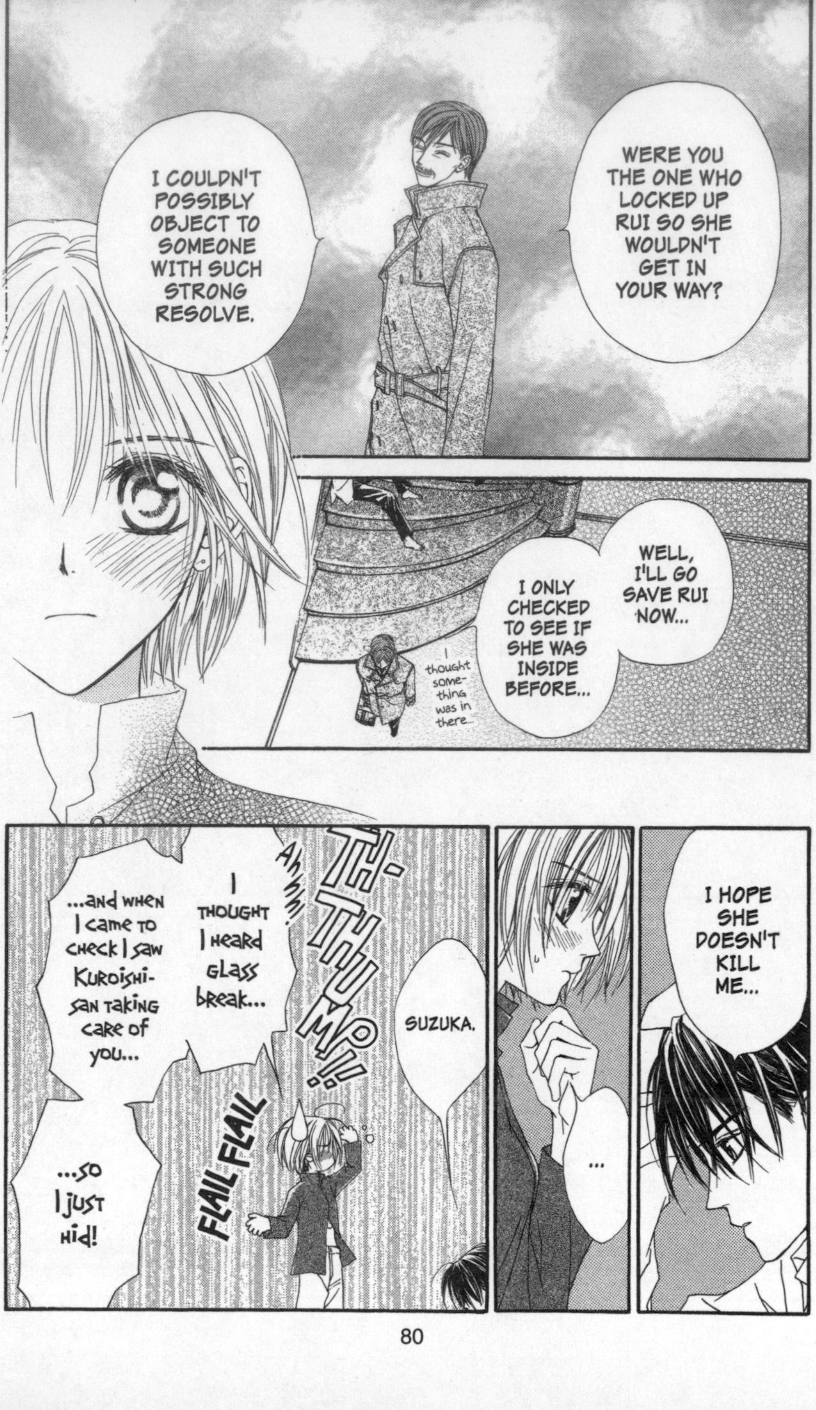
WERE YOU THE ONE WHO LOCKED UP RUI SO SHE WOULDN'T GET IN YOUR WAY?
I COULDN'T POSSIBLY OBJECT TO SOMEONE WITH SUCH STRONG RESOLVE.
WELL, I'LL GO SAVE RUI NOW...
I ONLY CHECKED TO SEE IF SHE WAS INSIDE BEFORE...
I thought something was in there...
I HOPE SHE DOESN'T KILL ME...
...
SUZUKA.
TH-THUMP!!!
Ahhh!
I THOUGHT I HEARD GLASS BREAK...
...and when I came to check I saw Kuroishi-san taking care of you...
...so I just hid!
FLAIL FLAIL

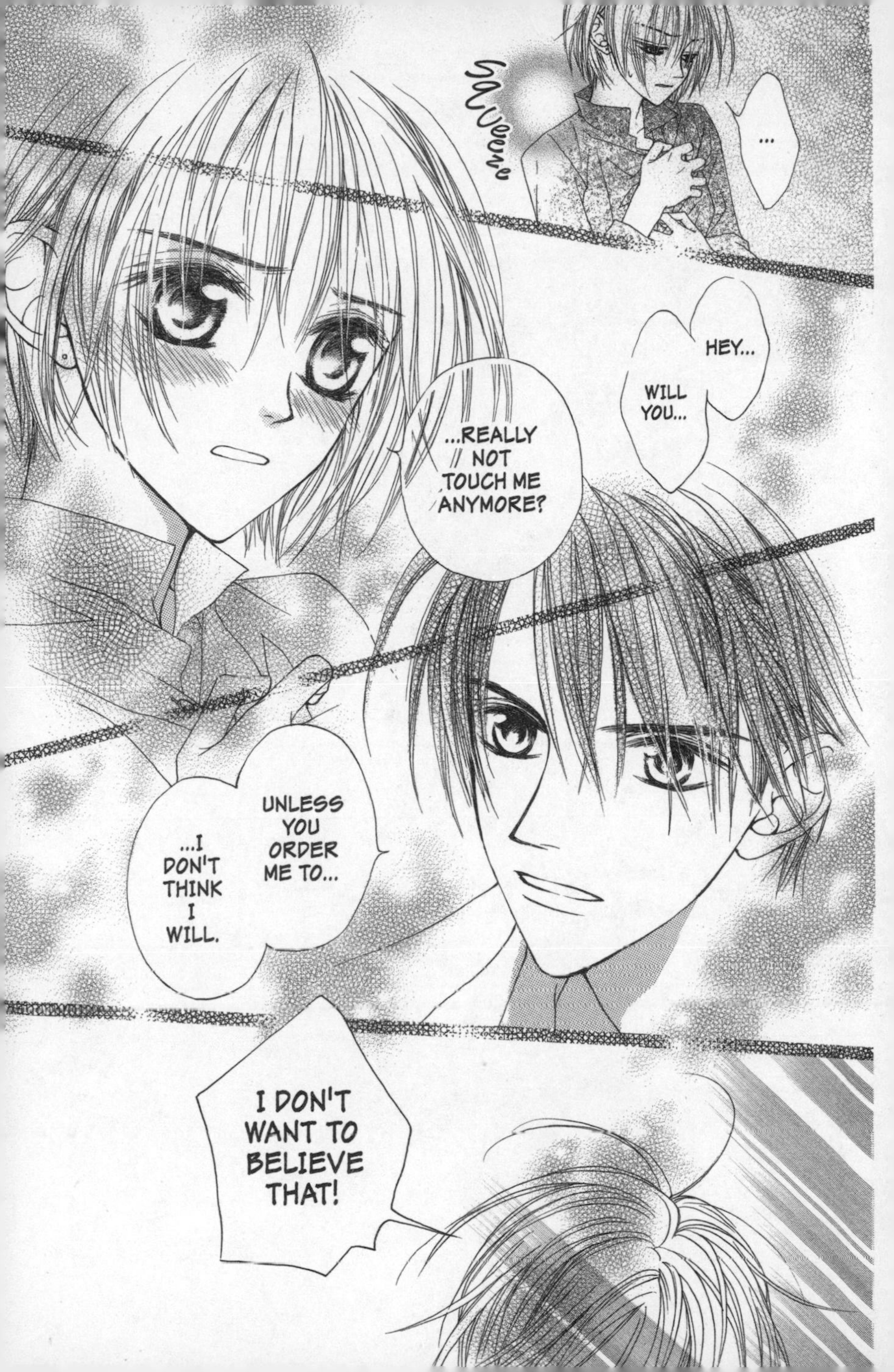
...
SQUEEZE
HEY... WILL YOU...
...REALLY NOT TOUCH ME ANYMORE?
UNLESS YOU ORDER ME TO...
...I DON'T THINK I WILL.
I DON'T WANT TO BELIEVE THAT!

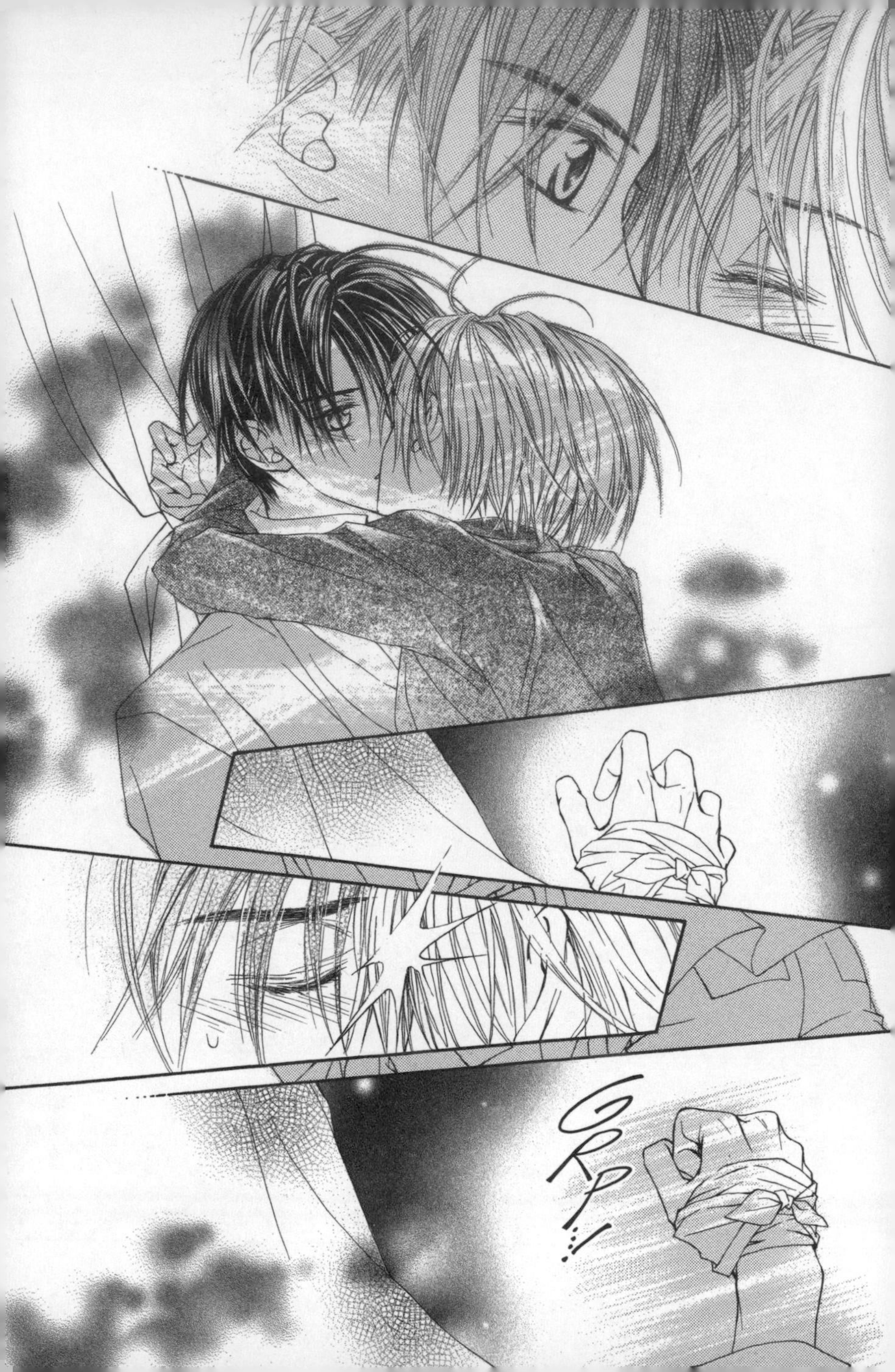
GRIP...!

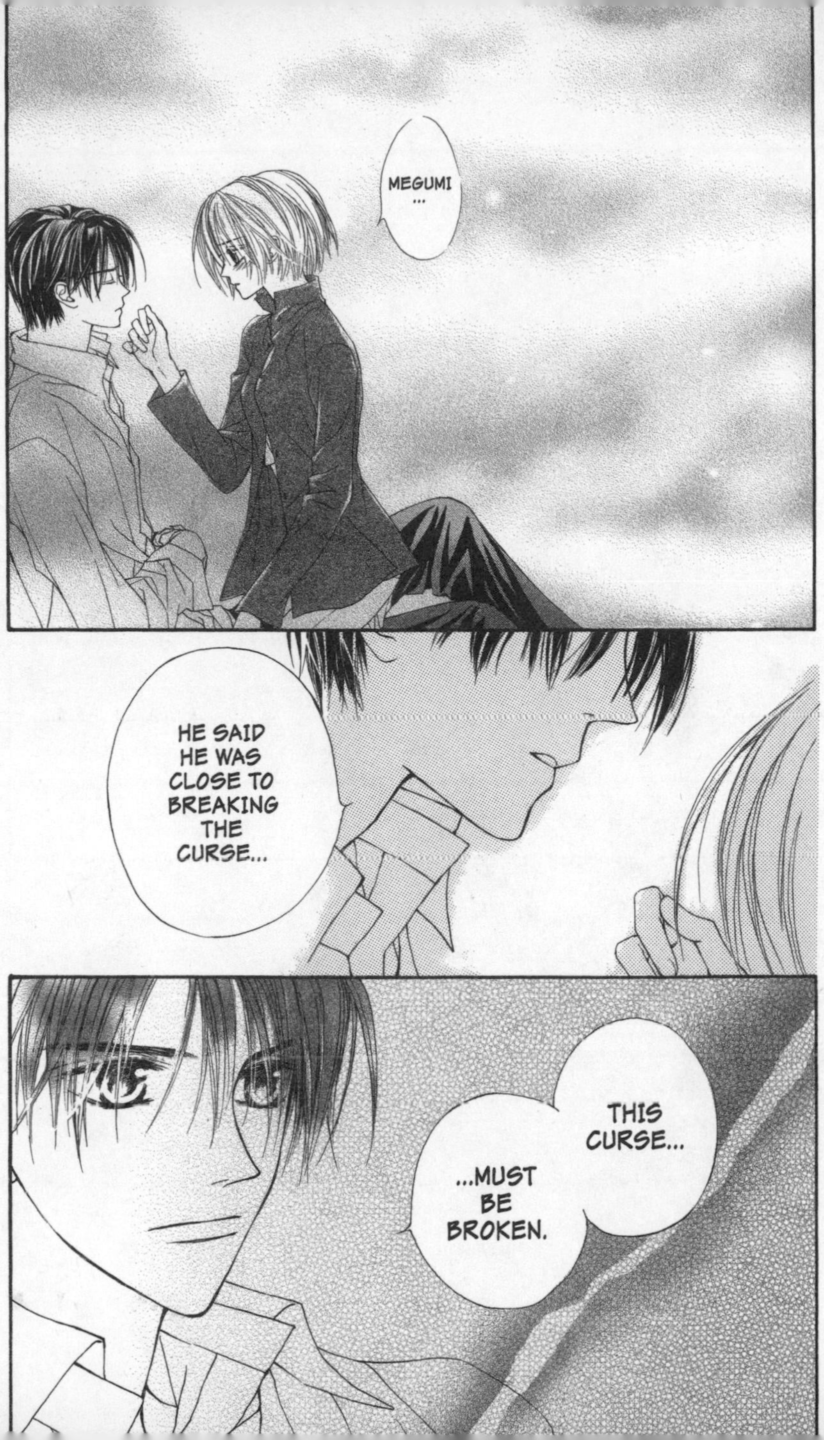
MEGUMI ...
HE SAID HE WAS CLOSE TO BREAKING THE CURSE...
THIS CURSE...
...MUST BE BROKEN.

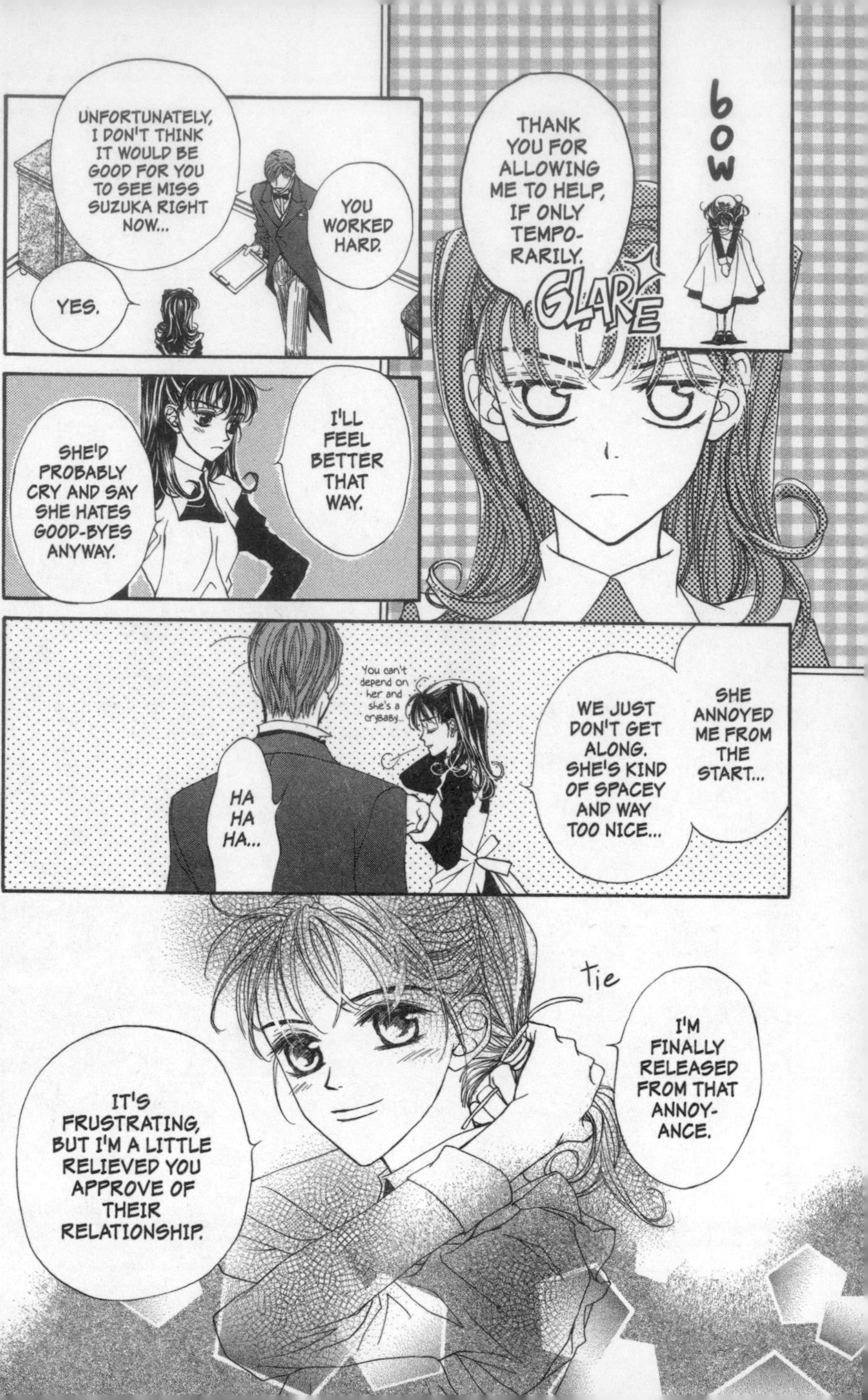
BOW
THANK YOU FOR ALLOWING ME TO HELP, IF ONLY TEMPO-RARILY.
GLARE
YOU WORKED HARD.
UNFORTUNATELY, I DON'T THINK IT WOULD BE GOOD FOR YOU TO SEE MISS SUZUKA RIGHT NOW...
YES.
I'LL FEEL BETTER THAT WAY.
SHE'D PROBABLY CRY AND SAY SHE HATES GOOD-BYES ANYWAY.
SHE ANNOYED ME FROM THE START...
WE JUST DON'T GET ALONG. SHE'S KIND OF SPACEY AND WAY TOO NICE...
You can't depend on her and she's a crybaby...
HA HA HA...
tie
I'M FINALLY RELEASED FROM THAT ANNOY-ANCE.
IT'S FRUSTRATING, BUT I'M A LITTLE RELIEVED YOU APPROVE OF THEIR RELATIONSHIP.

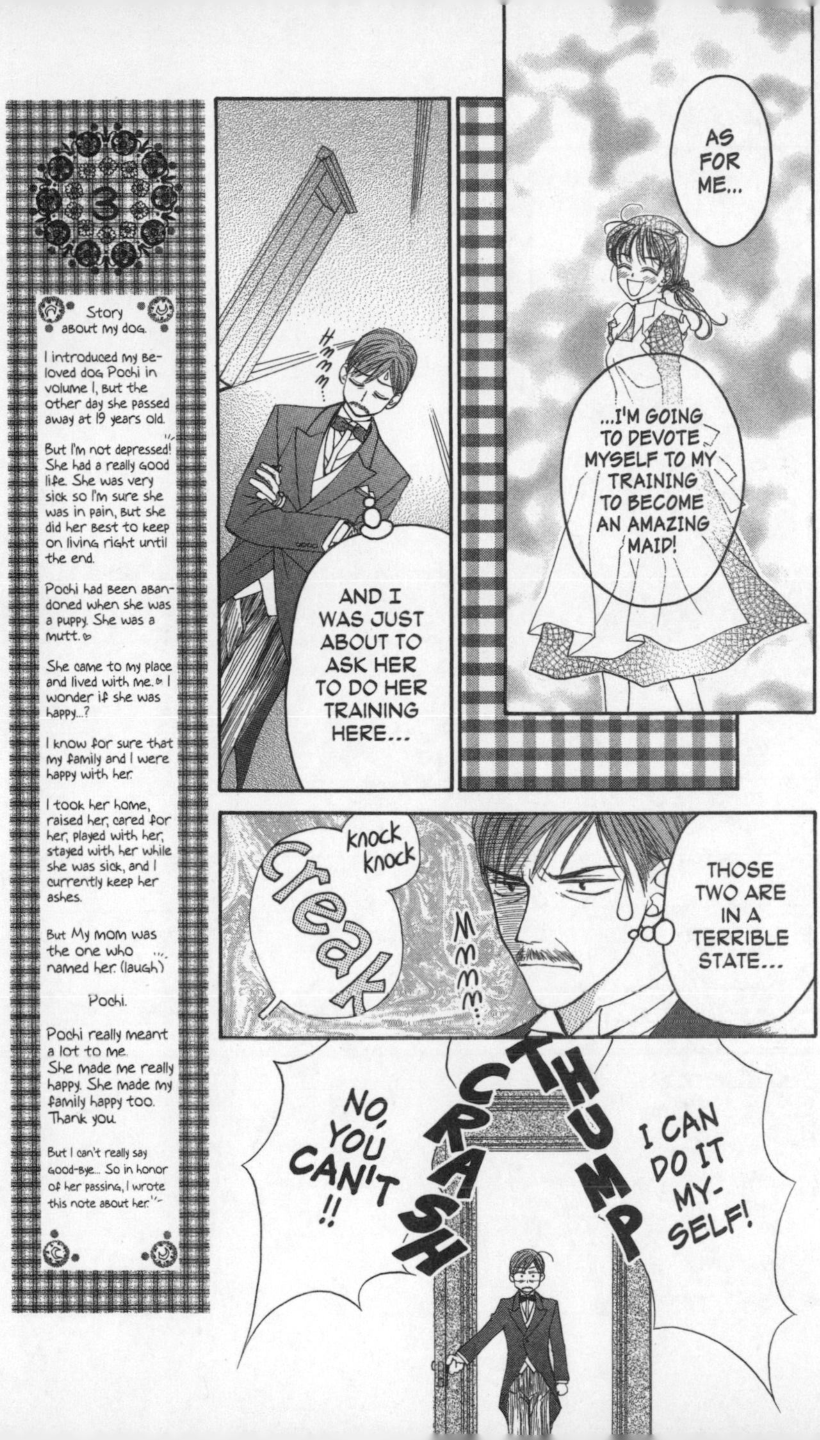
AS FOR ME...
...I'M GOING TO DEVOTE MYSELF TO MY TRAINING TO BECOME AN AMAZING MAID!
Hmmm...
AND I WAS JUST ABOUT TO ASK HER TO DO HER TRAINING HERE...
THOSE TWO ARE IN A TERRIBLE STATE...
Mmmm...
knock knock
creak
I CAN DO IT MY-SELF!
THUMP
CRASH
NO, YOU CAN'T!!

3

Story about my dog.

I introduced my beloved dog Pochi in volume 1, but the other day she passed away at 19 years old.

But I'm not depressed! She had a really good life. She was very sick so I'm sure she was in pain, but she did her best to keep on living right until the end.

Pochi had been abandoned when she was a puppy. She was a mutt.♡

She came to my place and lived with me.♡ I wonder if she was happy...?

I know for sure that my family and I were happy with her.

I took her home, raised her, cared for her, played with her, stayed with her while she was sick, and I currently keep her ashes.

But my mom was the one who named her. (laugh)

Pochi.

Pochi really meant a lot to me.
She made me really happy. She made my family happy too.
Thank you.

But I can't really say good-bye... So in honor of her passing, I wrote this note about her.

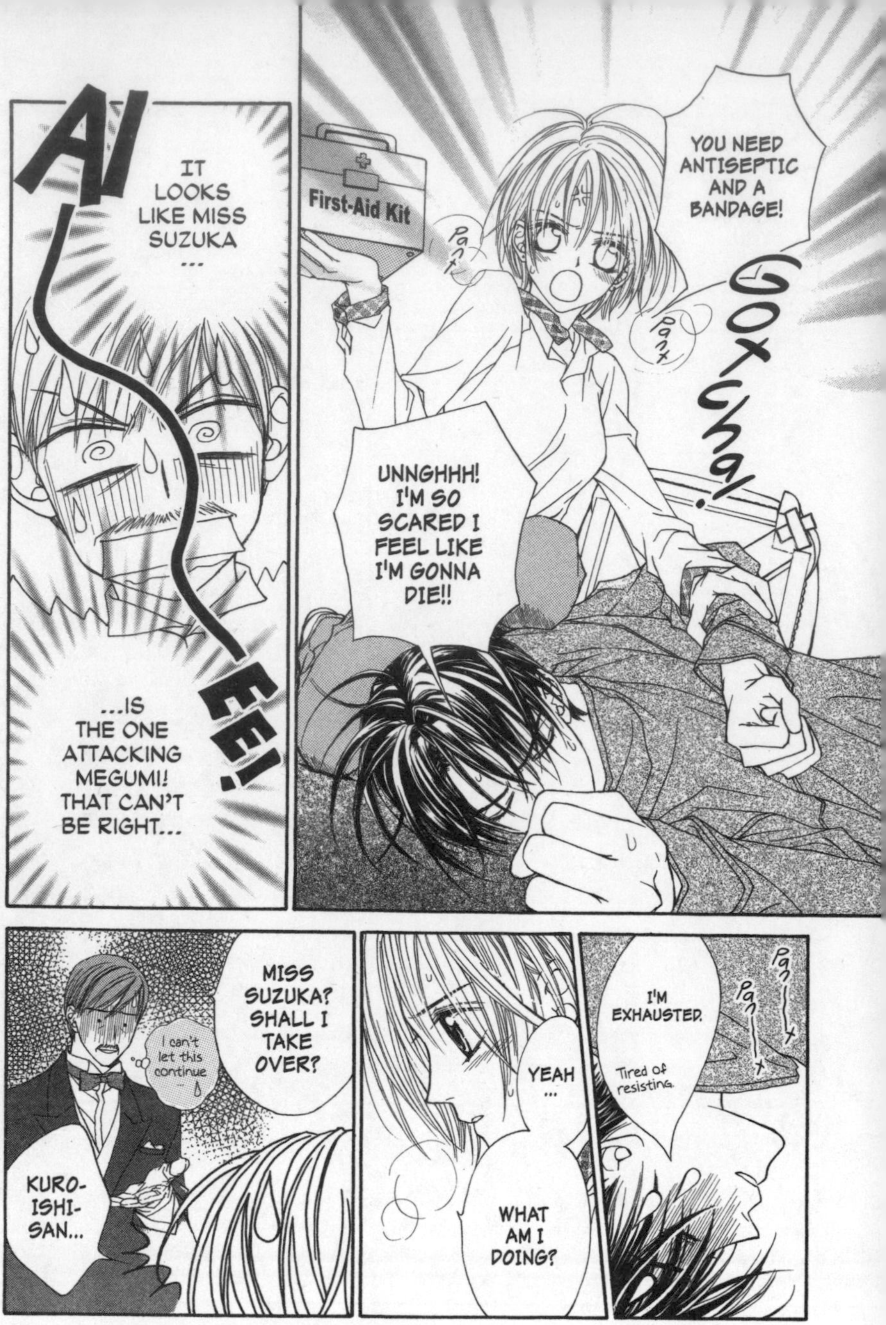
YOU NEED ANTISEPTIC AND A BANDAGE!
GOTCHA!
Pant
Pant
First-Aid Kit
UNNGHHH! I'M SO SCARED I FEEL LIKE I'M GONNA DIE!!
AIEE!
IT LOOKS LIKE MISS SUZUKA ...
...IS THE ONE ATTACKING MEGUMI! THAT CAN'T BE RIGHT...
Pant Pant
I'M EXHAUSTED.
Tired of resisting.
YEAH ...
WHAT AM I DOING?
MISS SUZUKA? SHALL I TAKE OVER?
I can't let this continue ...
KURO-ISHI-SAN...

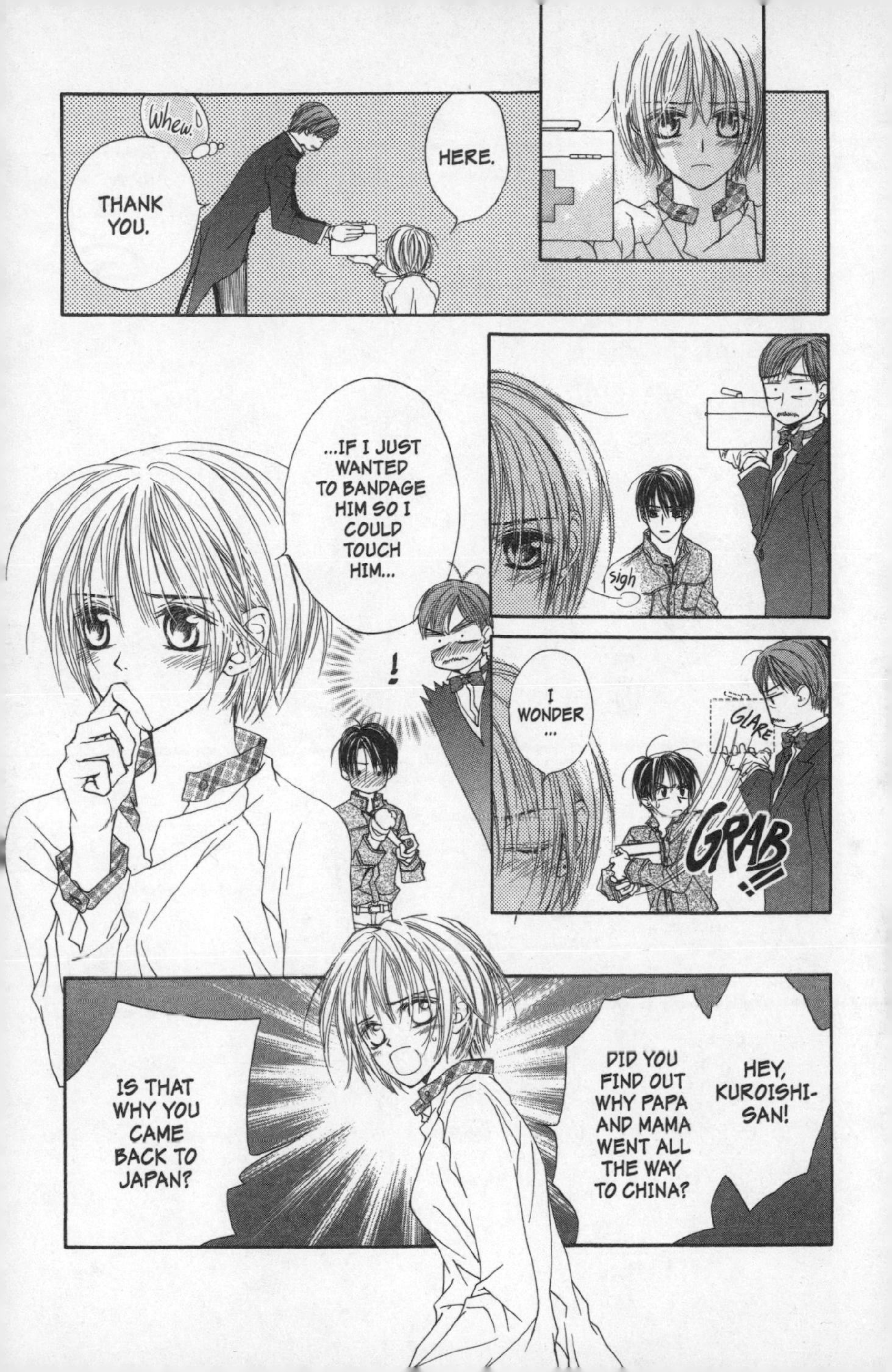
HERE.
Whew.
THANK YOU.
Sigh
I WONDER ...
GLARE
GRAB!!!
...IF I JUST WANTED TO BANDAGE HIM SO I COULD TOUCH HIM...
!
HEY, KUROISHI-SAN!
DID YOU FIND OUT WHY PAPA AND MAMA WENT ALL THE WAY TO CHINA?
IS THAT WHY YOU CAME BACK TO JAPAN?

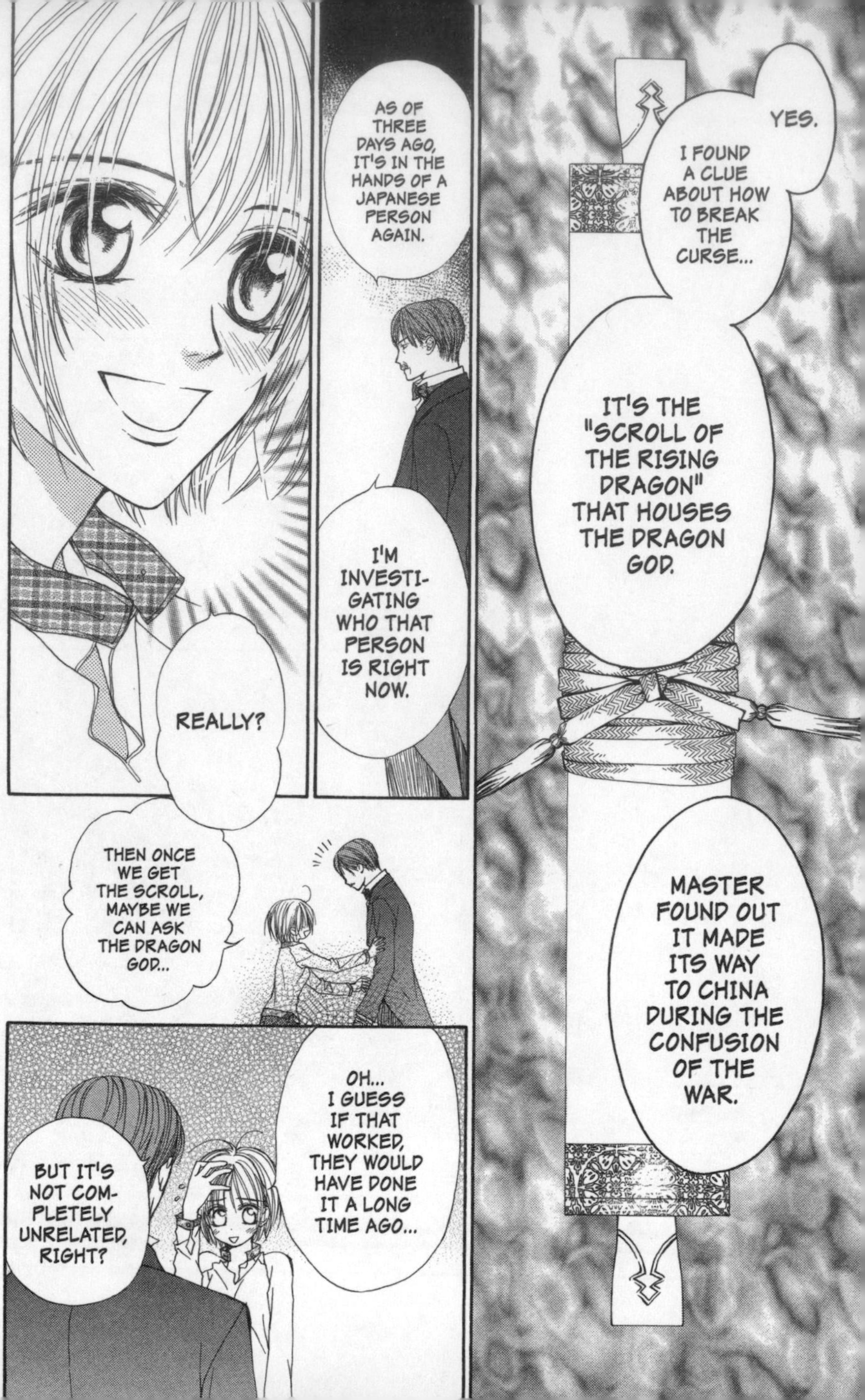
YES.
I FOUND A CLUE ABOUT HOW TO BREAK THE CURSE...
IT'S THE "SCROLL OF THE RISING DRAGON" THAT HOUSES THE DRAGON GOD.
MASTER FOUND OUT IT MADE ITS WAY TO CHINA DURING THE CONFUSION OF THE WAR.
AS OF THREE DAYS AGO, IT'S IN THE HANDS OF A JAPANESE PERSON AGAIN.
I'M INVESTI-GATING WHO THAT PERSON IS RIGHT NOW.
REALLY?
THEN ONCE WE GET THE SCROLL, MAYBE WE CAN ASK THE DRAGON GOD...
OH... I GUESS IF THAT WORKED, THEY WOULD HAVE DONE IT A LONG TIME AGO...
BUT IT'S NOT COM-PLETELY UNRELATED, RIGHT?

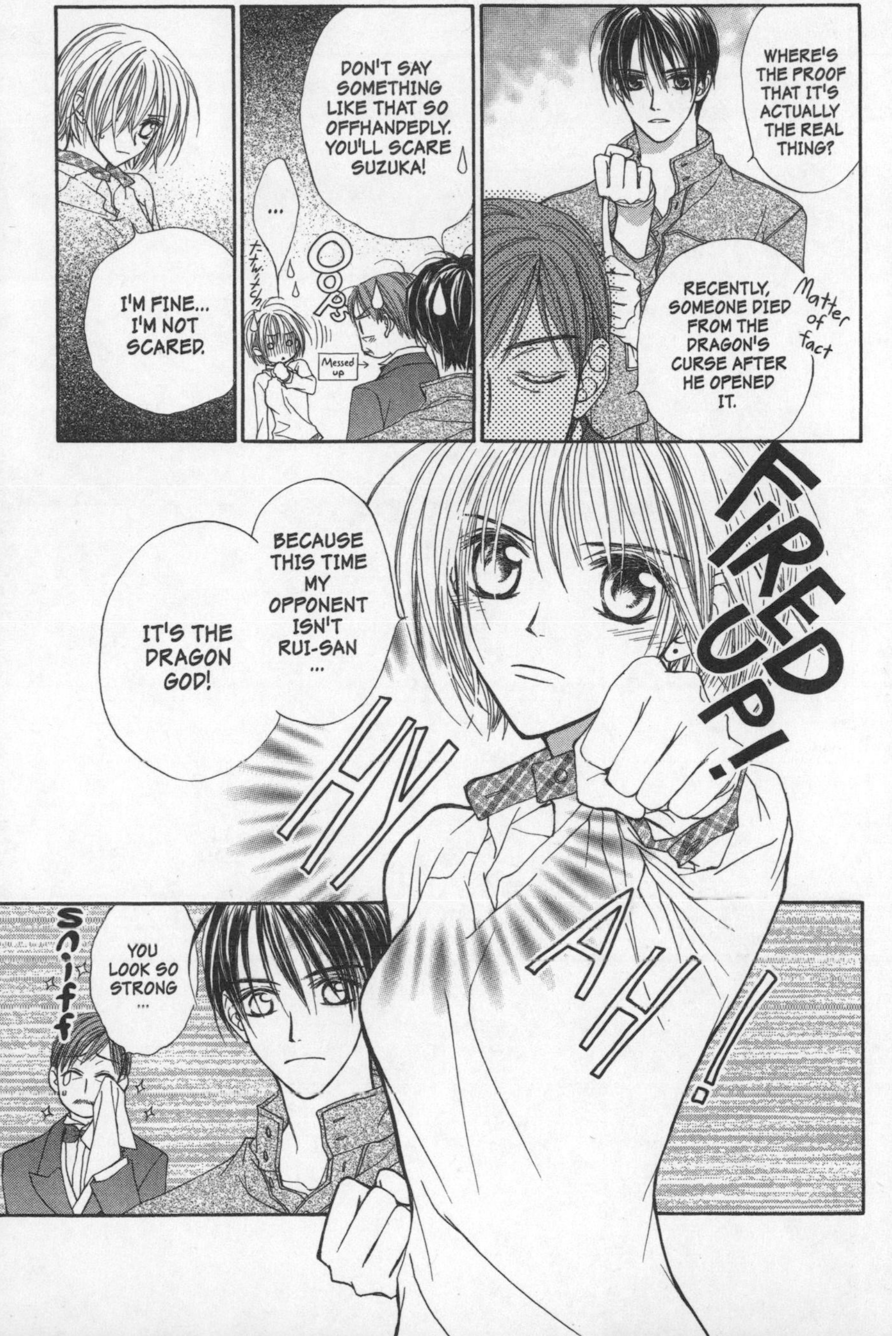
WHERE'S THE PROOF THAT IT'S ACTUALLY THE REAL THING?
RECENTLY, SOMEONE DIED FROM THE DRAGON'S CURSE AFTER HE OPENED IT.
Matter of fact
DON'T SAY SOMETHING LIKE THAT SO OFFHANDEDLY. YOU'LL SCARE SUZUKA!
Oops
...
Messed up
I'M FINE... I'M NOT SCARED.
FIRED UP!!
BECAUSE THIS TIME MY OPPONENT ISN'T RUI-SAN ...
IT'S THE DRAGON GOD!
HYAAH!!
YOU LOOK SO STRONG ...
sniff

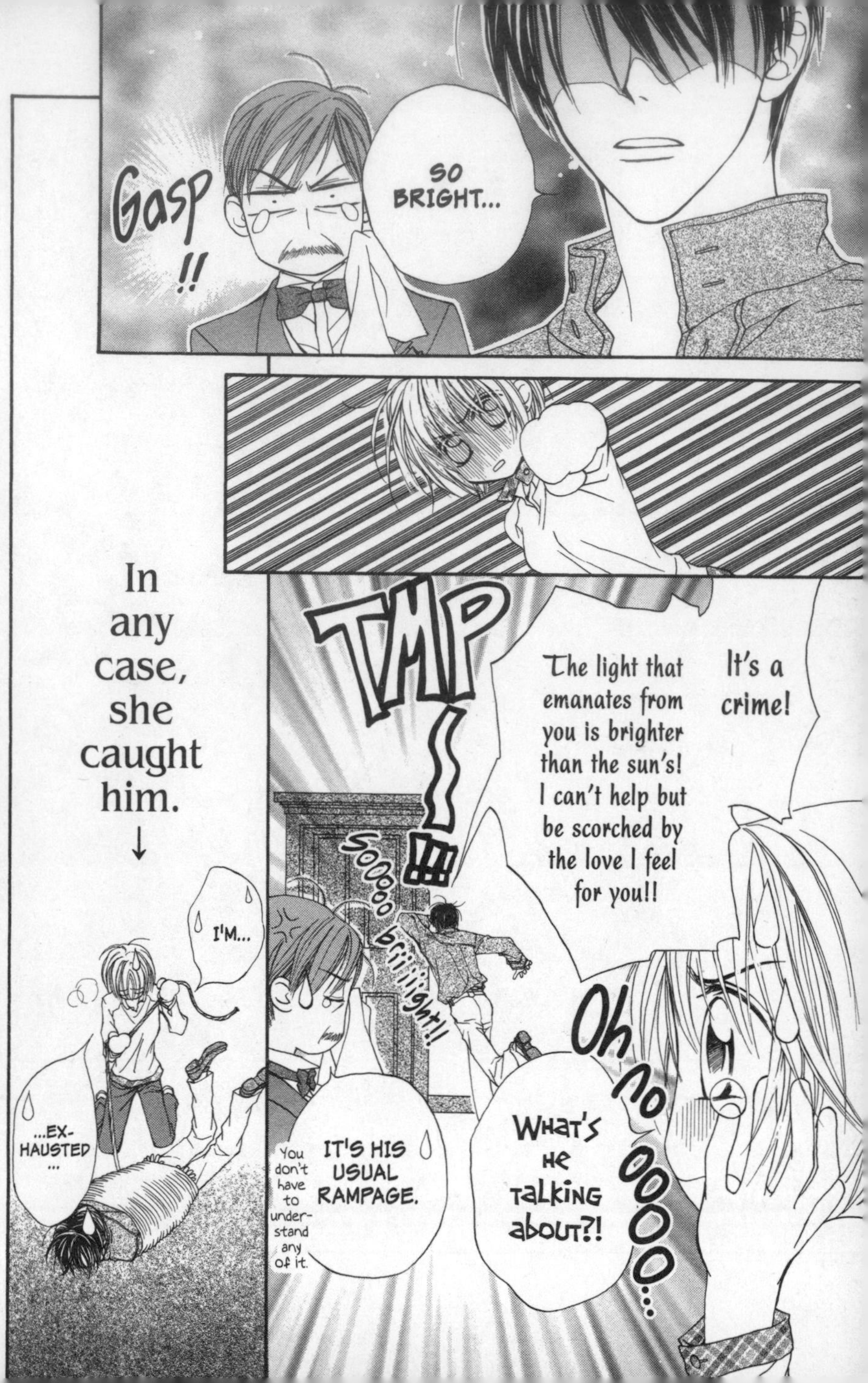

SO BRIGHT...
Gasp!!
It's a crime!
The light that emanates from you is brighter than the sun's! I can't help but be scorched by the love I feel for you!!
TMP!!!
Sooooo briiiiight!!
Oh nooooo...
What's he talking about?!
It's his usual rampage.
You don't have to understand any of it.
In any case, she caught him. ↓
I'm...
...exhausted...

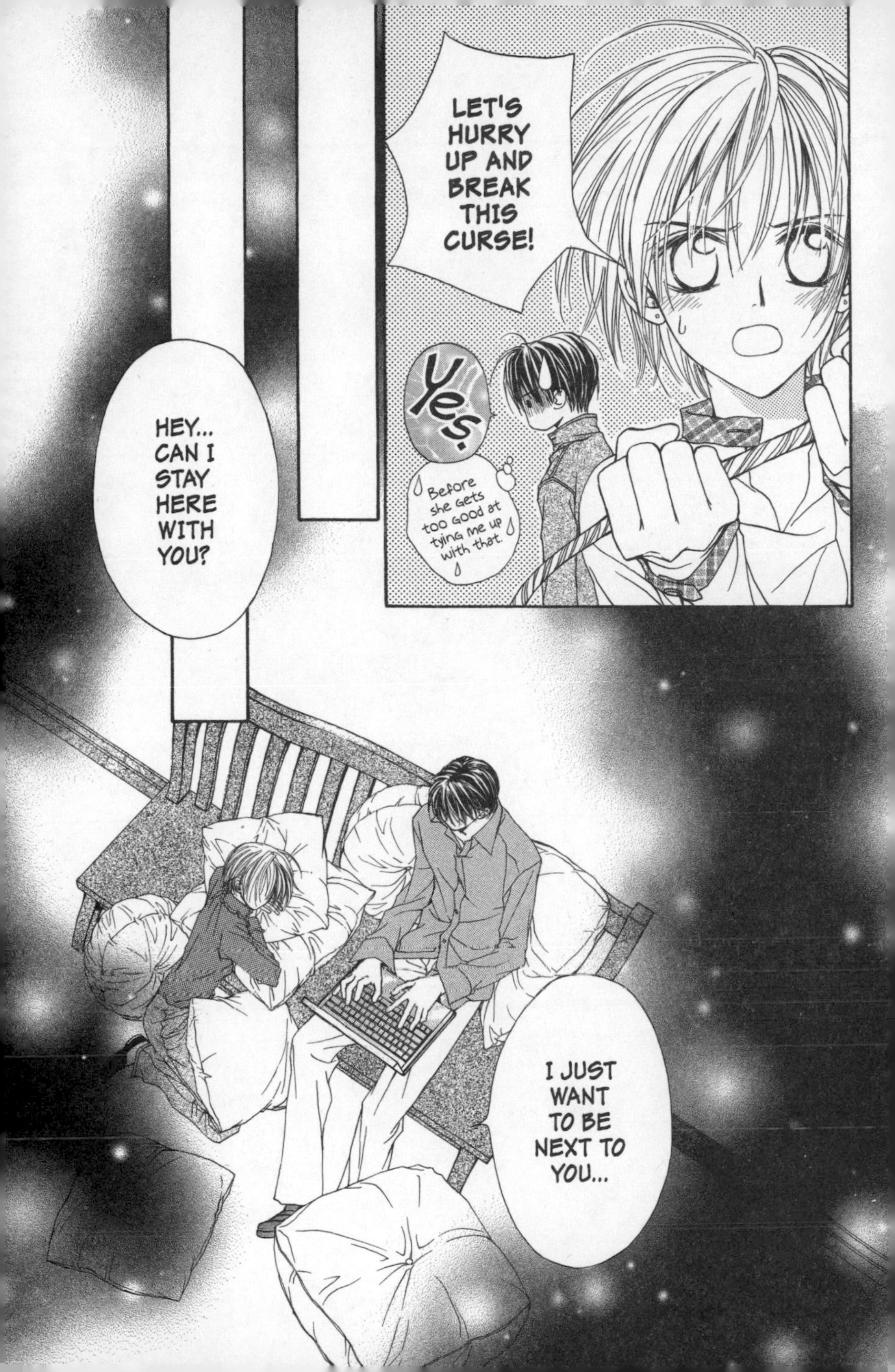
LET'S HURRY UP AND BREAK THIS CURSE!
Yes.
Before she gets too good at tying me up with that.
HEY... CAN I STAY HERE WITH YOU?
I JUST WANT TO BE NEXT TO YOU...

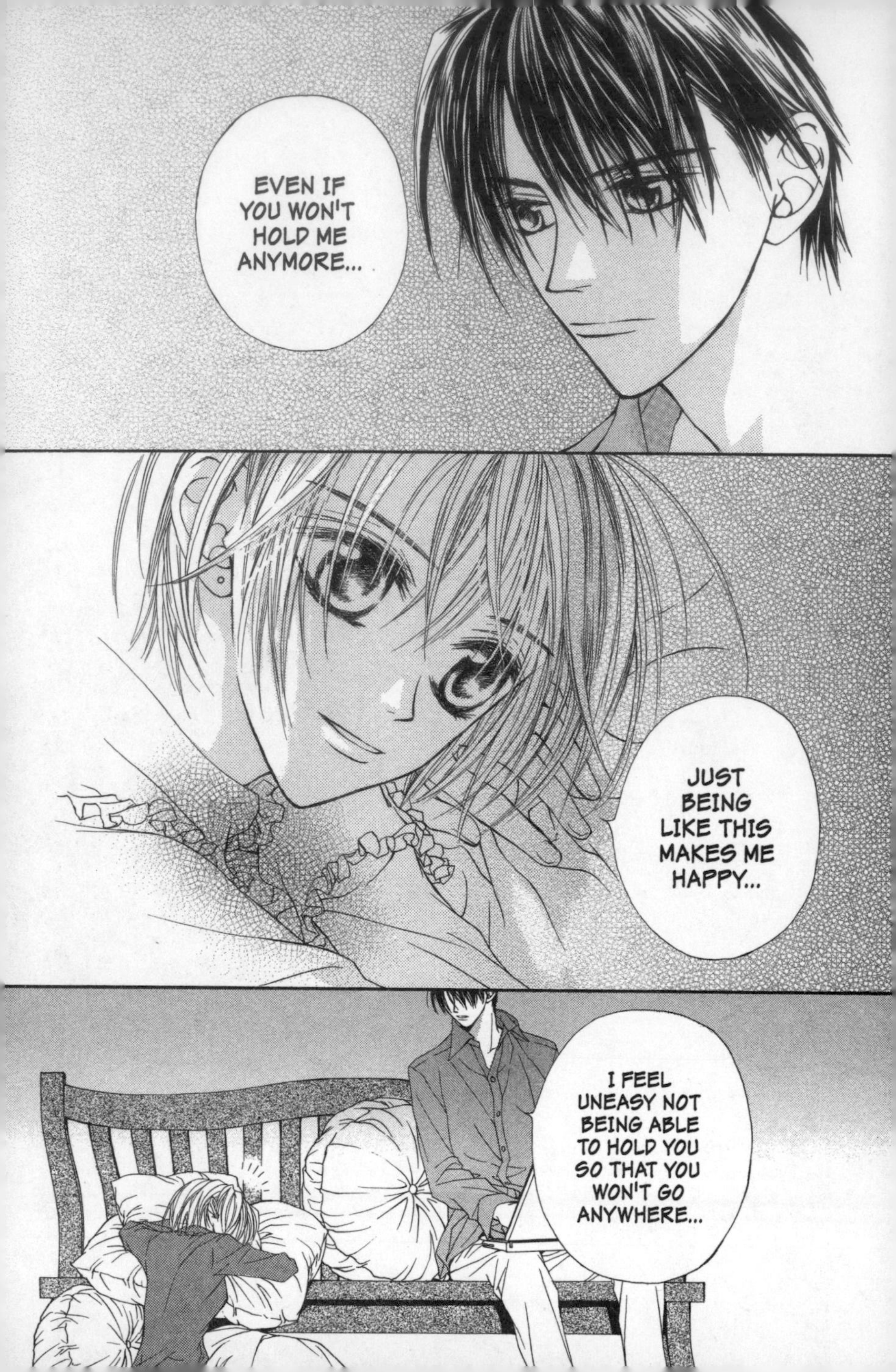
EVEN IF YOU WON'T HOLD ME ANYMORE...
JUST BEING LIKE THIS MAKES ME HAPPY...
I FEEL UNEASY NOT BEING ABLE TO HOLD YOU SO THAT YOU WON'T GO ANYWHERE...

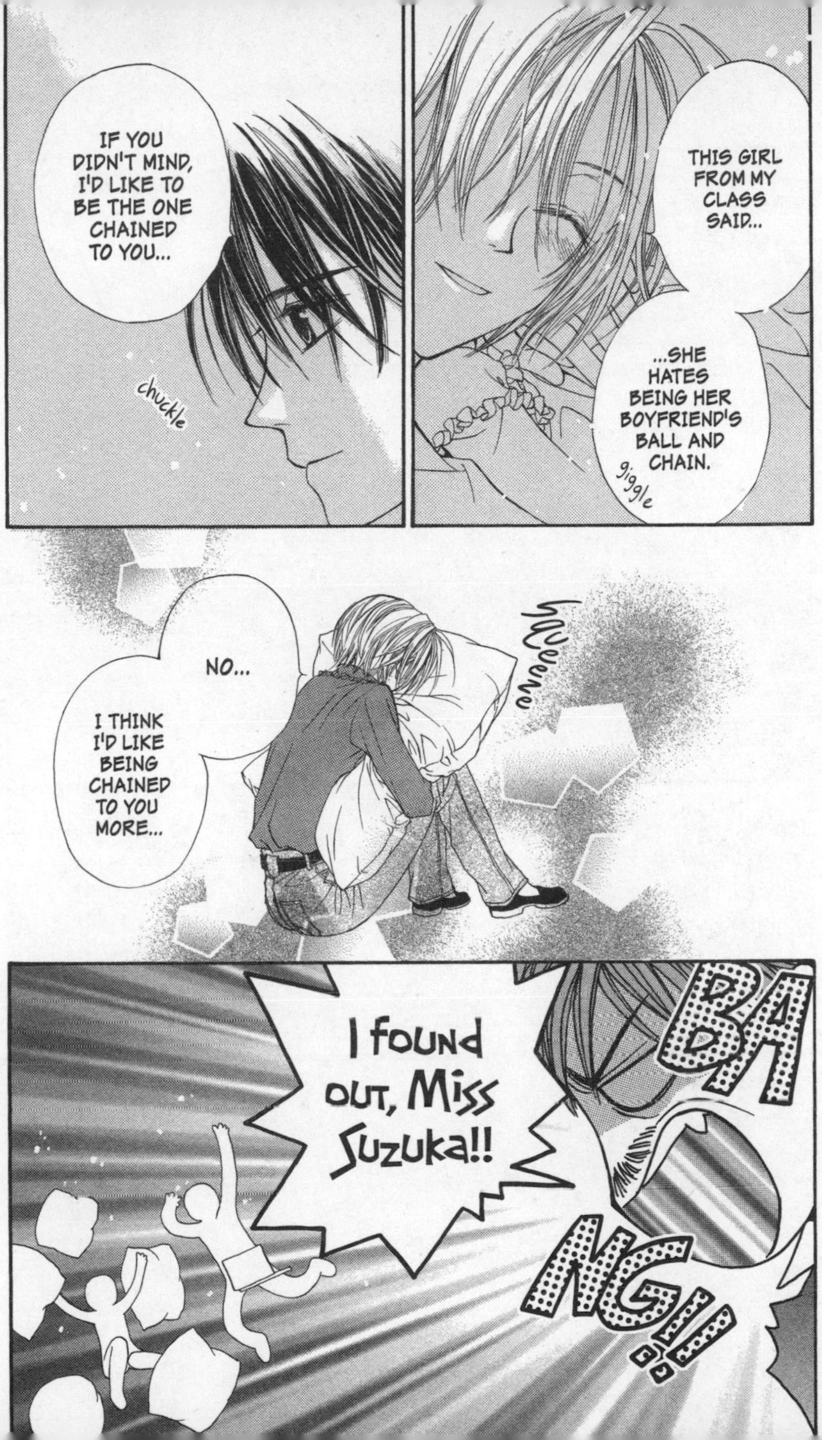
THIS GIRL FROM MY CLASS SAID...
...SHE HATES BEING HER BOYFRIEND'S BALL AND CHAIN.
giggle
IF YOU DIDN'T MIND, I'D LIKE TO BE THE ONE CHAINED TO YOU...
chuckle
NO...
I THINK I'D LIKE BEING CHAINED TO YOU MORE...
BANG!!
I found out, Miss Suzuka!!

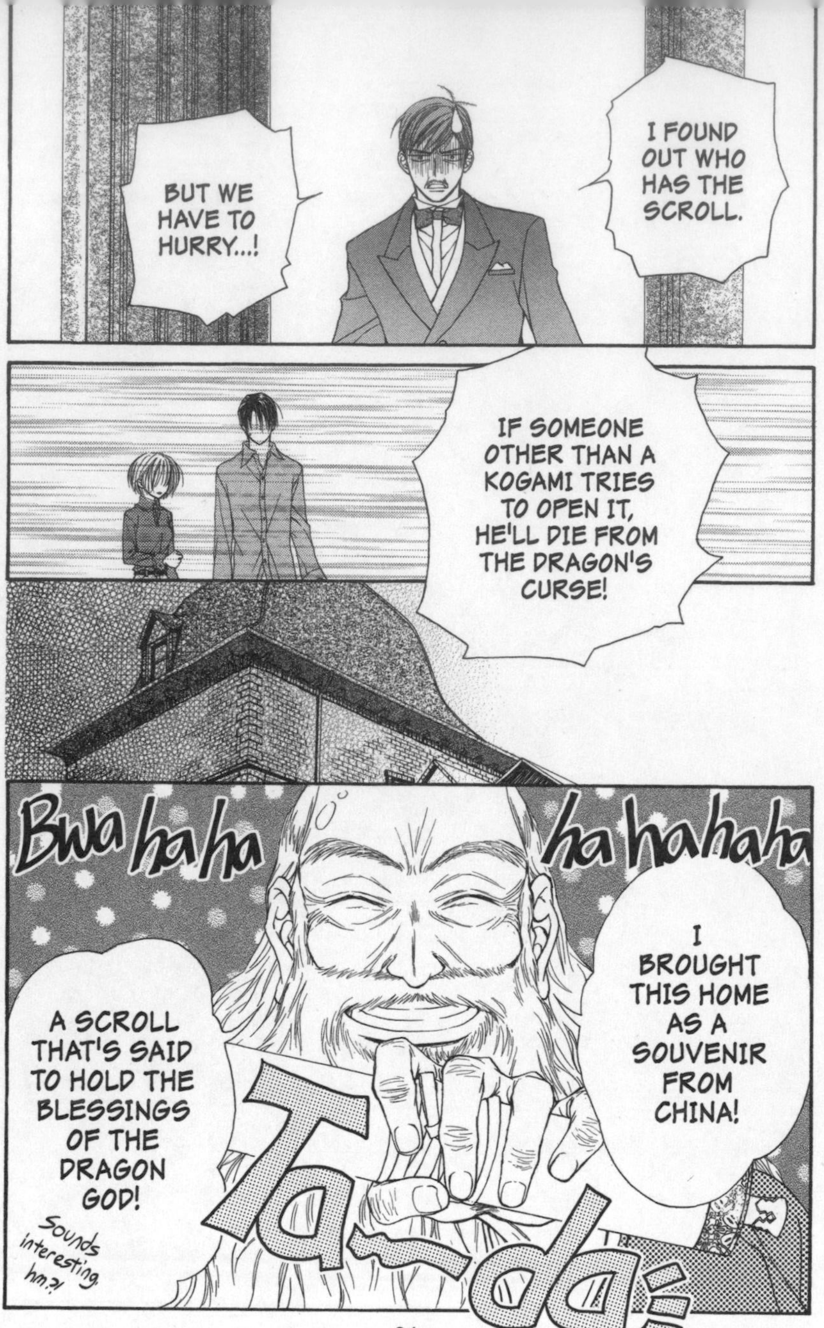

I FOUND OUT WHO HAS THE SCROLL.
BUT WE HAVE TO HURRY...!
IF SOMEONE OTHER THAN A KOGAMI TRIES TO OPEN IT, HE'LL DIE FROM THE DRAGON'S CURSE!
Bwa ha ha
ha ha ha ha ha
I BROUGHT THIS HOME AS A SOUVENIR FROM CHINA!
A SCROLL THAT'S SAID TO HOLD THE BLESSINGS OF THE DRAGON GOD!
Ta-da!!
Sounds interesting, hm?!

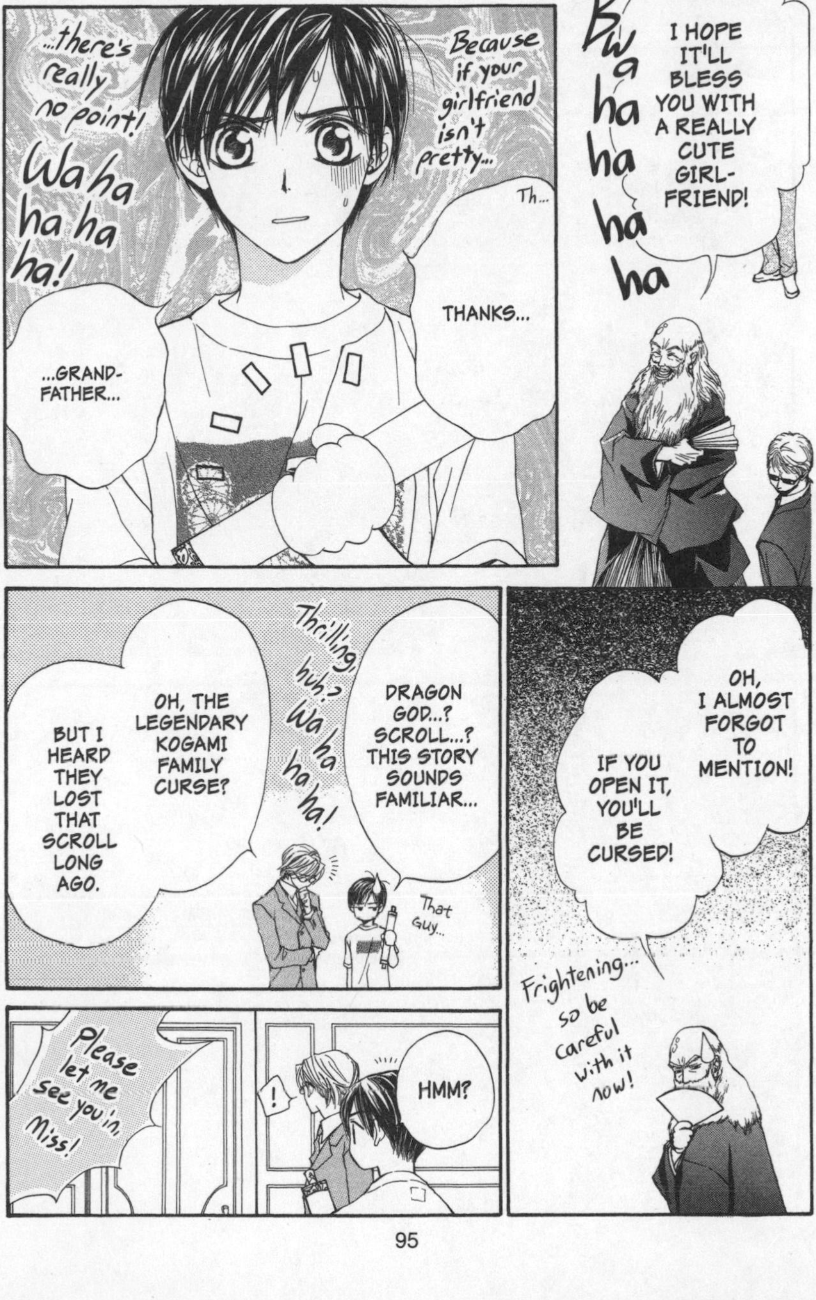
I HOPE IT'LL BLESS YOU WITH A REALLY CUTE GIRLFRIEND!
Bwa ha ha ha ha ha
Because if your girlfriend isn't pretty...
...there's really no point!
Wa ha ha ha ha ha!
Th...
THANKS...
...GRANDFATHER...
OH, I ALMOST FORGOT TO MENTION!
IF YOU OPEN IT, YOU'LL BE CURSED!
Frightening... so be careful with it now!
DRAGON GOD...? SCROLL...? THIS STORY SOUNDS FAMILIAR...
Thrilling, huh? Wa ha ha ha!
OH, THE LEGENDARY KOGAMI FAMILY CURSE?
BUT I HEARD THEY LOST THAT SCROLL LONG AGO.
That guy...
HMM?
Please let me see you in, Miss!

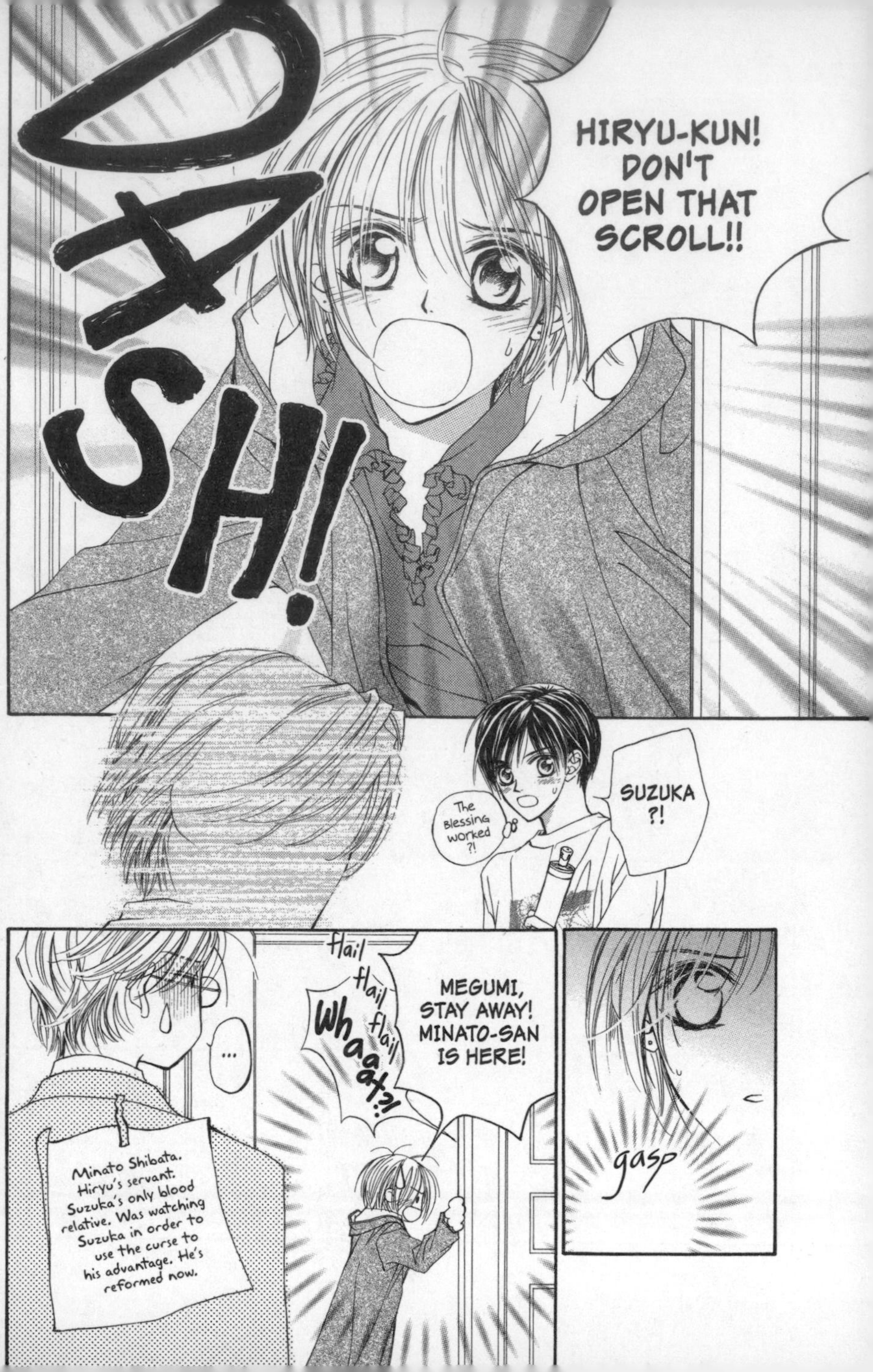
HIRYU-KUN! DON'T OPEN THAT SCROLL!!
DASH!
SUZUKA ?!
The blessing worked ?!
gasp
MEGUMI, STAY AWAY! MINATO-SAN IS HERE!
flail flail flail
Whaaat?!
...
Minato Shibata. Hiryu's servant. Suzuka's only blood relative. Was watching Suzuka in order to use the curse to his advantage. He's reformed now.

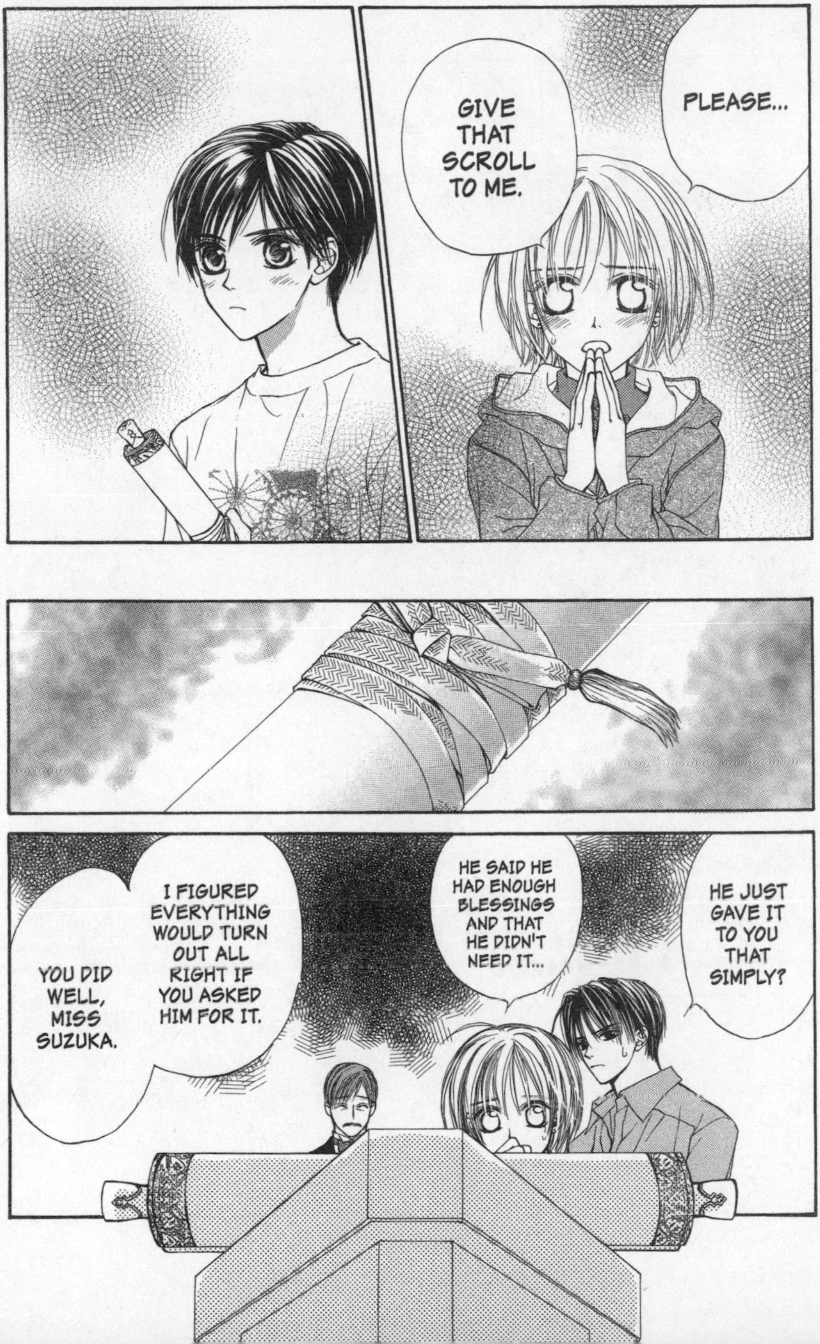
PLEASE...
GIVE THAT SCROLL TO ME.
HE JUST GAVE IT TO YOU THAT SIMPLY?
HE SAID HE HAD ENOUGH BLESSINGS AND THAT HE DIDN'T NEED IT...
YOU DID WELL, MISS SUZUKA.
I FIGURED EVERYTHING WOULD TURN OUT ALL RIGHT IF YOU ASKED HIM FOR IT.

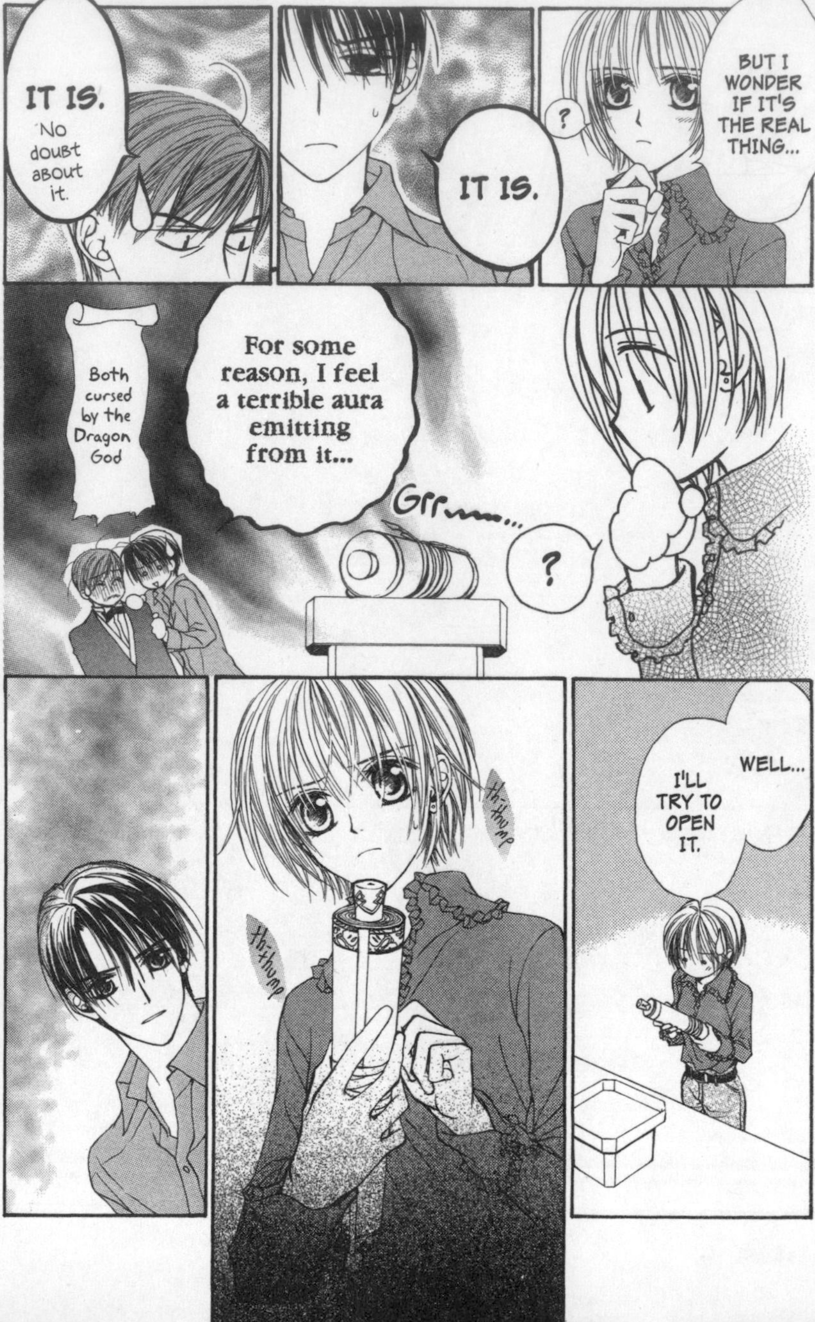
?
BUT I WONDER IF IT'S THE REAL THING...
IT IS.
IT IS.
No doubt about it.
For some reason, I feel a terrible aura emitting from it...
Both cursed by the Dragon God
Grr......
?
WELL...
I'LL TRY TO OPEN IT.
th-thump
th-thump

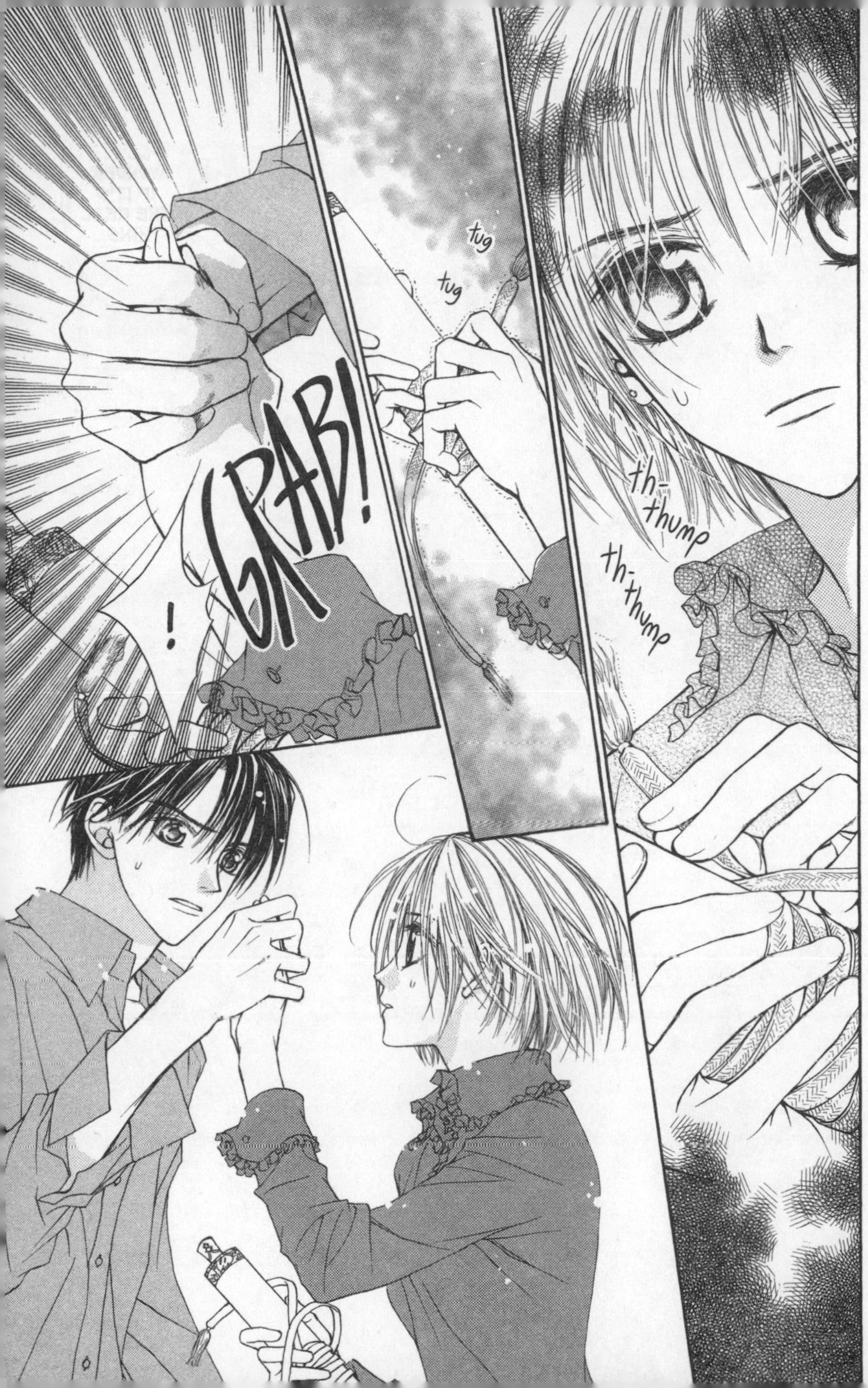
th-thump
th-thump
tug
tug
GRAB!
!

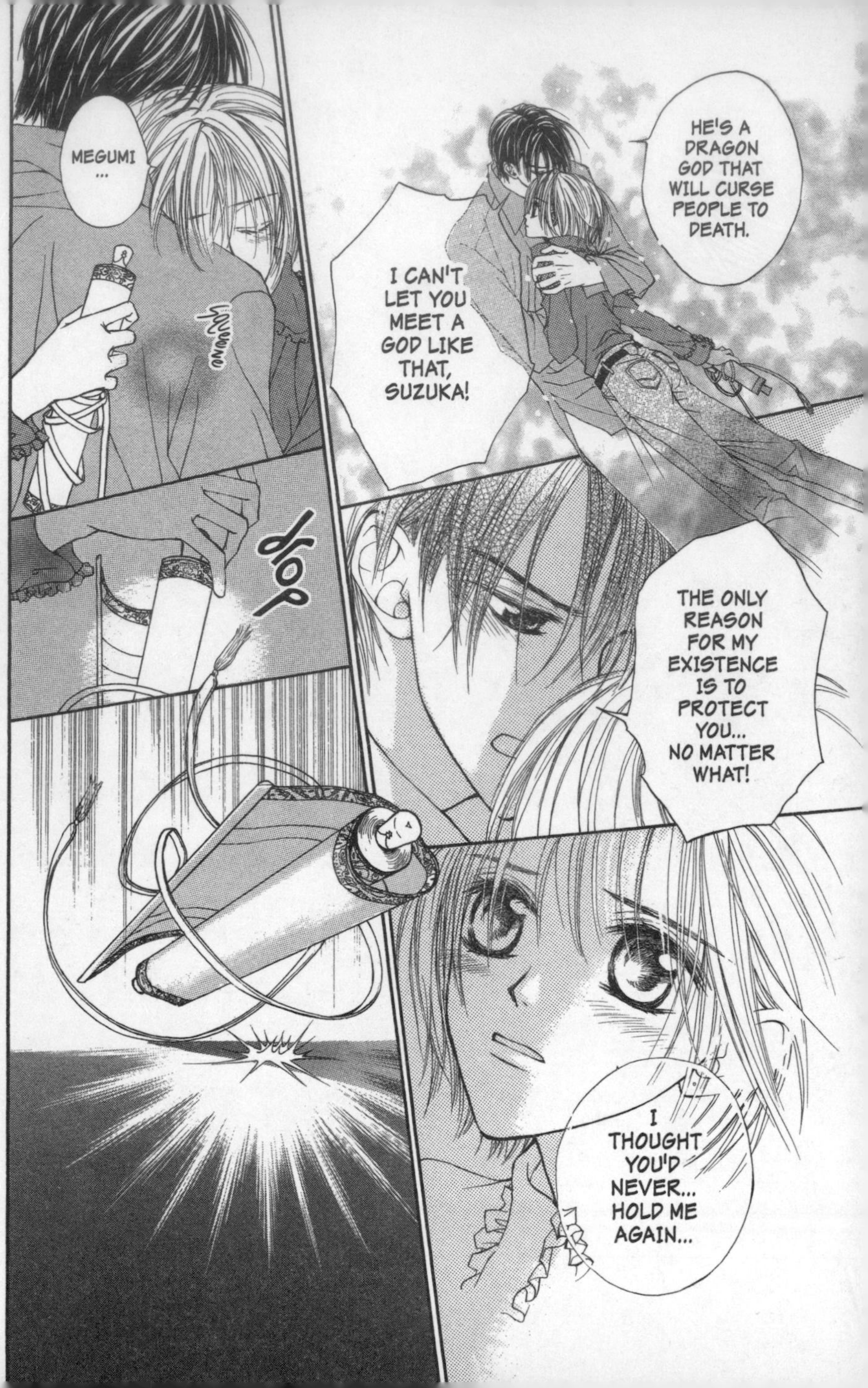
HE'S A DRAGON GOD THAT WILL CURSE PEOPLE TO DEATH.
I CAN'T LET YOU MEET A GOD LIKE THAT, SUZUKA!
MEGUMI ...
squeeze
THE ONLY REASON FOR MY EXISTENCE IS TO PROTECT YOU... NO MATTER WHAT!
drop
I THOUGHT YOU'D NEVER... HOLD ME AGAIN...

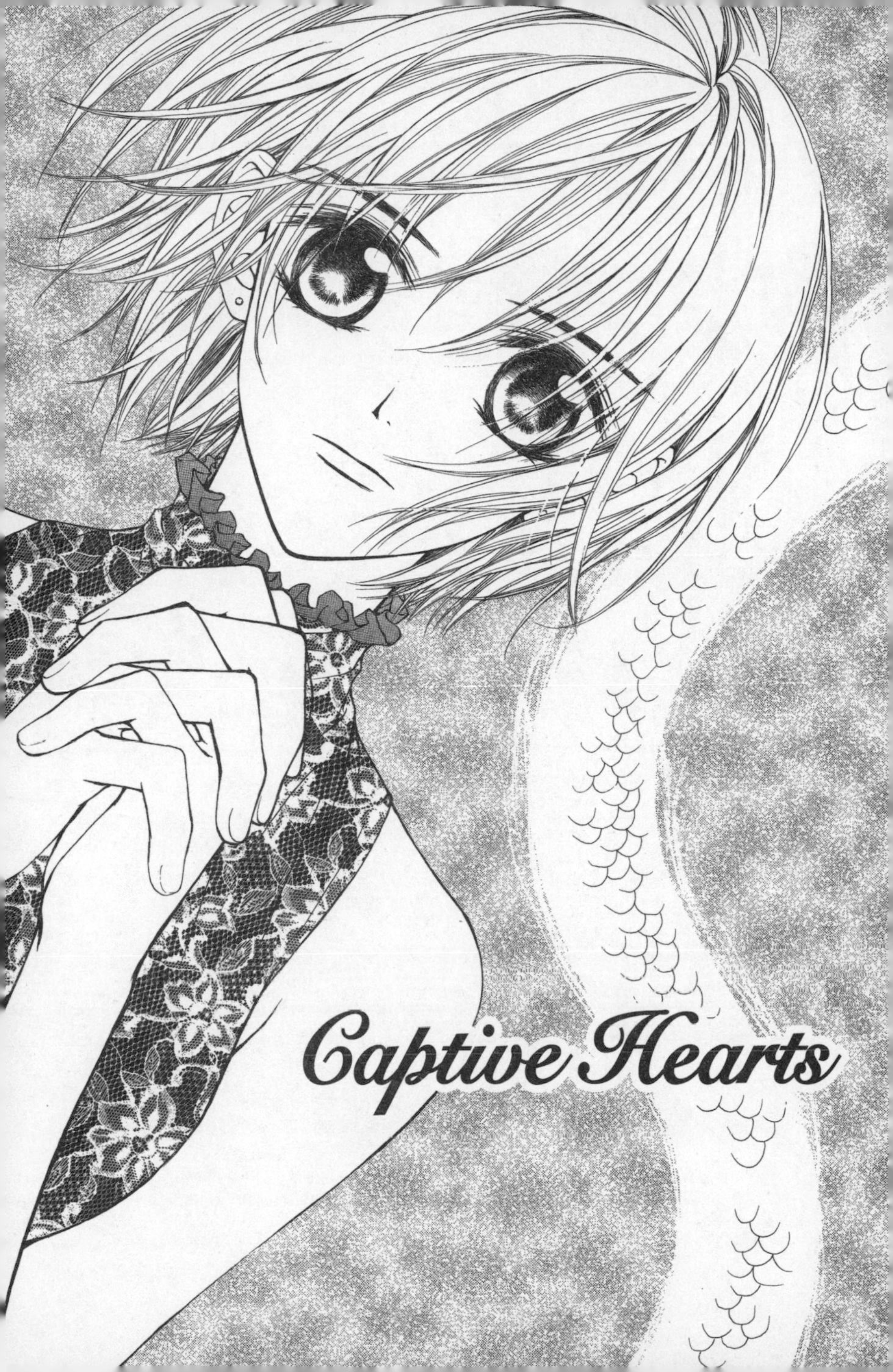
Captive Hearts

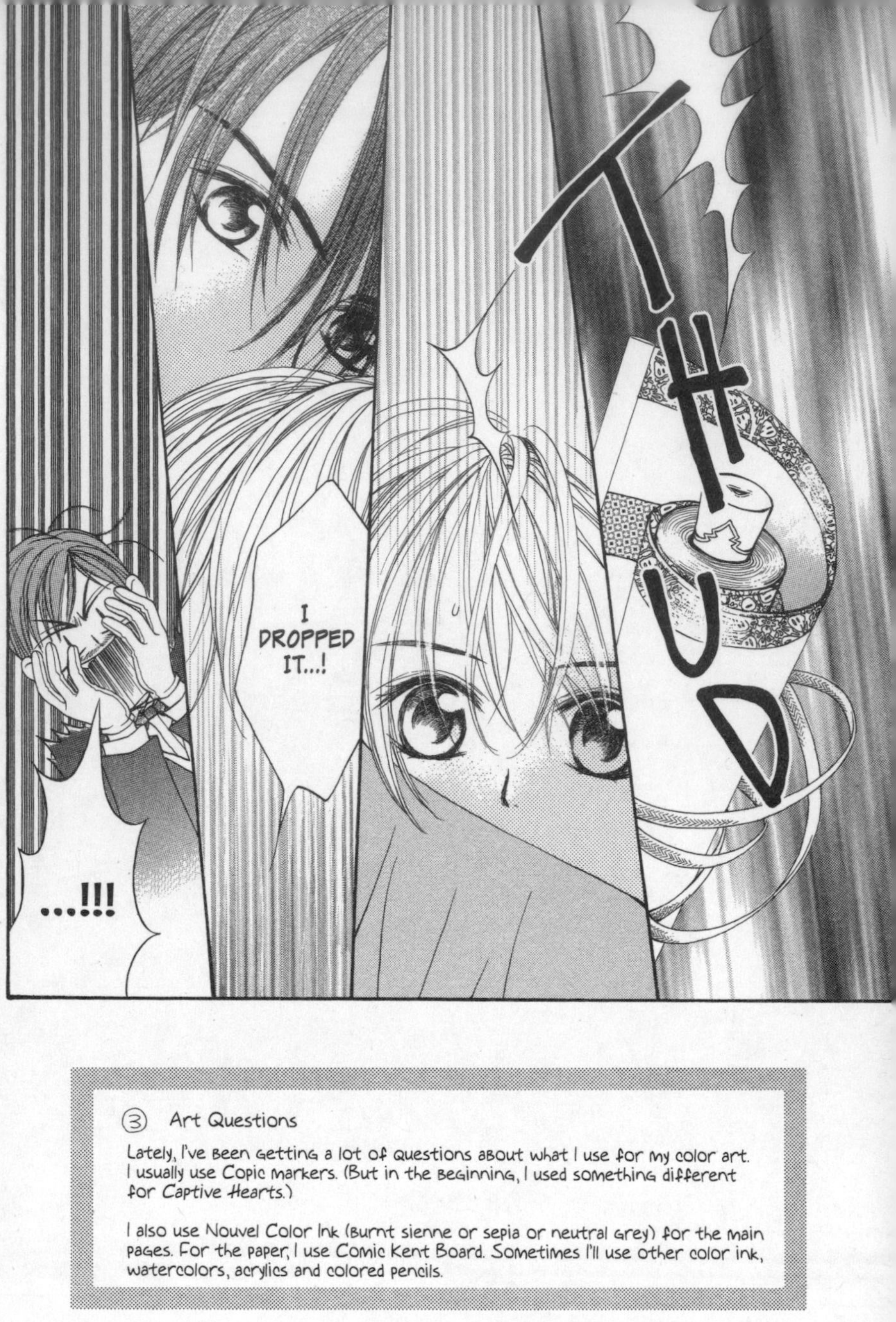
THUD
I DROPPED IT...!
...!!!

③ Art Questions

Lately, I've been getting a lot of questions about what I use for my color art. I usually use Copic markers. (But in the beginning, I used something different for *Captive Hearts*.)

I also use Nouvel Color Ink (burnt sienne or sepia or neutral grey) for the main pages. For the paper, I use Comic Kent Board. Sometimes I'll use other color ink, watercolors, acrylics and colored pencils.

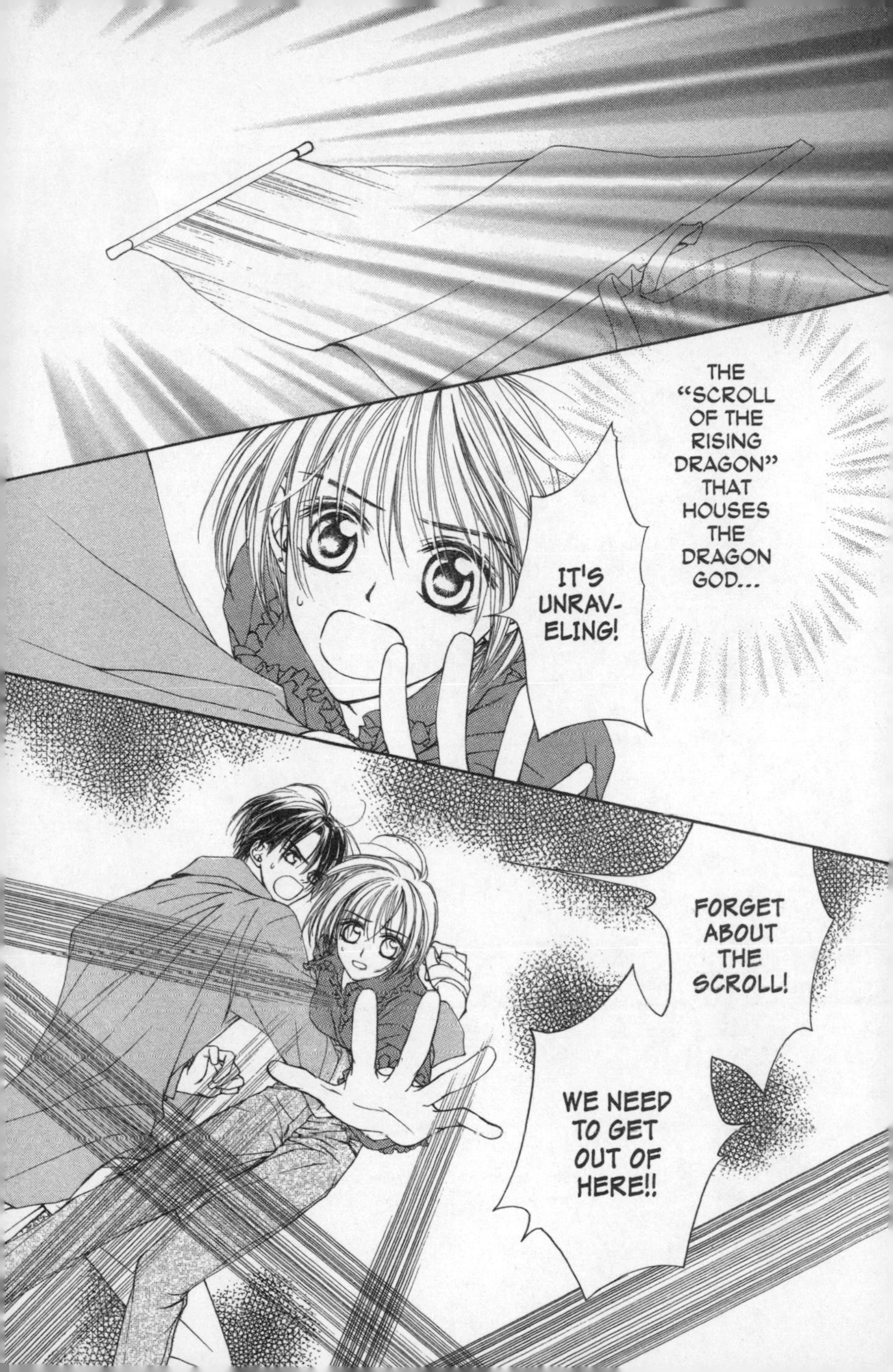
THE "SCROLL OF THE RISING DRAGON" THAT HOUSES THE DRAGON GOD...
IT'S UNRAV-ELING!
FORGET ABOUT THE SCROLL!
WE NEED TO GET OUT OF HERE!!

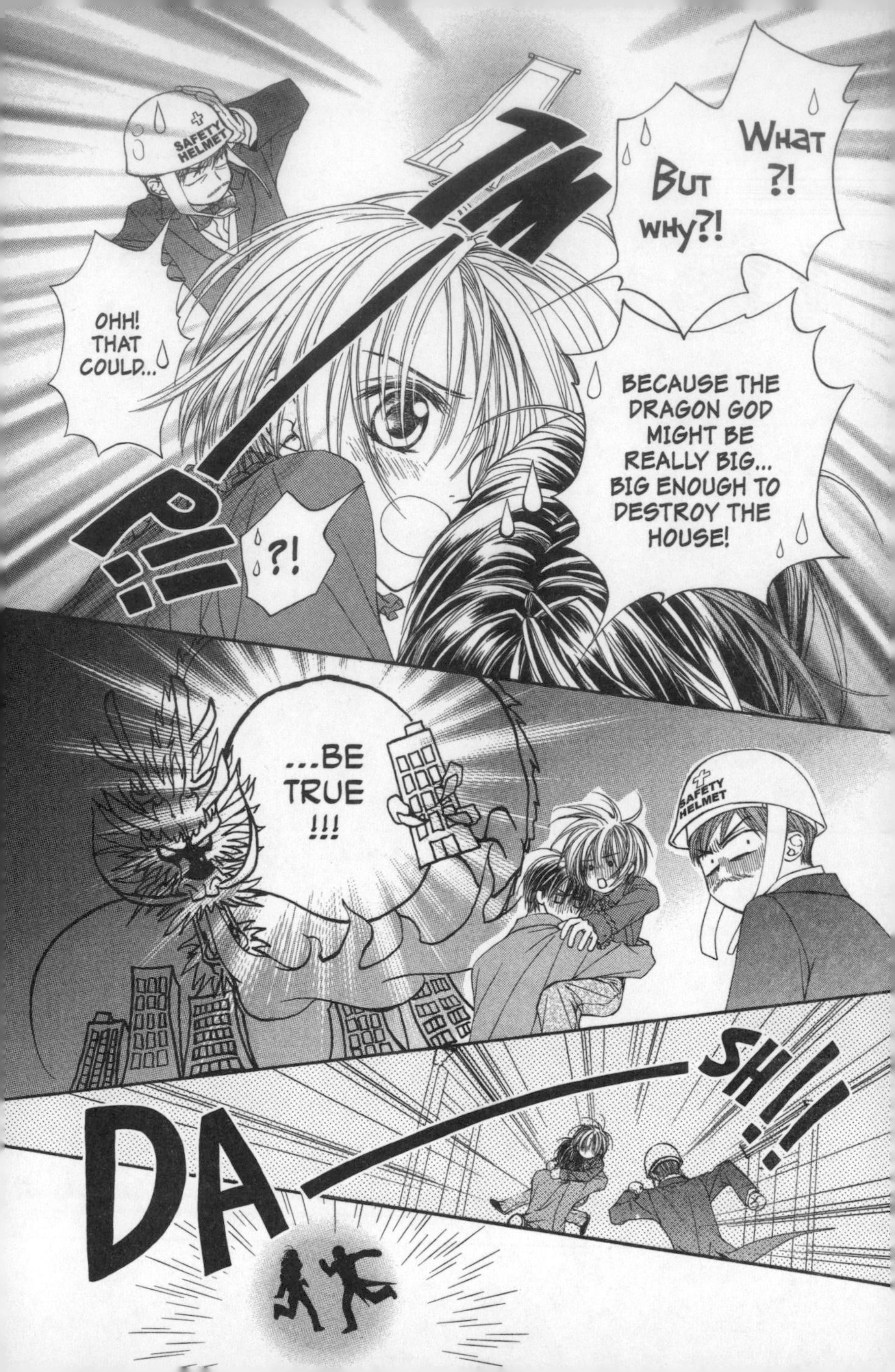

WHAT?! BUT WHY?!
BECAUSE THE DRAGON GOD MIGHT BE REALLY BIG... BIG ENOUGH TO DESTROY THE HOUSE!
TA—P!!
?!
OHH! THAT COULD...
...BE TRUE!!!
DA—SH!!!

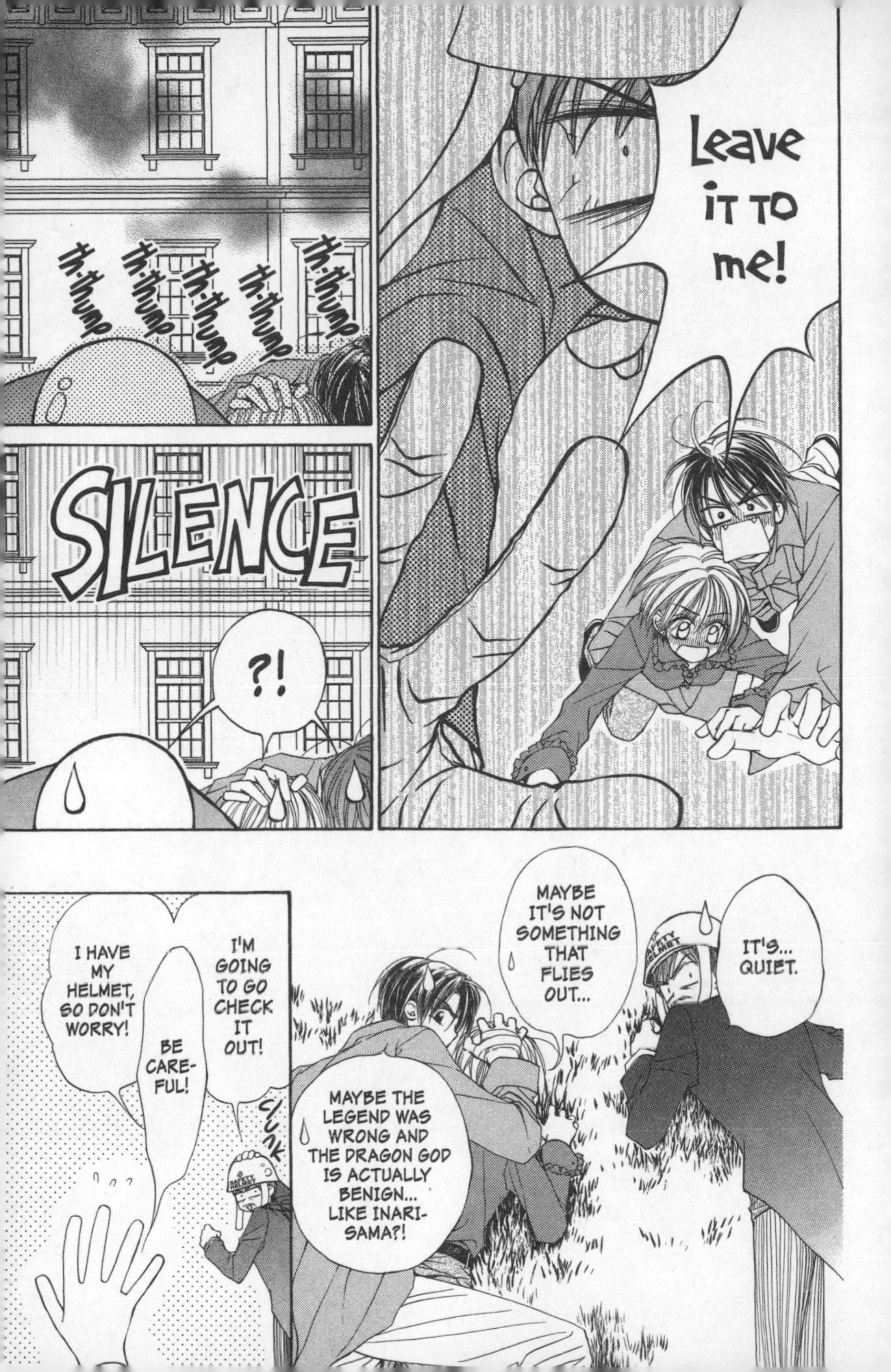
Leave it to me!
th-thump
th-thump
th-thump
th-thump
th-thump
SILENCE
?!
IT'S... QUIET.
MAYBE IT'S NOT SOMETHING THAT FLIES OUT...
SAFETY HELMET
MAYBE THE LEGEND WAS WRONG AND THE DRAGON GOD IS ACTUALLY BENIGN... LIKE INARI-SAMA?!
I'M GOING TO GO CHECK IT OUT!
BE CARE-FUL!
CLUNK
SAFETY HELMET
I HAVE MY HELMET, SO DON'T WORRY!

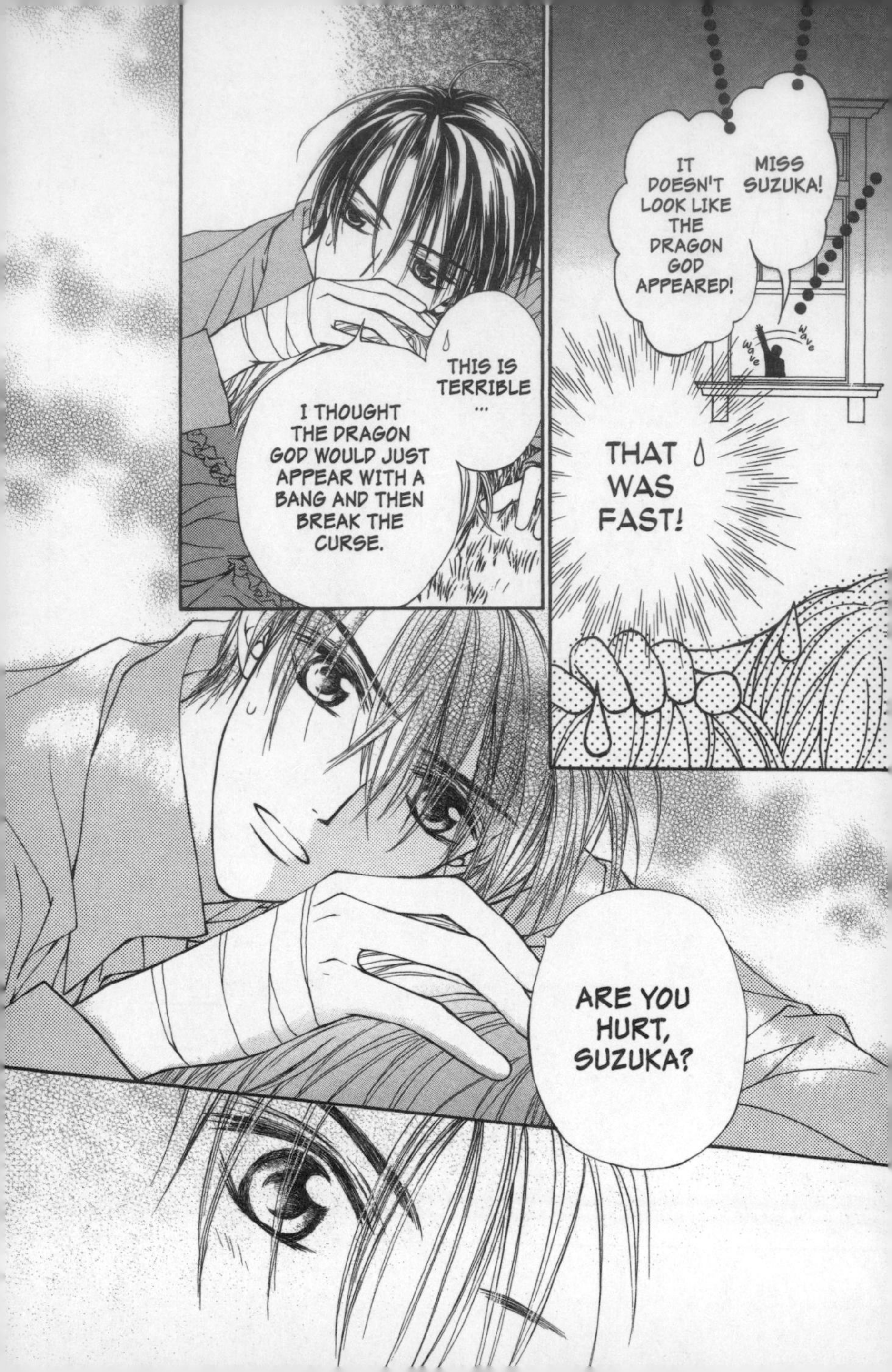
MISS SUZUKA!
IT DOESN'T LOOK LIKE THE DRAGON GOD APPEARED!
wave wave
THAT WAS FAST!
THIS IS TERRIBLE ...
I THOUGHT THE DRAGON GOD WOULD JUST APPEAR WITH A BANG AND THEN BREAK THE CURSE.
ARE YOU HURT, SUZUKA?

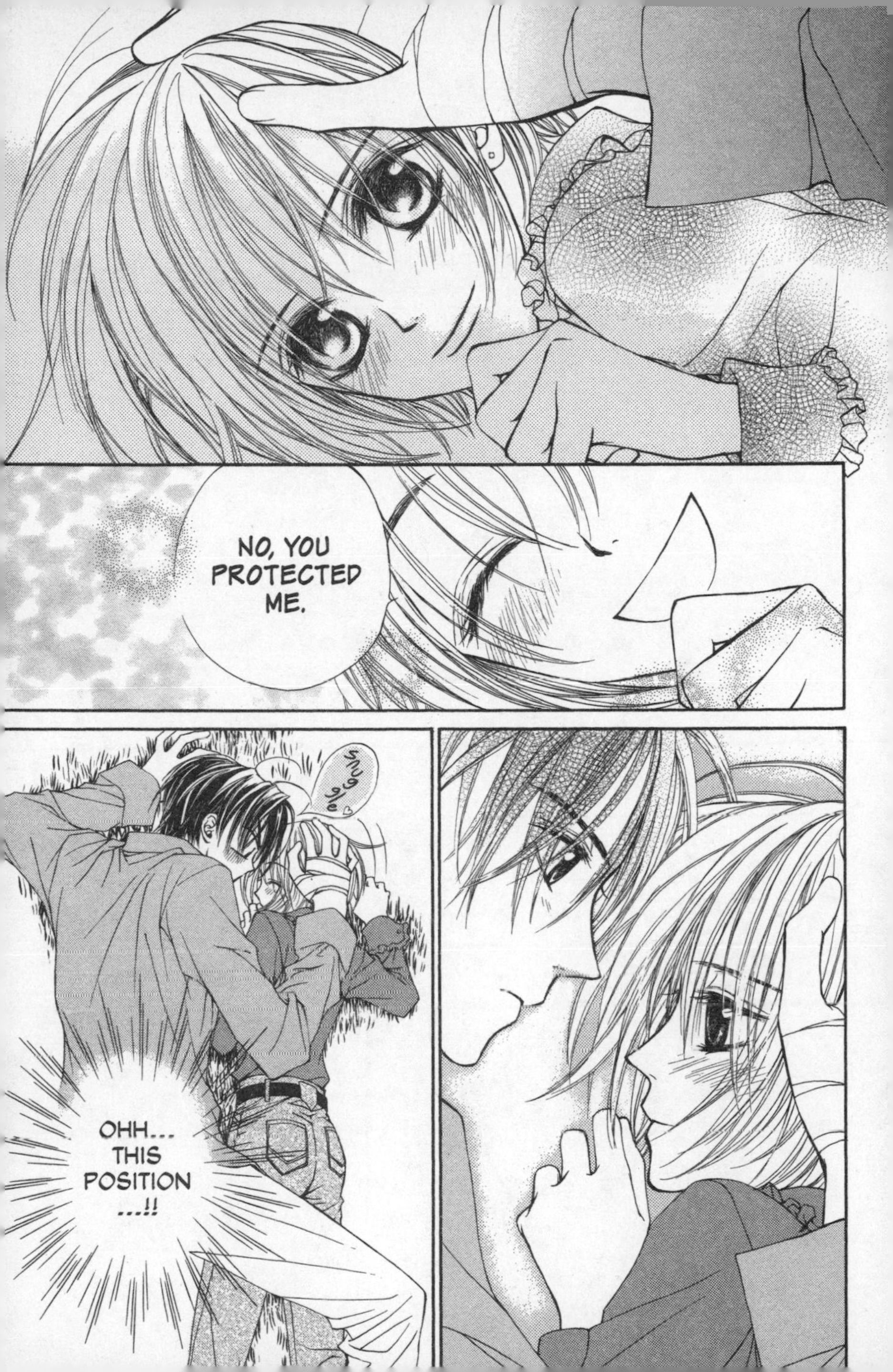
NO, YOU PROTECTED ME.
snuggle
OHH... THIS POSITION ...!!

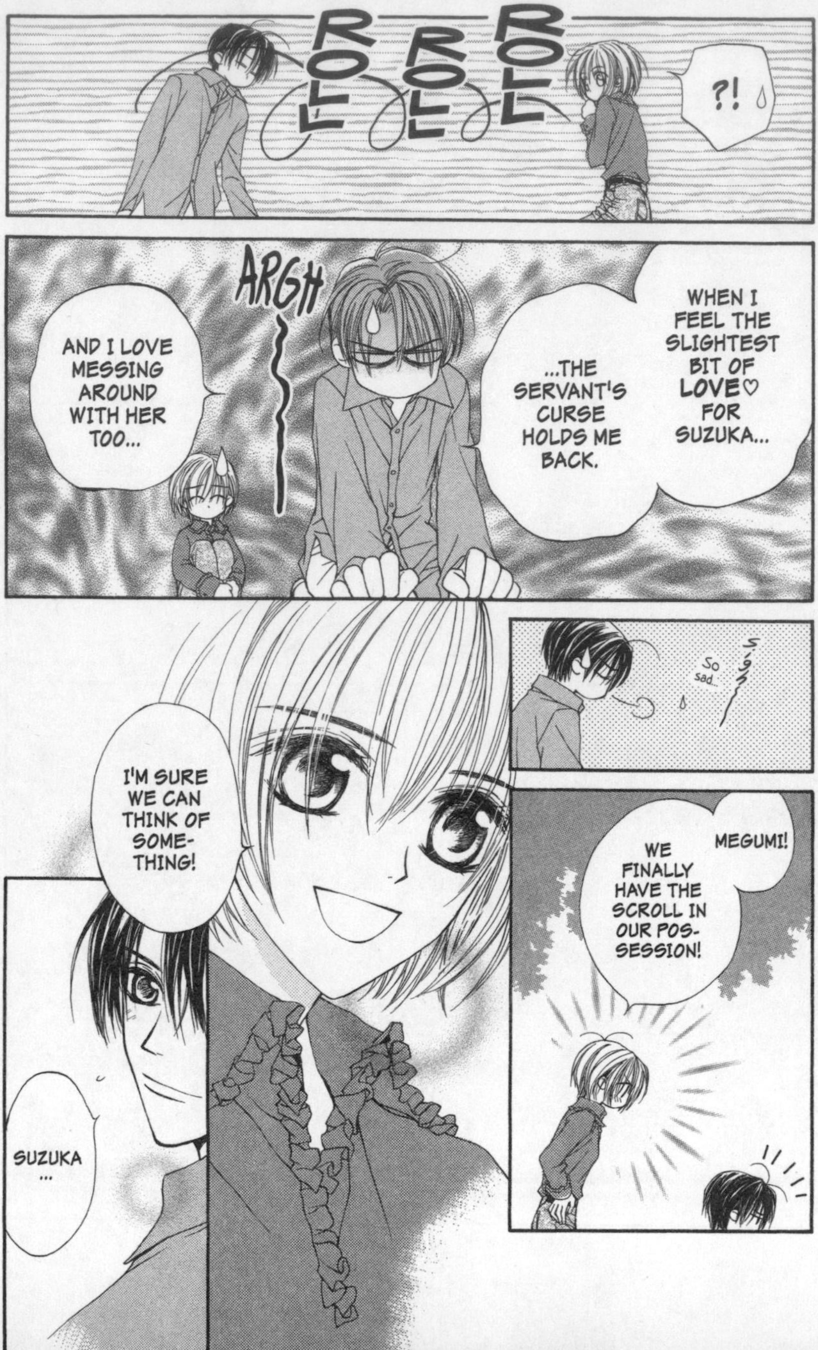

ROLL ROLL ROLL
?!
WHEN I FEEL THE SLIGHTEST BIT OF LOVE♡ FOR SUZUKA...
...THE SERVANT'S CURSE HOLDS ME BACK.
ARGH
AND I LOVE MESSING AROUND WITH HER TOO...
So sad...
Sigh
MEGUMI!
WE FINALLY HAVE THE SCROLL IN OUR POS-SESSION!
I'M SURE WE CAN THINK OF SOME-THING!
SUZUKA ...

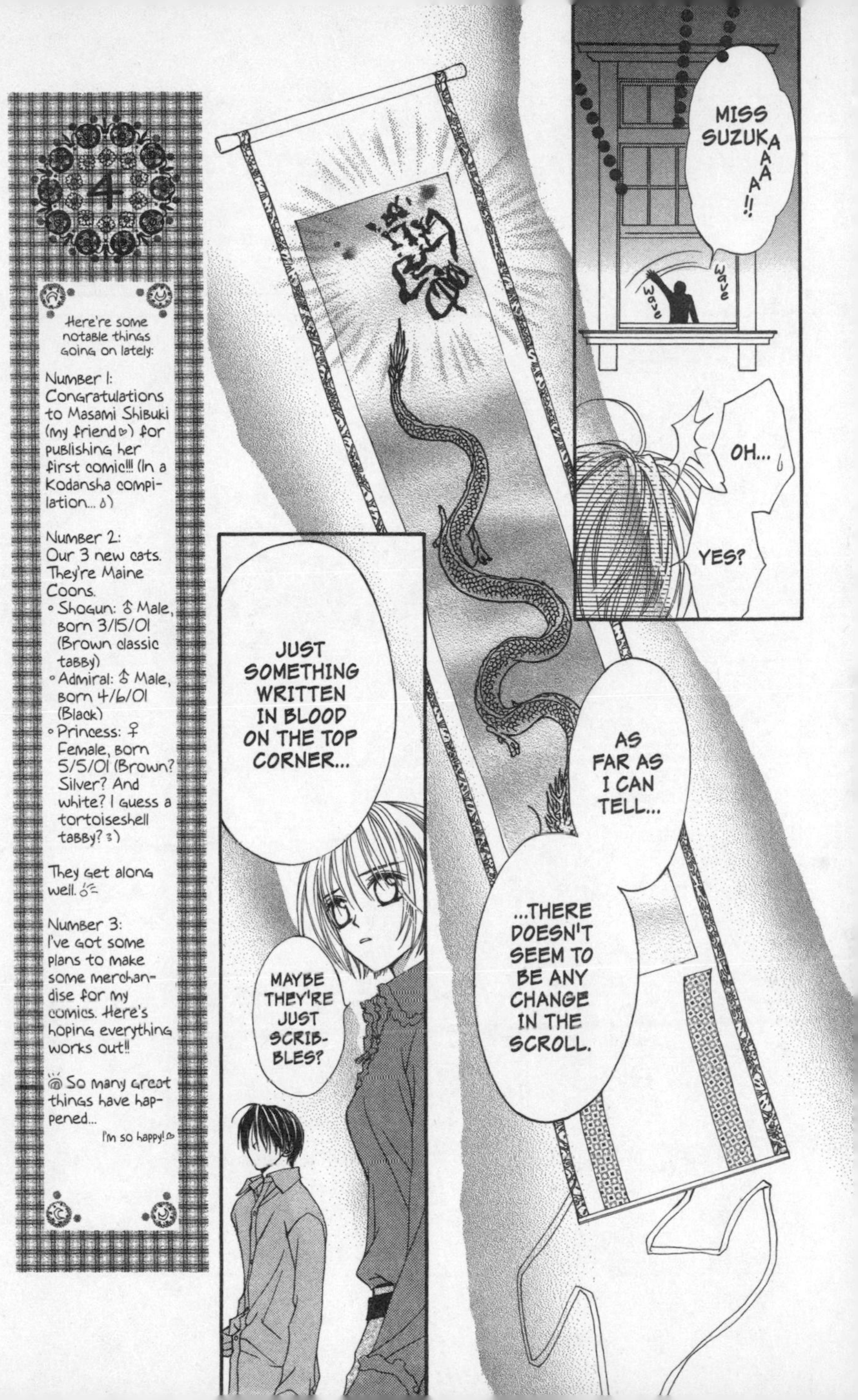
MISS SUZUKAAAA!!
wave wave
OH...
YES?
AS FAR AS I CAN TELL...
...THERE DOESN'T SEEM TO BE ANY CHANGE IN THE SCROLL.
JUST SOMETHING WRITTEN IN BLOOD ON THE TOP CORNER...
MAYBE THEY'RE JUST SCRIBBLES?

4

Here're some notable things going on lately:

Number 1: Congratulations to Masami Shibuki (my friend♡) for publishing her first comic!!! (In a Kodansha compilation...)

Number 2: Our 3 new cats. They're Maine Coons.

- Shogun: ♂ Male, born 3/15/01 (Brown classic tabby)
- Admiral: ♂ Male, born 4/6/01 (Black)
- Princess: ♀ Female, born 5/5/01 (Brown? Silver? And white? I guess a tortoiseshell tabby?)

They get along well.

Number 3: I've got some plans to make some merchandise for my comics. Here's hoping everything works out!!

So many great things have happened...

I'm so happy!♡

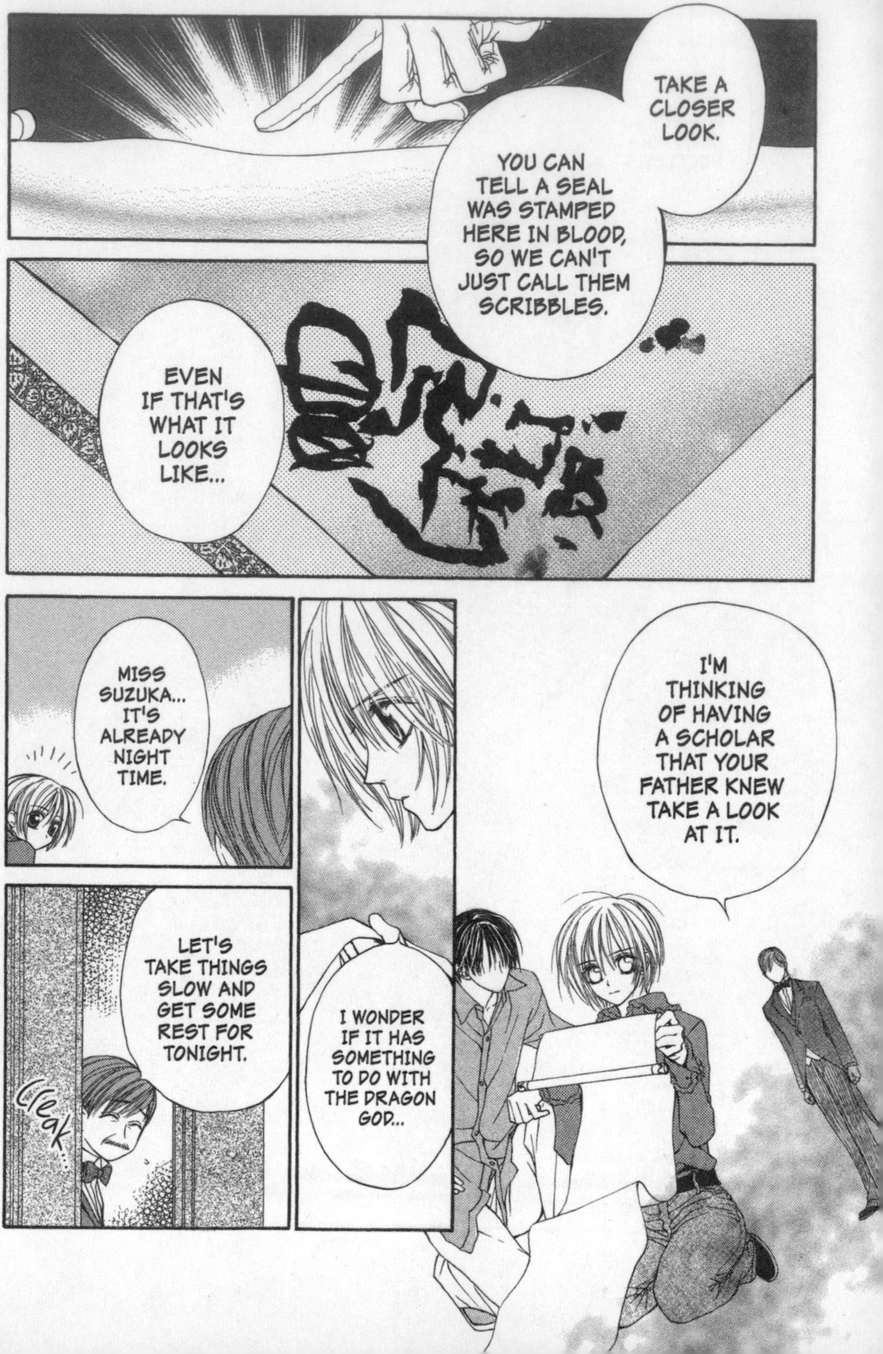
TAKE A CLOSER LOOK.
YOU CAN TELL A SEAL WAS STAMPED HERE IN BLOOD, SO WE CAN'T JUST CALL THEM SCRIBBLES.
EVEN IF THAT'S WHAT IT LOOKS LIKE...
I'M THINKING OF HAVING A SCHOLAR THAT YOUR FATHER KNEW TAKE A LOOK AT IT.
I WONDER IF IT HAS SOMETHING TO DO WITH THE DRAGON GOD...
MISS SUZUKA... IT'S ALREADY NIGHT TIME.
LET'S TAKE THINGS SLOW AND GET SOME REST FOR TONIGHT.
Creak...

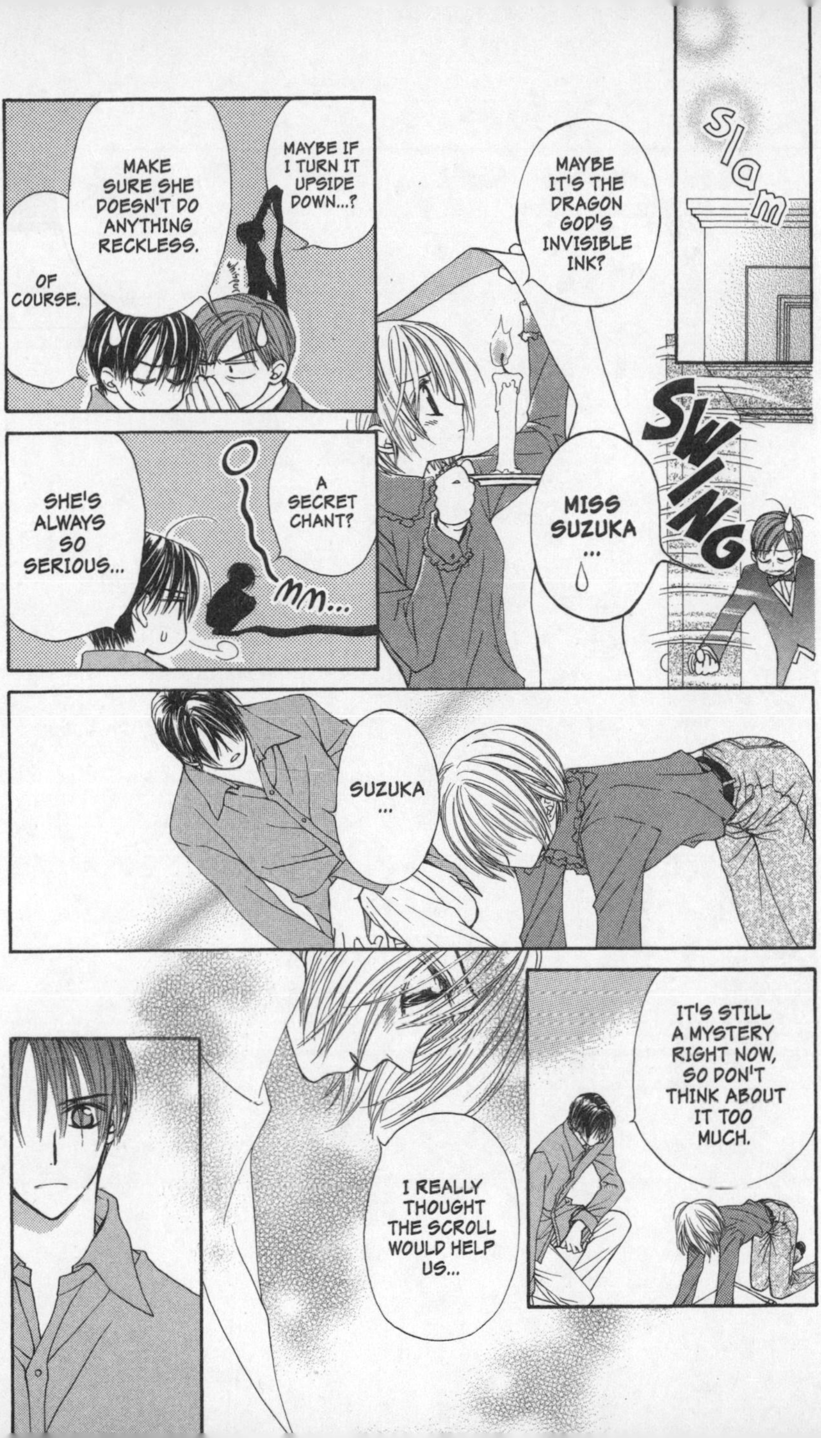
Slam
MAYBE IT'S THE DRAGON GOD'S INVISIBLE INK?
SWING
MISS SUZUKA ...
MAYBE IF I TURN IT UPSIDE DOWN...?
MAKE SURE SHE DOESN'T DO ANYTHING RECKLESS.
OF COURSE.
A SECRET CHANT?
mn...
SHE'S ALWAYS SO SERIOUS...
SUZUKA ...
IT'S STILL A MYSTERY RIGHT NOW, SO DON'T THINK ABOUT IT TOO MUCH.
I REALLY THOUGHT THE SCROLL WOULD HELP US...

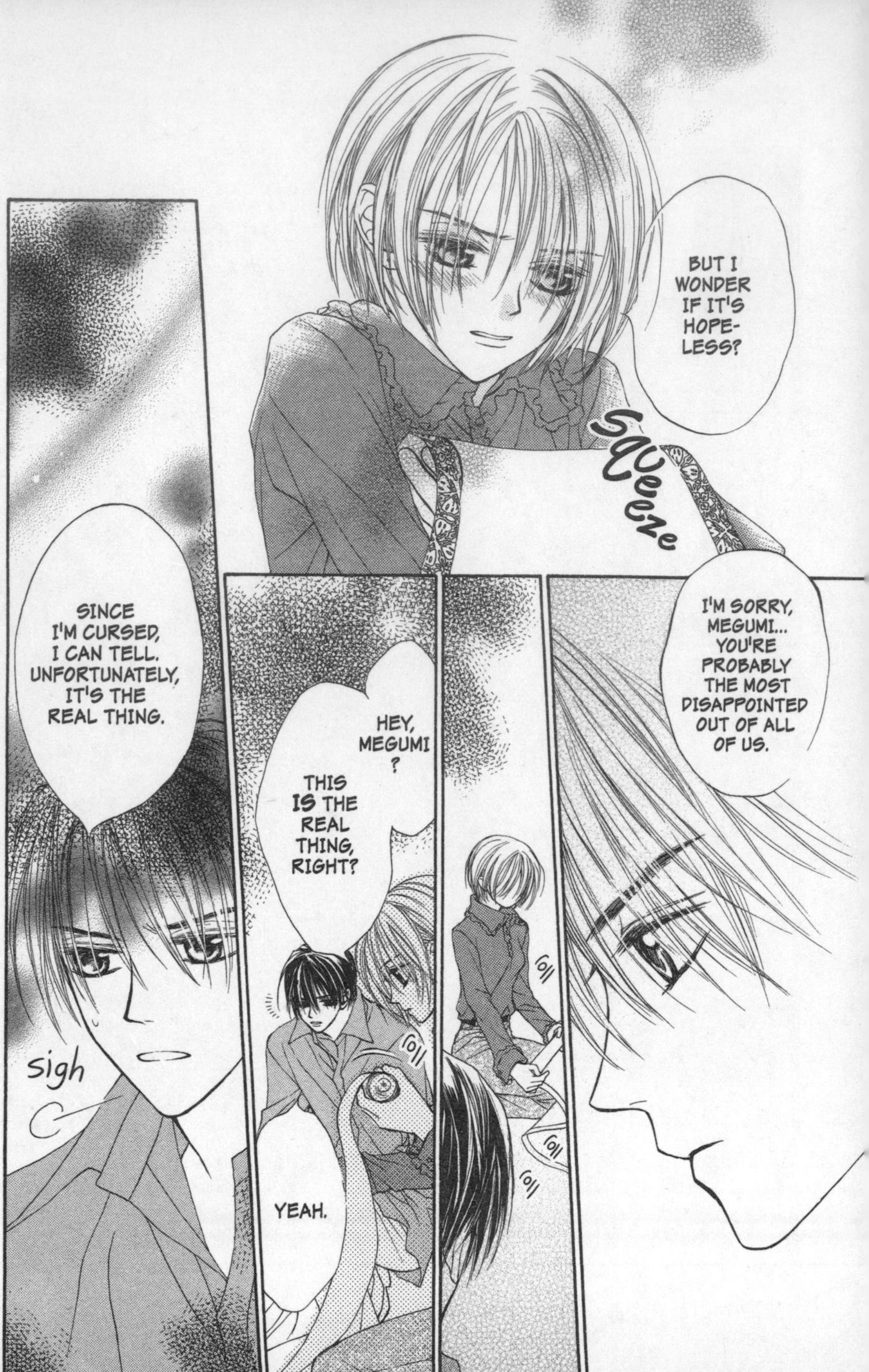

BUT I WONDER IF IT'S HOPE-LESS?
SQUEEZE
I'M SORRY, MEGUMI... YOU'RE PROBABLY THE MOST DISAPPOINTED OUT OF ALL OF US.
roll
roll
roll
HEY, MEGUMI?
THIS IS THE REAL THING, RIGHT?
roll
YEAH.
SINCE I'M CURSED, I CAN TELL. UNFORTUNATELY, IT'S THE REAL THING.
sigh

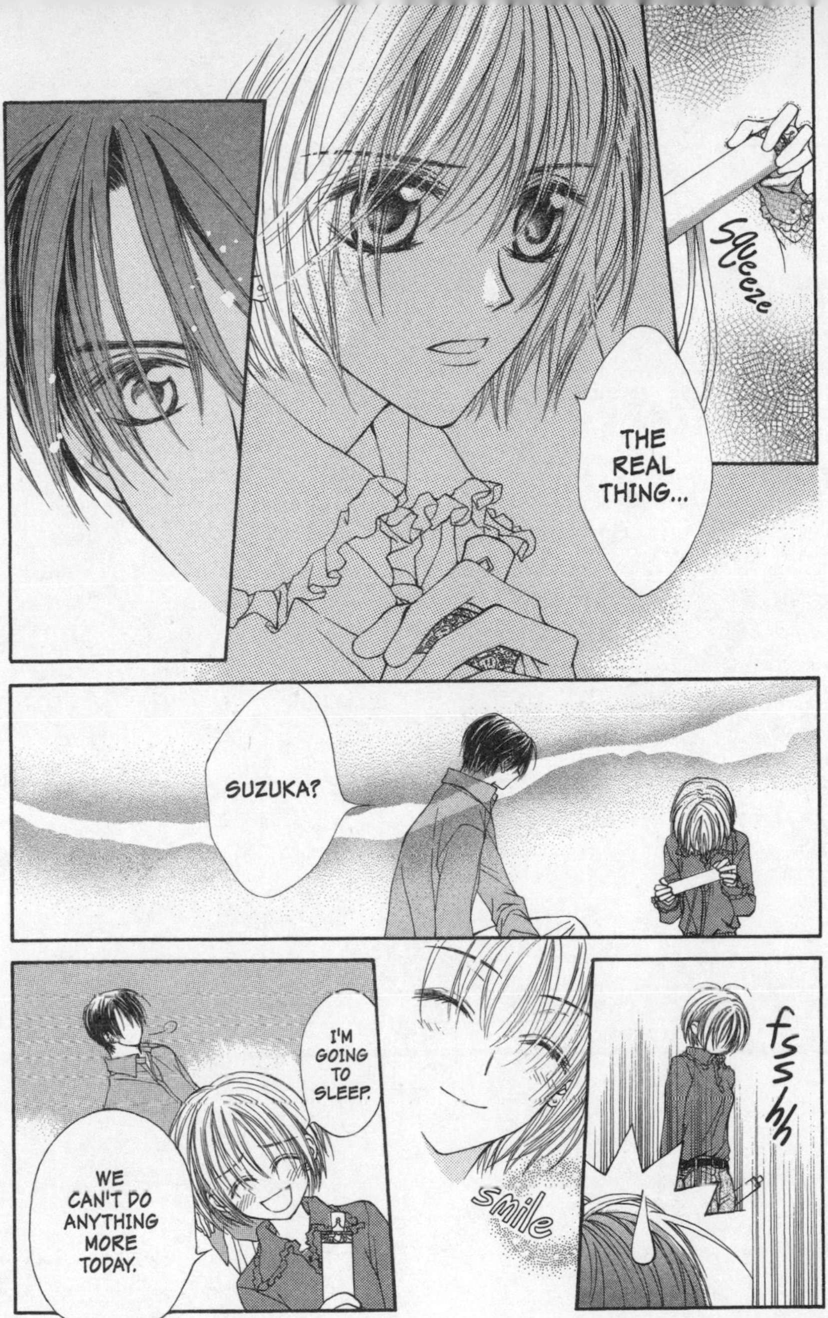
Squeeze
THE REAL THING...
SUZUKA?
fsshh
smile
I'M GOING TO SLEEP.
WE CAN'T DO ANYTHING MORE TODAY.

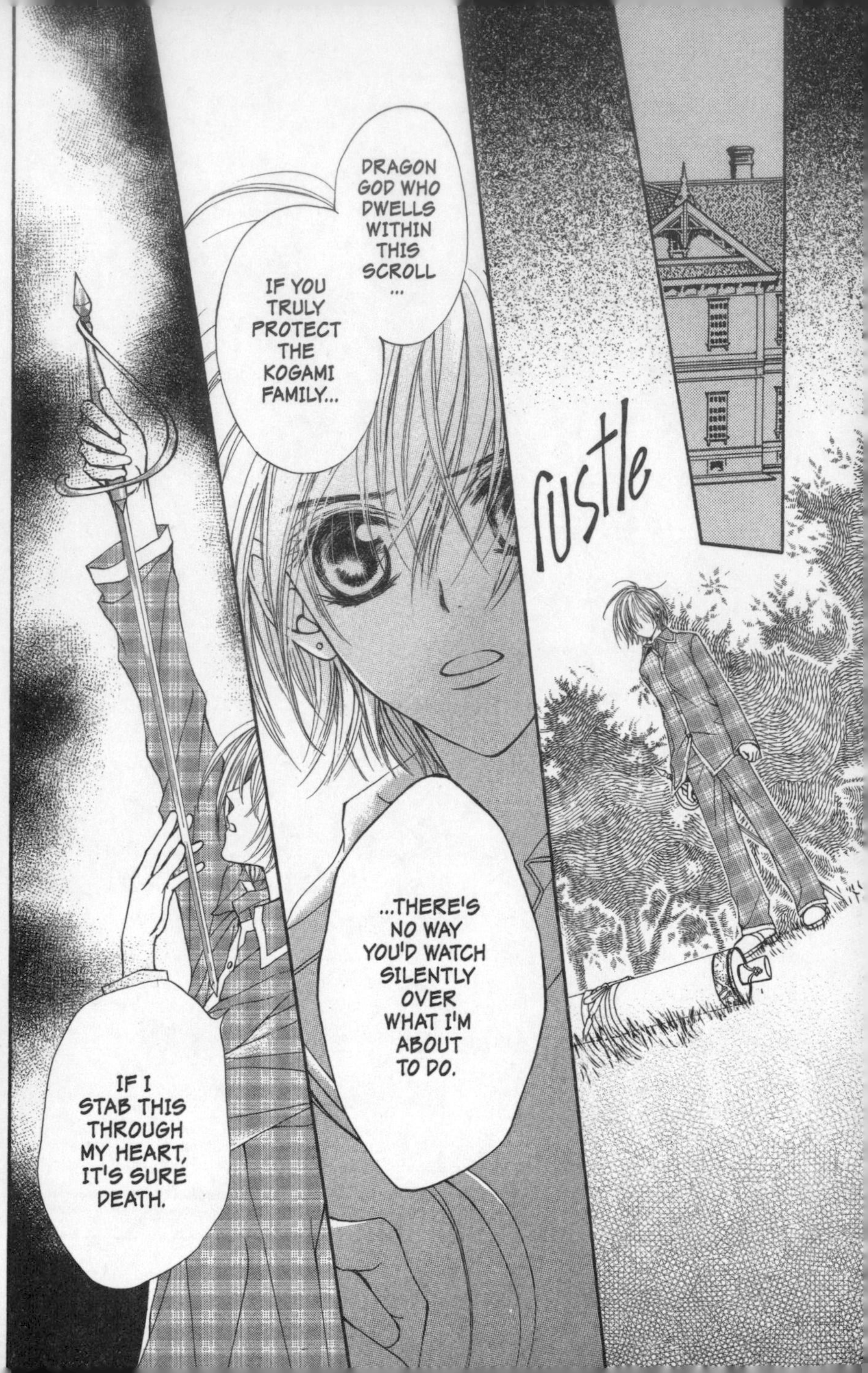
rustle
DRAGON GOD WHO DWELLS WITHIN THIS SCROLL...
IF YOU TRULY PROTECT THE KOGAMI FAMILY...
...THERE'S NO WAY YOU'D WATCH SILENTLY OVER WHAT I'M ABOUT TO DO.
IF I STAB THIS THROUGH MY HEART, IT'S SURE DEATH.

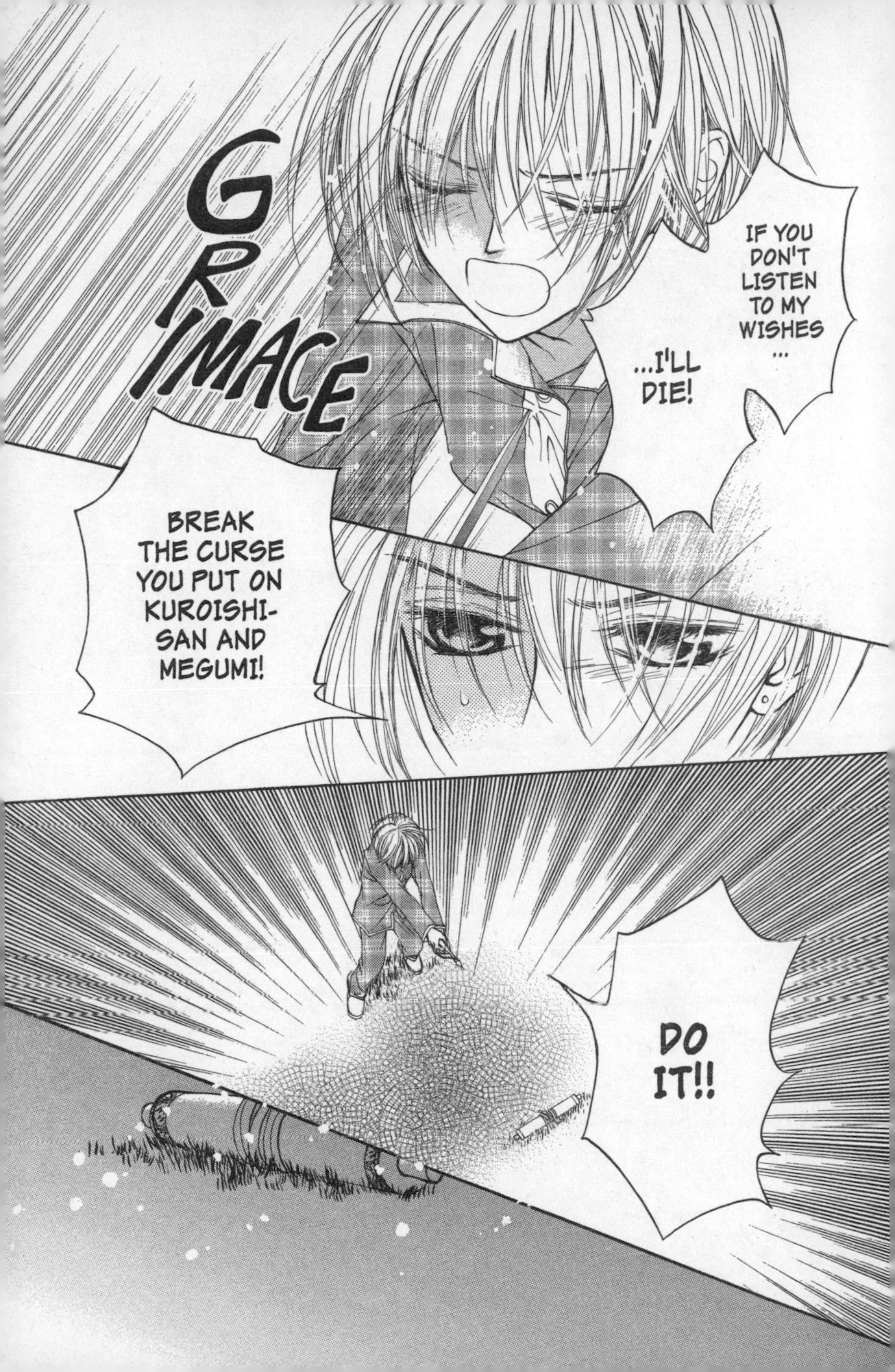
IF YOU DON'T LISTEN TO MY WISHES ...
...I'LL DIE!
GRIMACE
BREAK THE CURSE YOU PUT ON KUROISHI-SAN AND MEGUMI!
DO IT!!

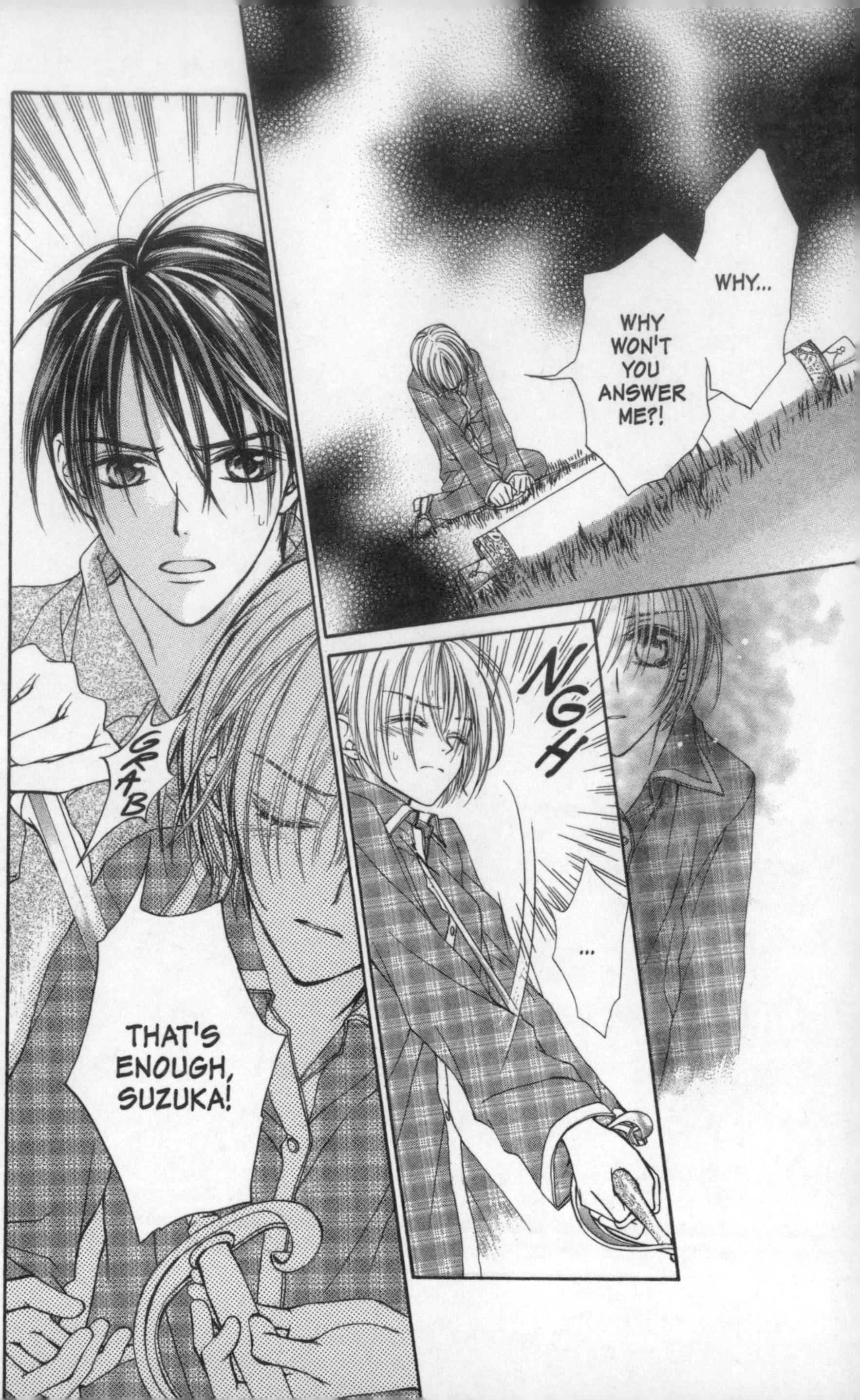
WHY...
WHY WON'T YOU ANSWER ME?!
NGH
...
GRAB
THAT'S ENOUGH, SUZUKA!

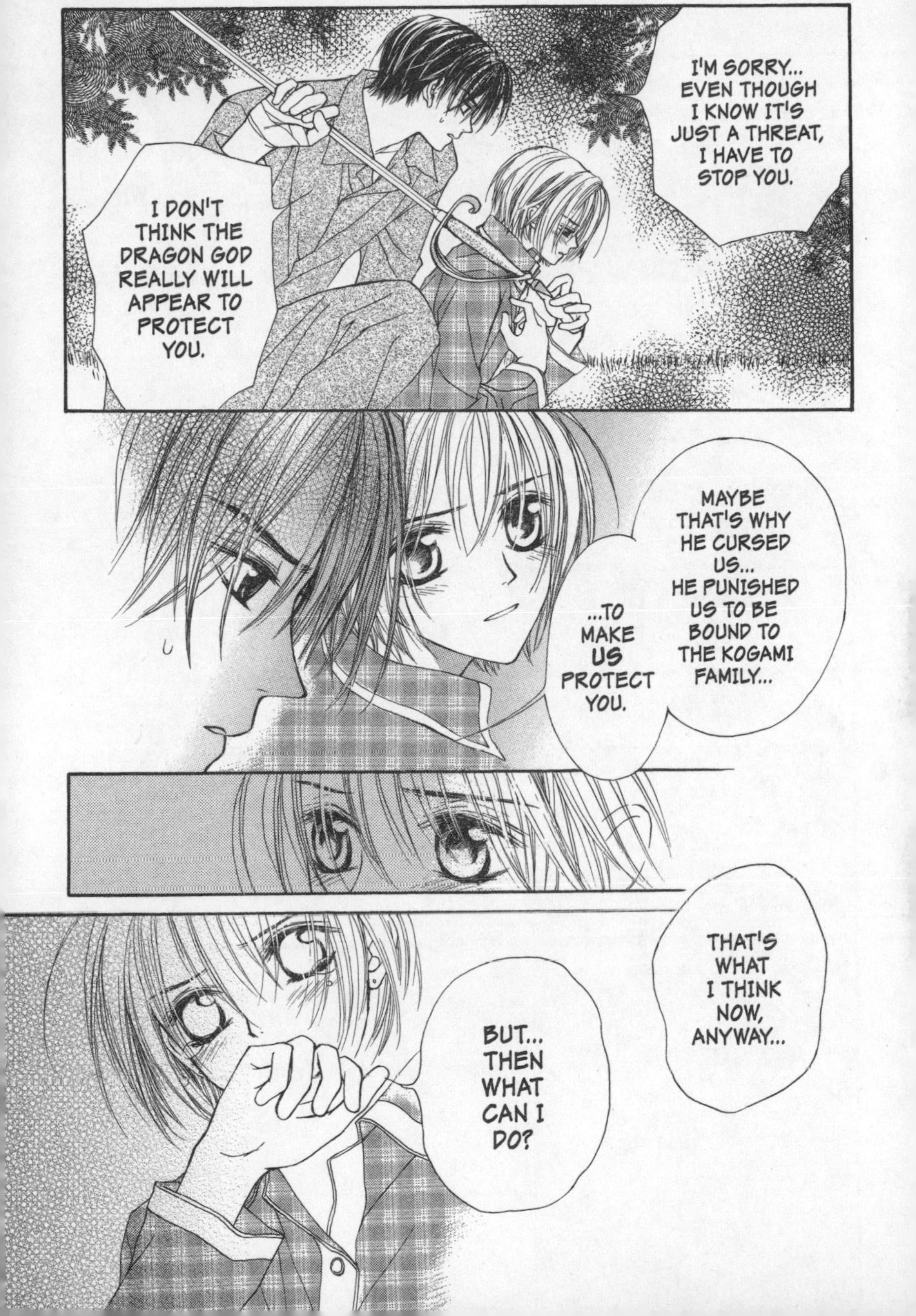
I'M SORRY... EVEN THOUGH I KNOW IT'S JUST A THREAT, I HAVE TO STOP YOU.
I DON'T THINK THE DRAGON GOD REALLY WILL APPEAR TO PROTECT YOU.
MAYBE THAT'S WHY HE CURSED US... HE PUNISHED US TO BE BOUND TO THE KOGAMI FAMILY...
...TO MAKE **US** PROTECT YOU.
THAT'S WHAT I THINK NOW, ANYWAY...
BUT... THEN WHAT CAN I DO?

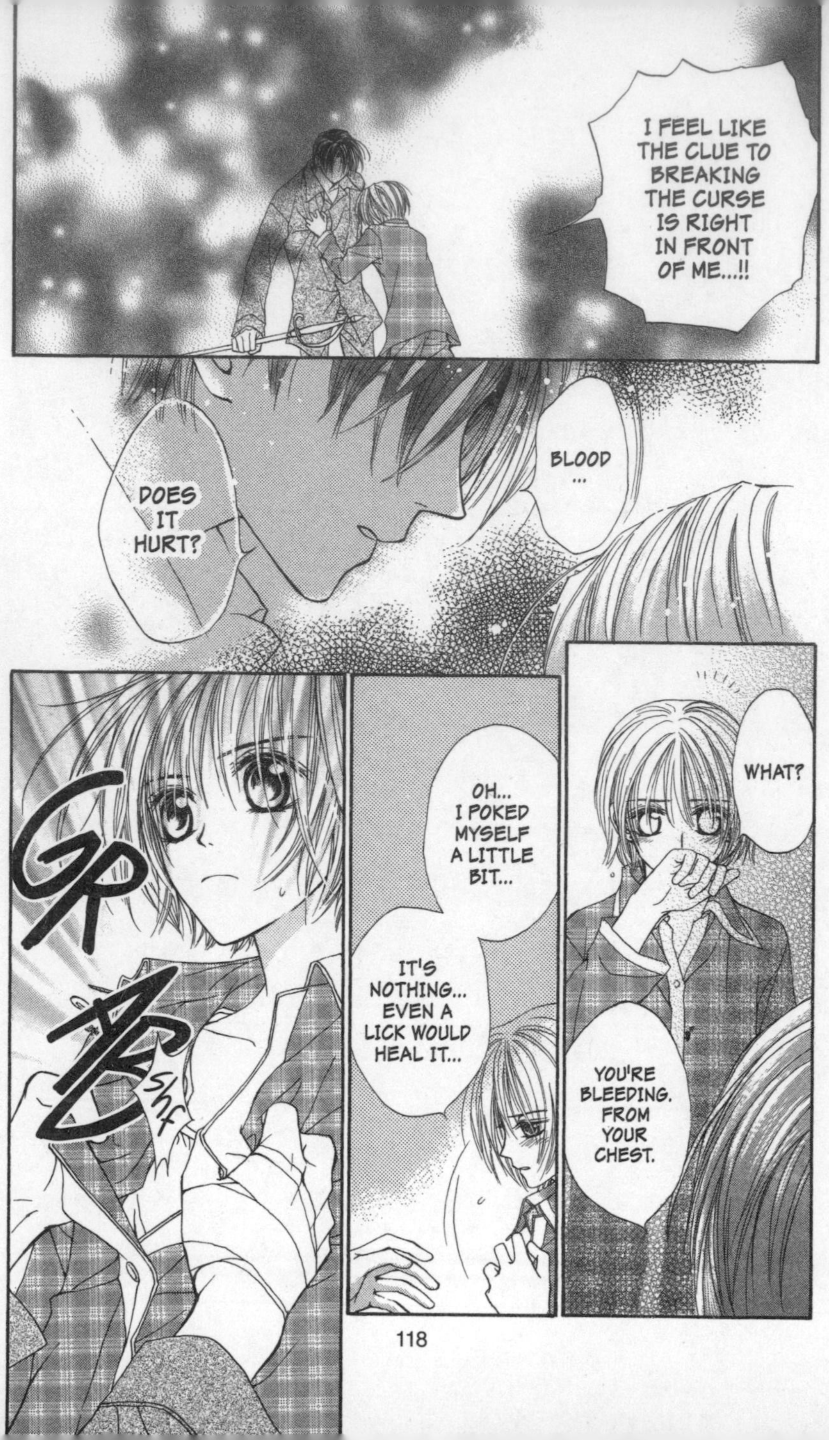
I FEEL LIKE THE CLUE TO BREAKING THE CURSE IS RIGHT IN FRONT OF ME...!!
BLOOD ...
DOES IT HURT?
WHAT?
YOU'RE BLEEDING. FROM YOUR CHEST.
OH... I POKED MYSELF A LITTLE BIT...
IT'S NOTHING... EVEN A LICK WOULD HEAL IT...
GRAB
shf

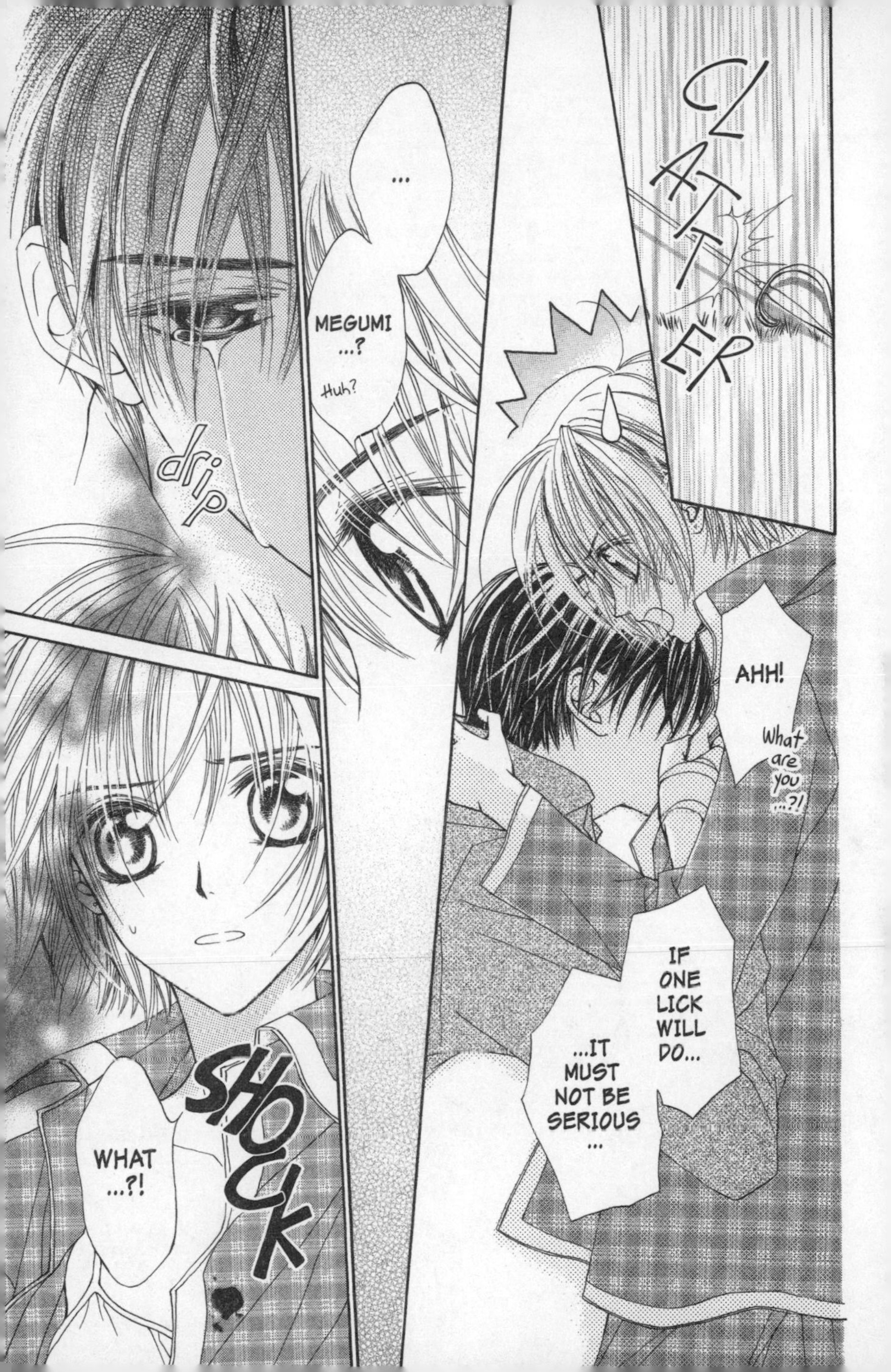
CLATTER
AHH!
What are you ...?!
IF ONE LICK WILL DO...
...IT MUST NOT BE SERIOUS ...
...
MEGUMI ...?
Huh?
drip
WHAT ...?!
SHOCK

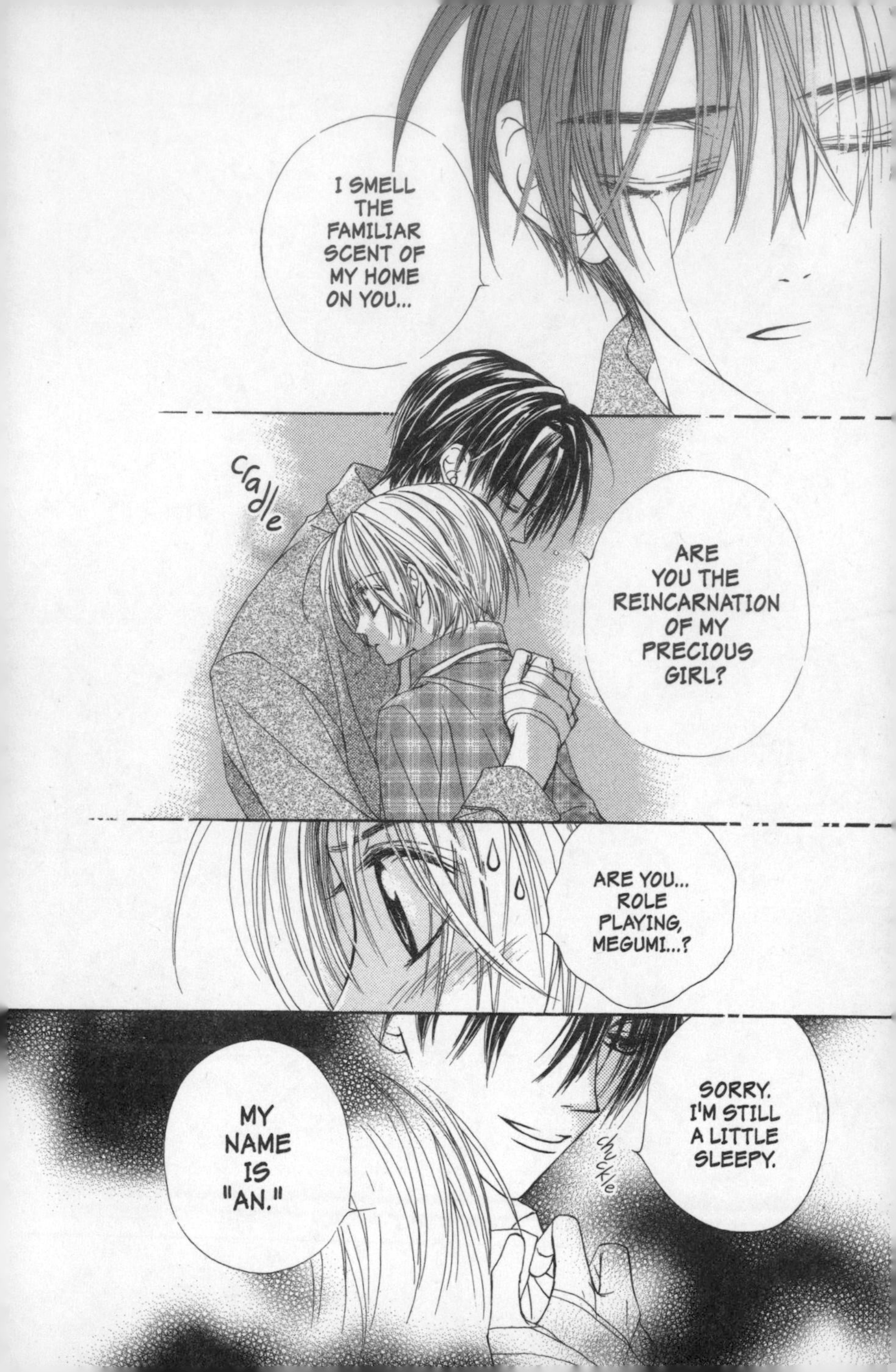
I SMELL THE FAMILIAR SCENT OF MY HOME ON YOU...
ARE YOU THE REINCARNATION OF MY PRECIOUS GIRL?
cradle
ARE YOU... ROLE PLAYING, MEGUMI...?
SORRY. I'M STILL A LITTLE SLEEPY.
chuckle
MY NAME IS "AN."

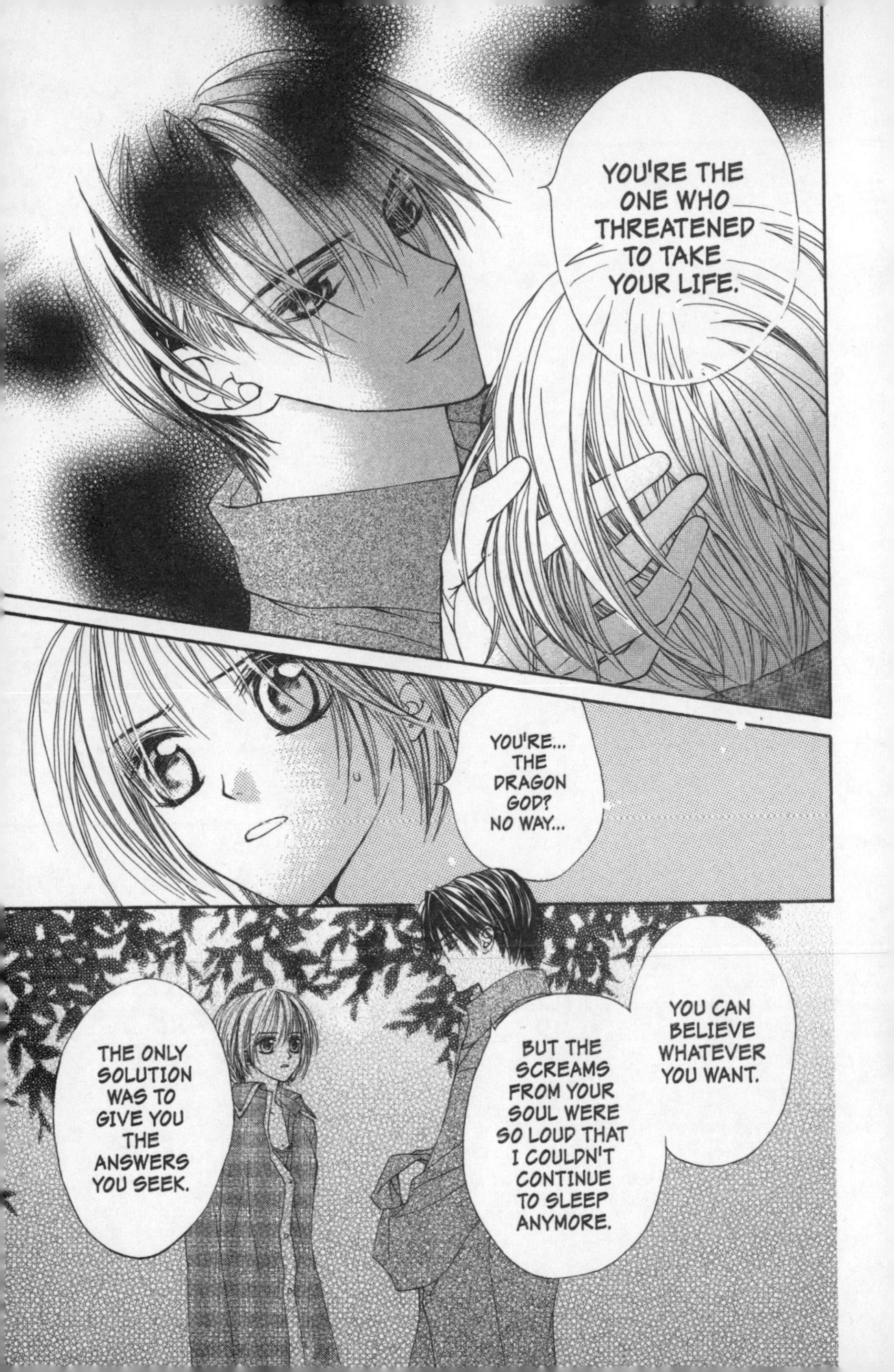
YOU'RE THE ONE WHO THREATENED TO TAKE YOUR LIFE.
YOU'RE... THE DRAGON GOD? NO WAY...
YOU CAN BELIEVE WHATEVER YOU WANT.
BUT THE SCREAMS FROM YOUR SOUL WERE SO LOUD THAT I COULDN'T CONTINUE TO SLEEP ANYMORE.
THE ONLY SOLUTION WAS TO GIVE YOU THE ANSWERS YOU SEEK.

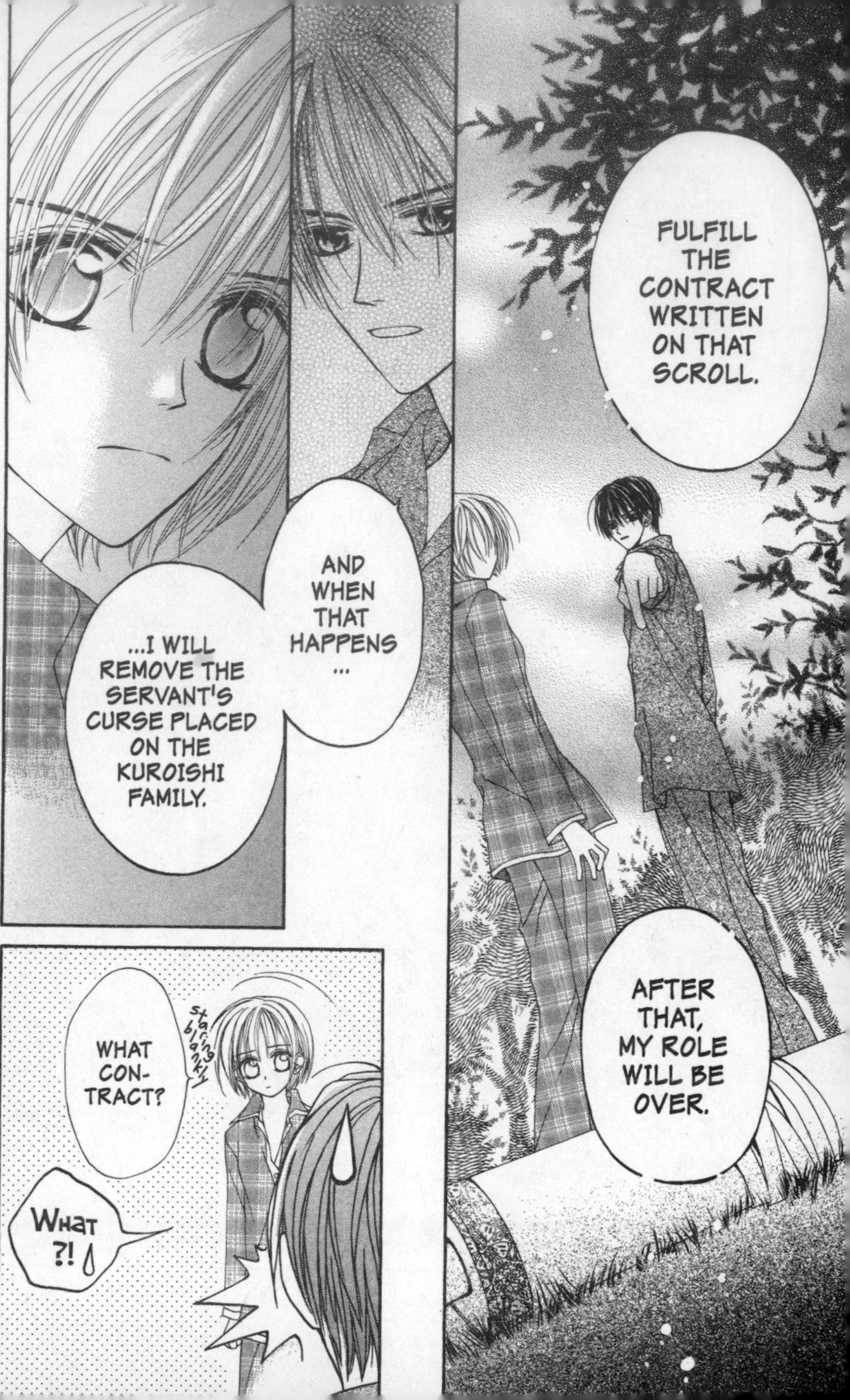
FULFILL THE CONTRACT WRITTEN ON THAT SCROLL.
AFTER THAT, MY ROLE WILL BE OVER.
AND WHEN THAT HAPPENS ...
...I WILL REMOVE THE SERVANT'S CURSE PLACED ON THE KUROISHI FAMILY.
WHAT CON-TRACT?
staring blankly
WHAT ?!

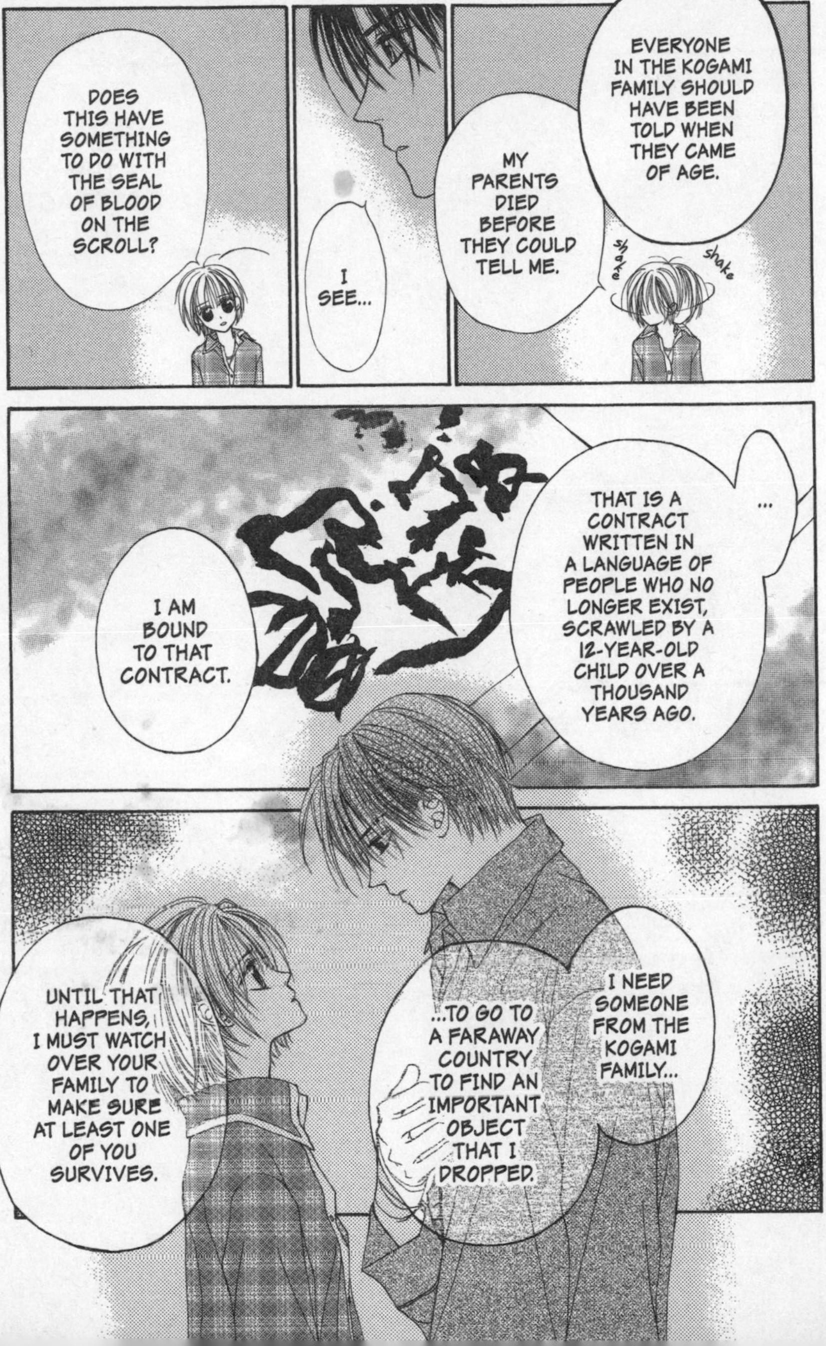
EVERYONE IN THE KOGAMI FAMILY SHOULD HAVE BEEN TOLD WHEN THEY CAME OF AGE.
MY PARENTS DIED BEFORE THEY COULD TELL ME.
shake
shake
I SEE...
DOES THIS HAVE SOMETHING TO DO WITH THE SEAL OF BLOOD ON THE SCROLL?
...
THAT IS A CONTRACT WRITTEN IN A LANGUAGE OF PEOPLE WHO NO LONGER EXIST, SCRAWLED BY A 12-YEAR-OLD CHILD OVER A THOUSAND YEARS AGO.
I AM BOUND TO THAT CONTRACT.
I NEED SOMEONE FROM THE KOGAMI FAMILY...
...TO GO TO A FARAWAY COUNTRY TO FIND AN IMPORTANT OBJECT THAT I DROPPED.
UNTIL THAT HAPPENS, I MUST WATCH OVER YOUR FAMILY TO MAKE SURE AT LEAST ONE OF YOU SURVIVES.

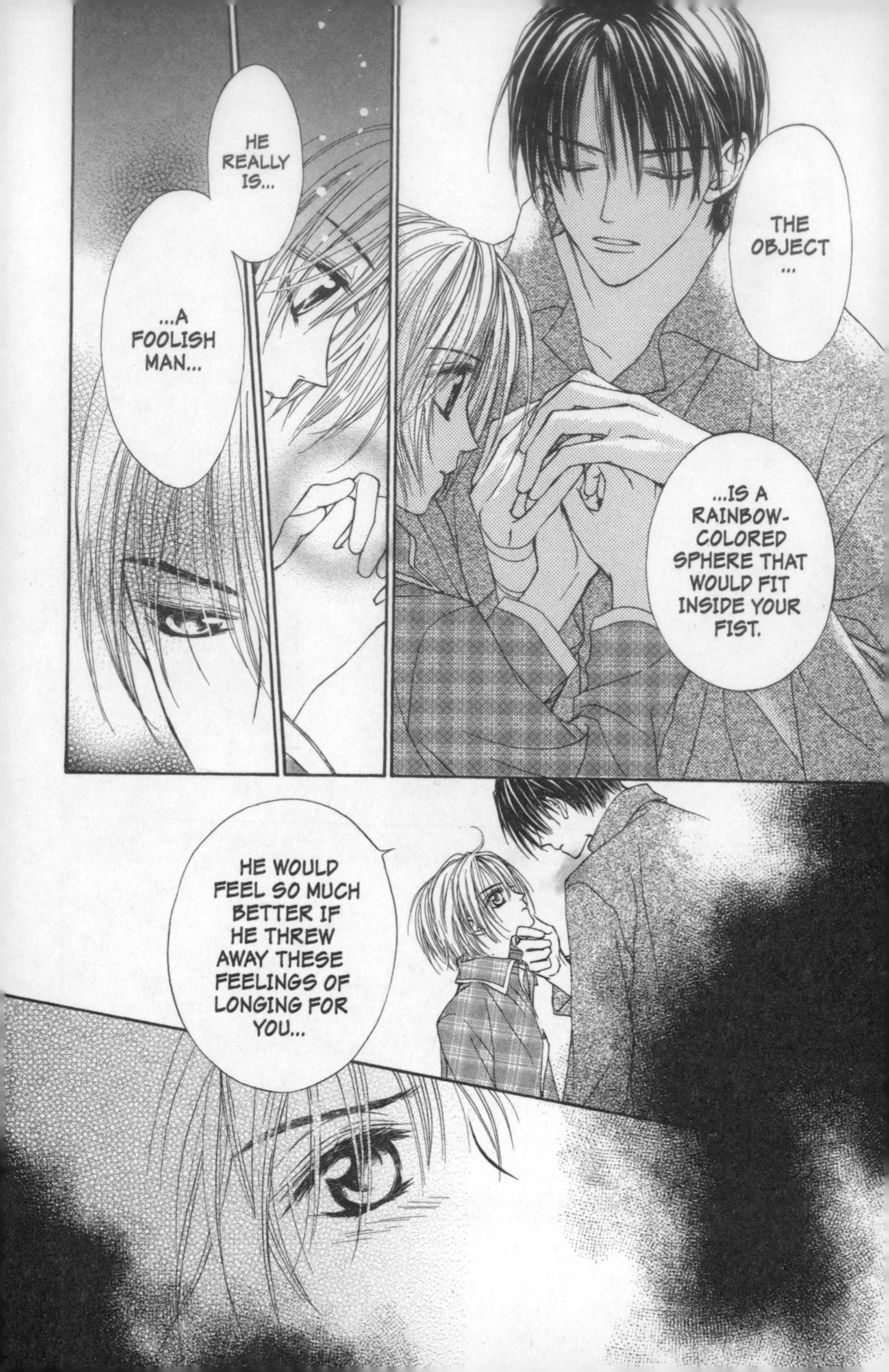
THE OBJECT...
...IS A RAINBOW-COLORED SPHERE THAT WOULD FIT INSIDE YOUR FIST.
HE REALLY IS...
...A FOOLISH MAN...
HE WOULD FEEL SO MUCH BETTER IF HE THREW AWAY THESE FEELINGS OF LONGING FOR YOU...

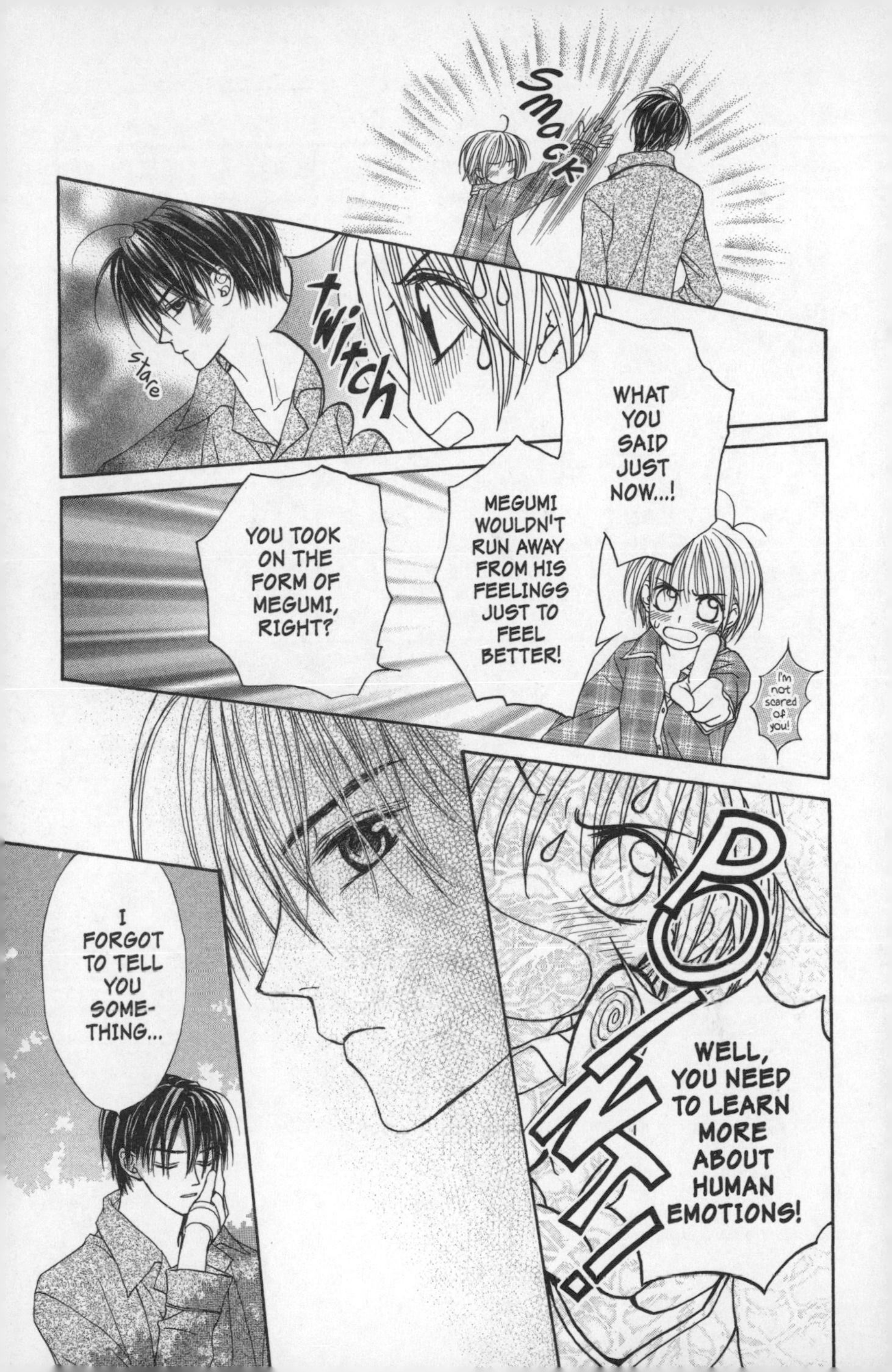
SMACK
WHAT YOU SAID JUST NOW...!
twitch
stare
MEGUMI WOULDN'T RUN AWAY FROM HIS FEELINGS JUST TO FEEL BETTER!
I'm not scared of you!
YOU TOOK ON THE FORM OF MEGUMI, RIGHT?
BONK!!
WELL, YOU NEED TO LEARN MORE ABOUT HUMAN EMOTIONS!
I FORGOT TO TELL YOU SOMETHING...

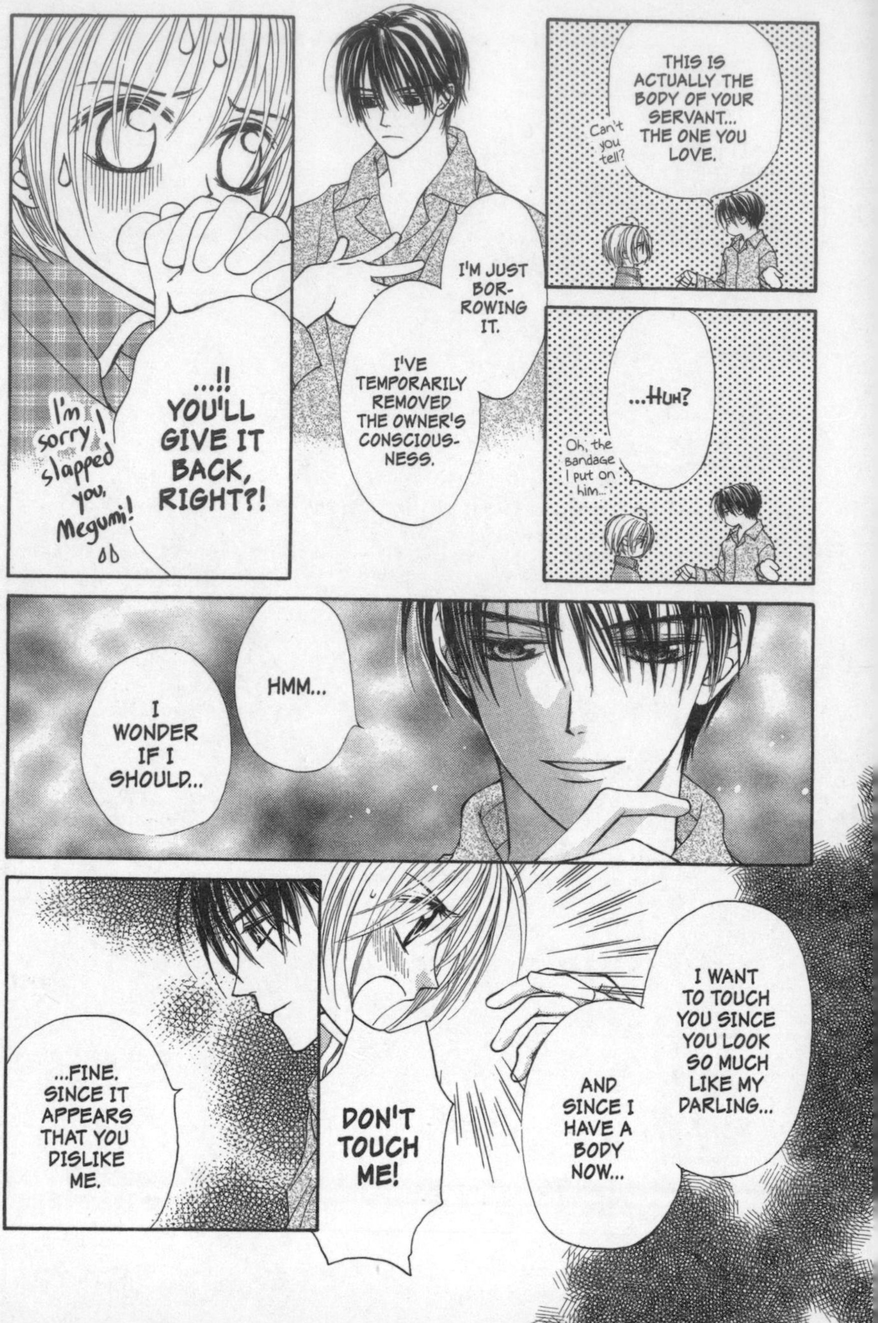
THIS IS ACTUALLY THE BODY OF YOUR SERVANT... THE ONE YOU LOVE.
Can't you tell?
...HUH?
Oh, the bandage I put on him...
I'M JUST BOR-ROWING IT.
I'VE TEMPORARILY REMOVED THE OWNER'S CONSCIOUS-NESS.
...!! YOU'LL GIVE IT BACK, RIGHT?!
I'm sorry I slapped you, Megumi!
HMM...
I WONDER IF I SHOULD...
I WANT TO TOUCH YOU SINCE YOU LOOK SO MUCH LIKE MY DARLING...
AND SINCE I HAVE A BODY NOW...
DON'T TOUCH ME!
...FINE. SINCE IT APPEARS THAT YOU DISLIKE ME.

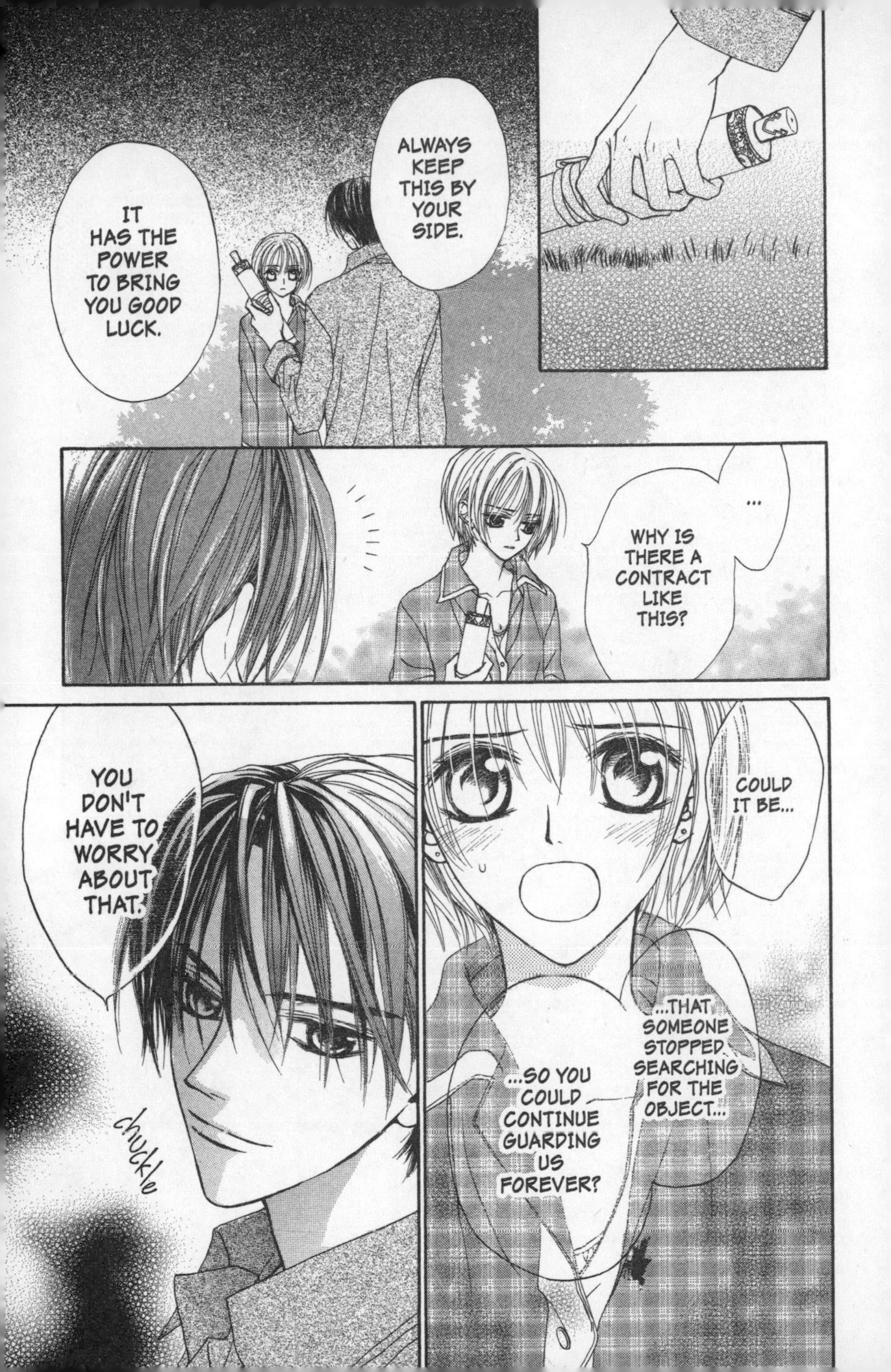
ALWAYS KEEP THIS BY YOUR SIDE.
IT HAS THE POWER TO BRING YOU GOOD LUCK.
...
WHY IS THERE A CONTRACT LIKE THIS?
COULD IT BE...
...THAT SOMEONE STOPPED SEARCHING FOR THE OBJECT...
...SO YOU COULD CONTINUE GUARDING US FOREVER?
YOU DON'T HAVE TO WORRY ABOUT THAT.
chuckle

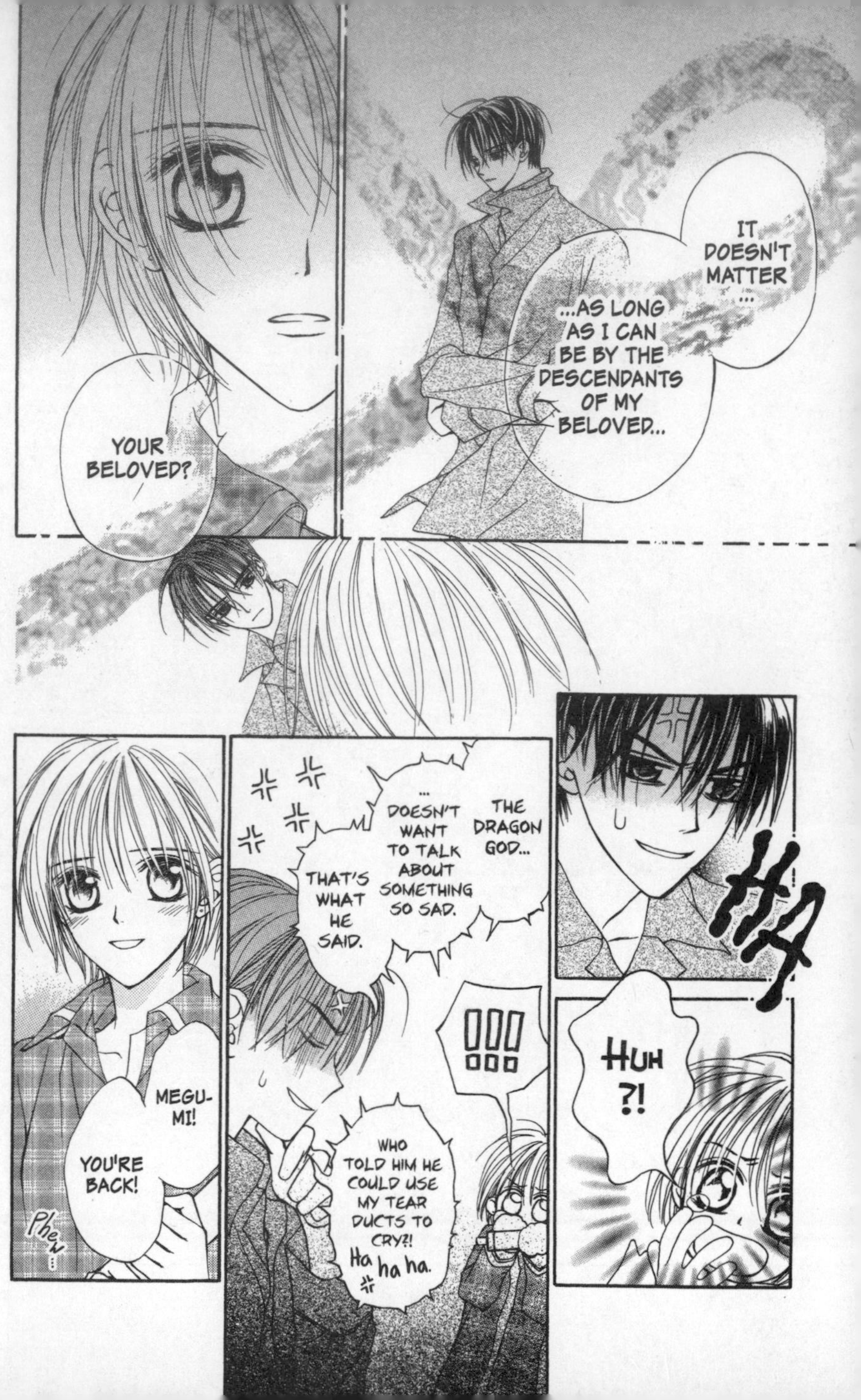
IT DOESN'T MATTER...
...AS LONG AS I CAN BE BY THE DESCENDANTS OF MY BELOVED...
YOUR BELOVED?
HUH ?!
THE DRAGON GOD...
...DOESN'T WANT TO TALK ABOUT SOMETHING SO SAD.
THAT'S WHAT HE SAID.
!!!
WHO TOLD HIM HE COULD USE MY TEAR DUCTS TO CRY?!
Ha ha ha.
MEGUMI!
YOU'RE BACK!
Phew...

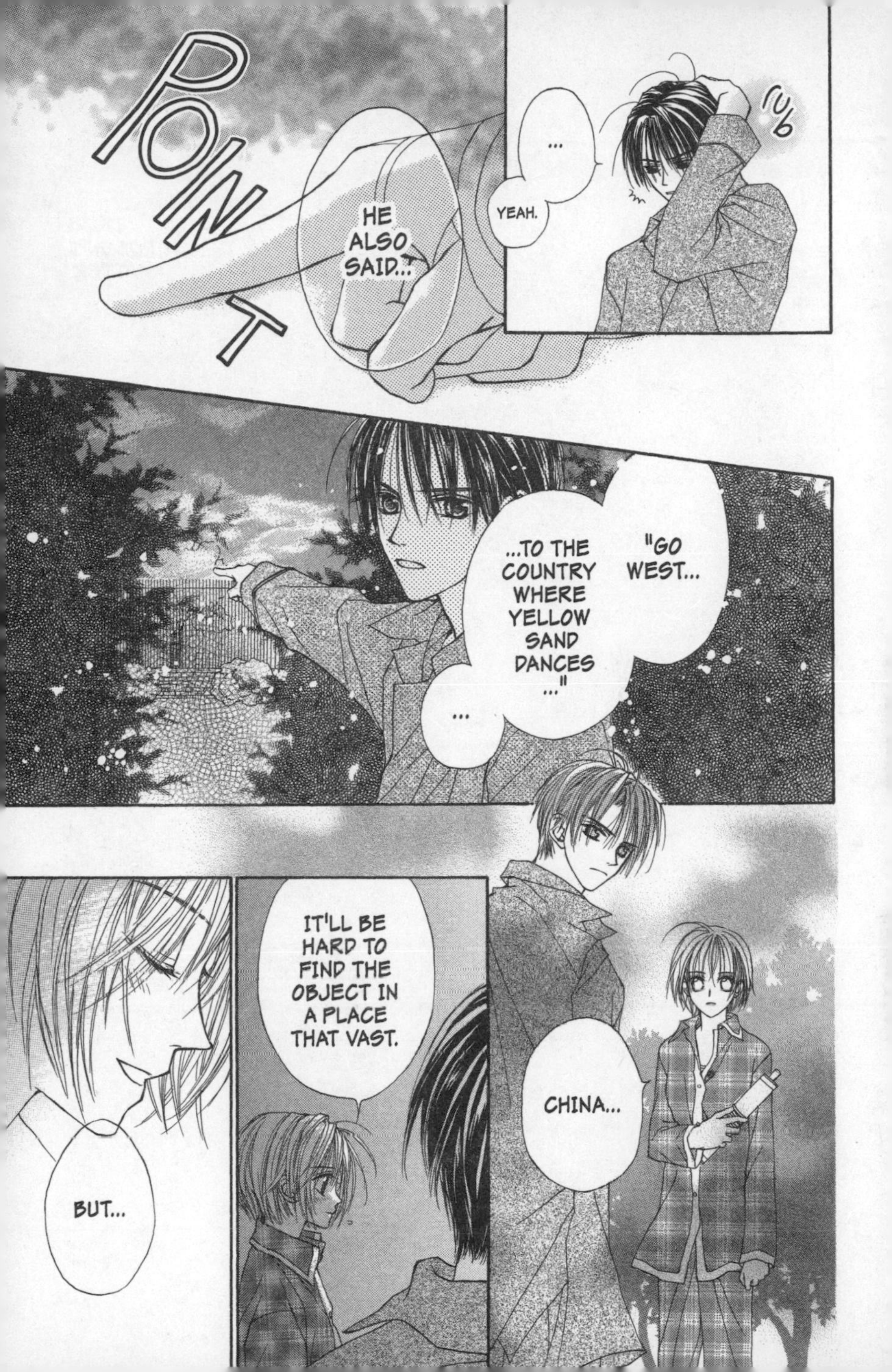
rub
...
YEAH.
POINT
HE ALSO SAID...
"GO WEST...
...TO THE COUNTRY WHERE YELLOW SAND DANCES..."
...
CHINA...
IT'LL BE HARD TO FIND THE OBJECT IN A PLACE THAT VAST.
BUT...

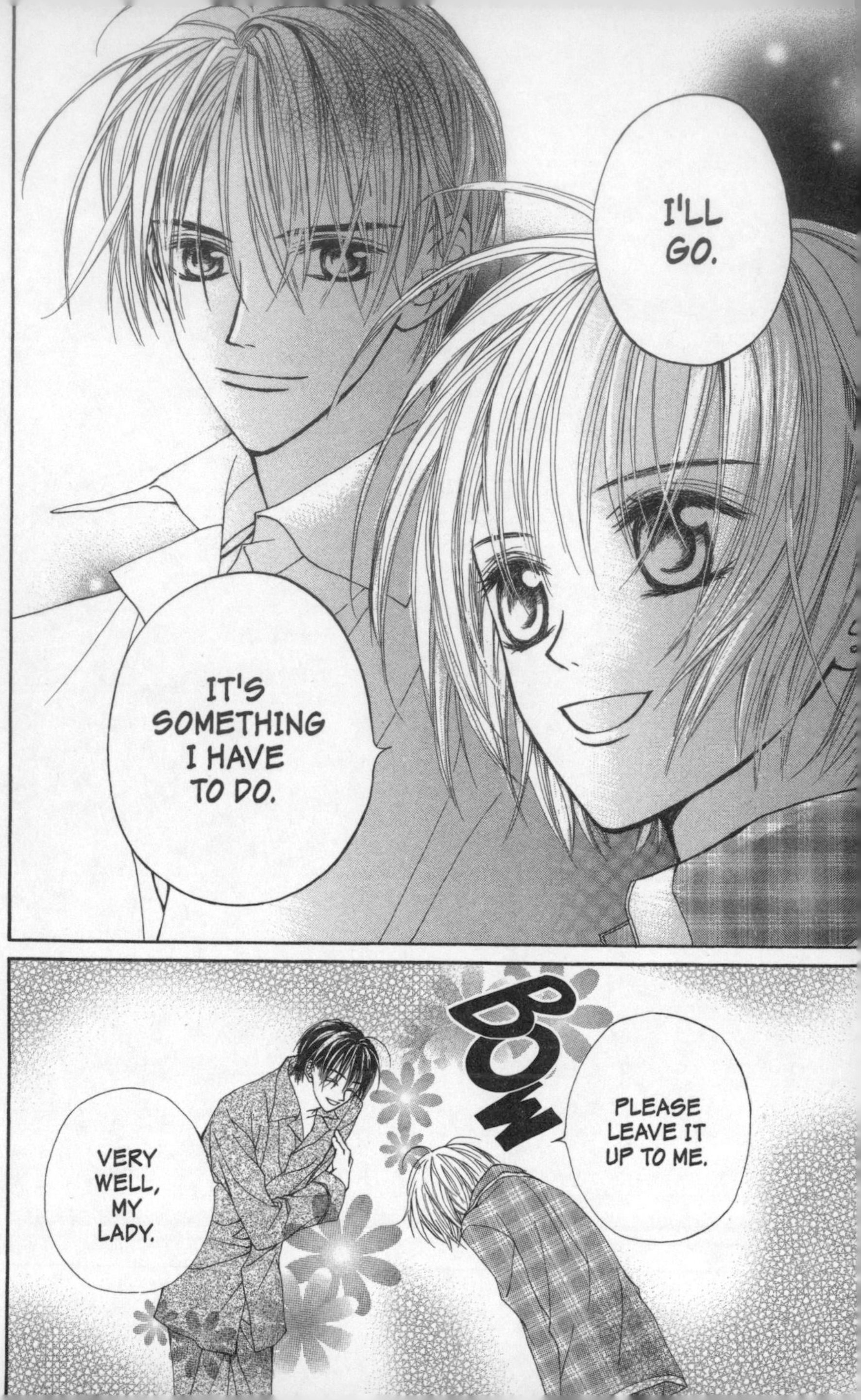
I'LL GO.
IT'S SOMETHING I HAVE TO DO.
BOW
PLEASE LEAVE IT UP TO ME.
VERY WELL, MY LADY.

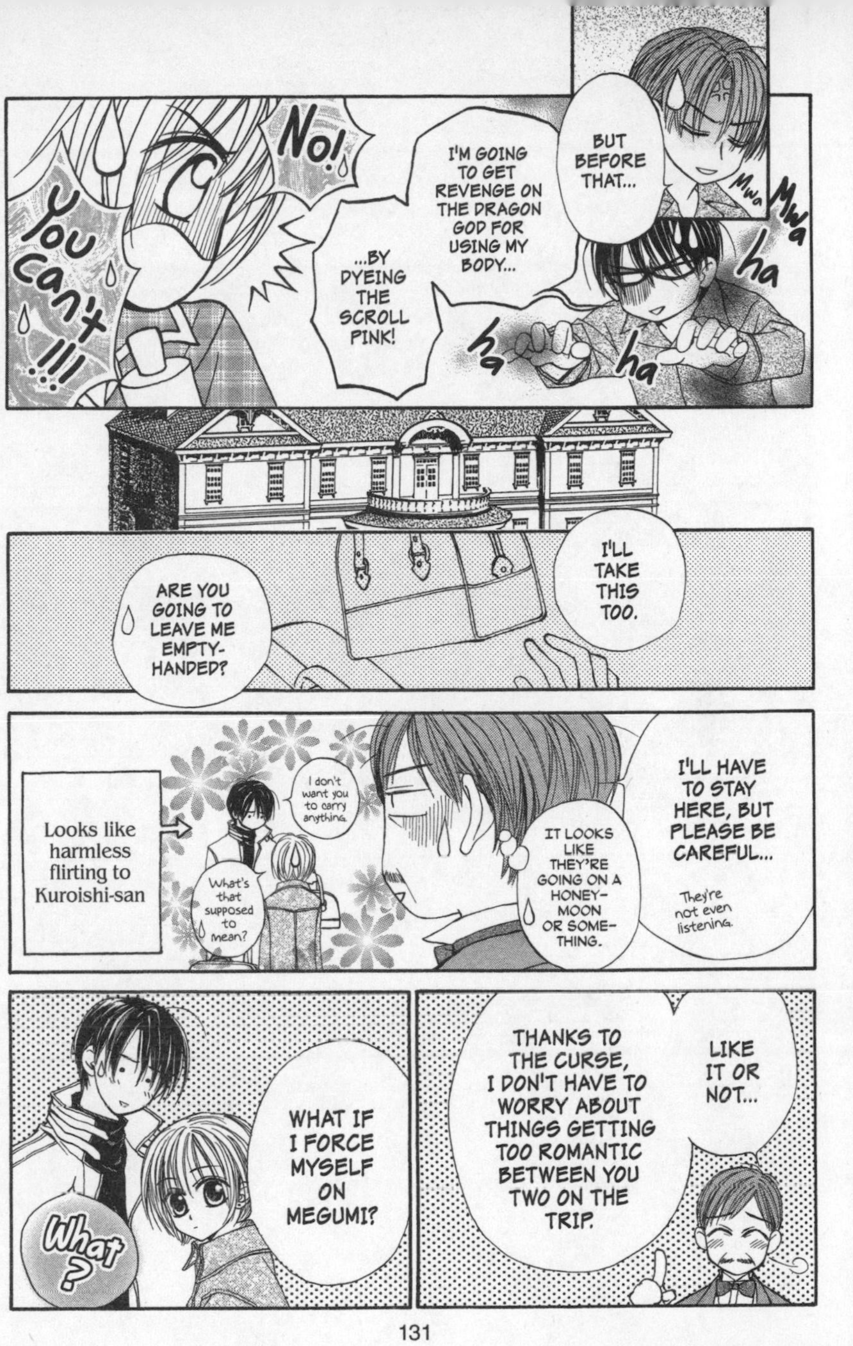
BUT BEFORE THAT...
I'M GOING TO GET REVENGE ON THE DRAGON GOD FOR USING MY BODY...
...BY DYEING THE SCROLL PINK!
Mwa Mwa ha ha ha ha
No!
You can't!!!
I'LL TAKE THIS TOO.
ARE YOU GOING TO LEAVE ME EMPTY-HANDED?
I'LL HAVE TO STAY HERE, BUT PLEASE BE CAREFUL...
They're not even listening.
IT LOOKS LIKE THEY'RE GOING ON A HONEY-MOON OR SOME-THING.
I don't want you to carry anything.
What's that supposed to mean?
Looks like harmless flirting to Kuroishi-san
LIKE IT OR NOT...
THANKS TO THE CURSE, I DON'T HAVE TO WORRY ABOUT THINGS GETTING TOO ROMANTIC BETWEEN YOU TWO ON THE TRIP.
WHAT IF I FORCE MYSELF ON MEGUMI?
What?

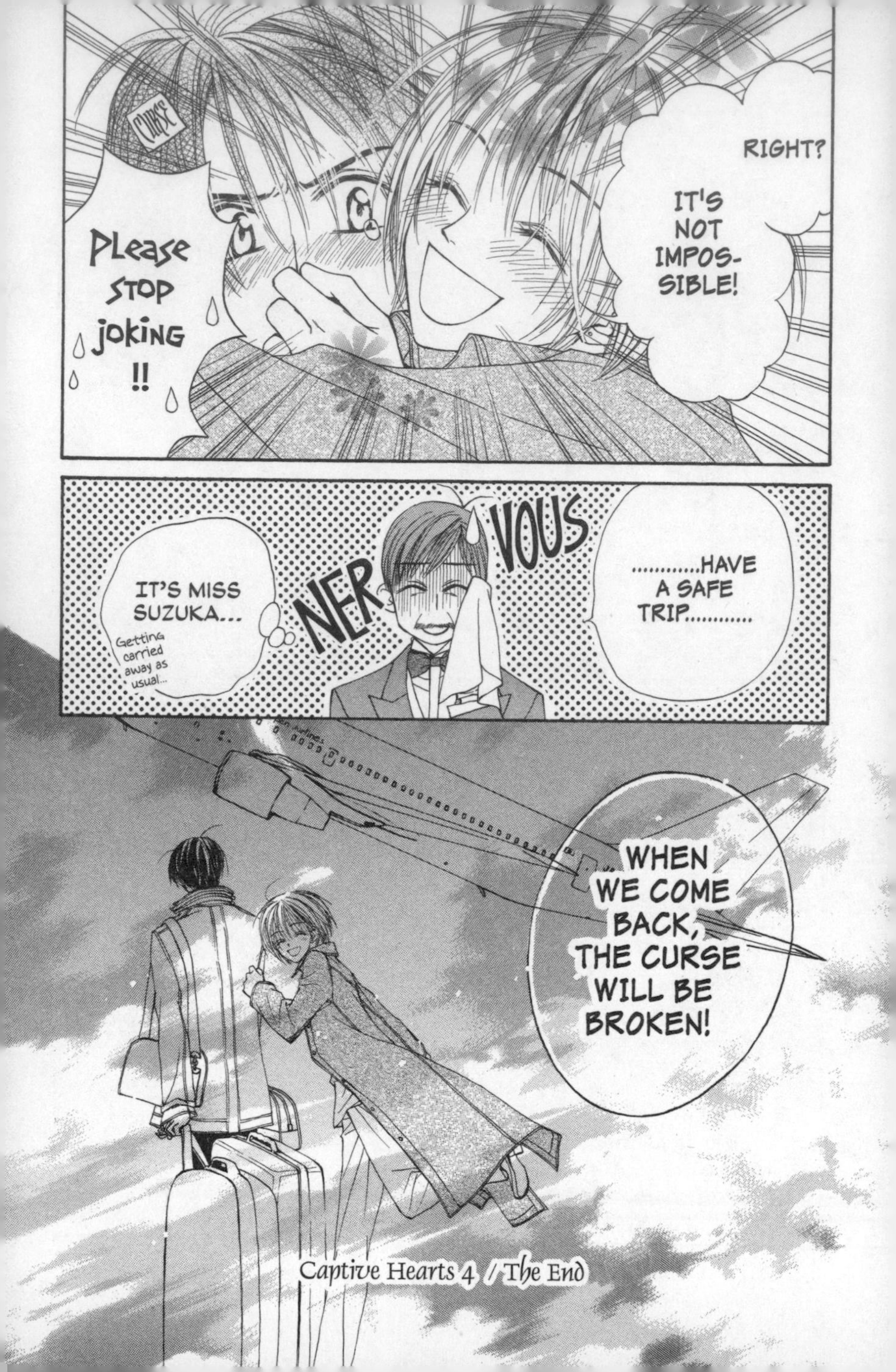
RIGHT?
IT'S NOT IMPOS-SIBLE!
CURSE
Please stop joking !!
............HAVE A SAFE TRIP............
NERVOUS
IT'S MISS SUZUKA...
Getting carried away as usual...
WHEN WE COME BACK, THE CURSE WILL BE BROKEN!
Captive Hearts 4 / The End

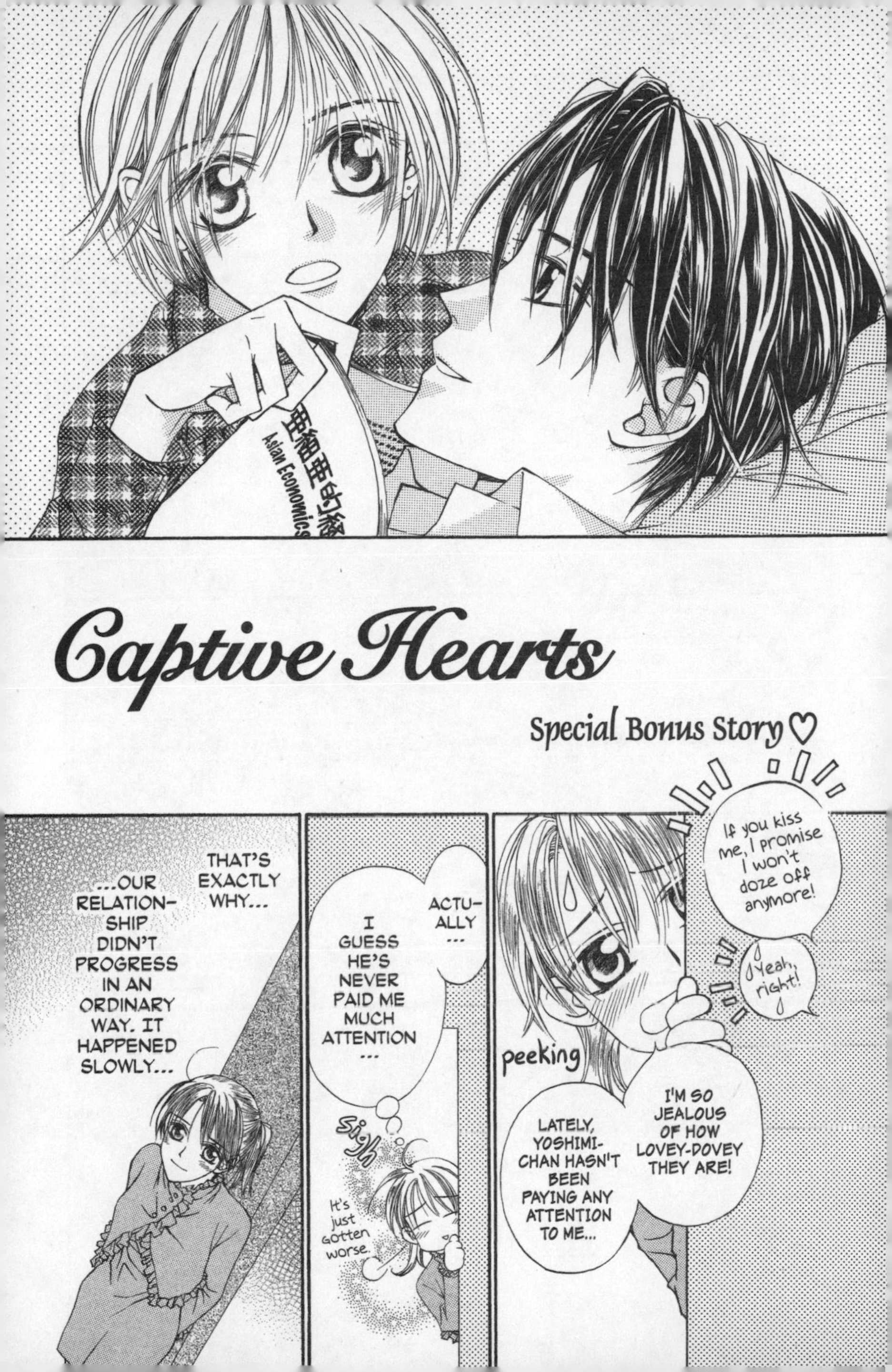
Asian Economics
Captive Hearts
Special Bonus Story ♡
If you kiss me, I promise I won't doze off anymore!
Yeah, right!
peeking
I'M SO JEALOUS OF HOW LOVEY-DOVEY THEY ARE!
LATELY, YOSHIMI-CHAN HASN'T BEEN PAYING ANY ATTENTION TO ME...
ACTU-ALLY...
I GUESS HE'S NEVER PAID ME MUCH ATTENTION...
Sigh
It's just gotten worse.
THAT'S EXACTLY WHY...
...OUR RELATION-SHIP DIDN'T PROGRESS IN AN ORDINARY WAY. IT HAPPENED SLOWLY...

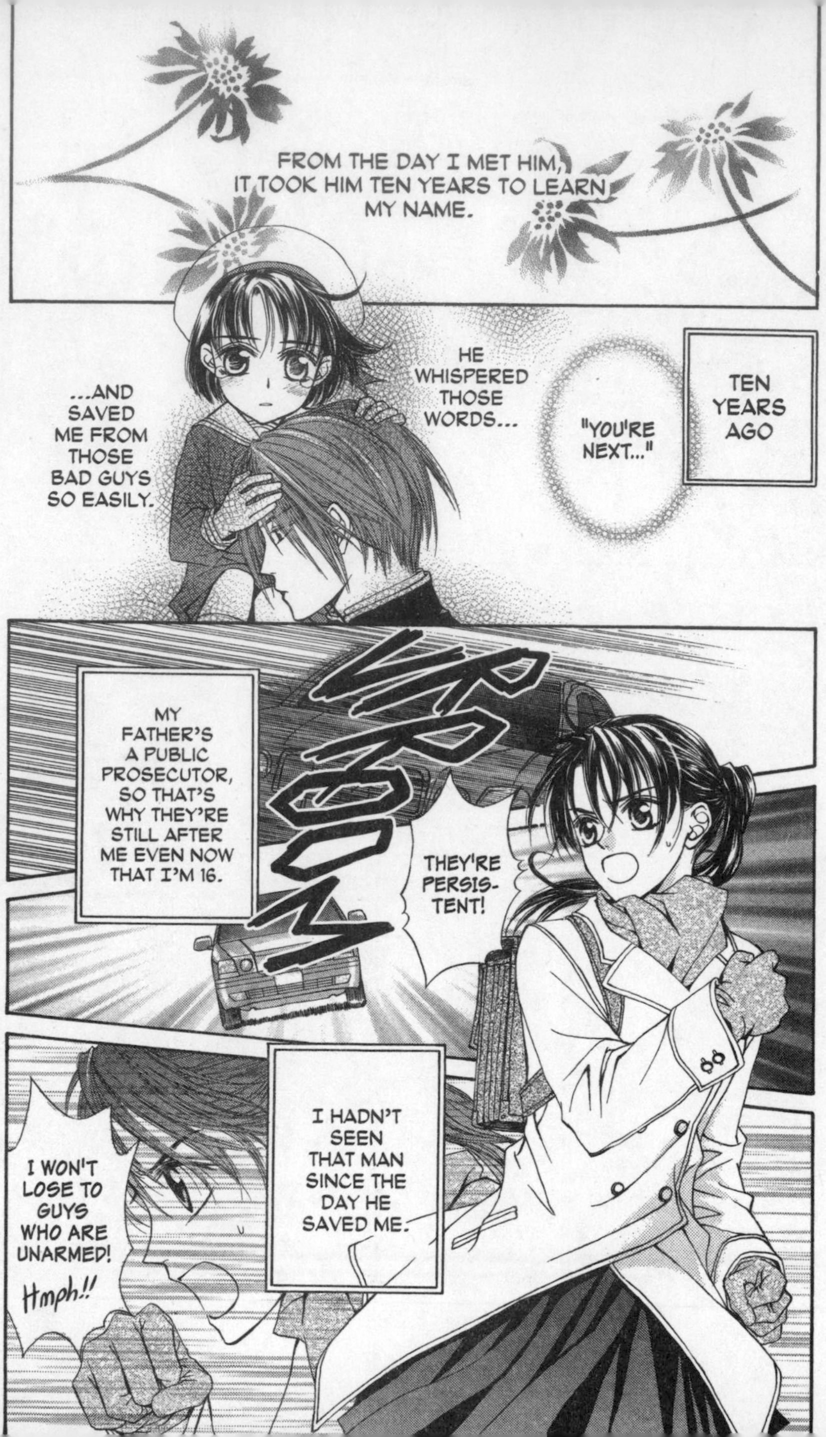
FROM THE DAY I MET HIM, IT TOOK HIM TEN YEARS TO LEARN MY NAME.
TEN YEARS AGO
"YOU'RE NEXT..."
HE WHISPERED THOSE WORDS...
...AND SAVED ME FROM THOSE BAD GUYS SO EASILY.
VROOM
THEY'RE PERSIS-TENT!
MY FATHER'S A PUBLIC PROSECUTOR, SO THAT'S WHY THEY'RE STILL AFTER ME EVEN NOW THAT I'M 16.
I HADN'T SEEN THAT MAN SINCE THE DAY HE SAVED ME.
I WON'T LOSE TO GUYS WHO ARE UNARMED!
Hmph!!

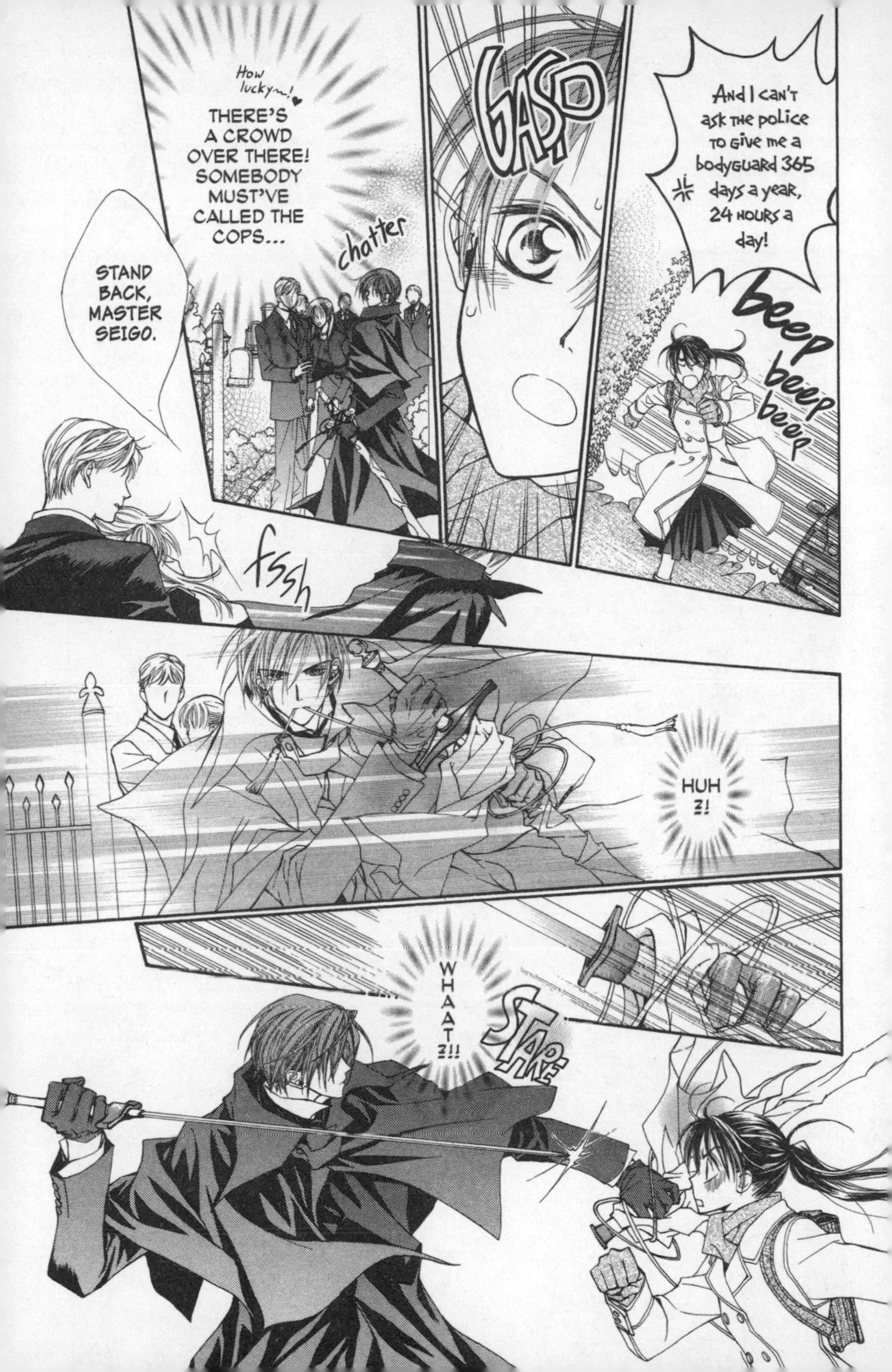
And I can't ask the police to give me a bodyguard 365 days a year, 24 hours a day!
beep beep beep
GASP
THERE'S A CROWD OVER THERE! SOMEBODY MUST'VE CALLED THE COPS...
How lucky~!
chatter
STAND BACK, MASTER SEIGO.
fssh
HUH?!
WHAAT?!!

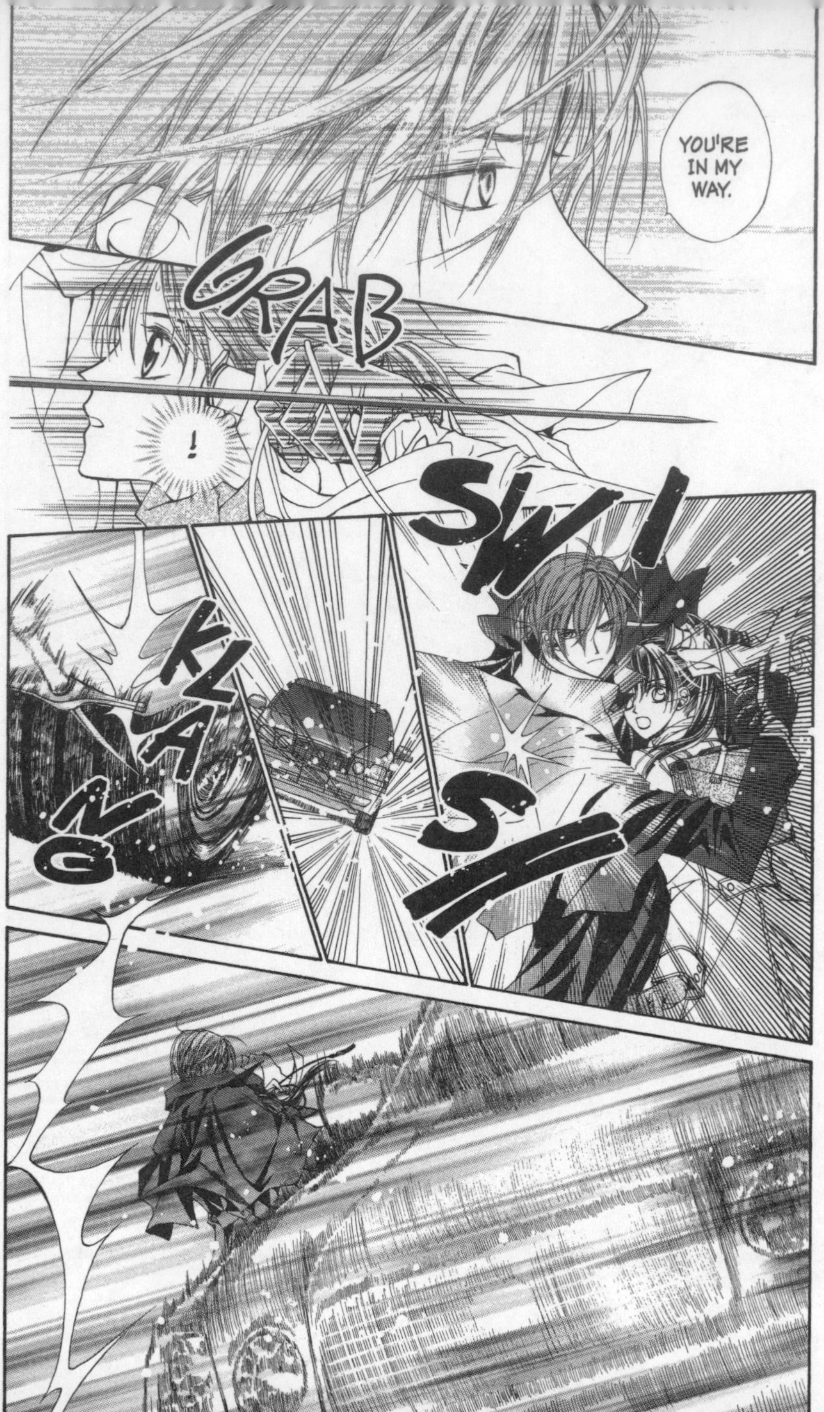
YOU'RE IN MY WAY.
GRAB
!
SWISH
KLANG

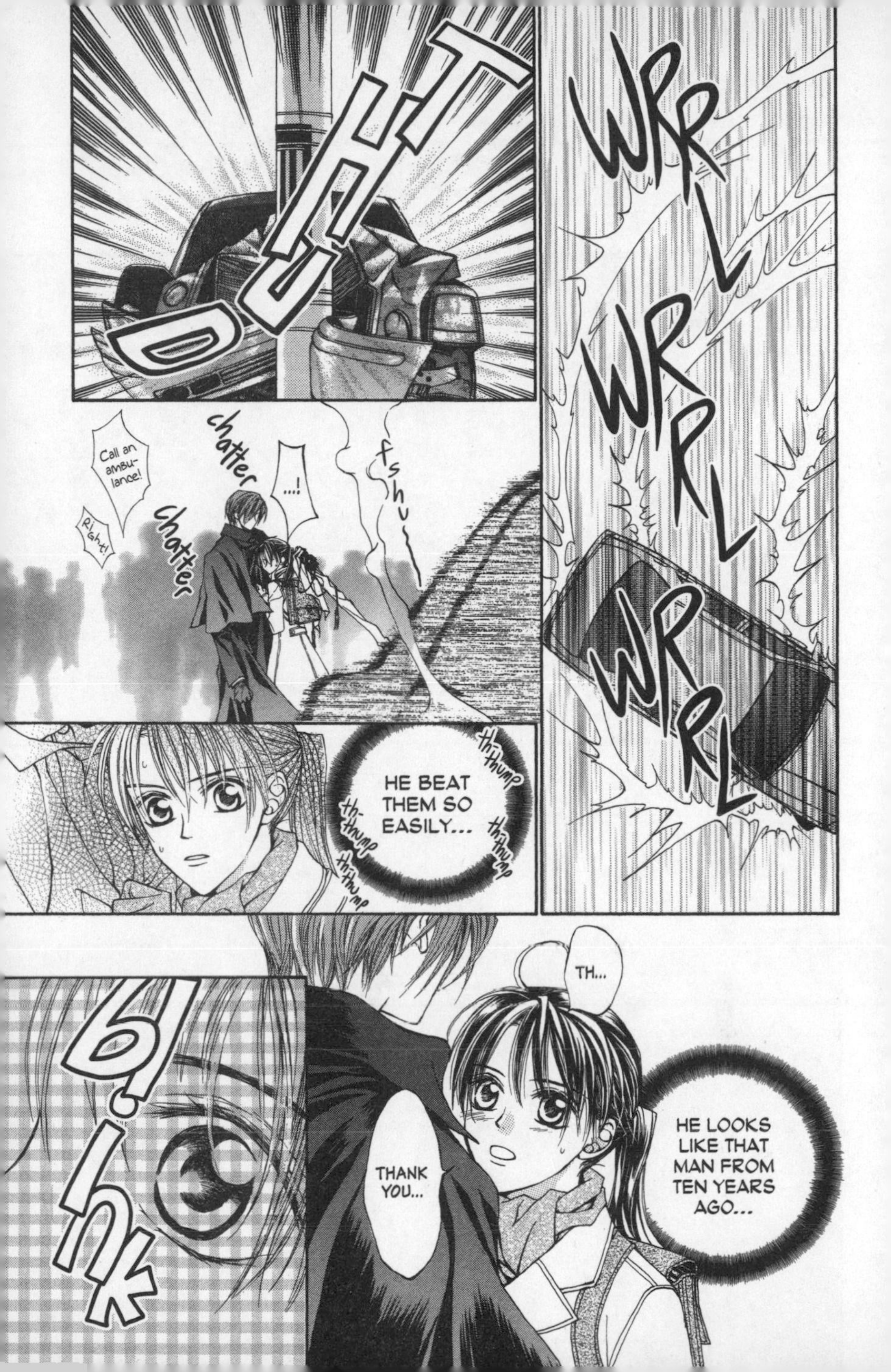

WRRL WRRL WRRL
THUD
fshu~
...!
chatter chatter
Call an ambulance!
Right!
th-thump th-thump th-thump th-thump
HE BEAT THEM SO EASILY...
TH...
THANK YOU...
HE LOOKS LIKE THAT MAN FROM TEN YEARS AGO...
blink

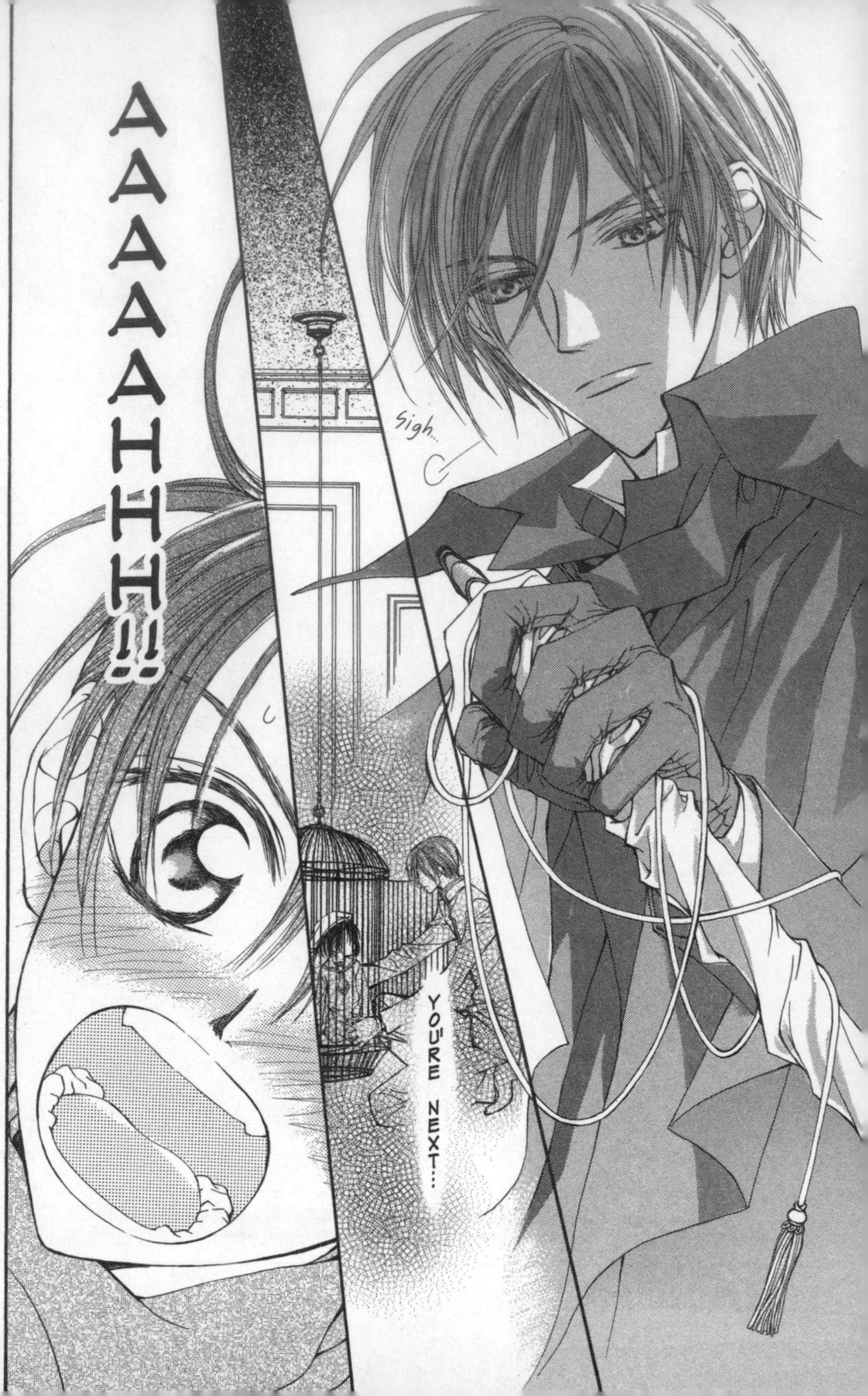
Sigh...
YOU'RE NEXT...
AAAAAHHH!!

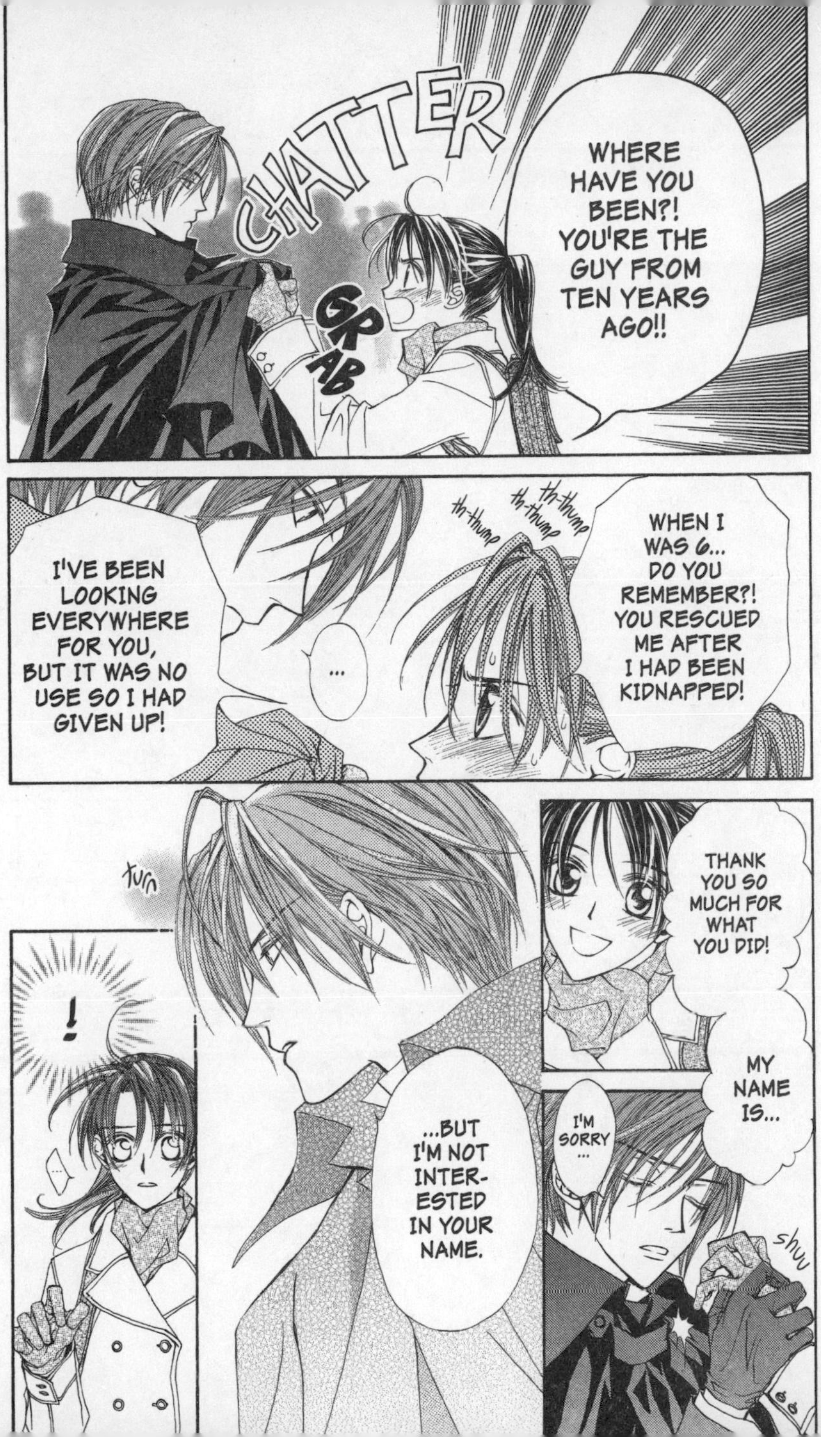
WHERE HAVE YOU BEEN?! YOU'RE THE GUY FROM TEN YEARS AGO!!
CHATTER
GRAB
th-thump th-thump
th-thump
WHEN I WAS 6... DO YOU REMEMBER?! YOU RESCUED ME AFTER I HAD BEEN KIDNAPPED!
...
I'VE BEEN LOOKING EVERYWHERE FOR YOU, BUT IT WAS NO USE SO I HAD GIVEN UP!
THANK YOU SO MUCH FOR WHAT YOU DID!
MY NAME IS...
I'M SORRY...
shuu
turn
...BUT I'M NOT INTER-ESTED IN YOUR NAME.
!
...

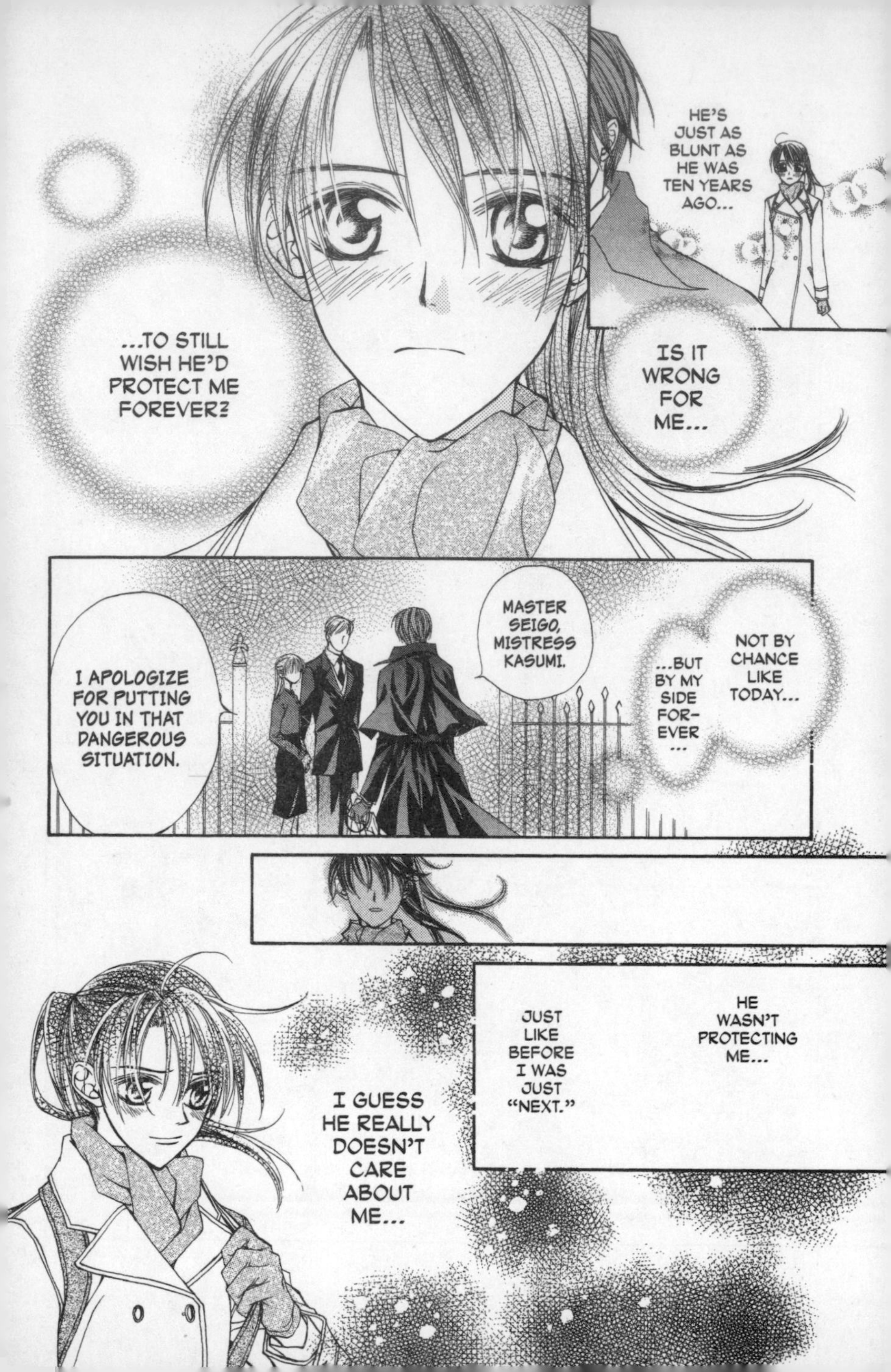
HE'S JUST AS BLUNT AS HE WAS TEN YEARS AGO...
IS IT WRONG FOR ME...
...TO STILL WISH HE'D PROTECT ME FOREVER?
NOT BY CHANCE LIKE TODAY...
...BUT BY MY SIDE FOR-EVER...
MASTER SEIGO, MISTRESS KASUMI.
I APOLOGIZE FOR PUTTING YOU IN THAT DANGEROUS SITUATION.
HE WASN'T PROTECTING ME...
JUST LIKE BEFORE I WAS JUST "NEXT."
I GUESS HE REALLY DOESN'T CARE ABOUT ME...

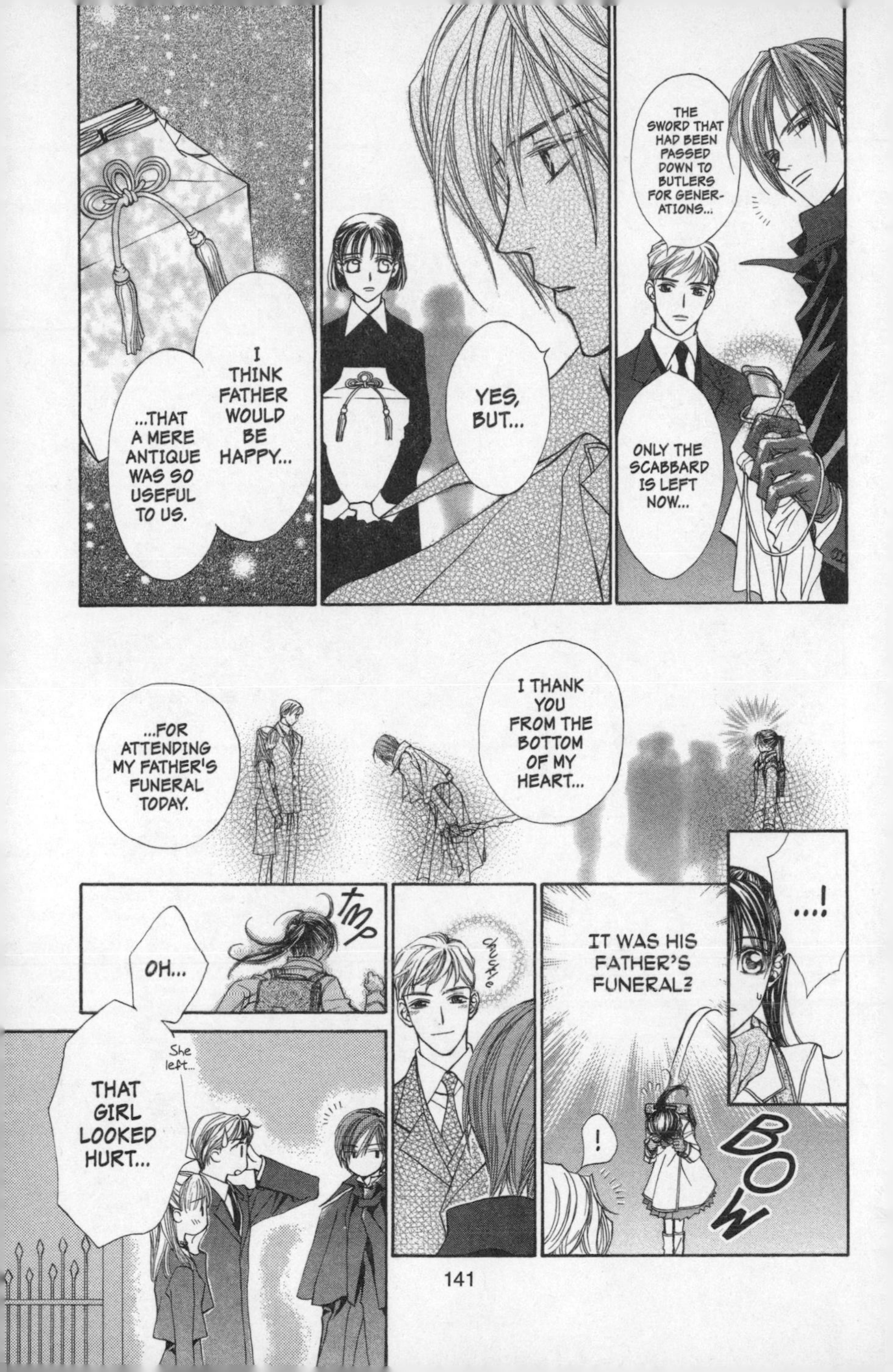
THE SWORD THAT HAD BEEN PASSED DOWN TO BUTLERS FOR GENERATIONS...
ONLY THE SCABBARD IS LEFT NOW...
YES, BUT...
I THINK FATHER WOULD BE HAPPY...
...THAT A MERE ANTIQUE WAS SO USEFUL TO US.
I THANK YOU FROM THE BOTTOM OF MY HEART...
...FOR ATTENDING MY FATHER'S FUNERAL TODAY.
...!
IT WAS HIS FATHER'S FUNERAL?
BOW
!
chuckle
tmp
OH...
She left...
THAT GIRL LOOKED HURT...

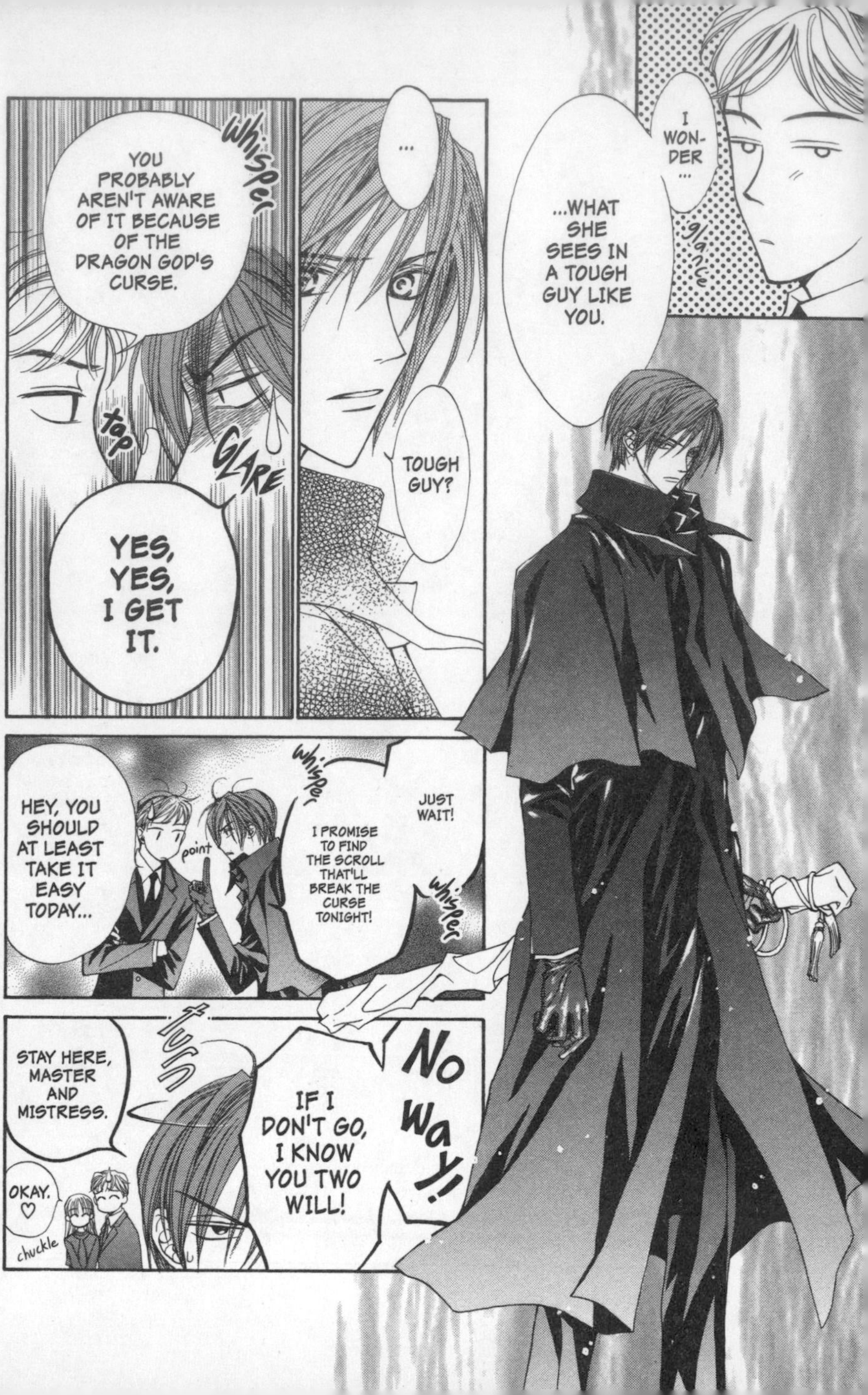
I WONDER...
glance
...WHAT SHE SEES IN A TOUGH GUY LIKE YOU.
...
TOUGH GUY?
whisper
YOU PROBABLY AREN'T AWARE OF IT BECAUSE OF THE DRAGON GOD'S CURSE.
tap
GLARE
YES, YES, I GET IT.
whisper
JUST WAIT!
I PROMISE TO FIND THE SCROLL THAT'LL BREAK THE CURSE TONIGHT!
whisper
HEY, YOU SHOULD AT LEAST TAKE IT EASY TODAY...
point
No way!
IF I DON'T GO, I KNOW YOU TWO WILL!
turn
STAY HERE, MASTER AND MISTRESS.
OKAY. ♡
chuckle

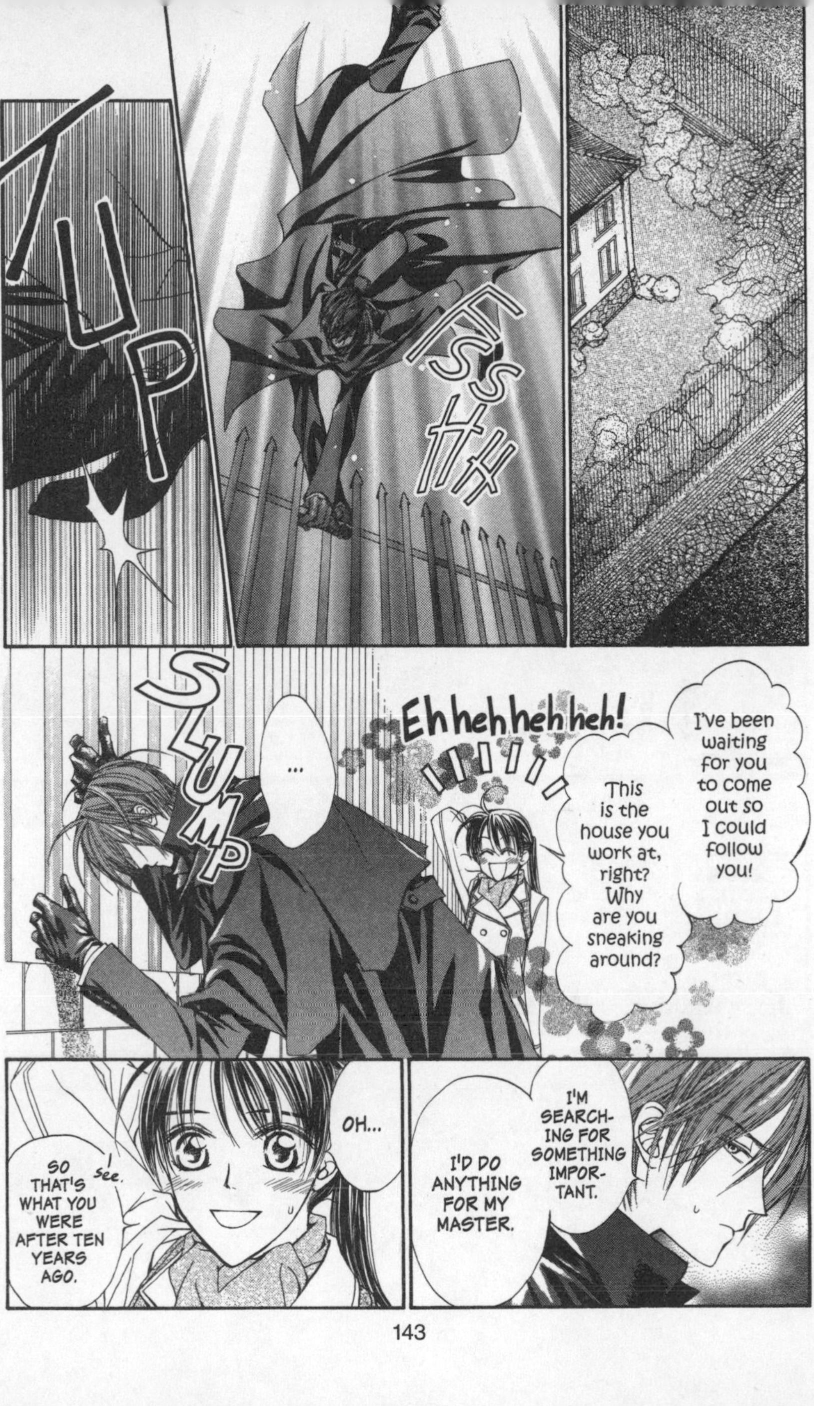
FSSHH
TUP
I've been waiting for you to come out so I could follow you!
This is the house you work at, right? Why are you sneaking around?
Eh heh heh heh!
...
SLUMP
I'M SEARCHING FOR SOMETHING IMPORTANT.
I'D DO ANYTHING FOR MY MASTER.
OH...
I see.
SO THAT'S WHAT YOU WERE AFTER TEN YEARS AGO.

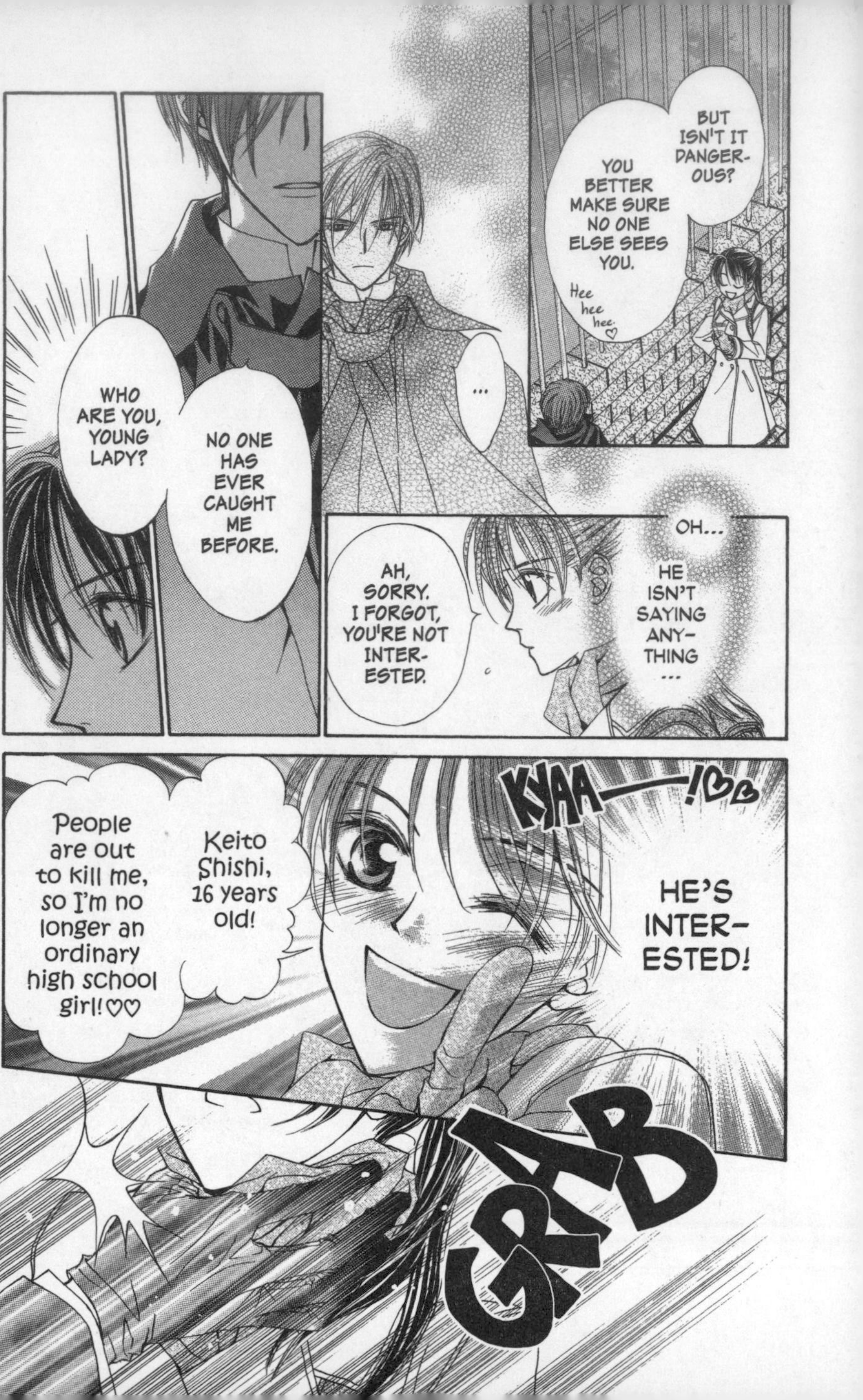
BUT ISN'T IT DANGER-OUS?
YOU BETTER MAKE SURE NO ONE ELSE SEES YOU.
Hee hee hee♡
...
OH...
HE ISN'T SAYING ANY-THING...
AH, SORRY. I FORGOT, YOU'RE NOT INTER-ESTED.
WHO ARE YOU, YOUNG LADY?
NO ONE HAS EVER CAUGHT ME BEFORE.
KYAA—!♡♡
HE'S INTER-ESTED!
Keito Shishi, 16 years old!
People are out to kill me, so I'm no longer an ordinary high school girl!♡♡
GRAB

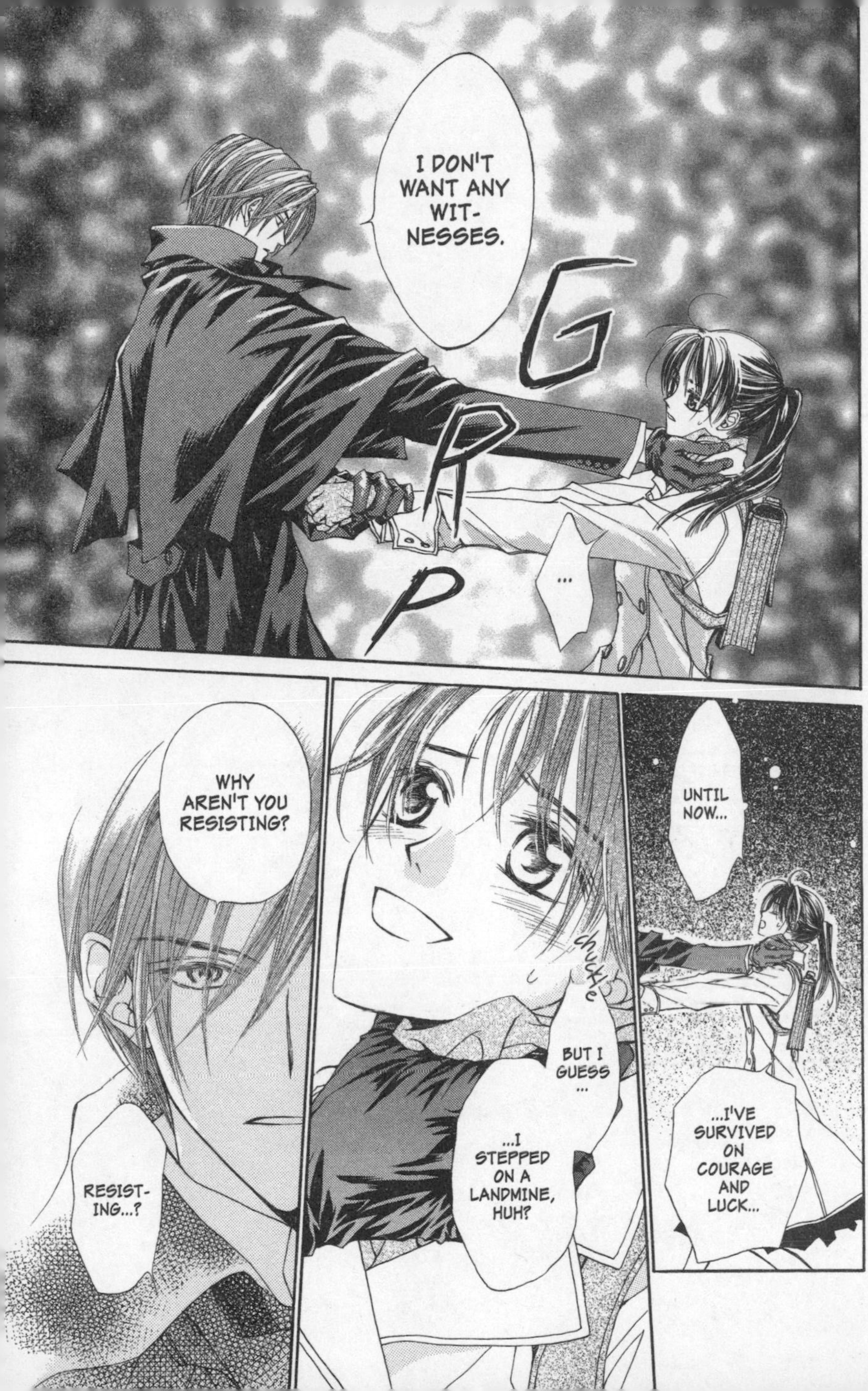
I DON'T WANT ANY WIT-NESSES.
GRIP
...
UNTIL NOW...
...I'VE SURVIVED ON COURAGE AND LUCK...
chuckle
BUT I GUESS ...
...I STEPPED ON A LANDMINE, HUH?
WHY AREN'T YOU RESISTING?
RESIST-ING...?

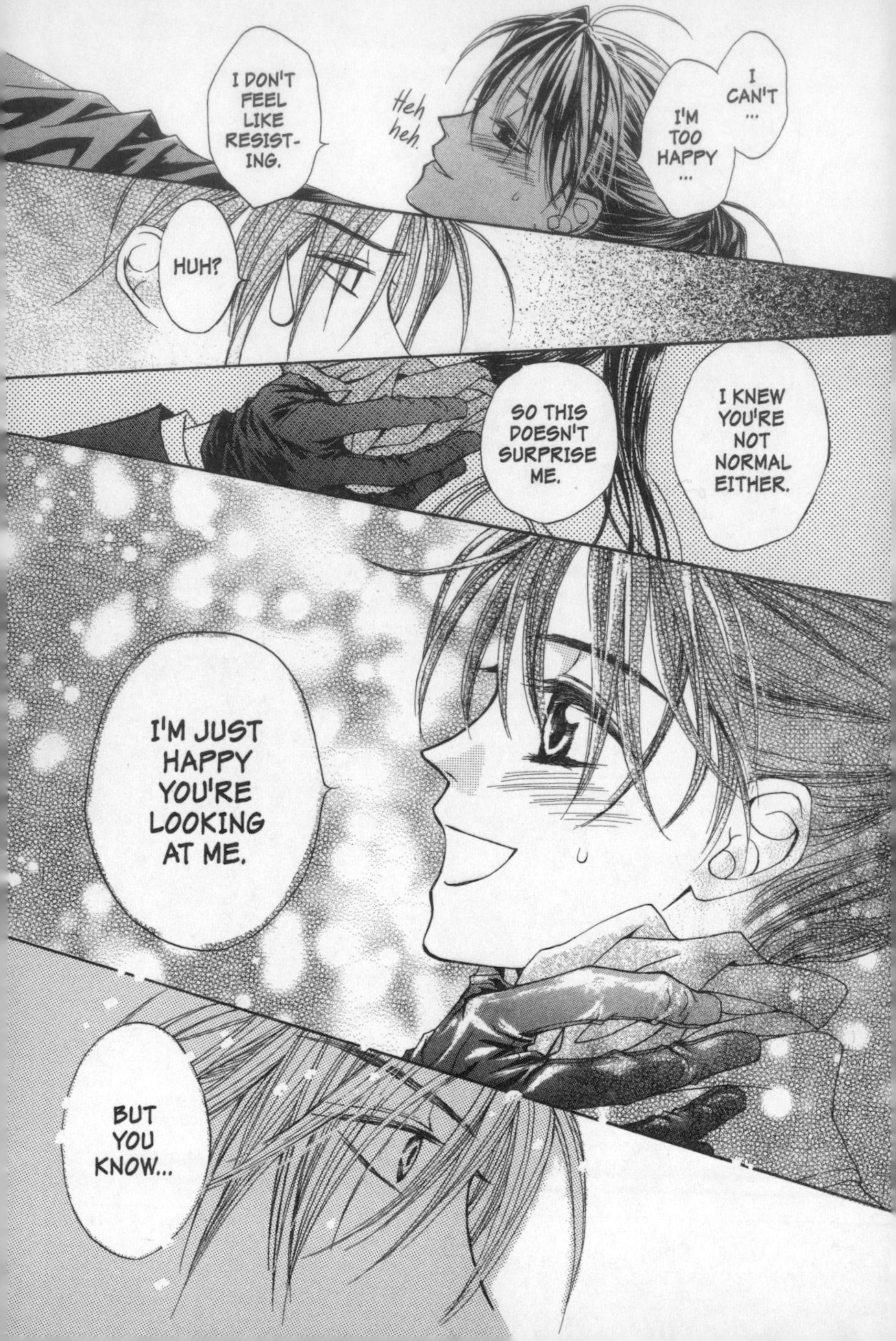
I CAN'T ...
I'M TOO HAPPY ...
Heh heh.
I DON'T FEEL LIKE RESIST-ING.
HUH?
I KNEW YOU'RE NOT NORMAL EITHER.
SO THIS DOESN'T SURPRISE ME.
I'M JUST HAPPY YOU'RE LOOKING AT ME.
BUT YOU KNOW...

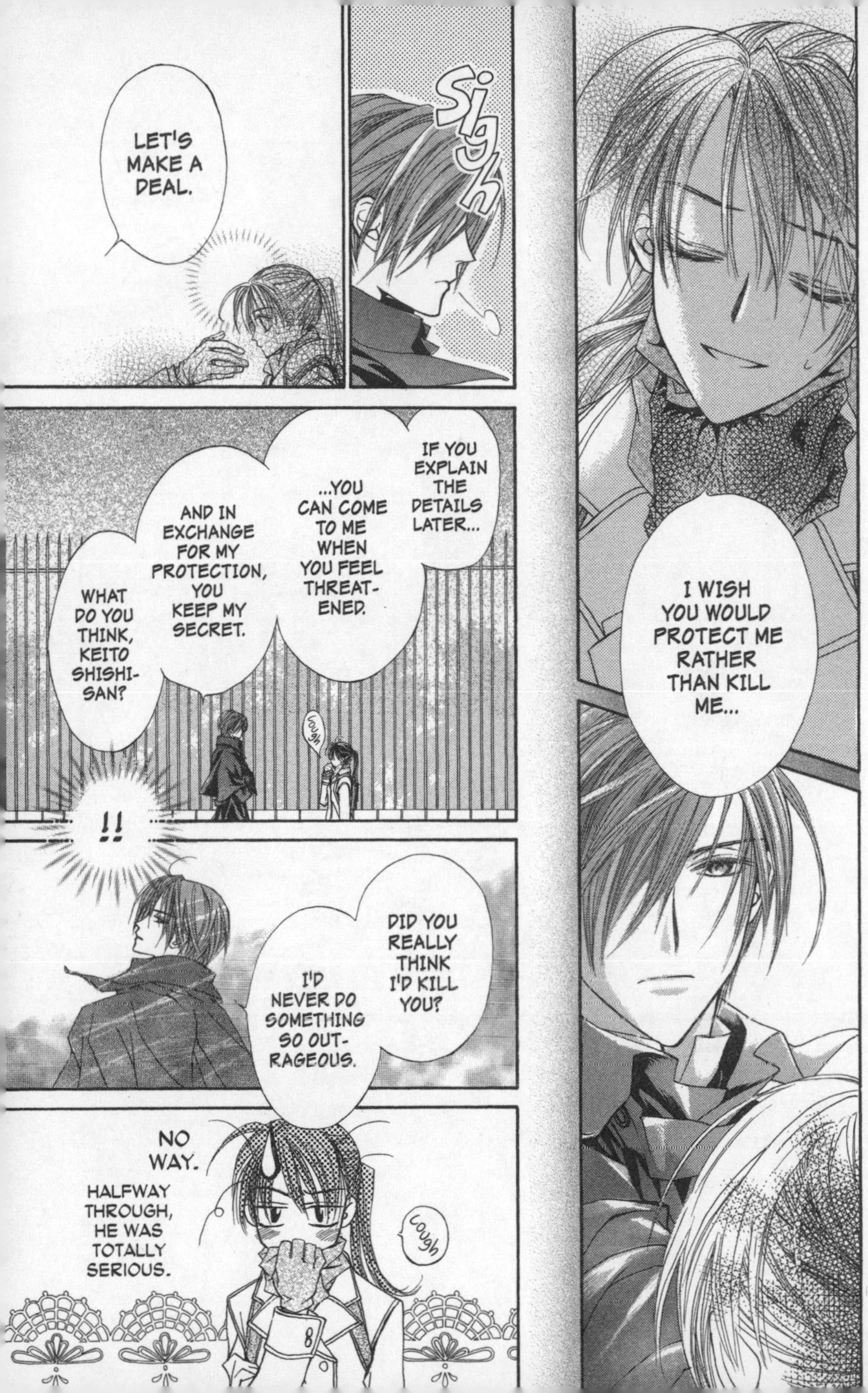
I WISH YOU WOULD PROTECT ME RATHER THAN KILL ME...
Sigh
LET'S MAKE A DEAL.
IF YOU EXPLAIN THE DETAILS LATER...
...YOU CAN COME TO ME WHEN YOU FEEL THREAT-ENED.
AND IN EXCHANGE FOR MY PROTECTION, YOU KEEP MY SECRET.
WHAT DO YOU THINK, KEITO SHISHI-SAN?
cough
!!
DID YOU REALLY THINK I'D KILL YOU?
I'D NEVER DO SOMETHING SO OUT-RAGEOUS.
cough
NO WAY.
HALFWAY THROUGH, HE WAS TOTALLY SERIOUS.

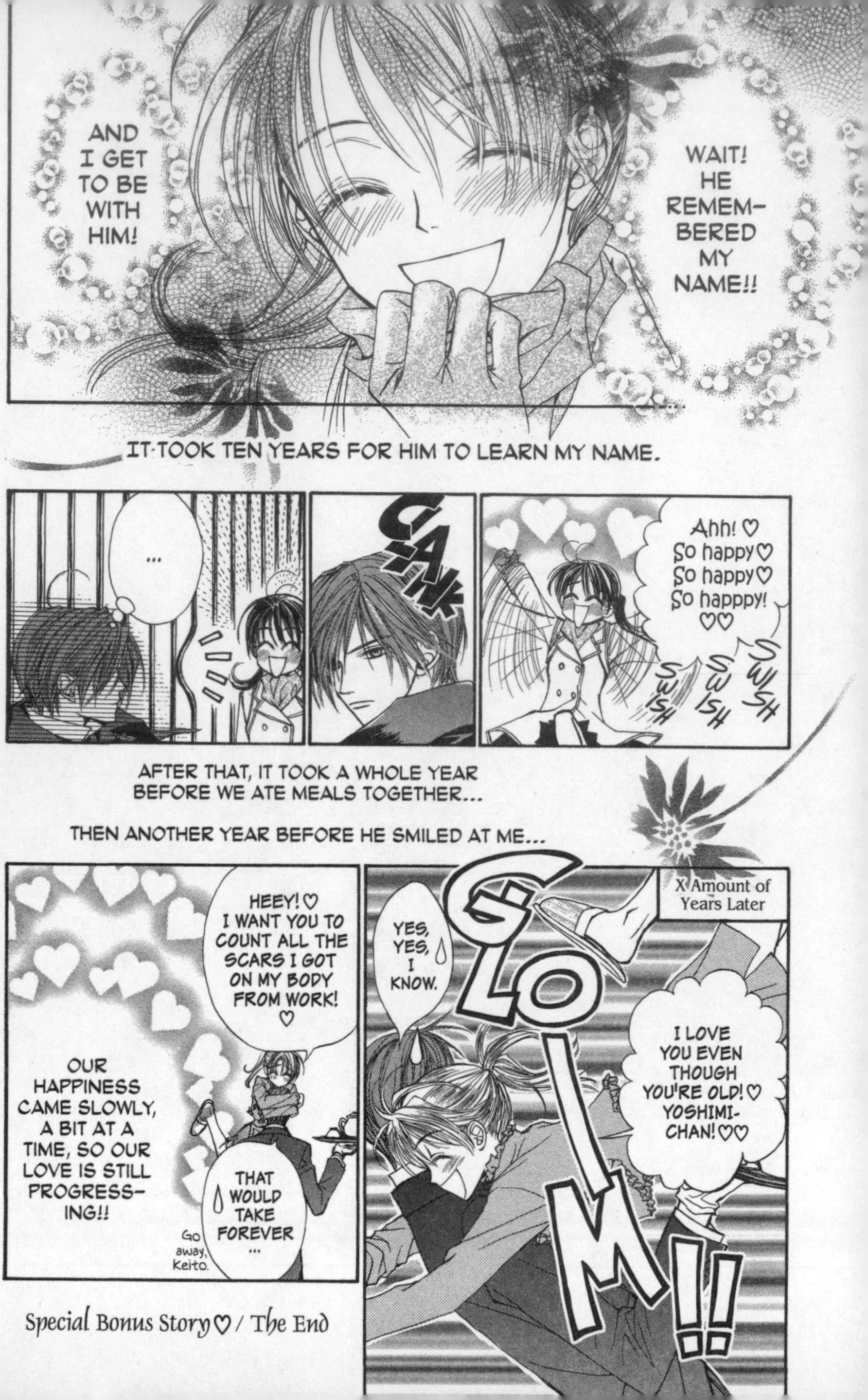
WAIT! HE REMEM-BERED MY NAME!!
AND I GET TO BE WITH HIM!
IT TOOK TEN YEARS FOR HIM TO LEARN MY NAME.
Ahh! ♡ So happy♡ So happy♡ So happpy! ♡♡
SWISH SWISH SWISH
CLANK
...
AFTER THAT, IT TOOK A WHOLE YEAR BEFORE WE ATE MEALS TOGETHER...
THEN ANOTHER YEAR BEFORE HE SMILED AT ME...
X Amount of Years Later
GLOMP!!
I LOVE YOU EVEN THOUGH YOU'RE OLD! ♡ YOSHIMI-CHAN! ♡♡
YES, YES, I KNOW.
HEEY! ♡ I WANT YOU TO COUNT ALL THE SCARS I GOT ON MY BODY FROM WORK! ♡
OUR HAPPINESS CAME SLOWLY, A BIT AT A TIME, SO OUR LOVE IS STILL PROGRESS-ING!!
THAT WOULD TAKE FOREVER...
Go away, Keito.

Special Bonus Story ♡ / The End

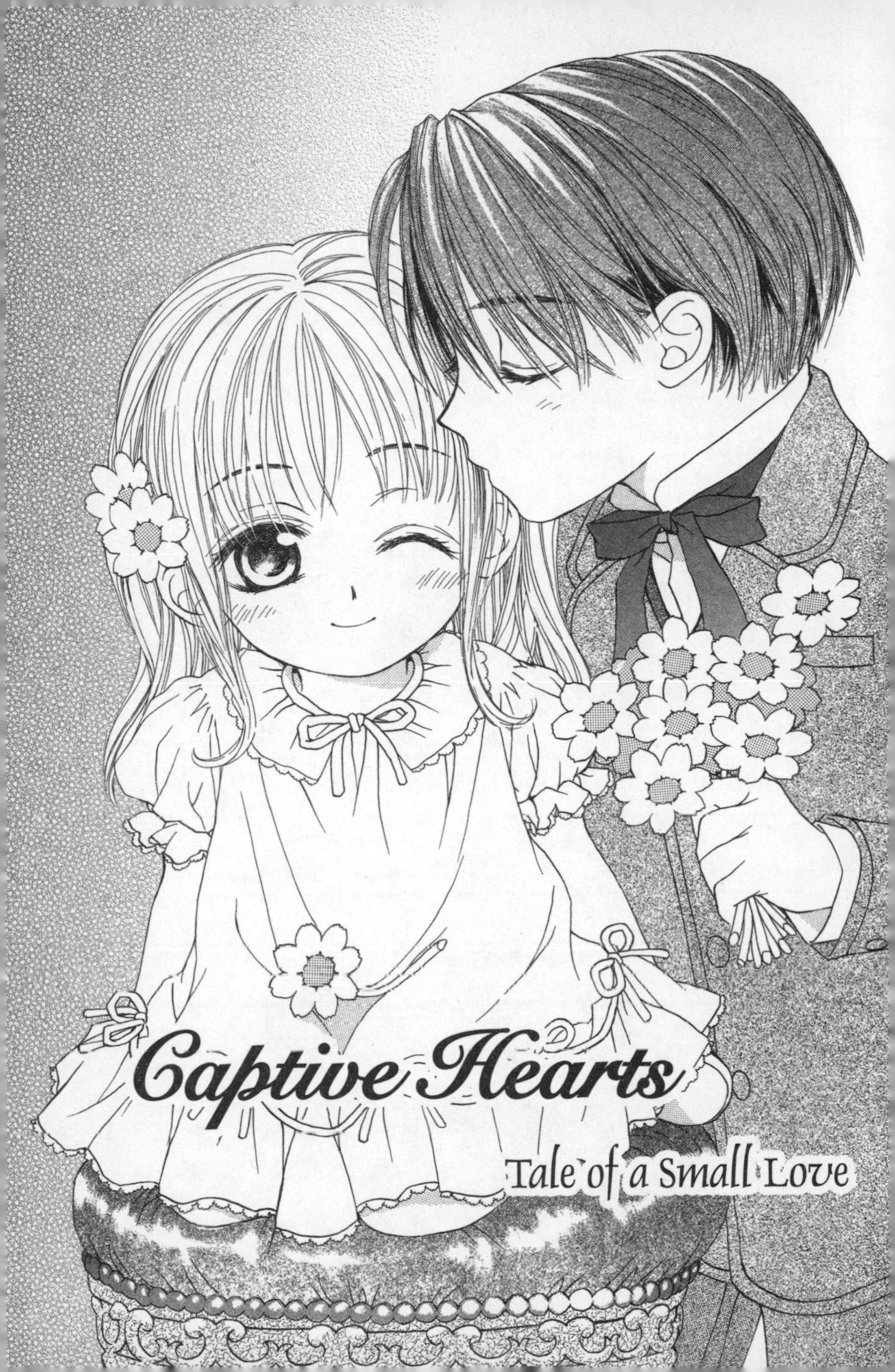
Captive Hearts
Tale of a Small Love

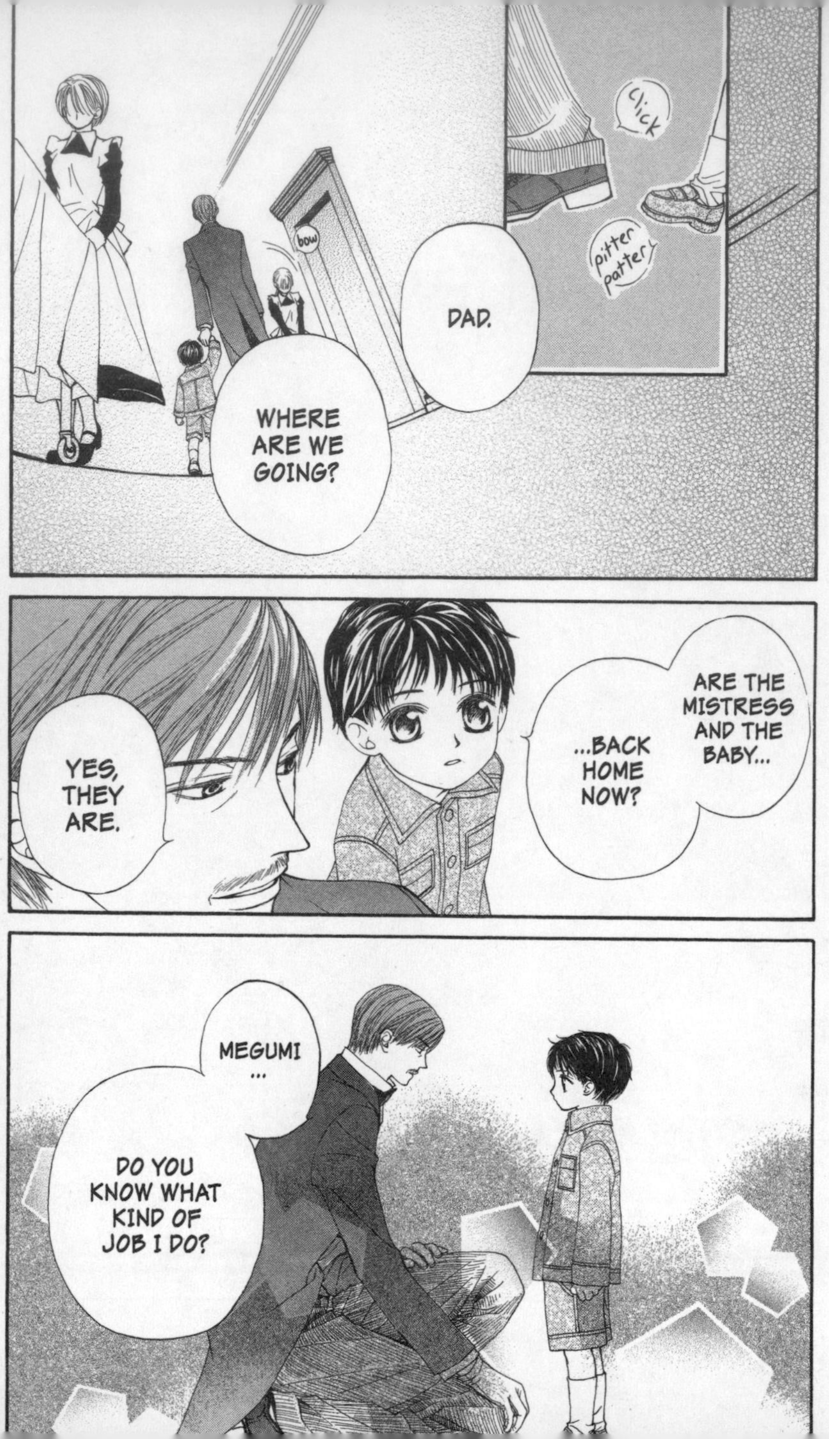
click
pitter patter
DAD.
WHERE ARE WE GOING?
bow
ARE THE MISTRESS AND THE BABY...
...BACK HOME NOW?
YES, THEY ARE.
MEGUMI...
DO YOU KNOW WHAT KIND OF JOB I DO?

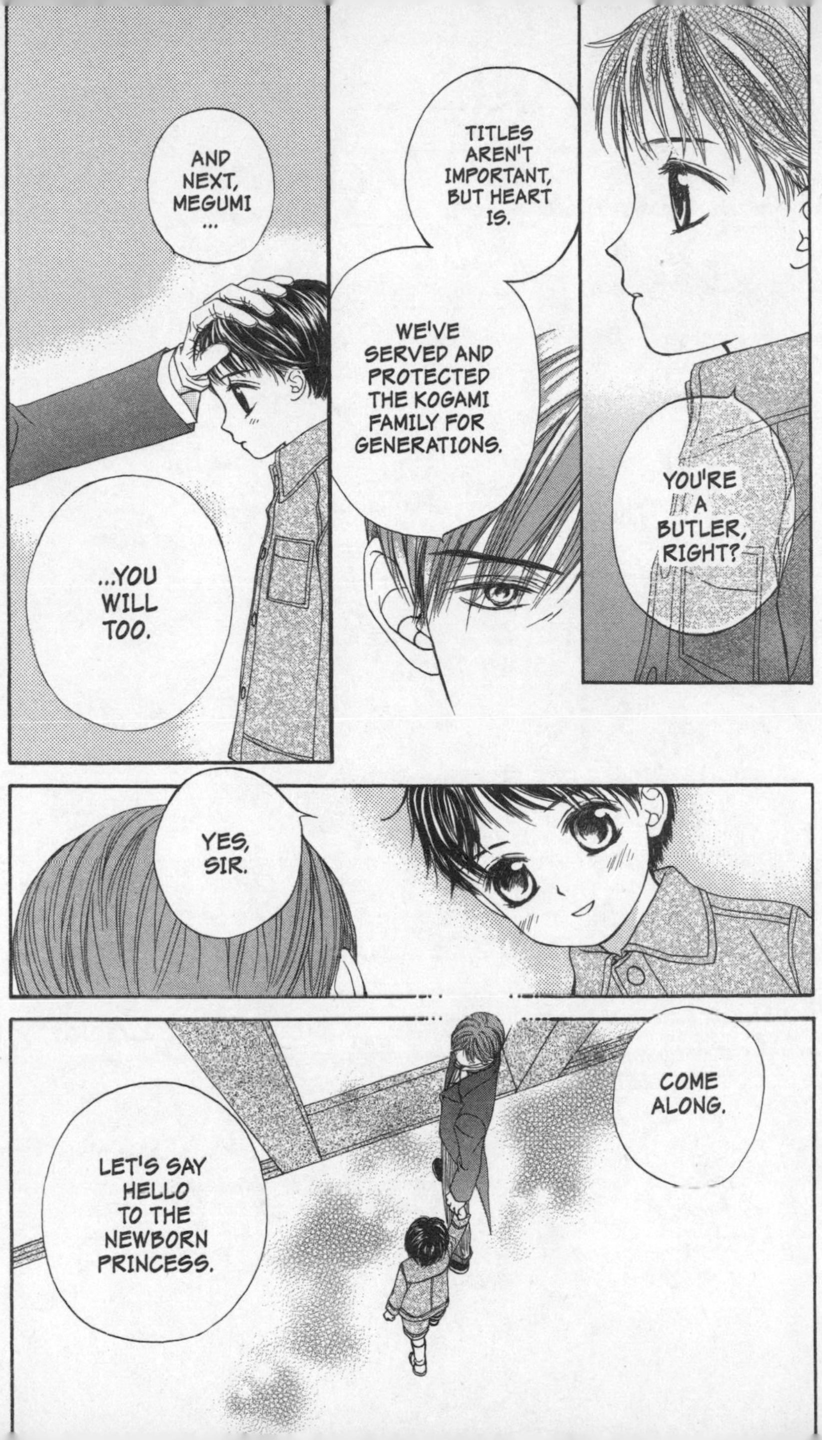
YOU'RE A BUTLER, RIGHT?
TITLES AREN'T IMPORTANT, BUT HEART IS.
WE'VE SERVED AND PROTECTED THE KOGAMI FAMILY FOR GENERATIONS.
AND NEXT, MEGUMI ...
...YOU WILL TOO.
YES, SIR.
COME ALONG.
LET'S SAY HELLO TO THE NEWBORN PRINCESS.

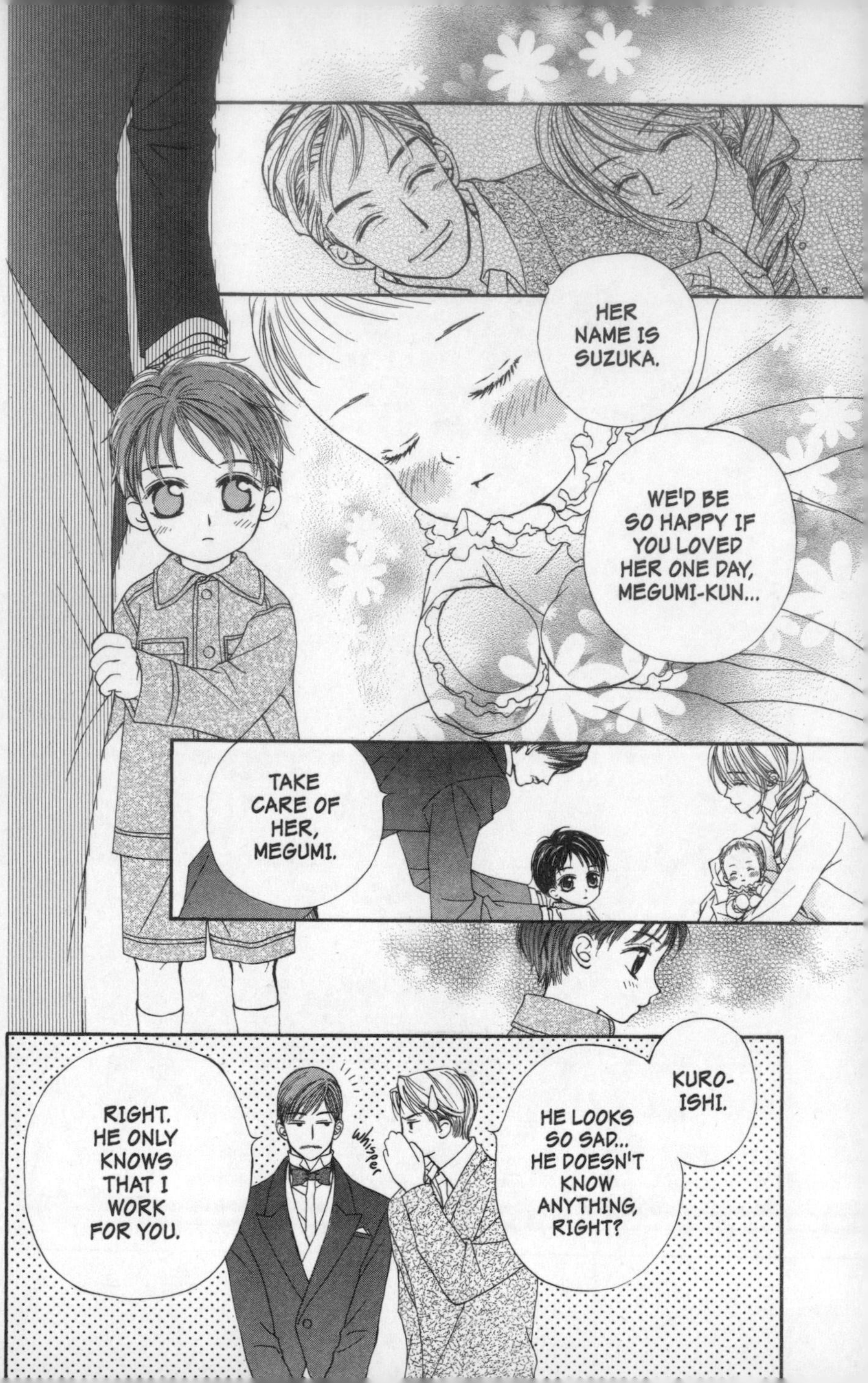
HER NAME IS SUZUKA.
WE'D BE SO HAPPY IF YOU LOVED HER ONE DAY, MEGUMI-KUN...
TAKE CARE OF HER, MEGUMI.
KURO-ISHI.
HE LOOKS SO SAD... HE DOESN'T KNOW ANYTHING, RIGHT?
whisper
RIGHT. HE ONLY KNOWS THAT I WORK FOR YOU.

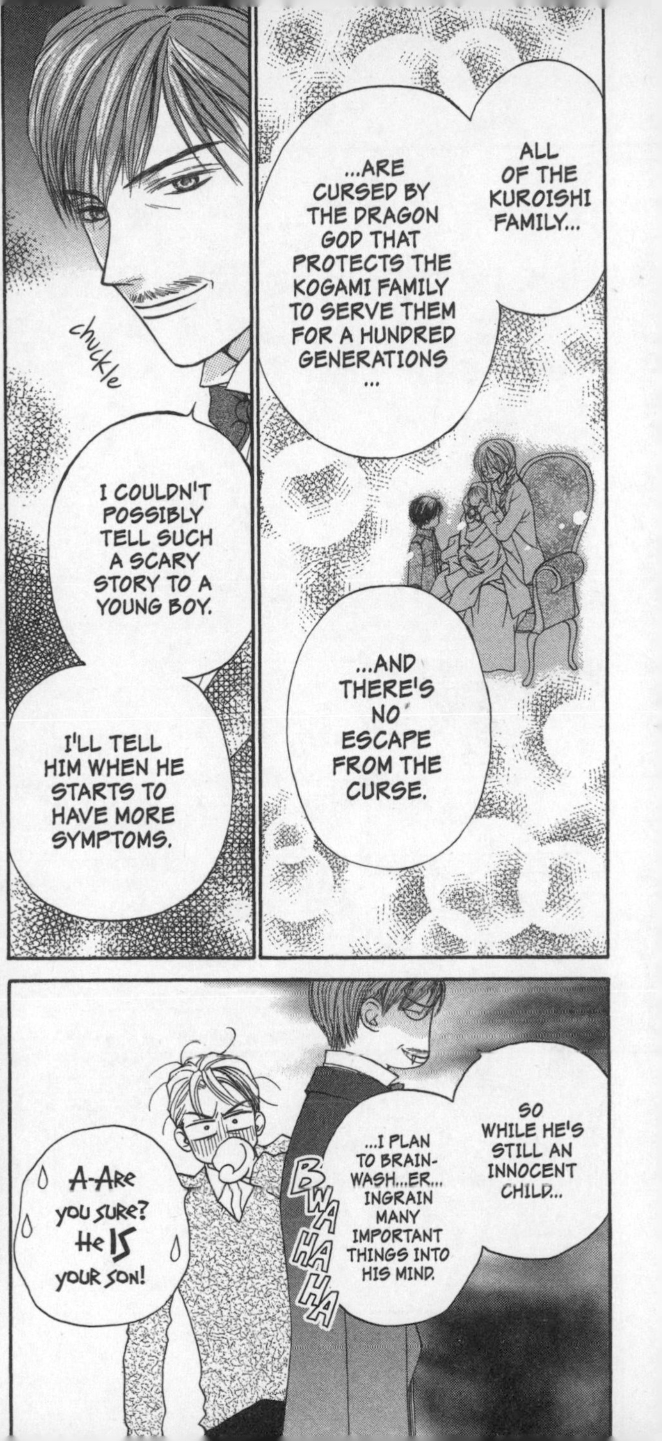
ALL OF THE KUROISHI FAMILY...
...ARE CURSED BY THE DRAGON GOD THAT PROTECTS THE KOGAMI FAMILY TO SERVE THEM FOR A HUNDRED GENERATIONS ...
...AND THERE'S NO ESCAPE FROM THE CURSE.
chuckle
I COULDN'T POSSIBLY TELL SUCH A SCARY STORY TO A YOUNG BOY.
I'LL TELL HIM WHEN HE STARTS TO HAVE MORE SYMPTOMS.
SO WHILE HE'S STILL AN INNOCENT CHILD...
...I PLAN TO BRAIN-WASH...ER... INGRAIN MANY IMPORTANT THINGS INTO HIS MIND.
BWAHAHAHA
A-Are you sure? He IS your son!

5

I've come this far drawing *Captive Hearts* because of all the readers who support me! I've gotten so much joy in continuing this series, and now as I prepare to write the final volume, I really want to do my best for you...!

I'll try to make it a really enjoyable story. So I'm going to think long and hard about the best way to end it. Or I'll just flip a coin and see what happens. Yeah.

I'm finally breaking into the core of what I envisioned *Captive Hearts* to be (from when it was serialized and how I had planned it). I feel like a countdown has started inside of me towards the final volume. I'm not sure what'll happen! ♪ But I want to keep enjoying it until the very end.

By the way, I had a lot of fun writing these three extra stories. Someone told me they could feel it seeping out from the pages! ♪ (laugh)

This is my last column for this volume, but I wanted to say that even though I haven't answered fan mail in a while, I'm definitely reading it! ♡ If you have any comments, please send them to me!

See you next time!

Matsuri Hino

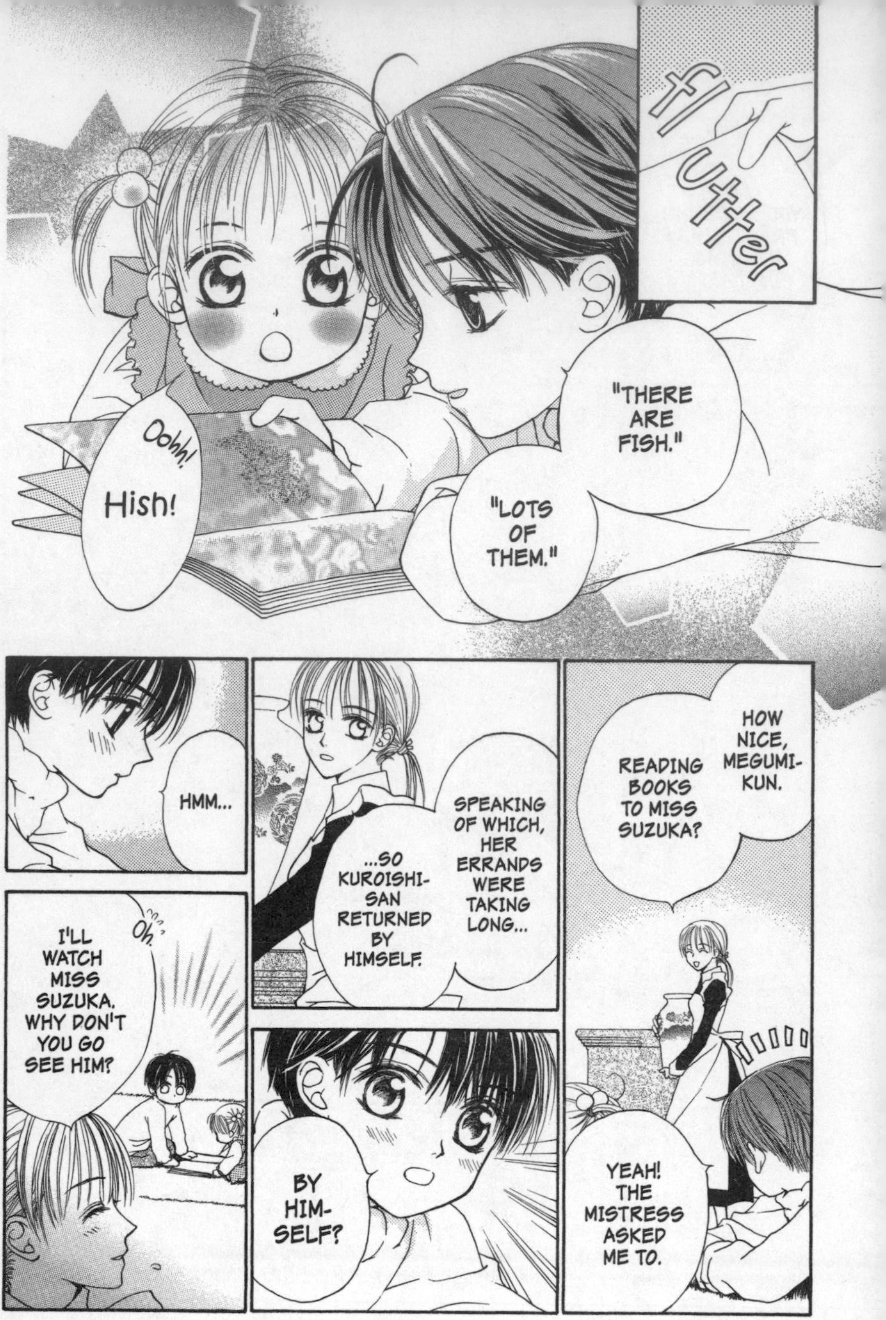
flutter
"THERE ARE FISH."
"LOTS OF THEM."
Oohh!
Hish!
HOW NICE, MEGUMI-KUN.
READING BOOKS TO MISS SUZUKA?
YEAH! THE MISTRESS ASKED ME TO.
SPEAKING OF WHICH, HER ERRANDS WERE TAKING LONG...
...SO KUROISHI-SAN RETURNED BY HIMSELF.
HMM...
BY HIM-SELF?
Oh.
I'LL WATCH MISS SUZUKA. WHY DON'T YOU GO SEE HIM?

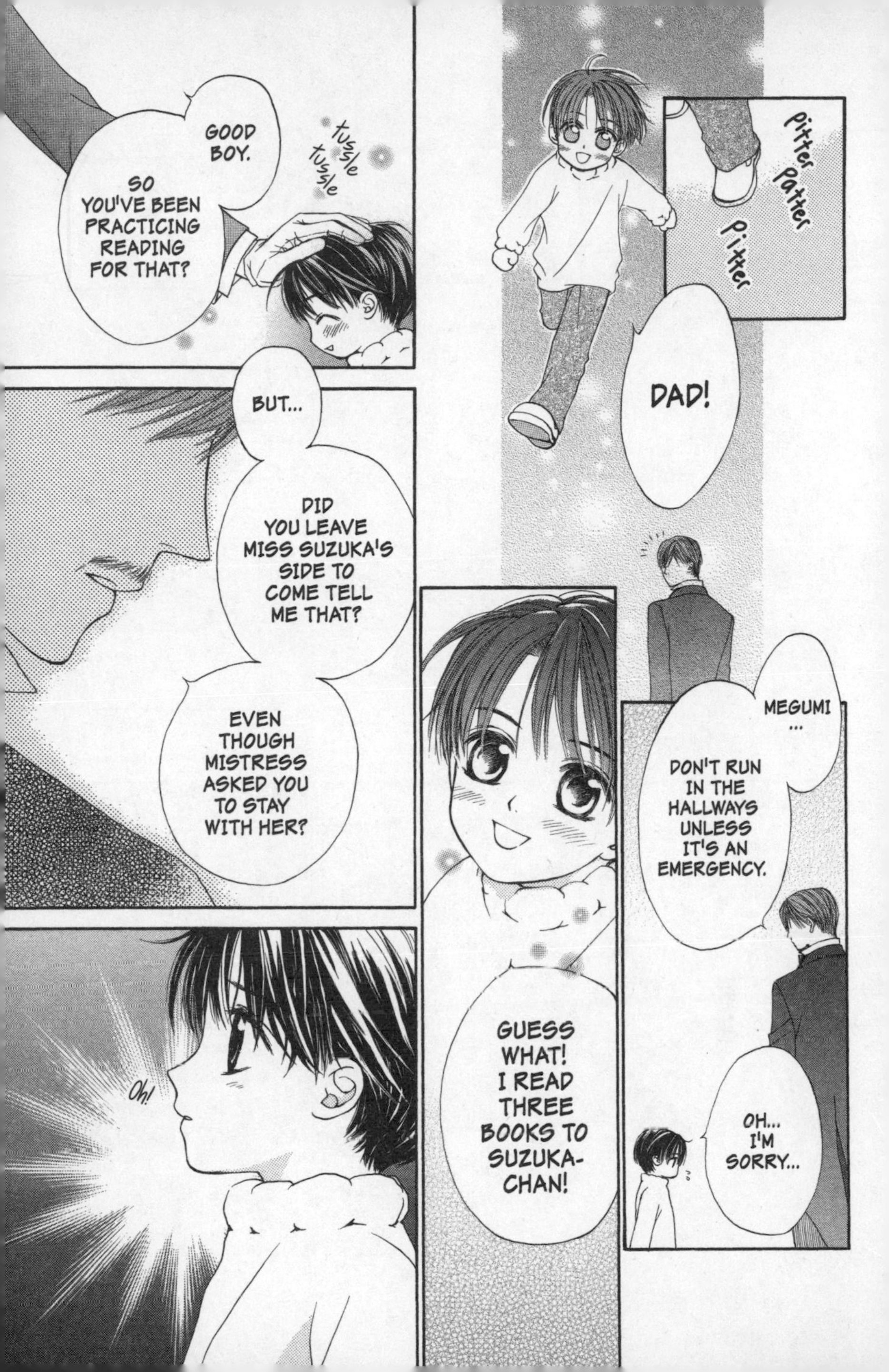
pitter patter pitter
DAD!
MEGUMI...
DON'T RUN IN THE HALLWAYS UNLESS IT'S AN EMERGENCY.
OH... I'M SORRY...
GUESS WHAT! I READ THREE BOOKS TO SUZUKA-CHAN!
GOOD BOY.
SO YOU'VE BEEN PRACTICING READING FOR THAT?
tusle tusle
BUT...
DID YOU LEAVE MISS SUZUKA'S SIDE TO COME TELL ME THAT?
EVEN THOUGH MISTRESS ASKED YOU TO STAY WITH HER?
Oh!

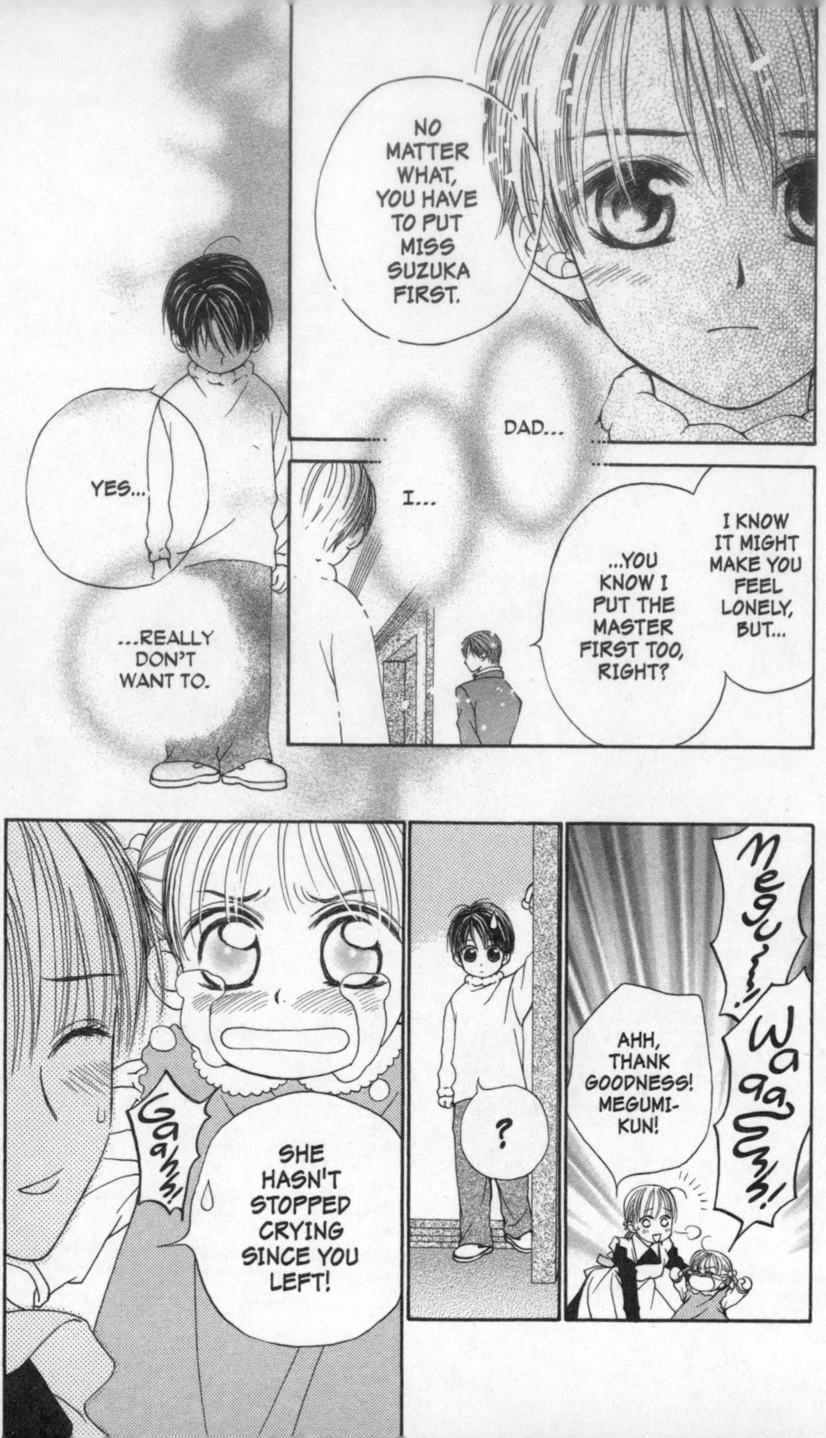
NO MATTER WHAT, YOU HAVE TO PUT MISS SUZUKA FIRST.
DAD...
I KNOW IT MIGHT MAKE YOU FEEL LONELY, BUT...
...YOU KNOW I PUT THE MASTER FIRST TOO, RIGHT?
I...
YES...
...REALLY DON'T WANT TO.
Megu~~!
Waaaahh!
AHH, THANK GOODNESS! MEGUMI-KUN!
?
Gaahh!
SHE HASN'T STOPPED CRYING SINCE YOU LEFT!

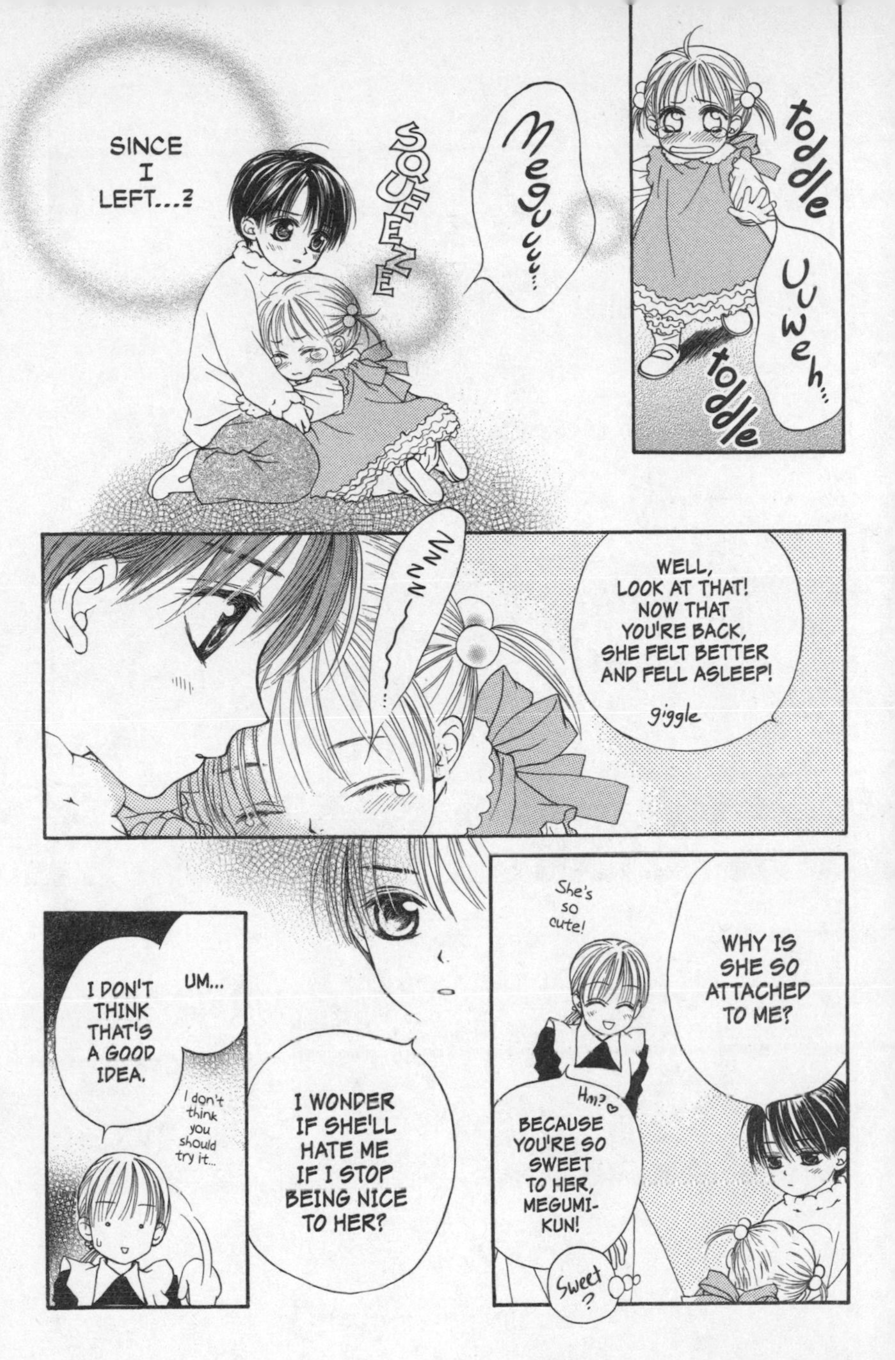
toddle
Uuweh...
toddle
Meguuu...
SQUEEZE
SINCE I LEFT...?
WELL, LOOK AT THAT! NOW THAT YOU'RE BACK, SHE FELT BETTER AND FELL ASLEEP!
giggle
Nnnn
WHY IS SHE SO ATTACHED TO ME?
She's so cute!
Hm?
BECAUSE YOU'RE SO SWEET TO HER, MEGUMI-KUN!
Sweet?
I WONDER IF SHE'LL HATE ME IF I STOP BEING NICE TO HER?
UM...
I DON'T THINK THAT'S A GOOD IDEA.
I don't think you should try it...

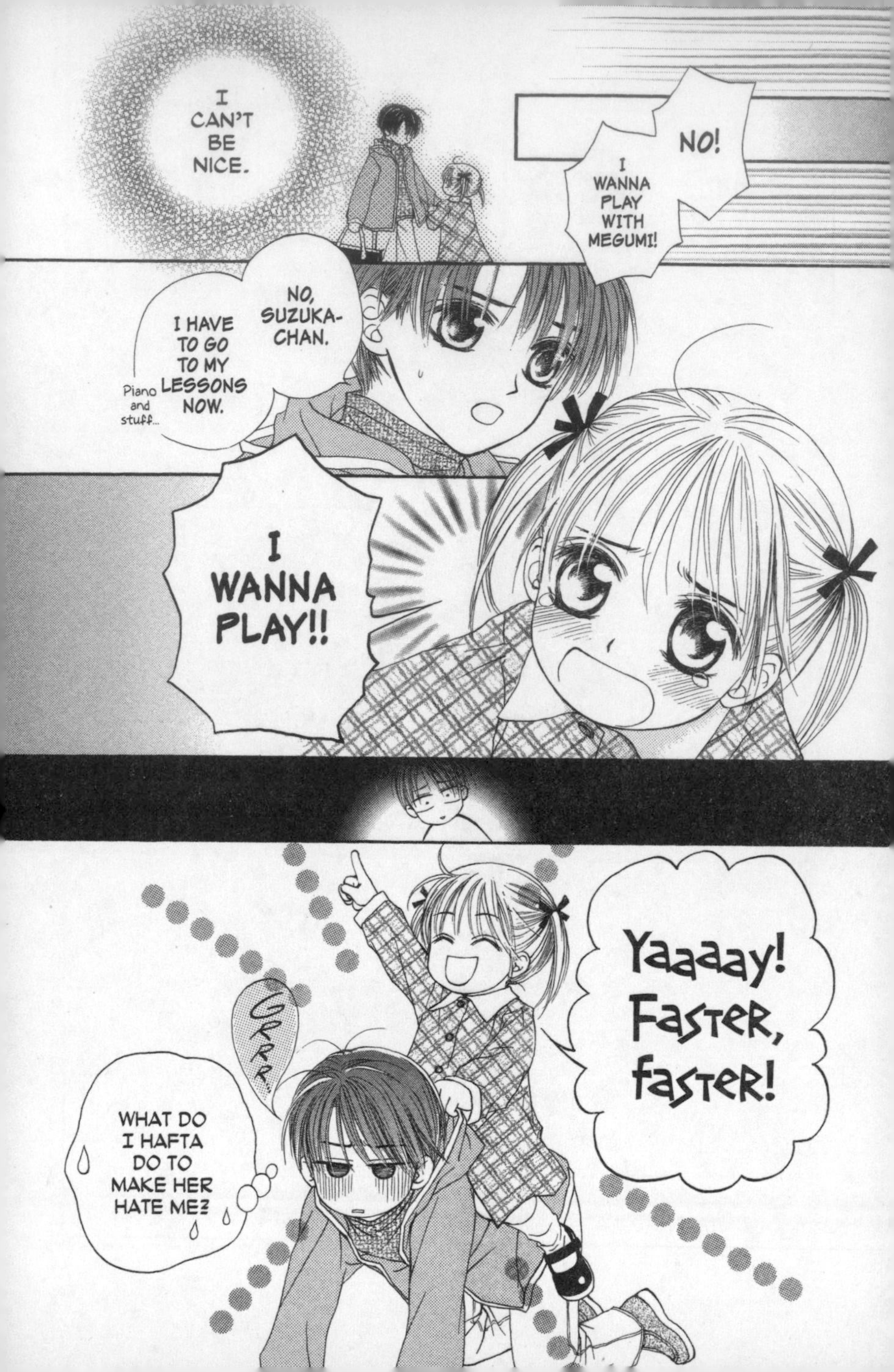
NO!
I WANNA PLAY WITH MEGUMI!
I CAN'T BE NICE.
NO, SUZUKA-CHAN.
I HAVE TO GO TO MY LESSONS NOW.
Piano and stuff...
I WANNA PLAY!!
Yaaaay! Faster, faster!
GRRR...
WHAT DO I HAFTA DO TO MAKE HER HATE ME?

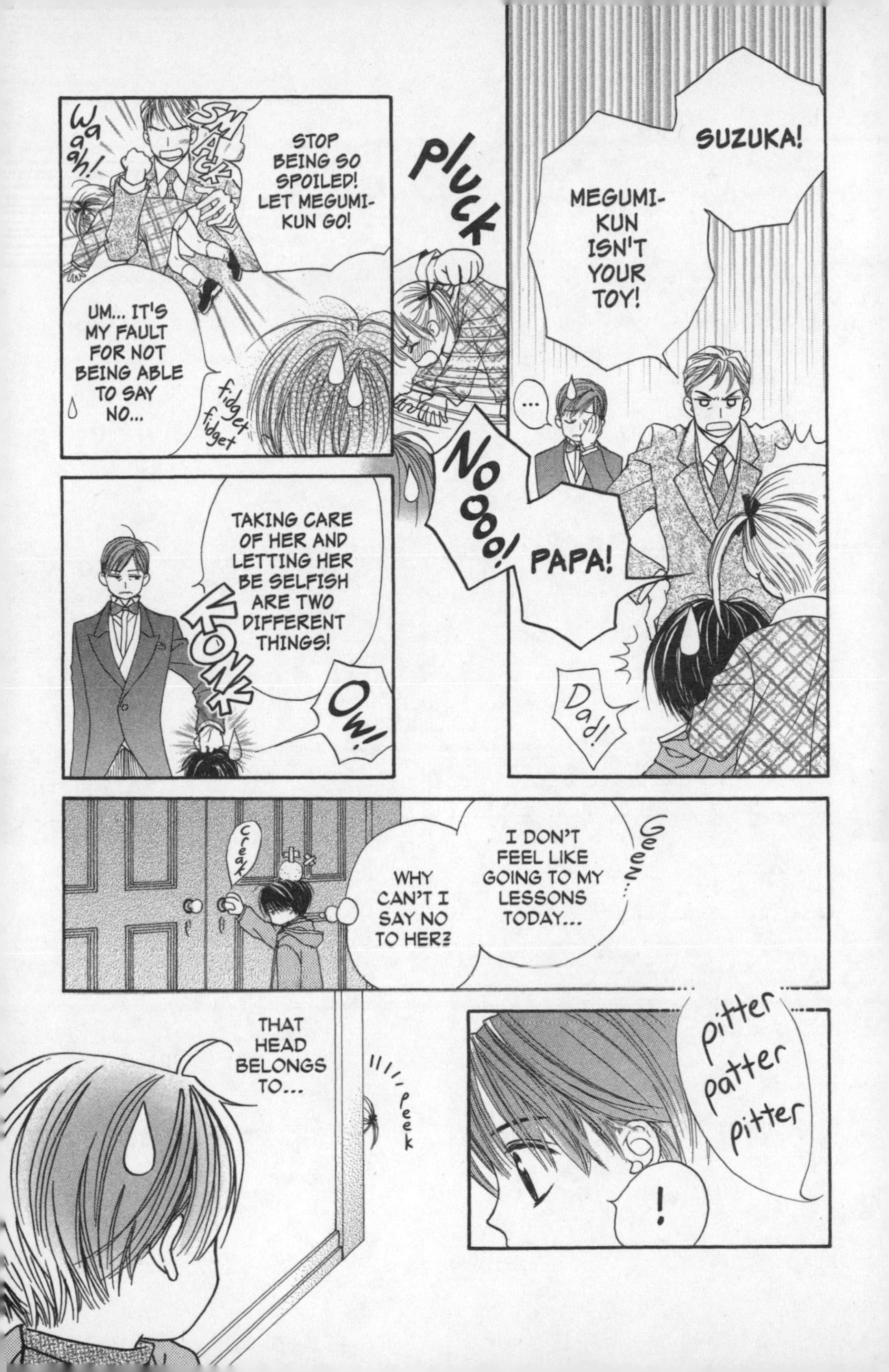
SUZUKA!
MEGUMI-KUN ISN'T YOUR TOY!
pluck
...
Noooo!
PAPA!
Dad!
Waaah!
SMACK
STOP BEING SO SPOILED! LET MEGUMI-KUN GO!
UM... IT'S MY FAULT FOR NOT BEING ABLE TO SAY NO...
fidget fidget
TAKING CARE OF HER AND LETTING HER BE SELFISH ARE TWO DIFFERENT THINGS!
KONK
Ow!
I DON'T FEEL LIKE GOING TO MY LESSONS TODAY...
Geez...
WHY CAN'T I SAY NO TO HER?
Creak
pitter patter pitter
!
THAT HEAD BELONGS TO...
Peek

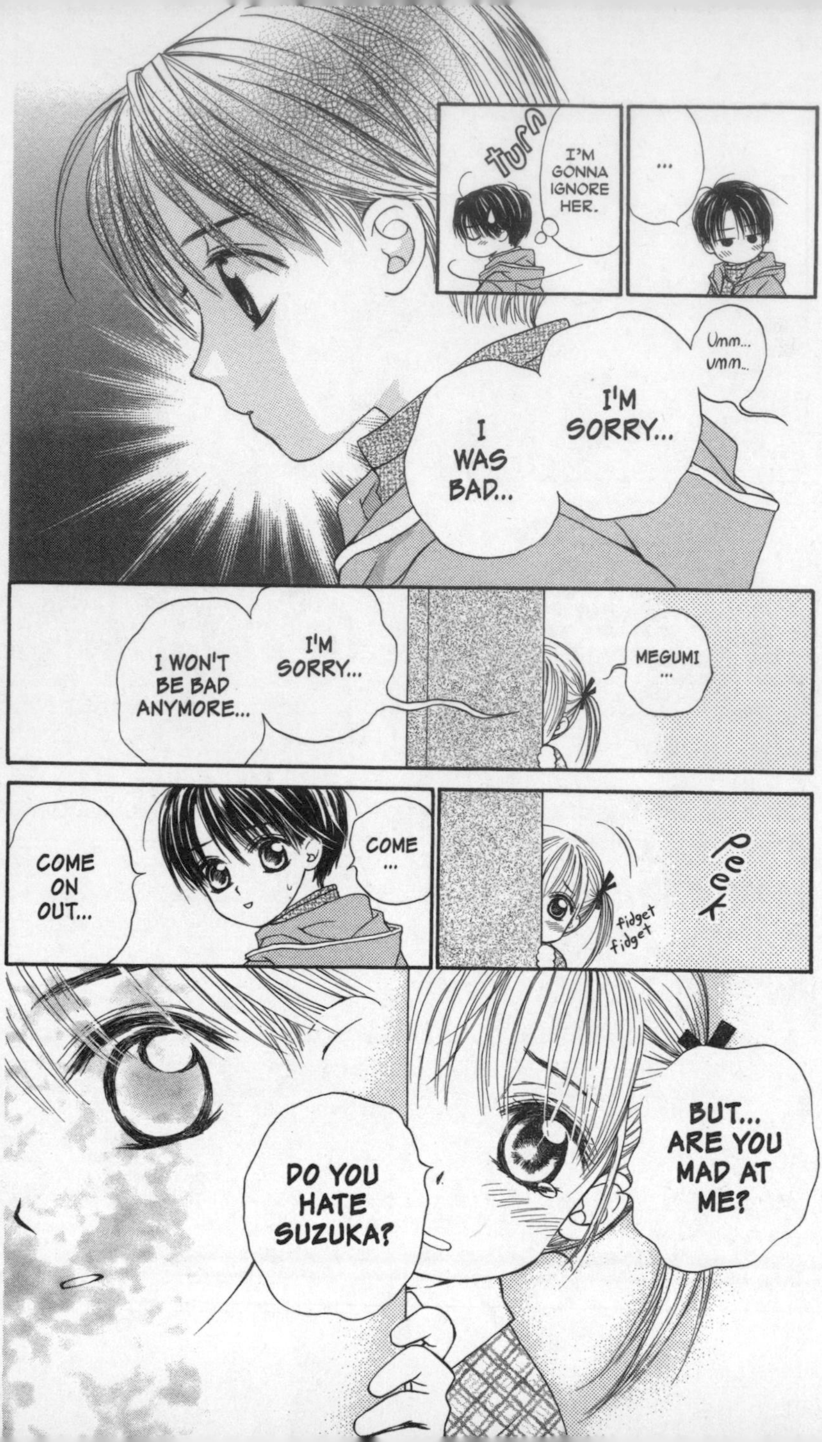
...
turn
I'M GONNA IGNORE HER.
Umm... umm...
I'M SORRY...
I WAS BAD...
MEGUMI ...
I'M SORRY...
I WON'T BE BAD ANYMORE...
peek
fidget fidget
COME ...
COME ON OUT...
BUT... ARE YOU MAD AT ME?
DO YOU HATE SUZUKA?

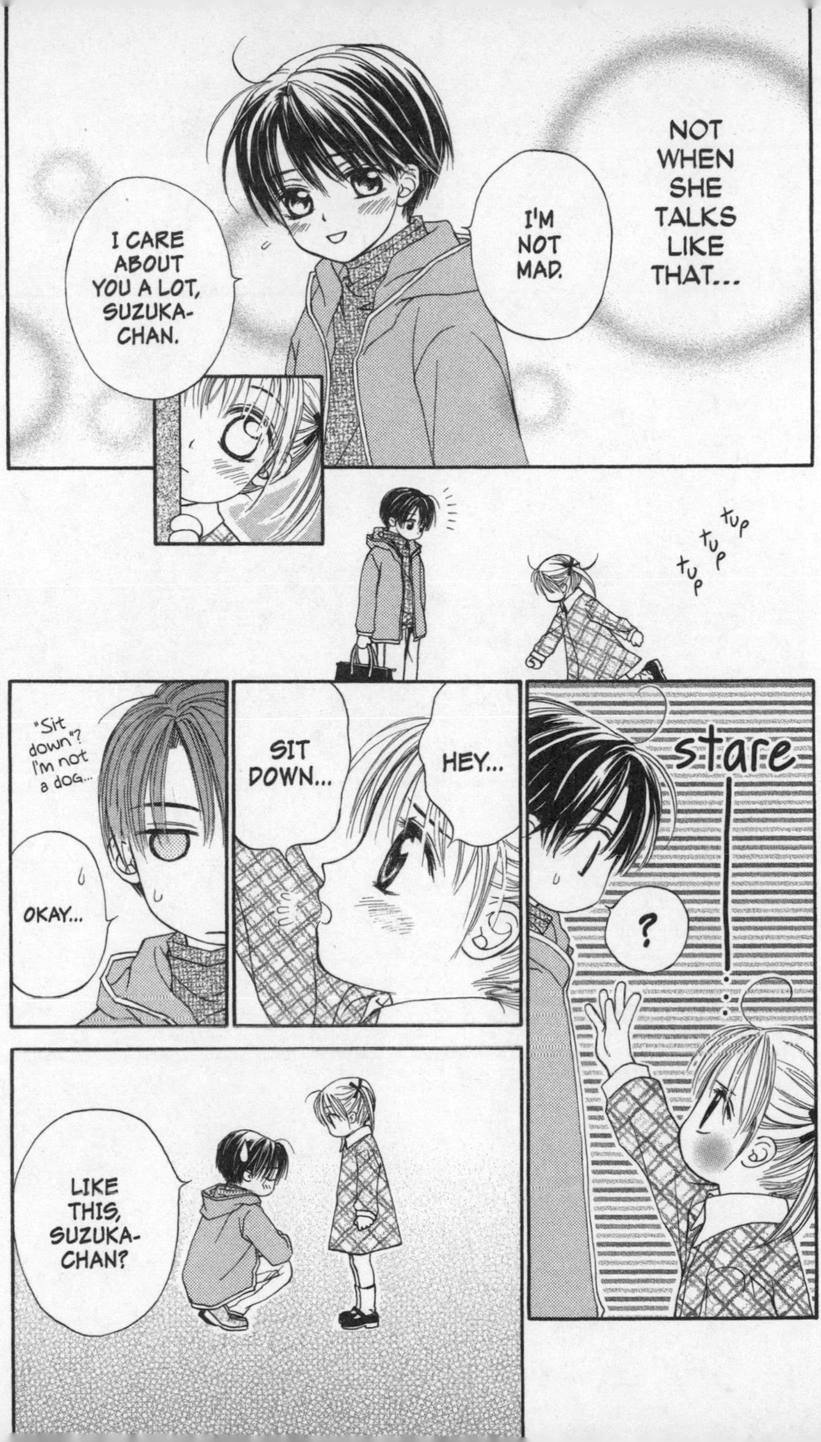
NOT WHEN SHE TALKS LIKE THAT...
I'M NOT MAD.
I CARE ABOUT YOU A LOT, SUZUKA-CHAN.
tup tup tup
stare
?
HEY...
SIT DOWN...
"Sit down"? I'm not a dog...
OKAY...
LIKE THIS, SUZUKA-CHAN?

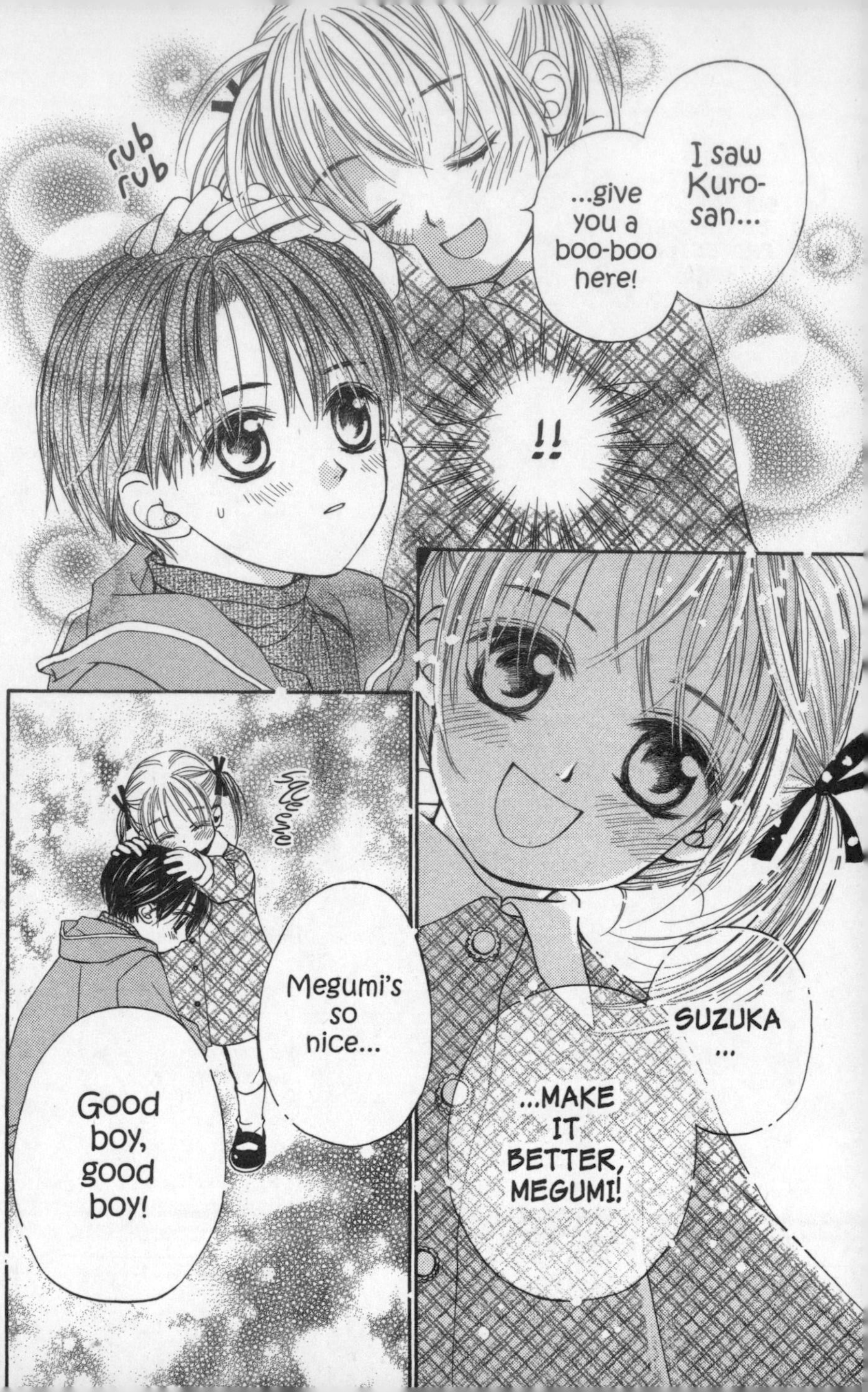
I saw Kuro-san...
...give you a boo-boo here!
rub rub
!!
SUZUKA ...
...MAKE IT BETTER, MEGUMI!
Megumi's so nice...
Good boy, good boy!

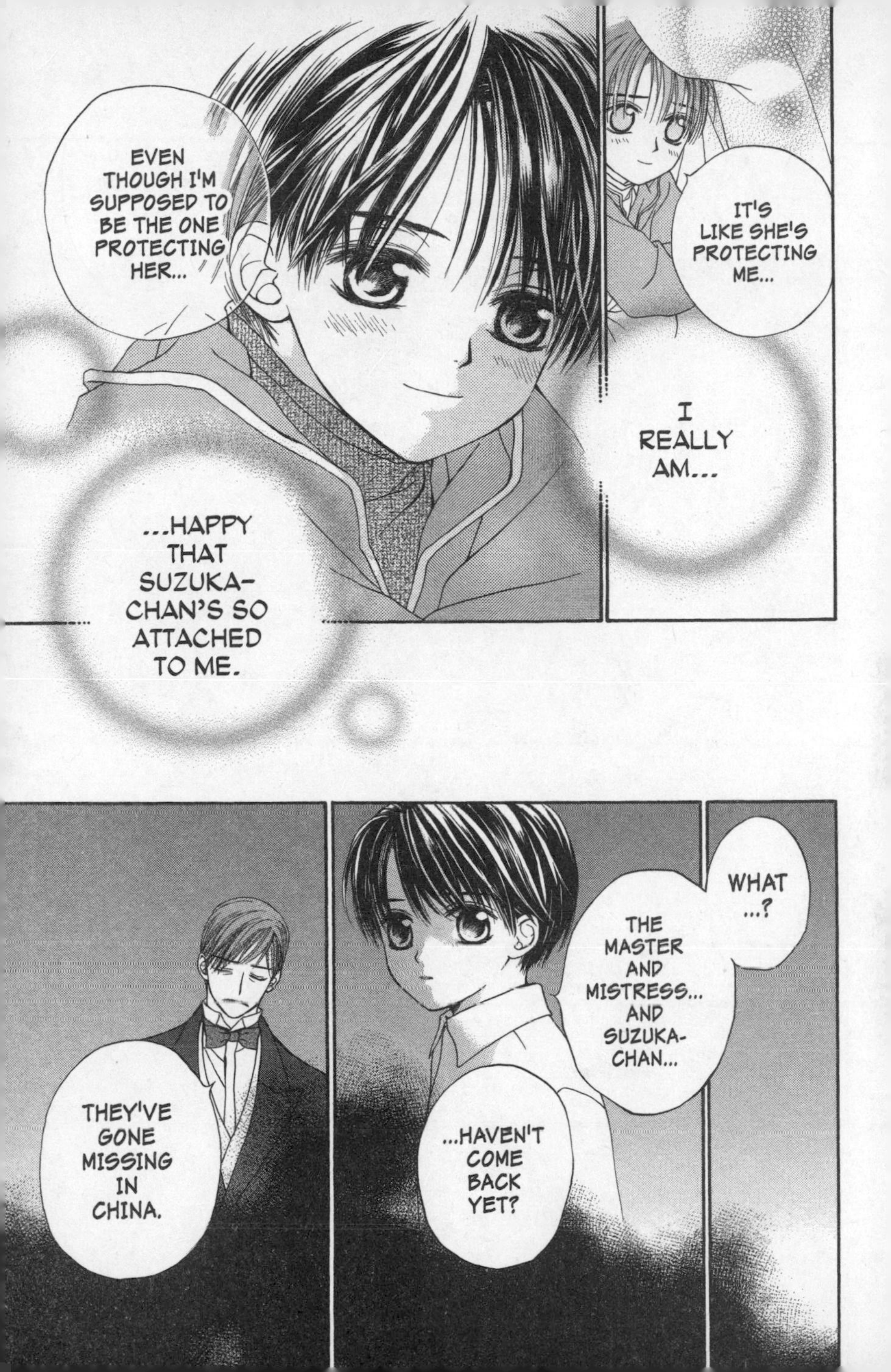
IT'S LIKE SHE'S PROTECTING ME...
I REALLY AM...
EVEN THOUGH I'M SUPPOSED TO BE THE ONE PROTECTING HER...
...HAPPY THAT SUZUKA-CHAN'S SO ATTACHED TO ME.
WHAT ...?
THE MASTER AND MISTRESS... AND SUZUKA-CHAN...
...HAVEN'T COME BACK YET?
THEY'VE GONE MISSING IN CHINA.

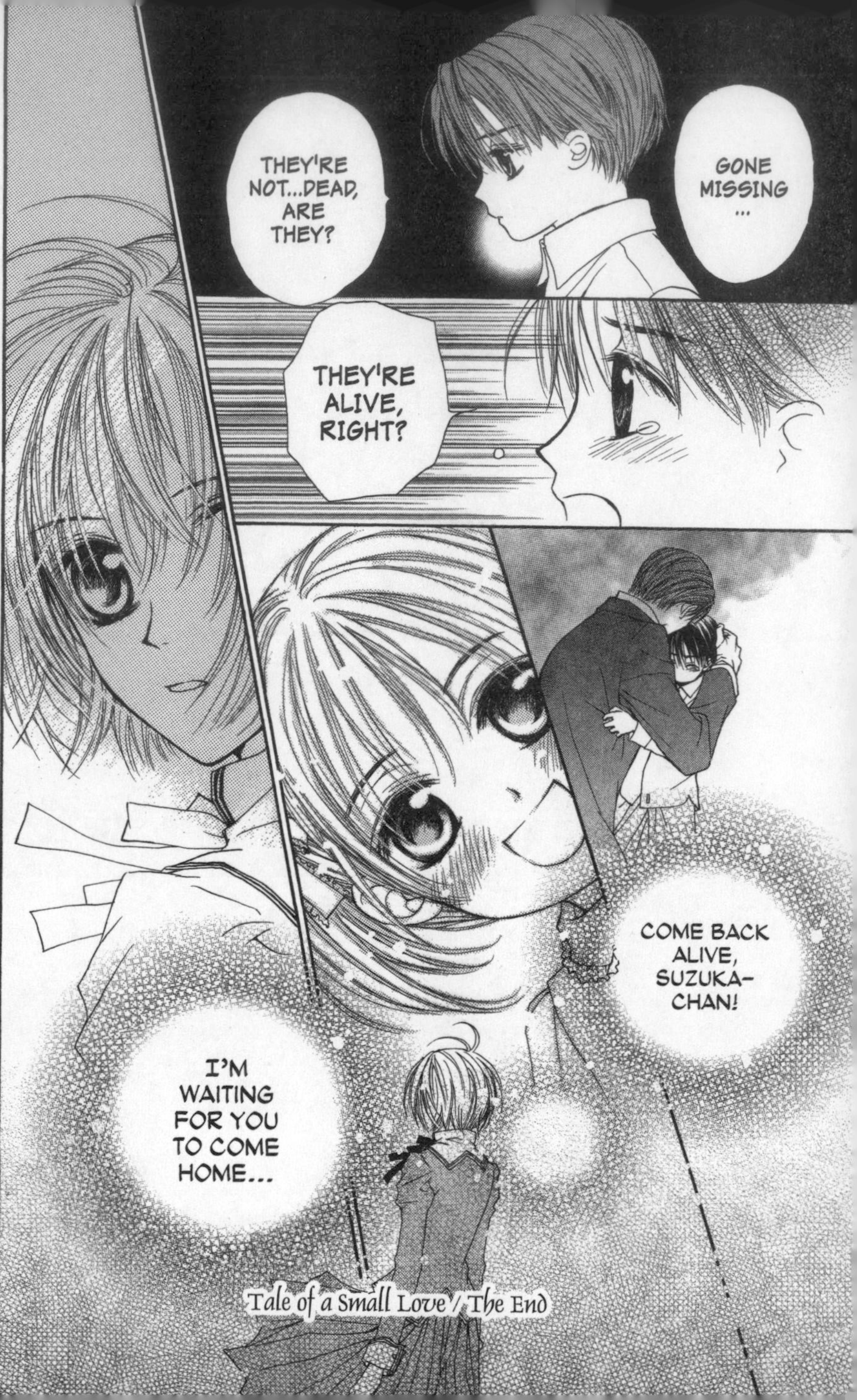
GONE MISSING ...
THEY'RE NOT...DEAD, ARE THEY?
THEY'RE ALIVE, RIGHT?
COME BACK ALIVE, SUZUKA-CHAN!
I'M WAITING FOR YOU TO COME HOME...
Tale of a Small Love / The End

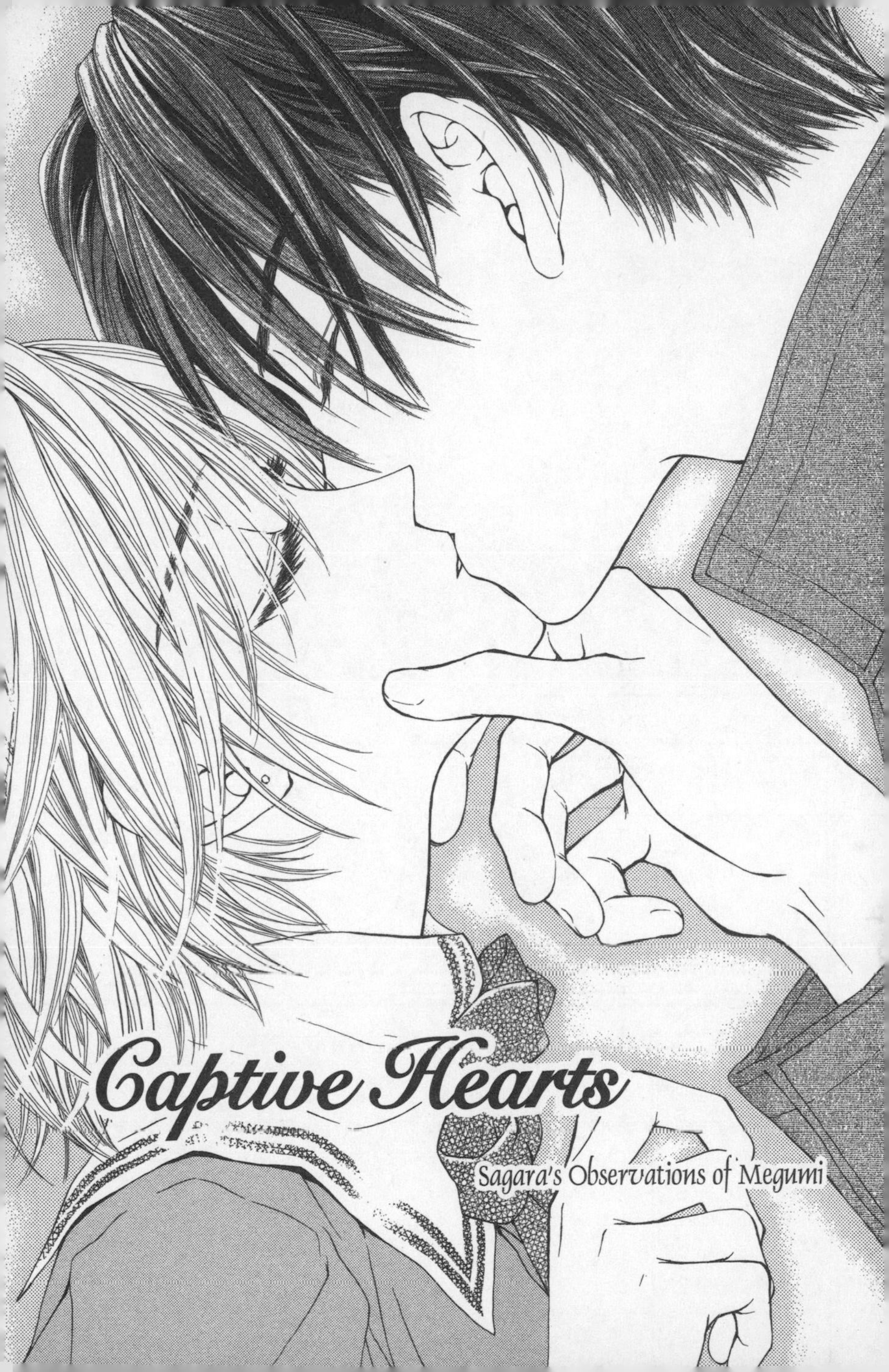
Captive Hearts
Sagara's Observations of Megumi

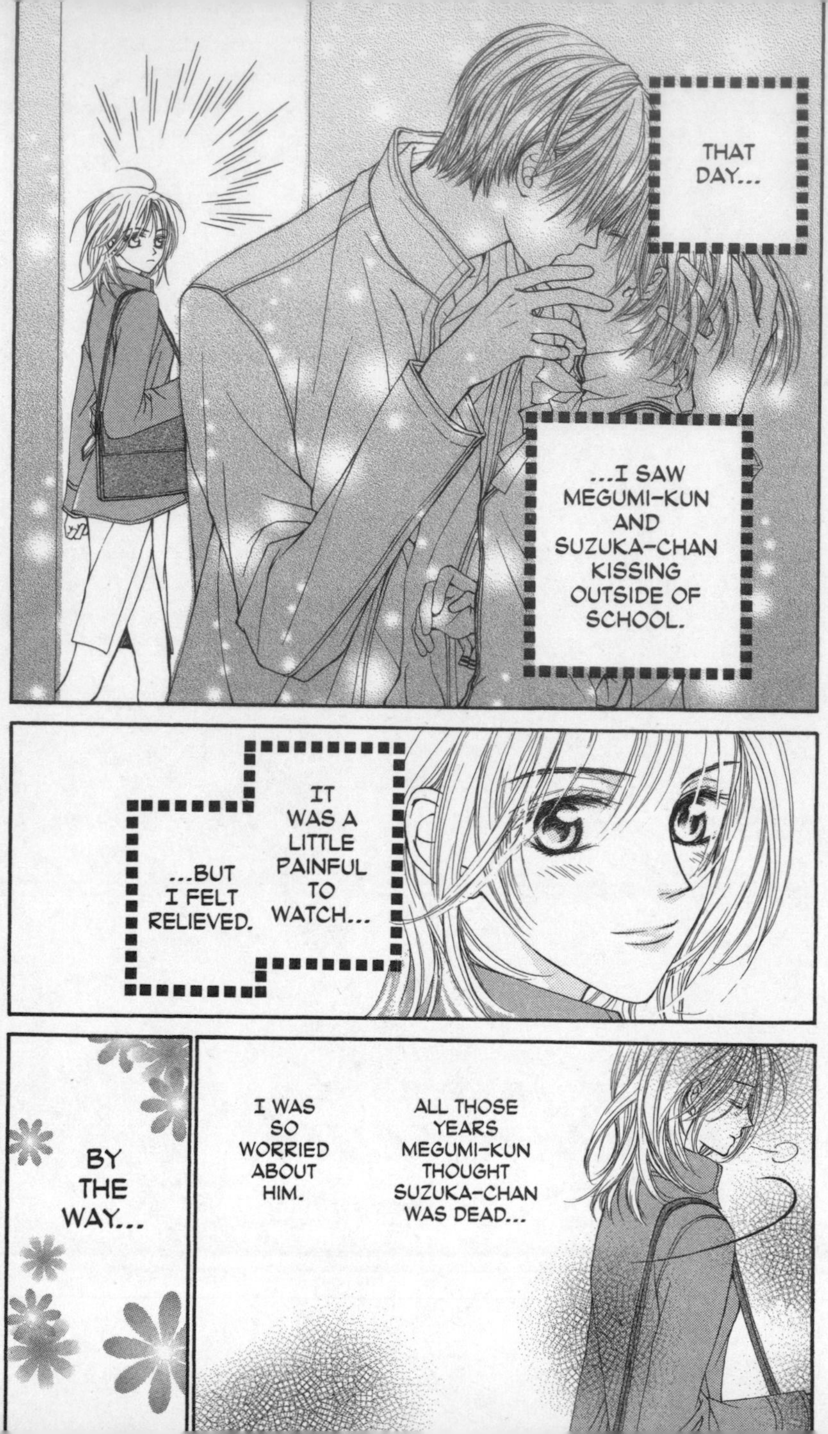
THAT DAY...
...I SAW MEGUMI-KUN AND SUZUKA-CHAN KISSING OUTSIDE OF SCHOOL.
IT WAS A LITTLE PAINFUL TO WATCH...
...BUT I FELT RELIEVED.
ALL THOSE YEARS MEGUMI-KUN THOUGHT SUZUKA-CHAN WAS DEAD...
I WAS SO WORRIED ABOUT HIM.
BY THE WAY...

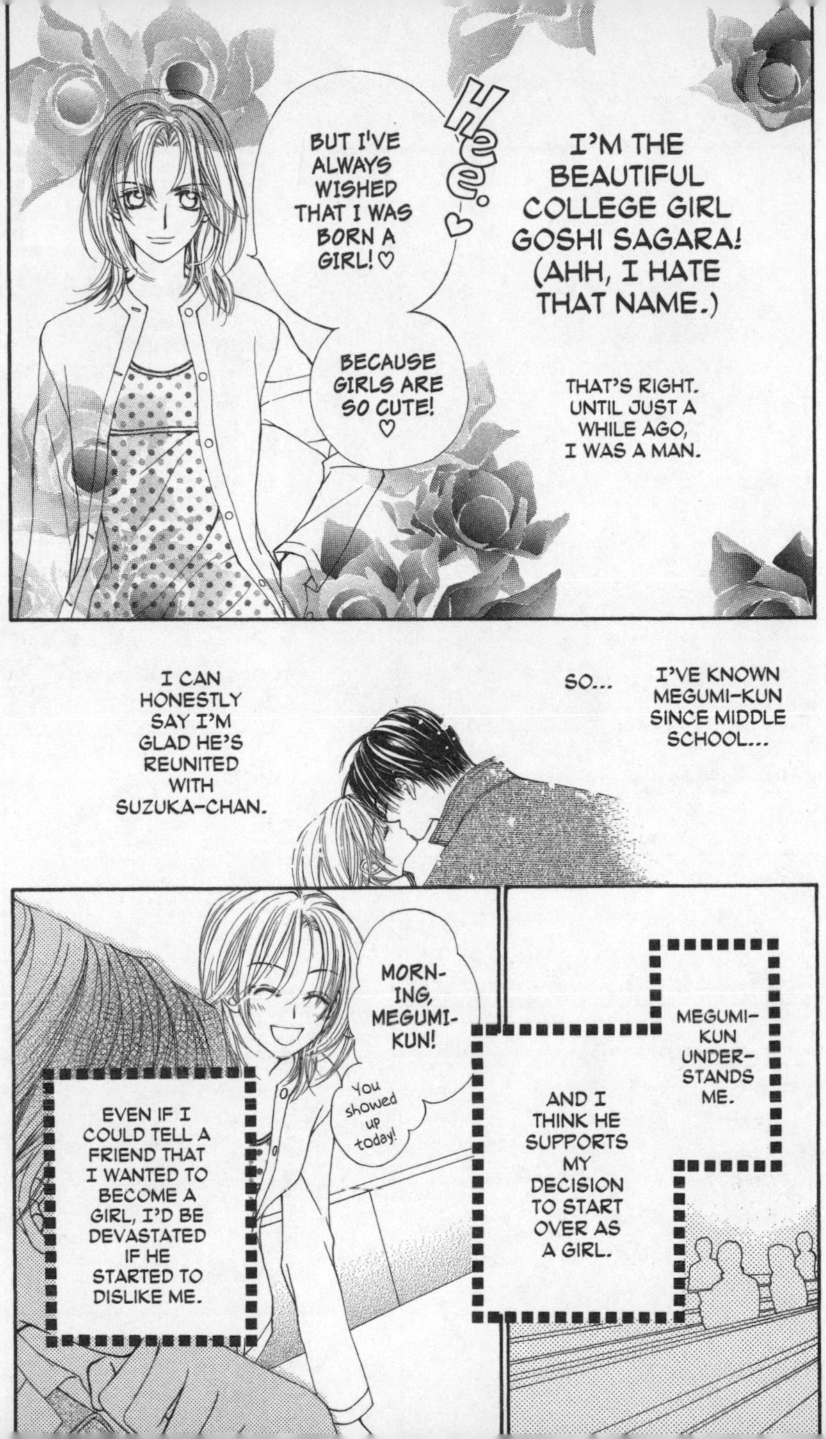
I'M THE BEAUTIFUL COLLEGE GIRL GOSHI SAGARA! (AHH, I HATE THAT NAME.)
Hee. ♡
BUT I'VE ALWAYS WISHED THAT I WAS BORN A GIRL! ♡
BECAUSE GIRLS ARE SO CUTE! ♡
THAT'S RIGHT. UNTIL JUST A WHILE AGO, I WAS A MAN.
I'VE KNOWN MEGUMI-KUN SINCE MIDDLE SCHOOL...
SO...
I CAN HONESTLY SAY I'M GLAD HE'S REUNITED WITH SUZUKA-CHAN.
MEGUMI-KUN UNDER-STANDS ME.
AND I THINK HE SUPPORTS MY DECISION TO START OVER AS A GIRL.
MORN-ING, MEGUMI-KUN!
You showed up today!
EVEN IF I COULD TELL A FRIEND THAT I WANTED TO BECOME A GIRL, I'D BE DEVASTATED IF HE STARTED TO DISLIKE ME.

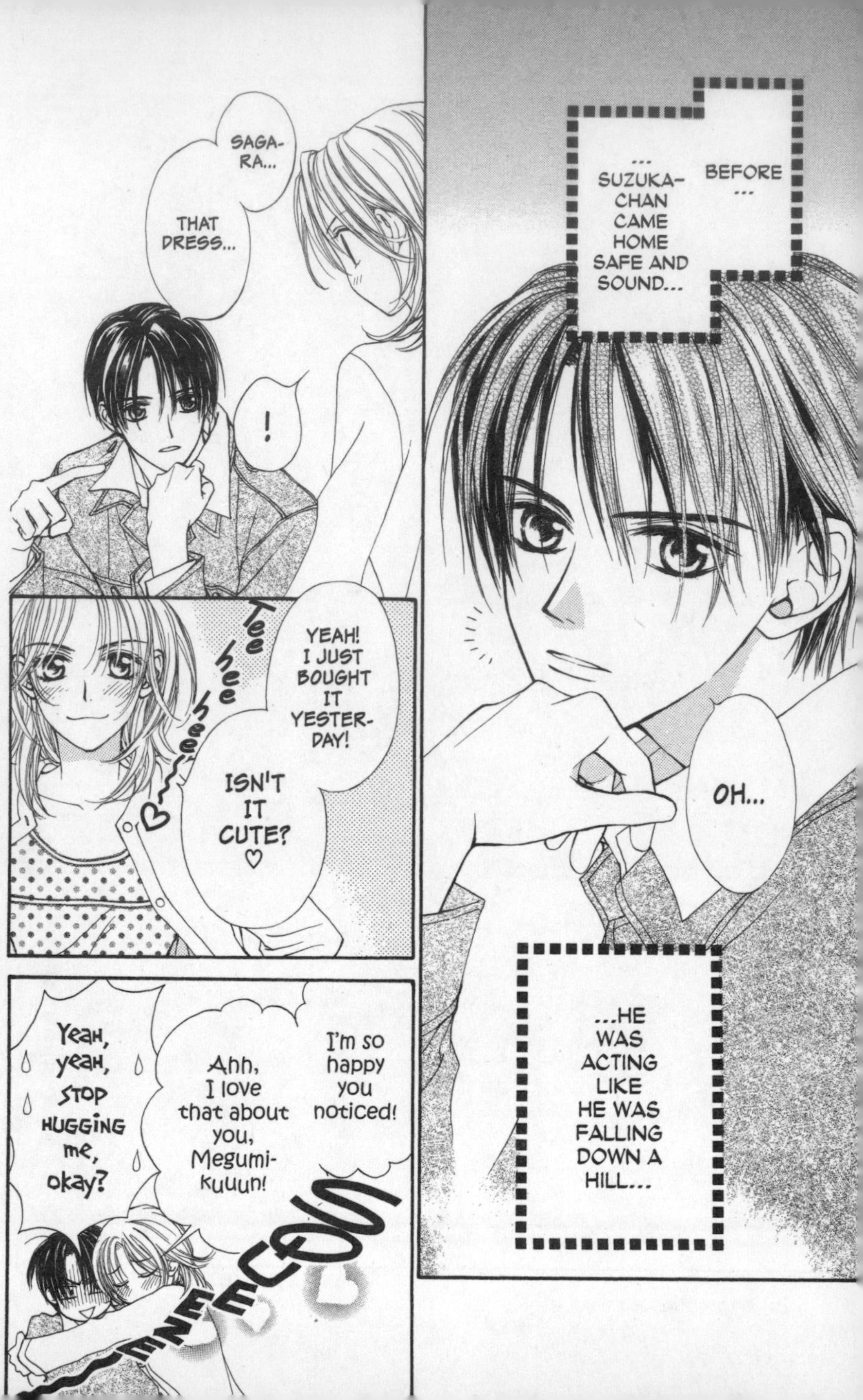
BEFORE ...
... SUZUKA-CHAN CAME HOME SAFE AND SOUND...
OH...
...HE WAS ACTING LIKE HE WAS FALLING DOWN A HILL...
SAGARA...
THAT DRESS...
!
YEAH! I JUST BOUGHT IT YESTER-DAY!
ISN'T IT CUTE? ♡
Tee hee hee ♥
I'm so happy you noticed!
Ahh, I love that about you, Megumi-kuuun!
Yeah, yeah, stop hugging me, okay?

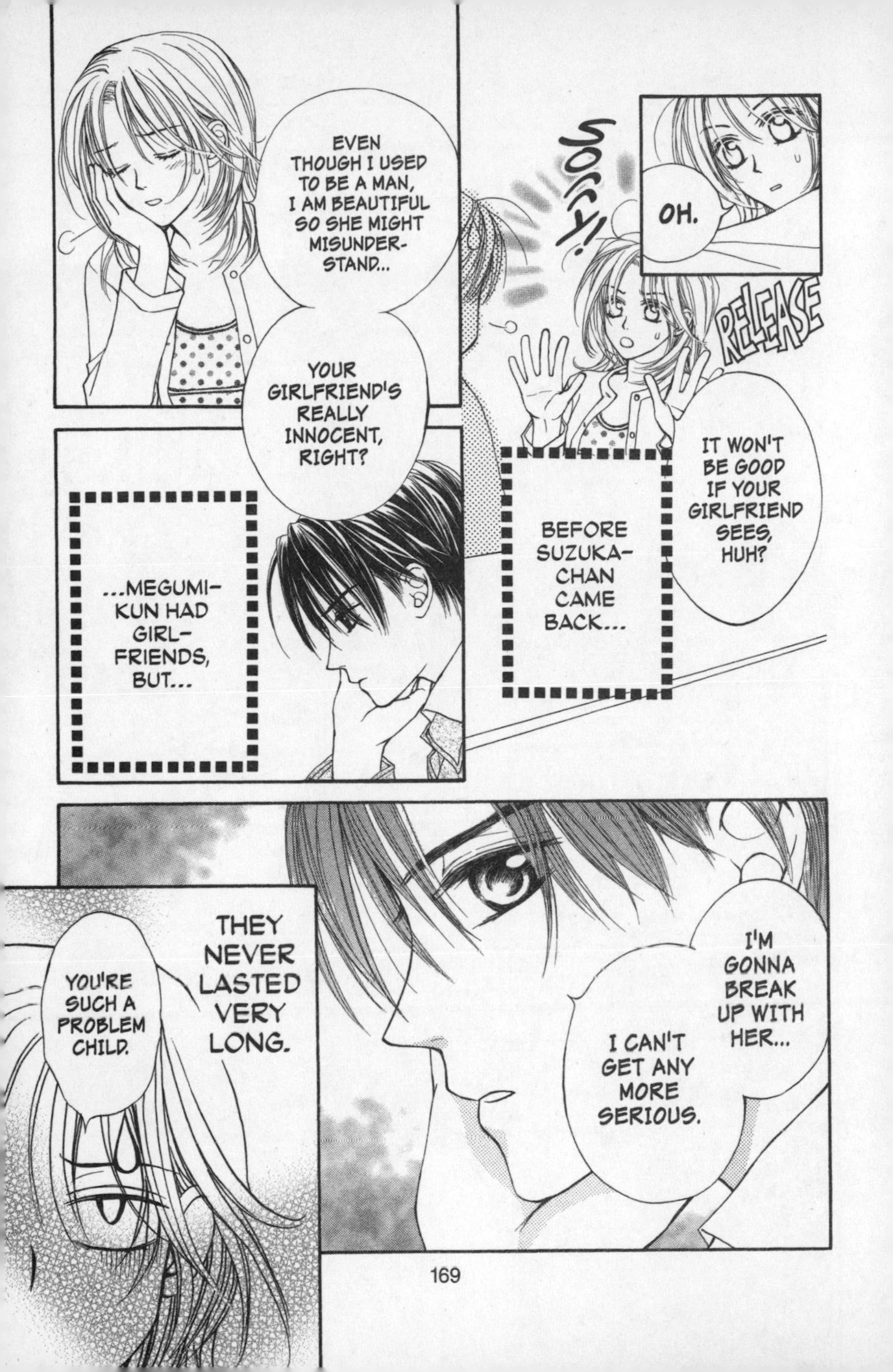
OH.
SORRY!
RELEASE
IT WON'T BE GOOD IF YOUR GIRLFRIEND SEES, HUH?
BEFORE SUZUKA-CHAN CAME BACK...
EVEN THOUGH I USED TO BE A MAN, I AM BEAUTIFUL SO SHE MIGHT MISUNDERSTAND...
YOUR GIRLFRIEND'S REALLY INNOCENT, RIGHT?
...MEGUMI-KUN HAD GIRL-FRIENDS, BUT...
I'M GONNA BREAK UP WITH HER...
I CAN'T GET ANY MORE SERIOUS.
THEY NEVER LASTED VERY LONG.
YOU'RE SUCH A PROBLEM CHILD.

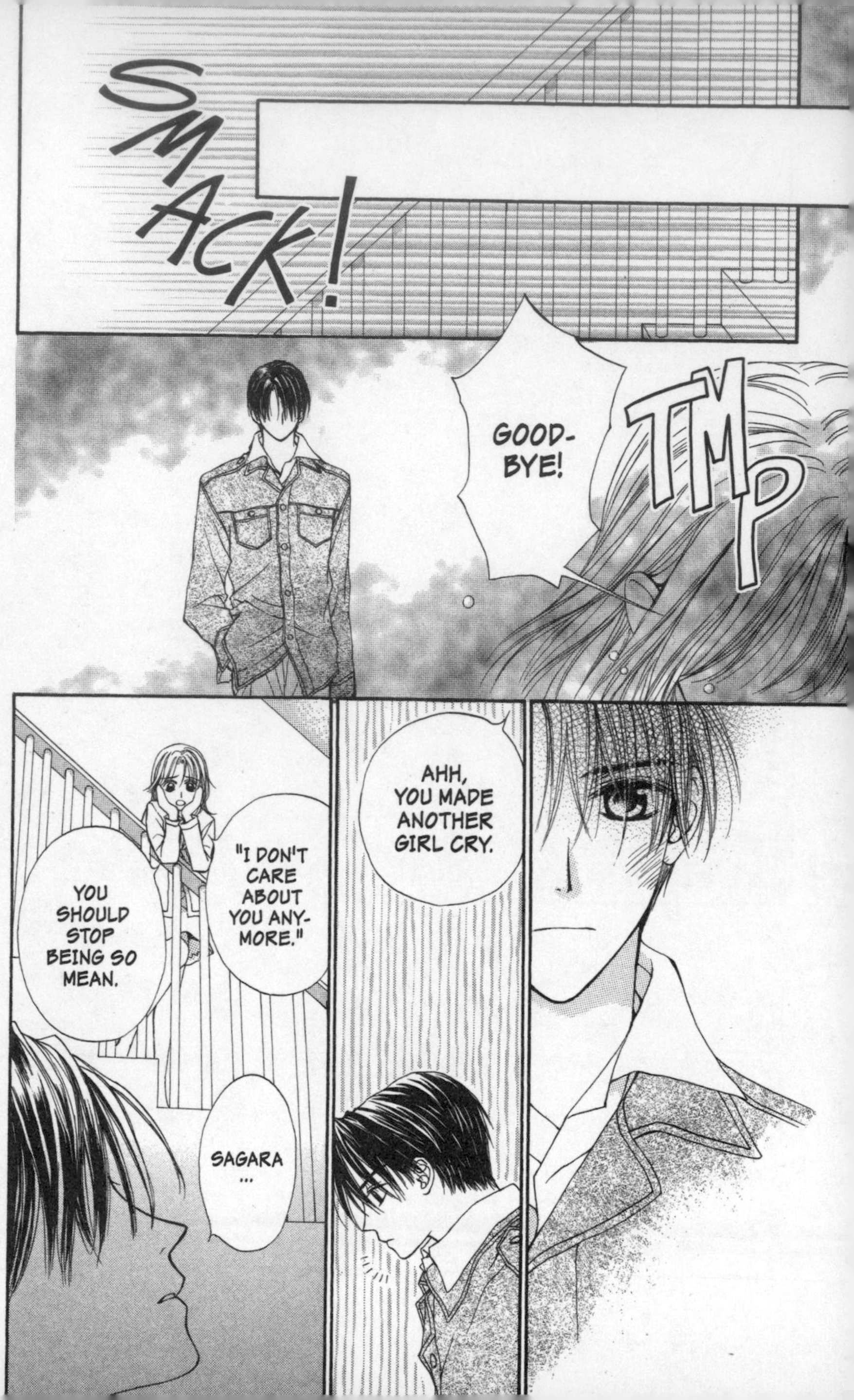
SMACK!
TMP
GOOD-BYE!
AHH, YOU MADE ANOTHER GIRL CRY.
"I DON'T CARE ABOUT YOU ANYMORE."
YOU SHOULD STOP BEING SO MEAN.
SAGARA ...

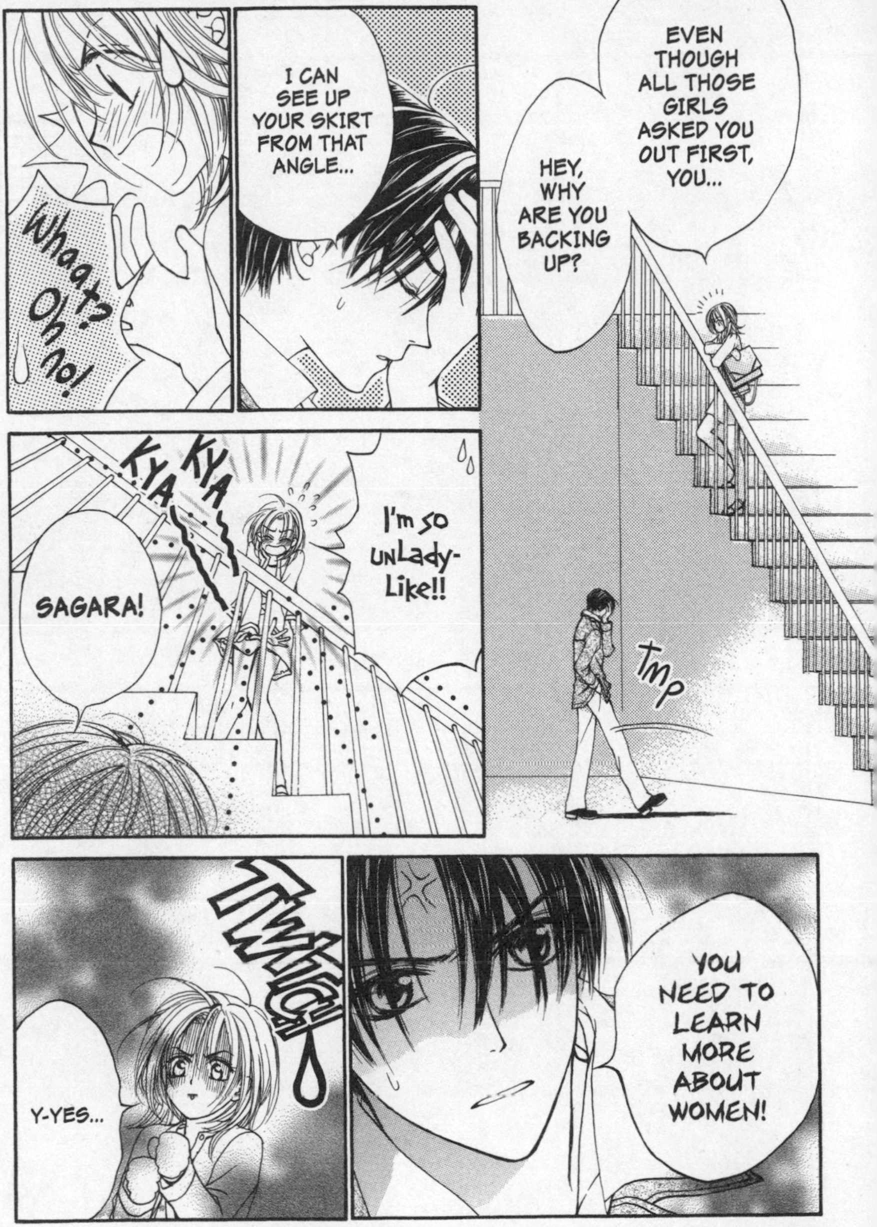
EVEN THOUGH ALL THOSE GIRLS ASKED YOU OUT FIRST, YOU...
HEY, WHY ARE YOU BACKING UP?
TMP
I CAN SEE UP YOUR SKIRT FROM THAT ANGLE...
Whaat? Oh no!
KYA KYA
I'm so unLady-Like!!
SAGARA!
YOU NEED TO LEARN MORE ABOUT WOMEN!
TWITCH
Y-YES...

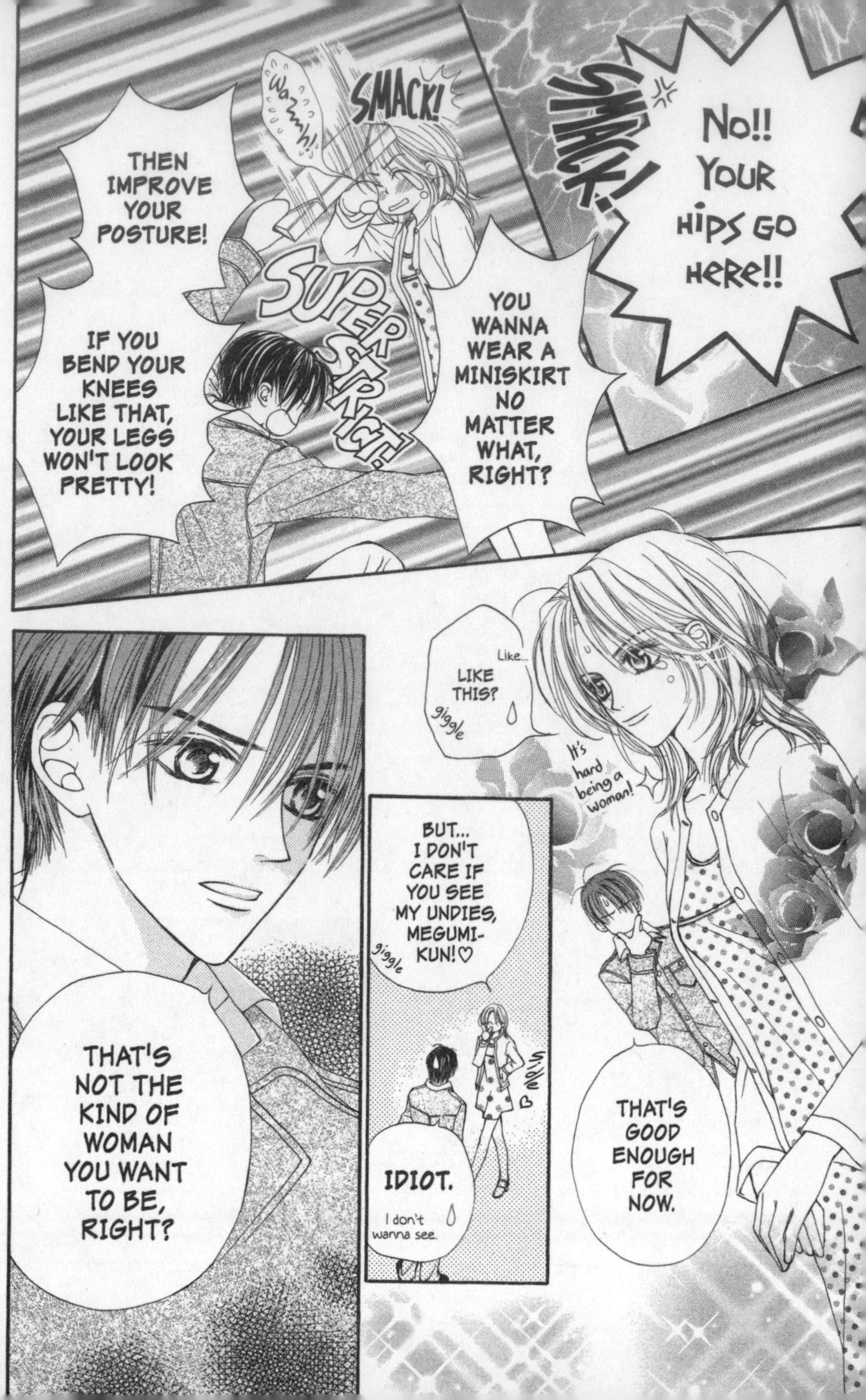
SMACK!
No!! YOUR HIPS GO HERE!!
SMACK!
THEN IMPROVE YOUR POSTURE!
SUPER STRICT!
YOU WANNA WEAR A MINISKIRT NO MATTER WHAT, RIGHT?
IF YOU BEND YOUR KNEES LIKE THAT, YOUR LEGS WON'T LOOK PRETTY!
Like...
LIKE THIS?
giggle
It's hard being a woman!
THAT'S GOOD ENOUGH FOR NOW.
BUT... I DON'T CARE IF YOU SEE MY UNDIES, MEGUMI-KUN!♡
giggle
giggle
IDIOT.
I don't wanna see.
THAT'S NOT THE KIND OF WOMAN YOU WANT TO BE, RIGHT?

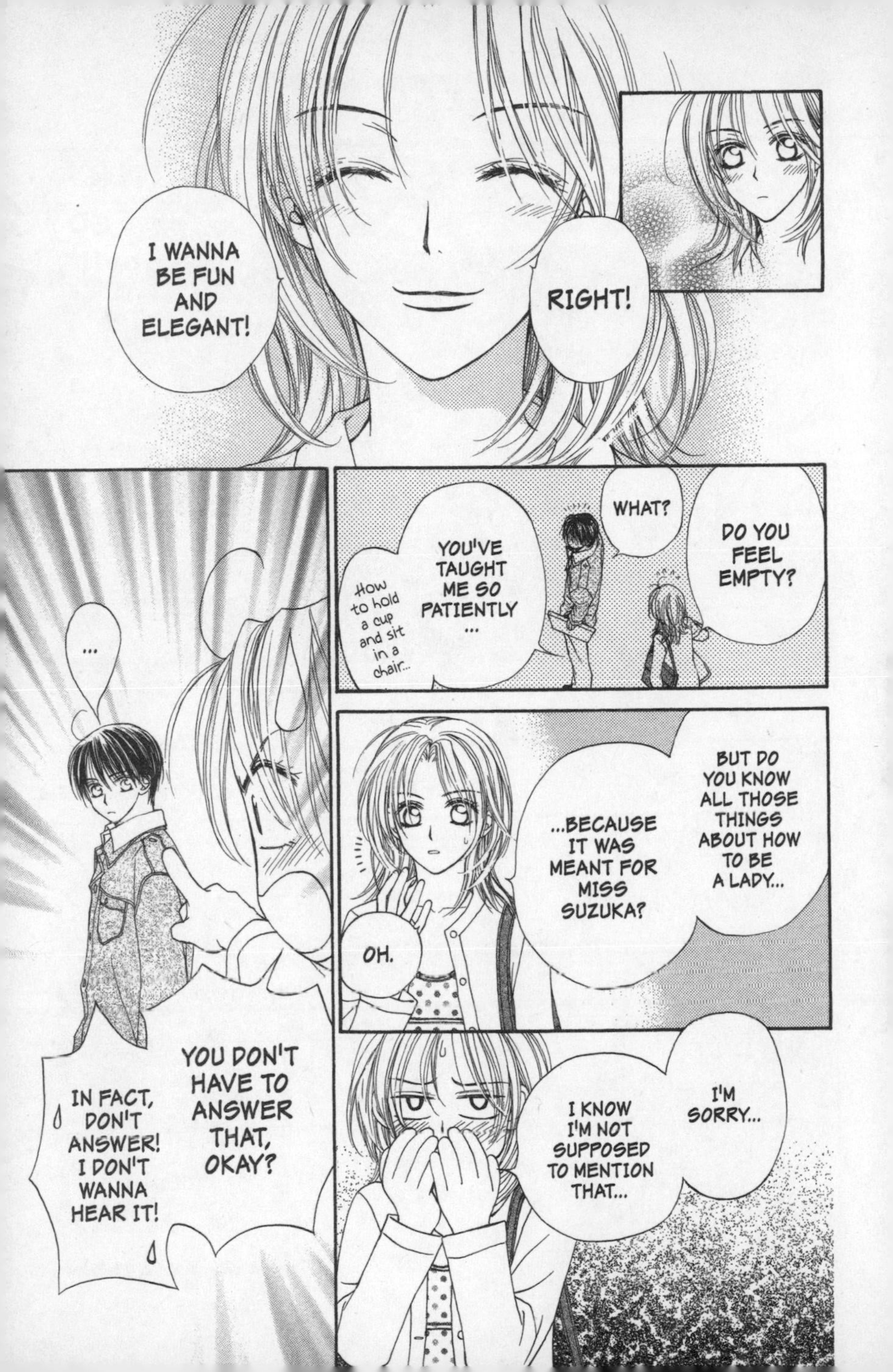
RIGHT!
I WANNA BE FUN AND ELEGANT!
DO YOU FEEL EMPTY?
WHAT?
YOU'VE TAUGHT ME SO PATIENTLY...
How to hold a cup and sit in a chair...
BUT DO YOU KNOW ALL THOSE THINGS ABOUT HOW TO BE A LADY...
...BECAUSE IT WAS MEANT FOR MISS SUZUKA?
OH.
I'M SORRY...
I KNOW I'M NOT SUPPOSED TO MENTION THAT...
...
YOU DON'T HAVE TO ANSWER THAT, OKAY?
IN FACT, DON'T ANSWER! I DON'T WANNA HEAR IT!

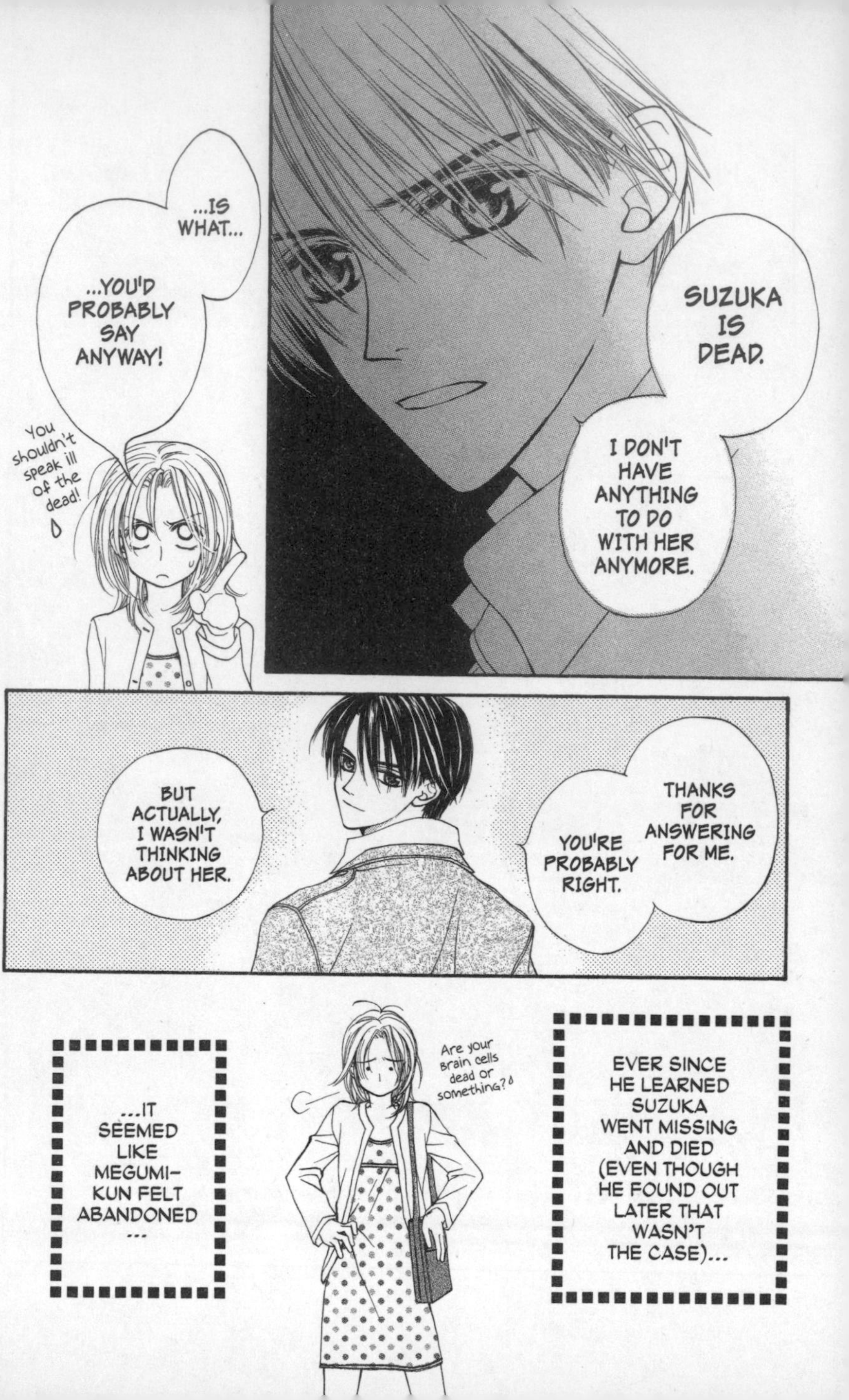
SUZUKA IS DEAD.
I DON'T HAVE ANYTHING TO DO WITH HER ANYMORE.
...IS WHAT...
...YOU'D PROBABLY SAY ANYWAY!
You shouldn't speak ill of the dead!
THANKS FOR ANSWERING FOR ME.
YOU'RE PROBABLY RIGHT.
BUT ACTUALLY, I WASN'T THINKING ABOUT HER.
EVER SINCE HE LEARNED SUZUKA WENT MISSING AND DIED (EVEN THOUGH HE FOUND OUT LATER THAT WASN'T THE CASE)...
Are your brain cells dead or something?
...IT SEEMED LIKE MEGUMI-KUN FELT ABANDONED ...

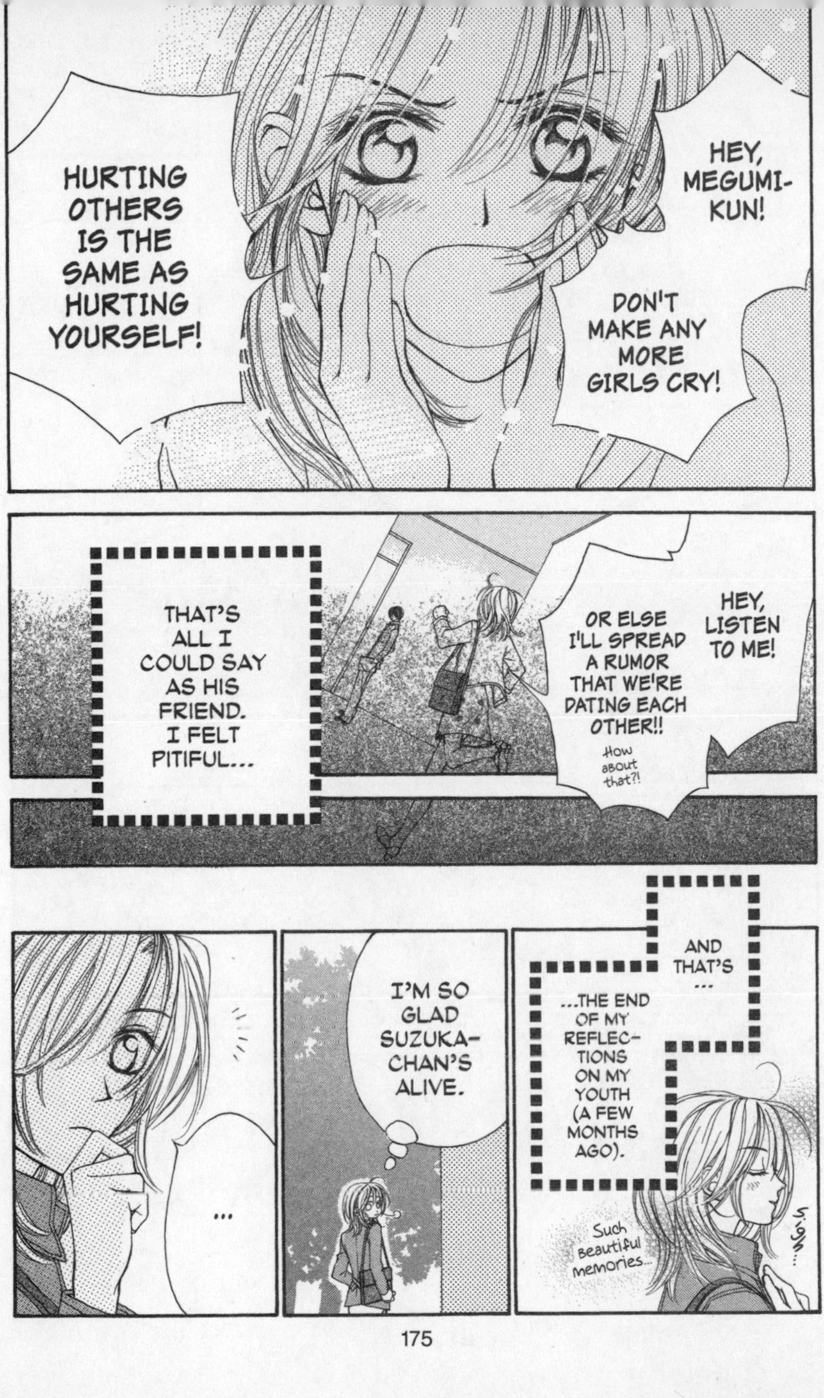
HEY, MEGUMI-KUN!
DON'T MAKE ANY MORE GIRLS CRY!
HURTING OTHERS IS THE SAME AS HURTING YOURSELF!
HEY, LISTEN TO ME!
OR ELSE I'LL SPREAD A RUMOR THAT WE'RE DATING EACH OTHER!!
How about that?!
THAT'S ALL I COULD SAY AS HIS FRIEND. I FELT PITIFUL...
AND THAT'S ...
...THE END OF MY REFLECTIONS ON MY YOUTH (A FEW MONTHS AGO).
Such Beautiful memories...
sigh...
I'M SO GLAD SUZUKA-CHAN'S ALIVE.
...

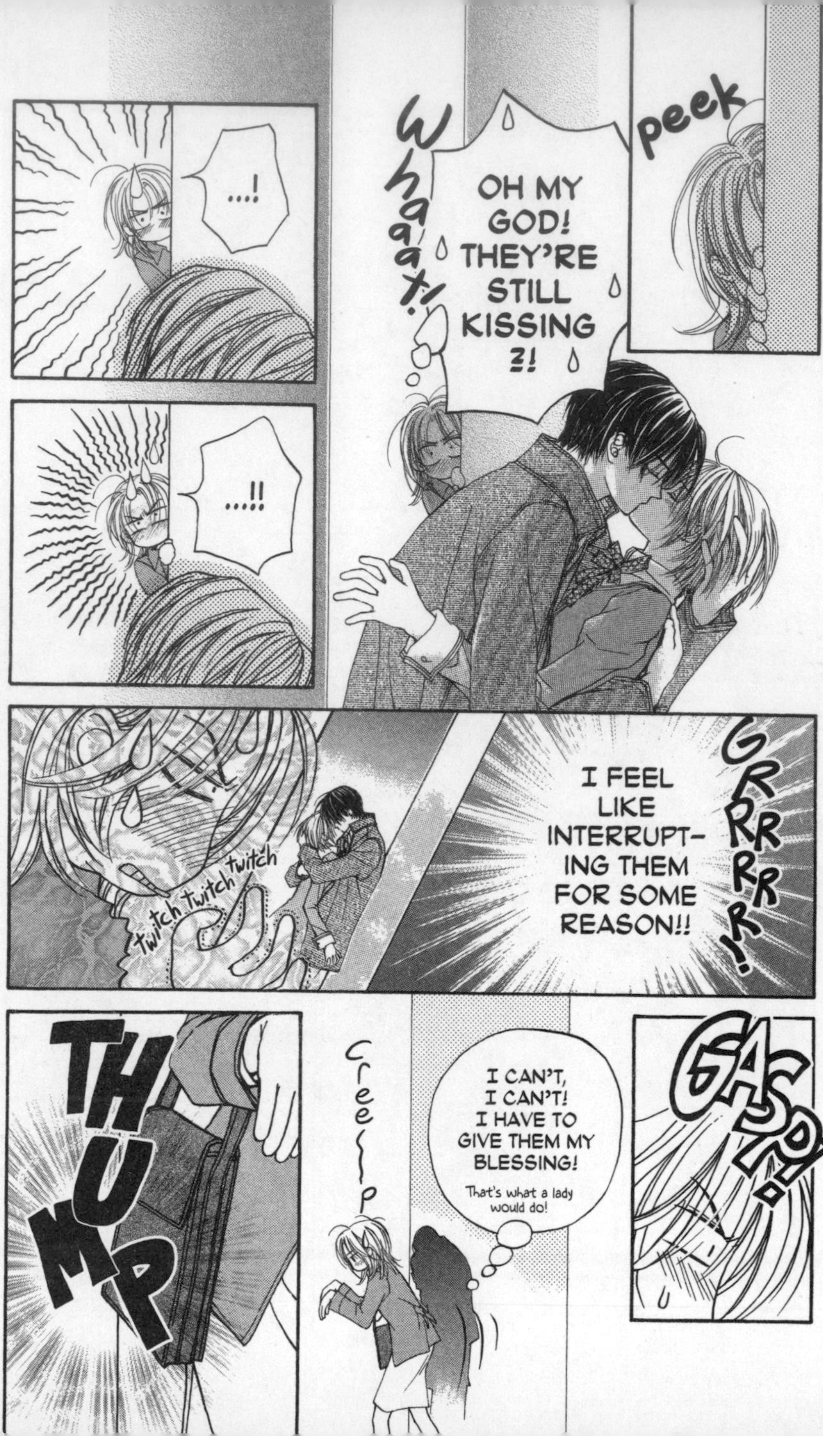

peek
Whaaat!
OH MY GOD! THEY'RE STILL KISSING?!
...!
...!!
GRRRRR!
I FEEL LIKE INTERRUPTING THEM FOR SOME REASON!!
twitch twitch twitch
GASP!
I CAN'T, I CAN'T! I HAVE TO GIVE THEM MY BLESSING!
That's what a lady would do!
Creee~p
THUMP

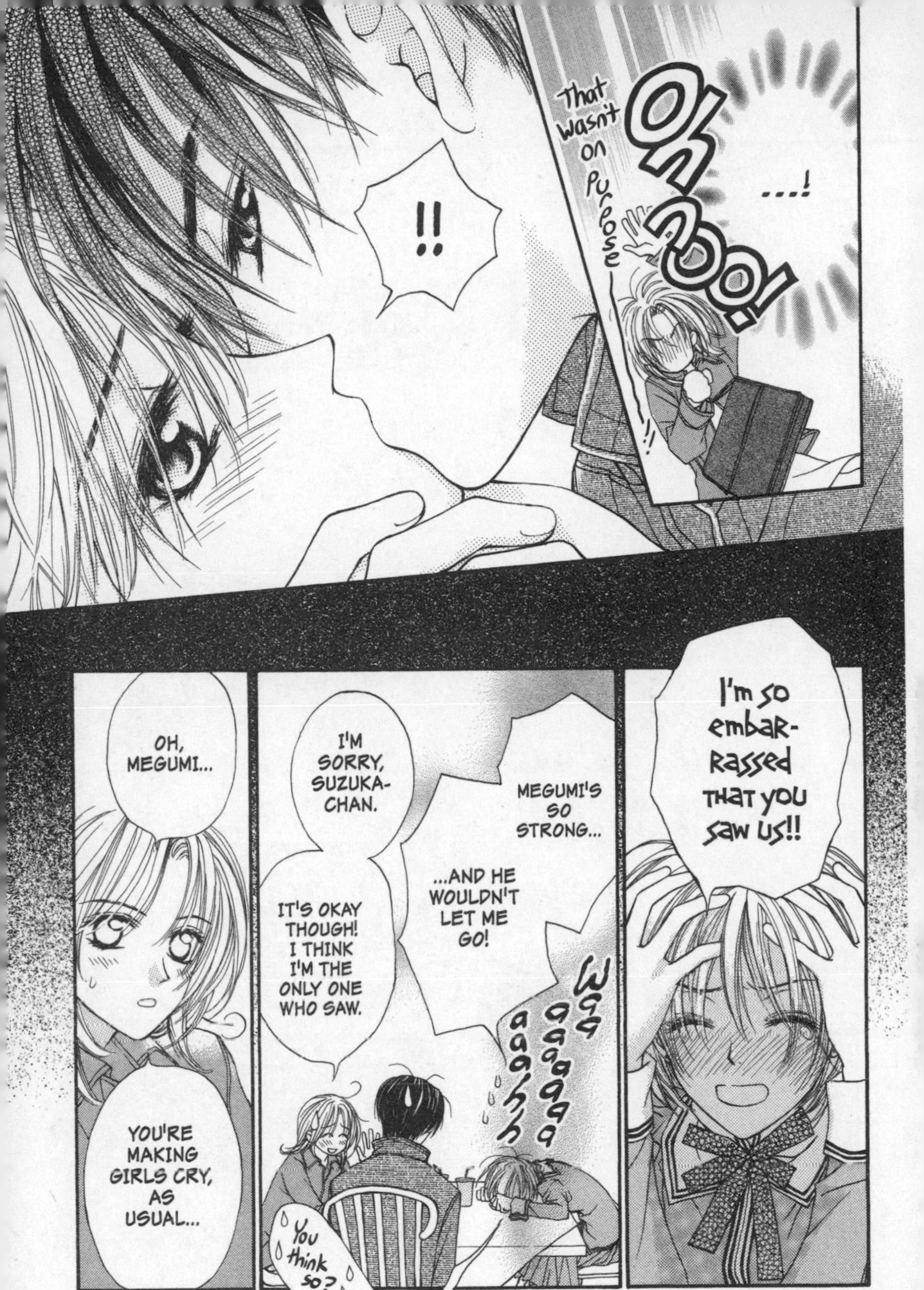
...!
Oh nooo!
That wasn't on purpose
!!
!!
I'm so embarrassed that you saw us!!
MEGUMI'S SO STRONG...
...AND HE WOULDN'T LET ME GO!
Waaaaaaaaaaaaahh
I'M SORRY, SUZUKA-CHAN.
IT'S OKAY THOUGH! I THINK I'M THE ONLY ONE WHO SAW.
You think so?
OH, MEGUMI...
YOU'RE MAKING GIRLS CRY, AS USUAL...

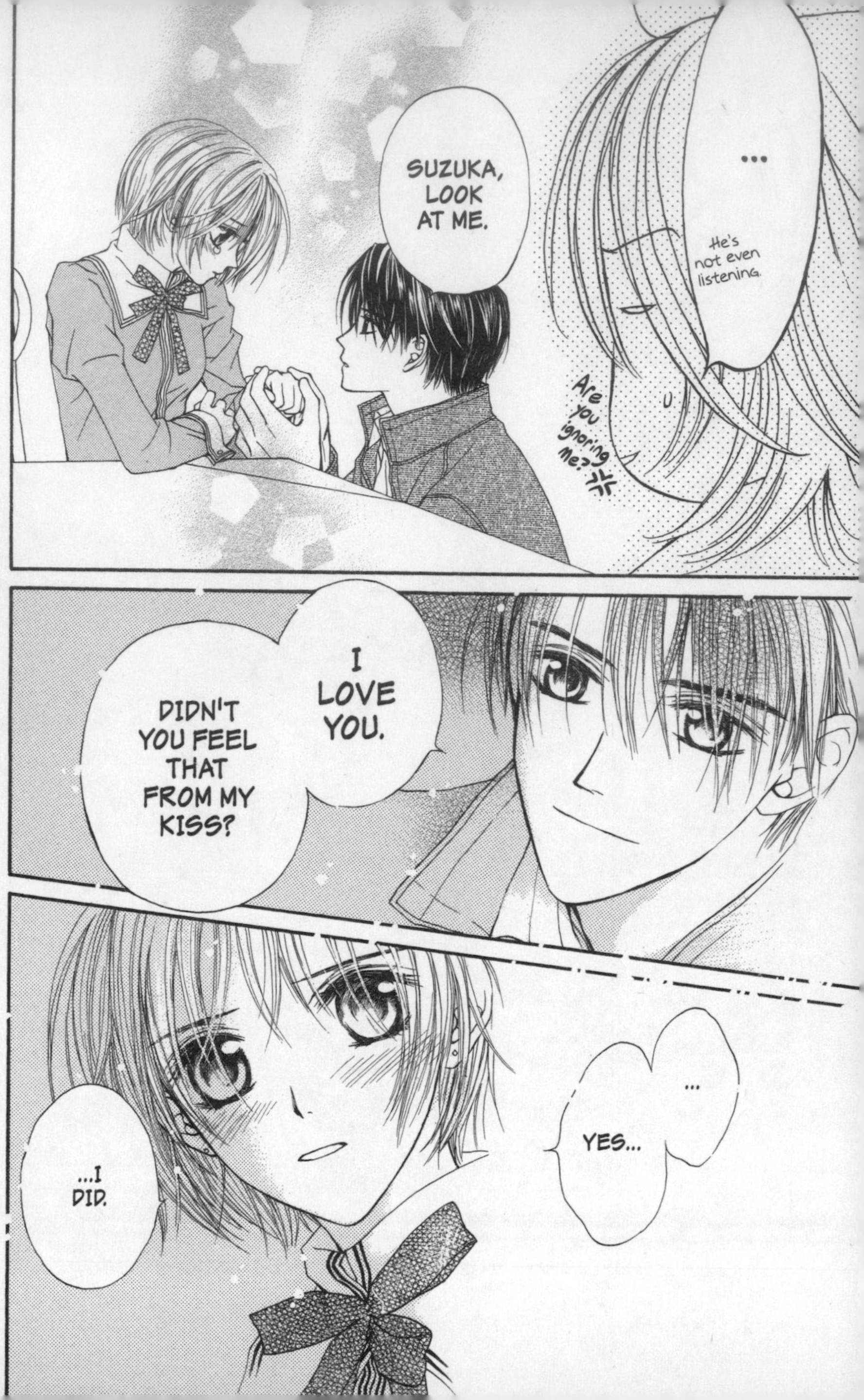
...
He's not even listening.
Are you ignoring me?
SUZUKA, LOOK AT ME.
I LOVE YOU.
DIDN'T YOU FEEL THAT FROM MY KISS?
... YES...
...I DID.

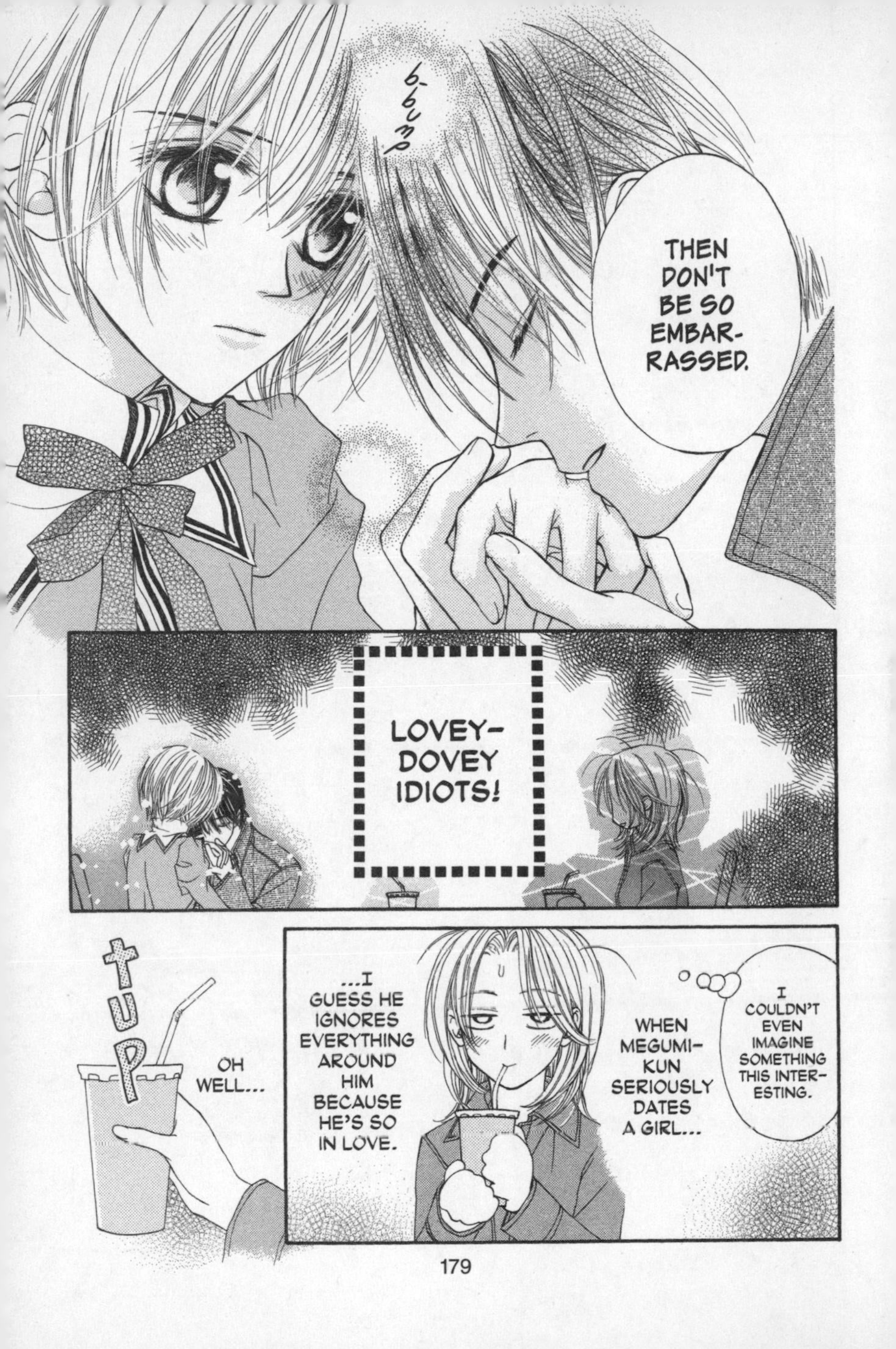
THEN DON'T BE SO EMBARRASSED.
b-bump
LOVEY-DOVEY IDIOTS!
I COULDN'T EVEN IMAGINE SOMETHING THIS INTERESTING.
WHEN MEGUMI-KUN SERIOUSLY DATES A GIRL...
...I GUESS HE IGNORES EVERYTHING AROUND HIM BECAUSE HE'S SO IN LOVE.
TUP
OH WELL...

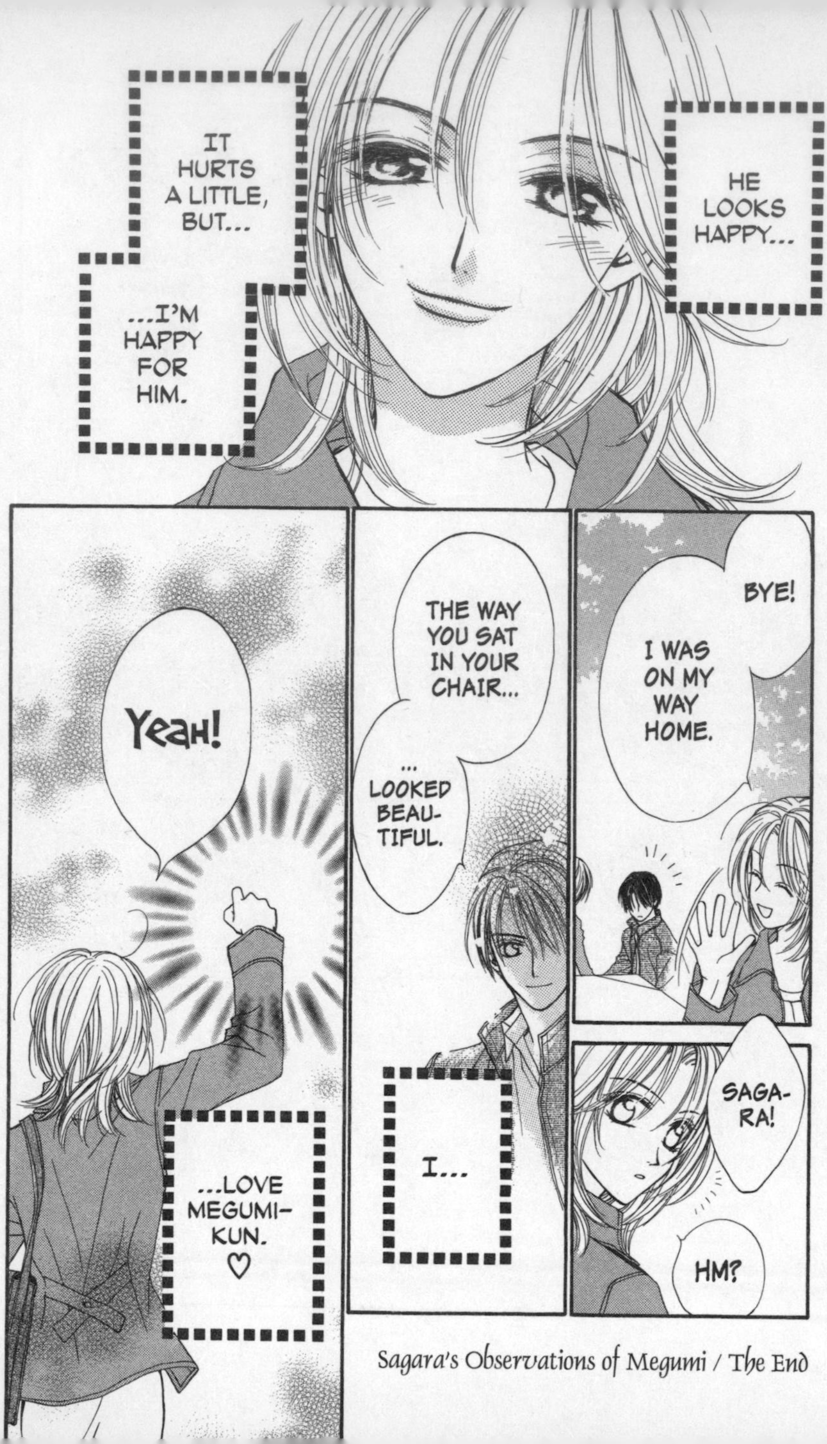
HE LOOKS HAPPY...
IT HURTS A LITTLE, BUT...
...I'M HAPPY FOR HIM.
BYE! I WAS ON MY WAY HOME.
SAGARA!
HM?
THE WAY YOU SAT IN YOUR CHAIR...
...LOOKED BEAUTIFUL.
I...
Yeah!
...LOVE MEGUMI-KUN. ♡

Sagara's Observations of Megumi / The End

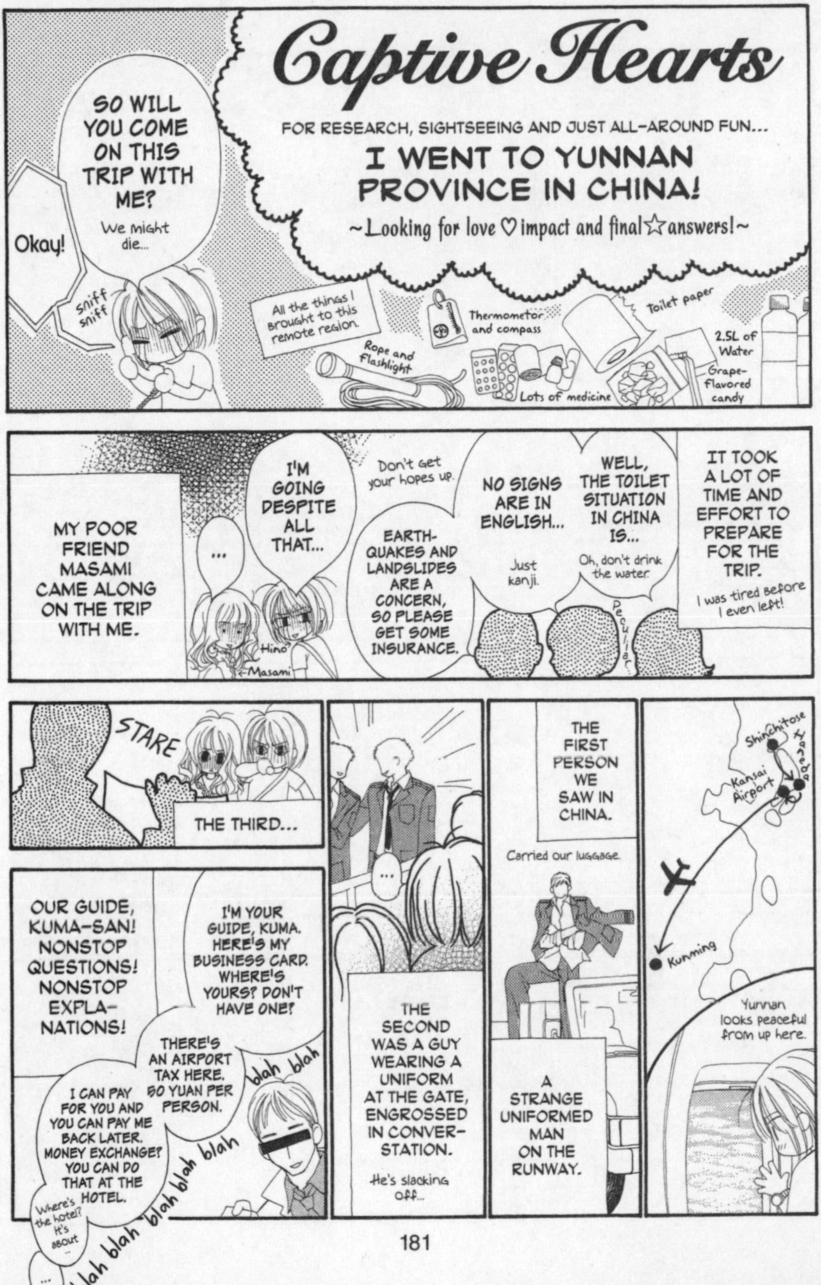

Captive Hearts
FOR RESEARCH, SIGHTSEEING AND JUST ALL-AROUND FUN...
I WENT TO YUNNAN PROVINCE IN CHINA!
~Looking for love ♡ impact and final ☆ answers!~
2.5L of Water
Toilet paper
Grape-flavored candy
Lots of medicine
Thermometer and compass
Rope and Flashlight
All the things I brought to this remote region.
SO WILL YOU COME ON THIS TRIP WITH ME?
We might die...
Okay!
sniff sniff
IT TOOK A LOT OF TIME AND EFFORT TO PREPARE FOR THE TRIP.
I was tired before I even left!
WELL, THE TOILET SITUATION IN CHINA IS...
Oh, don't drink the water.
Peculiar.
NO SIGNS ARE IN ENGLISH...
Just kanji.
Don't get your hopes up.
EARTH-QUAKES AND LANDSLIDES ARE A CONCERN, SO PLEASE GET SOME INSURANCE.
I'M GOING DESPITE ALL THAT...
...
Hino
←Masami
MY POOR FRIEND MASAMI CAME ALONG ON THE TRIP WITH ME.
Shinchitose
Haneda
Kansai Airport
Kunming
Yunnan looks peaceful from up here.
THE FIRST PERSON WE SAW IN CHINA.
Carried our luggage.
A STRANGE UNIFORMED MAN ON THE RUNWAY.
...
THE SECOND WAS A GUY WEARING A UNIFORM AT THE GATE, ENGROSSED IN CONVER-STATION.
He's slacking off...
STARE
THE THIRD...
I'M YOUR GUIDE, KUMA. HERE'S MY BUSINESS CARD. WHERE'S YOURS? DON'T HAVE ONE?
OUR GUIDE, KUMA-SAN! NONSTOP QUESTIONS! NONSTOP EXPLA-NATIONS!
THERE'S AN AIRPORT TAX HERE. 50 YUAN PER PERSON.
blah blah
I CAN PAY FOR YOU AND YOU CAN PAY ME BACK LATER. MONEY EXCHANGE? YOU CAN DO THAT AT THE HOTEL.
blah blah blah blah blah blah
Where's the hotel? It's about...
...

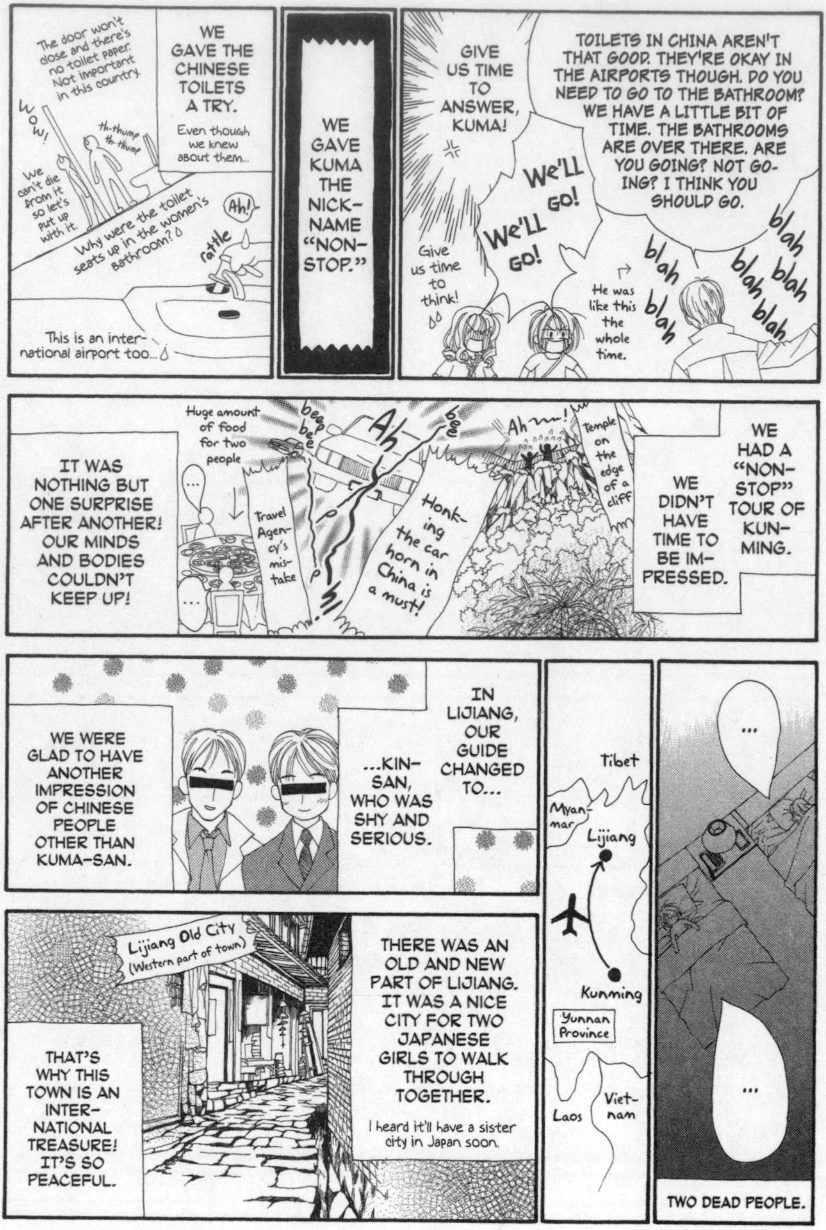
TOILETS IN CHINA AREN'T THAT GOOD. THEY'RE OKAY IN THE AIRPORTS THOUGH. DO YOU NEED TO GO TO THE BATHROOM? WE HAVE A LITTLE BIT OF TIME. THE BATHROOMS ARE OVER THERE. ARE YOU GOING? NOT GOING? I THINK YOU SHOULD GO.
GIVE US TIME TO ANSWER, KUMA!
We'LL GO!
We'LL GO!
Give us time to think!
blah blah blah blah
blah blah blah
He was like this the whole time.
WE GAVE KUMA THE NICKNAME "NON-STOP."
WE GAVE THE CHINESE TOILETS A TRY.
Even though we knew about them...
The door won't close and there's no toilet paper. Not important in this country.
Wow!
th-thump th-thump
We can't die from it so let's put up with it.
Why were the toilet seats up in the women's bathroom?
Ah!
rattle
This is an international airport too...
WE HAD A "NON-STOP" TOUR OF KUNMING.
WE DIDN'T HAVE TIME TO BE IMPRESSED.
Temple on the edge of a cliff
Ah~~!
bee bee
Ah
beep beep
Honking the car horn in China is a must!
Travel Agency's mistake
Huge amount of food for two people
...
...
IT WAS NOTHING BUT ONE SURPRISE AFTER ANOTHER! OUR MINDS AND BODIES COULDN'T KEEP UP!
...
...
TWO DEAD PEOPLE.
Tibet
Myanmar
Lijiang
Kunming
Yunnan Province
Laos
Vietnam
IN LIJIANG, OUR GUIDE CHANGED TO...
...KIN-SAN, WHO WAS SHY AND SERIOUS.
WE WERE GLAD TO HAVE ANOTHER IMPRESSION OF CHINESE PEOPLE OTHER THAN KUMA-SAN.
THERE WAS AN OLD AND NEW PART OF LIJIANG. IT WAS A NICE CITY FOR TWO JAPANESE GIRLS TO WALK THROUGH TOGETHER.
I heard it'll have a sister city in Japan soon.
Lijiang Old City (Western part of town)
THAT'S WHY THIS TOWN IS AN INTERNATIONAL TREASURE! IT'S SO PEACEFUL.

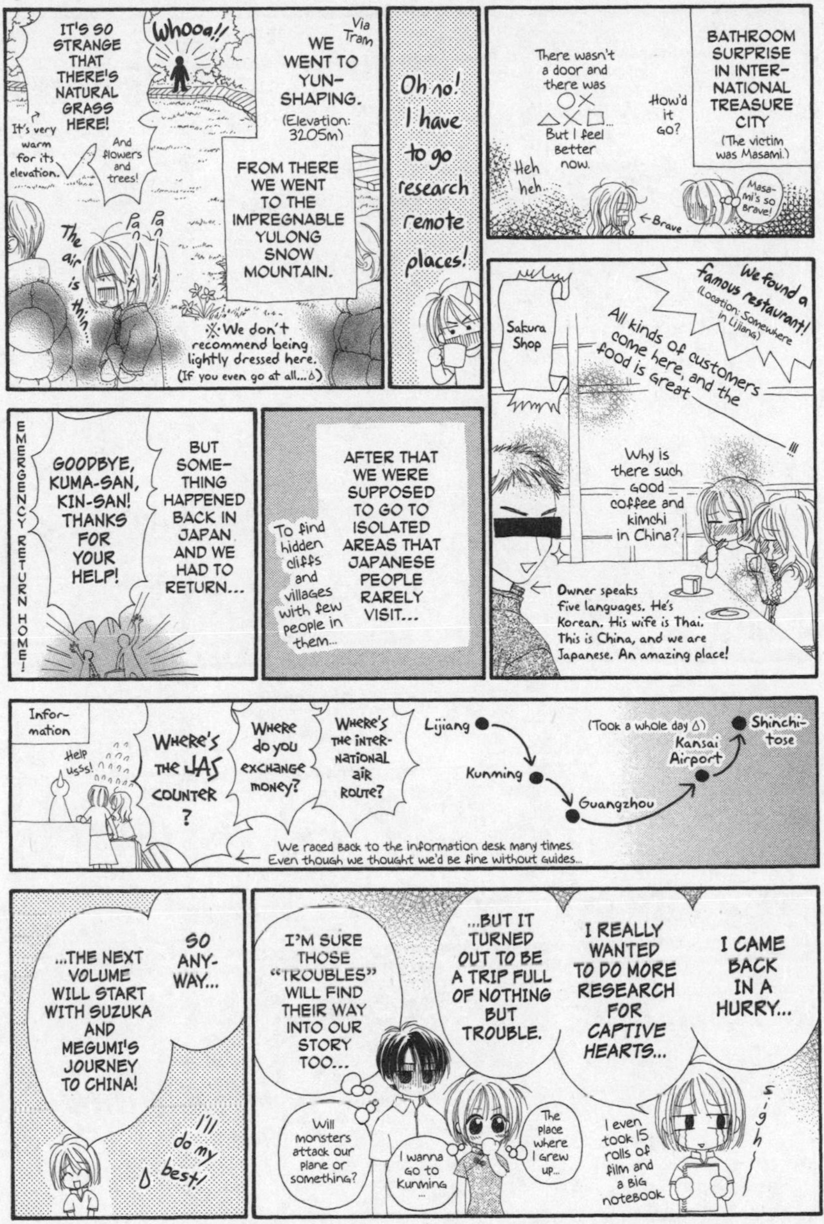
BATHROOM SURPRISE IN INTER-NATIONAL TREASURE CITY
(The victim was Masami.)
How'd it go?
There wasn't a door and there was ○× △×□... But I feel better now.
Heh heh.
Masami's so brave!
← Brave
Oh no! I have to go research remote places!
WE WENT TO YUN-SHAPING.
(Elevation: 3205m)
Via Tram
Whooa!!
IT'S SO STRANGE THAT THERE'S NATURAL GRASS HERE!
It's very warm for its elevation.
And flowers and trees!
FROM THERE WE WENT TO THE IMPREGNABLE YULONG SNOW MOUNTAIN.
The air is thin...
Pa n Pa n
※We don't recommend being lightly dressed here.
(If you even go at all...)
We found a famous restaurant!
(Location: Somewhere in Lijiang)
All kinds of customers come here, and the food is Great!!!
Sakura Shop
Why is there such good coffee and kimchi in China?
Owner speaks five languages. He's Korean. His wife is Thai. This is China, and we are Japanese. An amazing place!
AFTER THAT WE WERE SUPPOSED TO GO TO ISOLATED AREAS THAT JAPANESE PEOPLE RARELY VISIT...
To find hidden cliffs and villages with few people in them...
BUT SOME-THING HAPPENED BACK IN JAPAN AND WE HAD TO RETURN...
GOODBYE, KUMA-SAN, KIN-SAN! THANKS FOR YOUR HELP!
EMERGENCY RETURN HOME!
(Took a whole day)
Lijiang
Kunming
Guangzhou
Kansai Airport
Shinchi-tose
Where's the inter-national air route?
Where do you exchange money?
Where's the JAS counter?
Help usss!
Infor-mation
We raced back to the information desk many times.
Even though we thought we'd be fine without guides...
I CAME BACK IN A HURRY...
I REALLY WANTED TO DO MORE RESEARCH FOR CAPTIVE HEARTS...
...BUT IT TURNED OUT TO BE A TRIP FULL OF NOTHING BUT TROUBLE.
I'M SURE THOSE "TROUBLES" WILL FIND THEIR WAY INTO OUR STORY TOO...
sigh...
I even took 15 rolls of film and a BIG notebook
The place where I grew up...
I wanna go to Kunming...
Will monsters attack our plane or something?
SO ANY-WAY...
...THE NEXT VOLUME WILL START WITH SUZUKA AND MEGUMI'S JOURNEY TO CHINA!
I'll do my best!

Trip to Yunnan Province in China! / The End

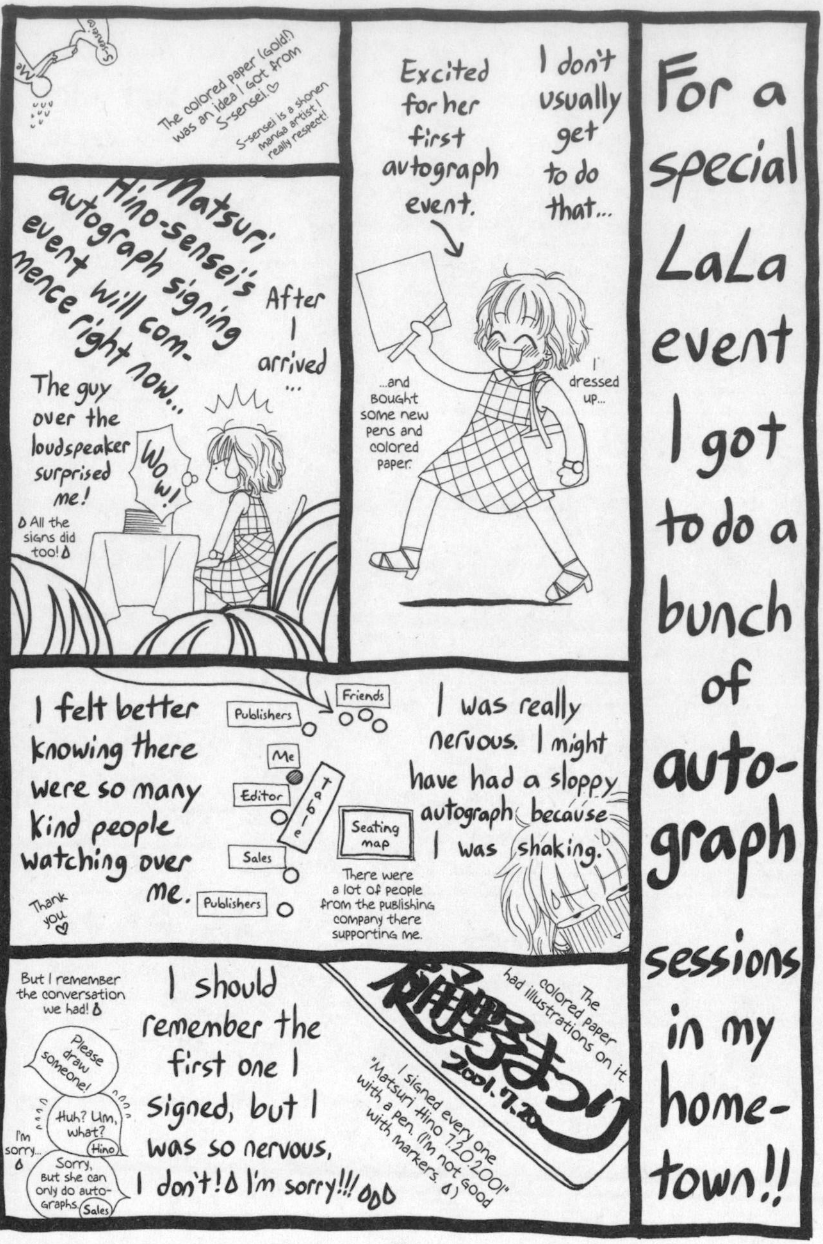

For a special LaLa event I got to do a bunch of autograph sessions in my hometown!!
I don't usually get to do that...
Excited for her first autograph event.
I dressed up...
...and bought some new pens and colored paper.
S-sensei
Me
The colored paper (Gold!) was an idea I got from S-sensei.
S-sensei is a shonen manga artist I really respect!
After I arrived...
Matsuri Hino-sensei's autograph signing event will commence right now...
WOW!
The guy over the loudspeaker surprised me!
All the signs did too!
I was really nervous. I might have had a sloppy autograph because I was shaking.
Friends
Publishers
Me
Table
Editor
Seating map
Sales
Publishers
There were a lot of people from the publishing company there supporting me.
I felt better knowing there were so many kind people watching over me.
Thank you
2001.7.20
The colored paper had illustrations on it.
I signed every one "Matsuri Hino 7.20.2001" with a pen. (I'm not good with markers.)
I should remember the first one I signed, but I was so nervous, I don't! I'm sorry!!!
But I remember the conversation we had!
Please draw someone!
Huh? Um, what? (Hino)
I'm sorry...
Sorry, but she can only do autographs. (Sales)

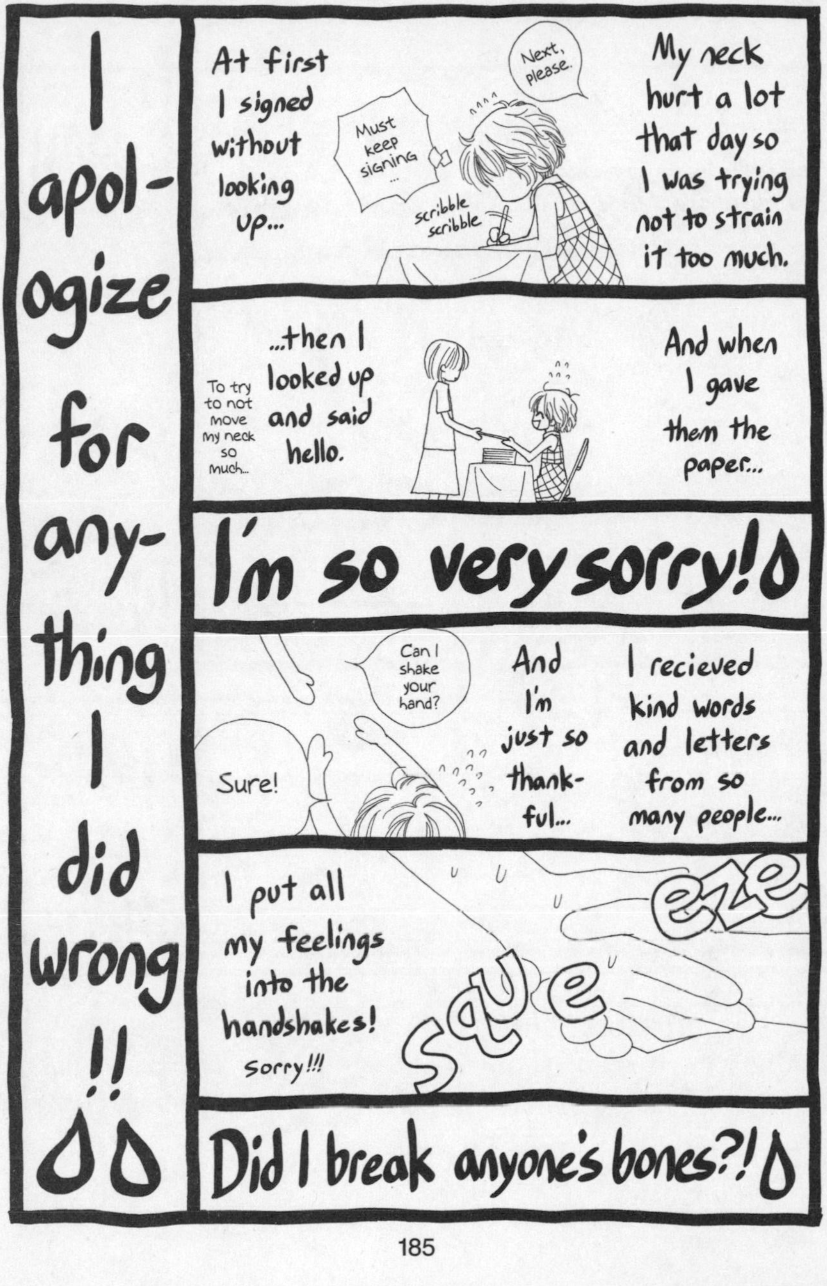
My neck hurt a lot that day so I was trying not to strain it too much.
Next, please.
Must keep signing ...
scribble scribble
At first I signed without looking up...
And when I gave them the paper...
...then I looked up and said hello.
To try to not move my neck so much...
I'm so very sorry!
I recieved kind words and letters from so many people...
And I'm just so thankful...
Can I shake your hand?
Sure!
squeeze
I put all my feelings into the handshakes!
Sorry!!!
Did I break anyone's bones?!
I apologize for anything I did wrong!!

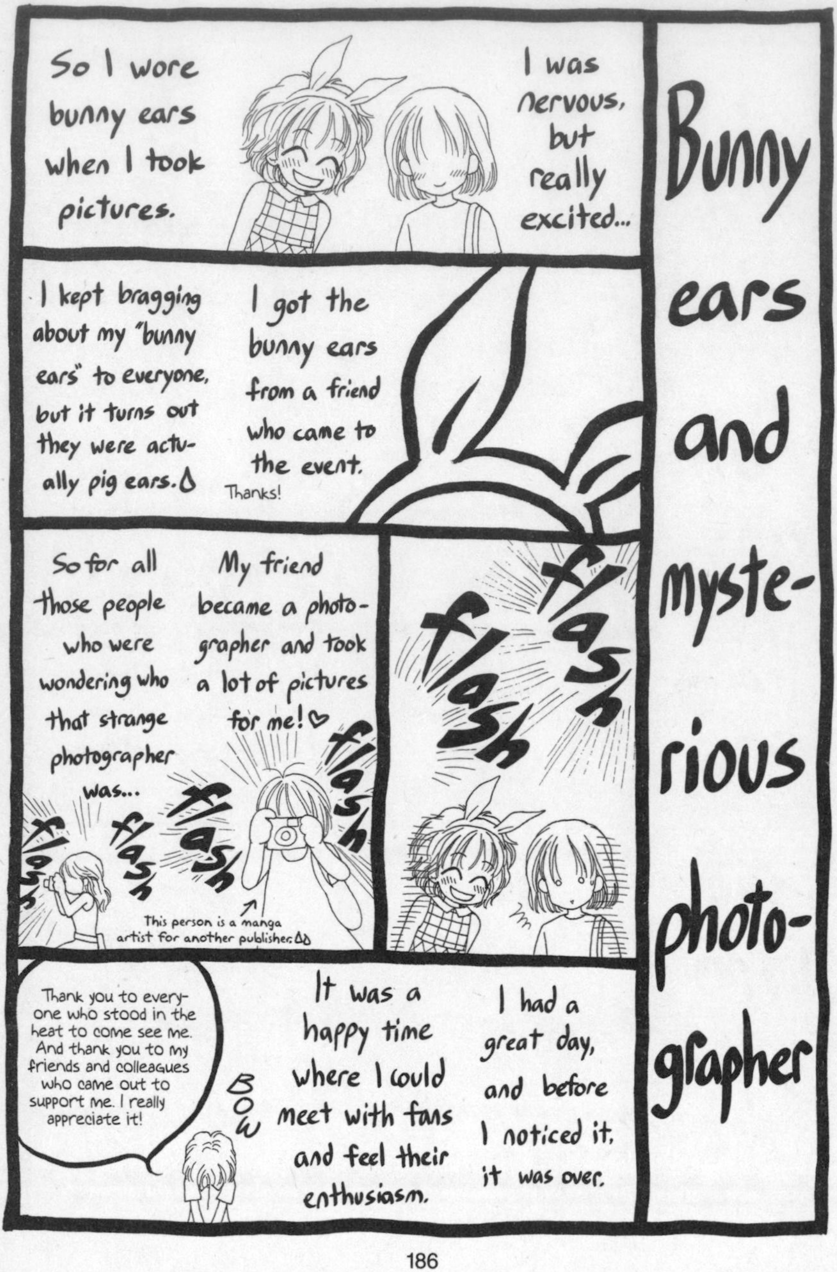
Bunny ears and myste-rious photo-grapher
I was nervous, but really excited...
So I wore bunny ears when I took pictures.
I got the bunny ears from a friend who came to the event.
Thanks!
I kept bragging about my "bunny ears" to everyone, but it turns out they were actu-ally pig ears.
flash
flash
My friend became a photo-grapher and took a lot of pictures for me! ♥
flash
So for all those people who were wondering who that strange photographer was...
flash
flash
flash
This person is a manga artist for another publisher.
I had a great day, and before I noticed it, it was over.
It was a happy time where I could meet with fans and feel their enthusiasm.
BOW
Thank you to every-one who stood in the heat to come see me. And thank you to my friends and colleagues who came out to support me. I really appreciate it!

Captivated by the story but confused by some of the terms? Here are some cultural notes to help you out!

HONORIFICS

Chan – an informal version of *san* used to address children and females.

Kun – an informal honorific used primarily for males; it can be used by people of more senior status addressing those junior to them or by anyone addressing boys or young men.

San – the most common honorific title; it is used to address people outside one's immediate family and close circle of friends.

Sama – the formal version of *san*; this honorific title is used primarily in addressing persons much higher in rank than oneself.

Sensei – honorific title used to address teachers as well as professionals such as doctors, lawyers and artists.

NOTES

Page 6, panel 1 – **Muromachi Era**
A division of Japanese history that ran from approximately 1336 to 1573. The period ended when the last shogun Ashikaga Yoshiaki was driven out of the capital Kyoto by Oda Nobunaga.

Page 13, panel 6 – **Oniisama**
Oniisan means "older brother," and swapping the "-san" honorific with "-sama" adds more respect. Rui is not literally calling Megumi her older brother. Rather, she feels close to him and respects him greatly.

Page 38, panel 4 – ***LaLa*** and ***LaLa DX***
Captive Hearts was originally serialized in *LaLa*, a Japanese shojo manga (girls' comics) magazine published monthly by Hakusensha. Some of the bonus stories in this volume ran in *LaLa DX*, *LaLa*'s sister magazine.

Page 105, panel 4 – **Inari-sama**
Also known as Uka no Mitama, the patron deity of agriculture (particularly rice). Megumi is suggesting that the Dragon God may actually be benevolent rather than destructive.

MATSURI HINO burst onto the manga scene with her title
Kono Yume ga Sametara (When This Dream Is Over), which was published
in *LaLa DX* magazine. Hino was a manga artist a mere nine months after
she decided to become one.

With the success of her popular series *Captive Hearts* and *MeruPuri*, Hino
has established herself as a major player in the world of shojo manga.
Vampire Knight is currently serialized in *LaLa* and *Shojo Beat* magazines.

Hino enjoys creative activities and has commented that she would
have been either an architect or an apprentice to traditional
Japanese craft masters if she had not become a manga artist.

Captive Hearts
Vol. 4

The Shojo Beat Manga Edition

STORY & ART BY
MATSURI HINO

Translation & Adaptation/Andria Cheng
Touch-up Art & Lettering/Sabrina Heep
Design/Amy Martin
Editor/Amy Yu

Editor in Chief, Books/Alvin Lu
Editor in Chief, Magazines/Marc Weidenbaum
VP, Publishing Licensing/Rika Inouye
VP, Sales & Product Marketing/Gonzalo Ferreyra
VP, Creative/Linda Espinosa
Publisher/Hyoe Narita

Toraware no Minoue by Matsuri Hino
© Matsuri Hino 2000
All rights reserved.
First published in Japan in 2001 by HAKUSENSHA, Inc., Tokyo.
English language translation rights arranged with Hakusensha, Inc., Tokyo.
The stories, characters and incidents mentioned in this publication are entirely fictional.

Printed in Canada

Published by VIZ Media, LLC
P.O. Box 77010
San Francisco, CA 94107

Shojo Beat Manga Edition
10 9 8 7 6 5 4 3 2 1
First printing, May 2009

store.viz.com